INNOVATIVE

EAST ASIA

The Future of Growth

SHAHID YUSUF

WITH

M. ANJUM ALTAF

BARRY EICHENGREEN

SUDARSHAN GOOPTU

KAORU NABESHIMA

CHARLES KENNY

DWIGHT H. PERKINS

MARC SHOTTEN

THE WORLD BANK
Washington, D.C.

A copublication of
the World Bank and
Oxford University Press

CONTENTS

Figures

Tables

FOREWORD

Ten years ago, the government of Japan and the World Bank collaboratively prepared a report that categorized East Asia's performance as a "miracle." The analysis contained in that report and the lessons it derived have provided the armature for much subsequent exegesis and debate, which have explicated the diversity of the development process within and beyond the East Asian region.

Over the past decade, this region has remained the global leader in terms of economic growth rates. However, since the crisis of 1997–98, several countries have struggled to sustain the earlier pace of development in the increasingly open, volatile, and competitive global environment; and even the economies growing strongly cannot afford to be complacent. Sound macroeconomic policies, manufacturing capability, and export prowess will remain the foundation for progress, but by themselves, they may not be sufficient in the future. The World Bank and the government of Japan share the view that East Asia must urgently attend to an agenda of institutional reforms and amplify its capacity for technological innovation in order to regain the dynamism and resilience of the miracle years.

Taking that view as its starting point, *Innovative East Asia: The Future of Growth* illuminates the road ahead for East Asia with a searching examination of recent experience. Deftly, and with reference to a wide array of pertinent research, this volume identifies the priorities for institutional reform—domestic and regional—needed to underwrite rapid growth. It convincingly establishes that whereas resource inputs were the principal sources of past growth, future growth in

East Asia rests on the emergence of an environment that enhances productivity and promotes innovation. The central achievement of the research is to define the elements of such an environment, to show how these elements interact, and to demonstrate their interdependence.

We are greatly pleased with the outcome of this cooperative venture by the World Bank and the government of Japan, and applaud the efforts of the authors. We are confident that this volume will be a valuable guide for policymakers, a stimulus for researchers, and a spur to thinking across the broad field of development.

James D. Wolfensohn
President
The World Bank Group

Haruhiko Kuroda
Vice Minister for
  International Affairs
Ministry of Finance
Government of Japan

PREFACE

This is the main volume in a series of publications based on a study cosponsored by the government of Japan and the World Bank to examine the future sources of economic growth in East Asia. The study was initiated in 2000 with the objective of identifying the most promising path to development in light of emerging global and regional changes, signaled by the crisis of 1997–98 and the challenges faced by the crisis-hit countries as they have sought to resume rapid growth.

The first volume, *Can East Asia Compete?*, provided an overview of the issues relevant to charting a strategic course for the future. This volume explores each issue and consequent policy choices in greater detail. The principal message is that sustained economic growth in East Asia will rest on retaining the strengths of the past—stability, openness, investment, human capital development—on overcoming the sources of current weaknesses—in the financial, corporate, judicial, and social sectors—and on implementing the changes required by the evolving economic environment. The two subsequent volumes in this series will present revised versions of papers prepared for this study, which are rich in insights and empirical details on topics ranging from venture capital to production networking. Later volumes will provide in-depth assessments of state enterprise reforms and the role of business services, whose importance is underscored in this volume.

Many interrelated developments at the global and regional levels suggest a future quite different from the past. They include increasing global integration, more open domestic markets, a slower growing Japanese economy, and the emergence of China as a strong competitor and promising market—all this amid a continuing technological revolution and transformation of the organization of global production. This book argues, based on a careful analysis of these changes, that unless East Asia moves toward a technological, rather than a factor-intensive, mode of production, it will experience slower growth in the future. It is imperative that East Asia prepare itself to move up the value chain, relying increasingly on productivity-enhancing innovations based on science and technology for its dominant source of growth.

The contribution of this book lies in its identifying the sources of change in the future and proposing strategies that would position East Asian economies to become much more innovative over time. However, this volume stresses the importance of a three-stranded formula for growth, in which retaining the strengths of the past and overcoming the weaknesses of the present are essential prerequisites for a successful strategy addressing the challenges of the future.

The financial backing of the government of Japan through its Policy and Human Resources Development Fund provided vital support for this project, as did senior public officials who gave generously of their time. We are deeply grateful to Haruhiko Kuroda, Masahiro Kawai, Kiyoashi Kodera, Rinataro Tamaki, Junichi Maruyama, and Takatoshi Ito. The quality and relevance of the research were closely monitored by members of the international steering committee of the study: Masahiko Aoki, Jemal-ud-din Kassum, Masahiro Kawai, Mohsin Khan, Homi Kharas, Gobind Nankani, Eisuke Sakakibara, Il SaKong, Tharman Shanmugaratnam, Nicholas Stern, Joseph Stiglitz, Tarrin Nimmanahaeminda, and Xiaochuan Zhou. We are indebted to them for their advice and insights. The staff of the World Bank's Tokyo office facilitated the reviews, and we greatly appreciate the assistance provided by Yukio Yoshimura, Shuzo Nakumura, Mika Iwasaki, Tomoko Hirai, and Hitomi Sasaki.

At the World Bank, the Development Research Group provided a home for the study, and the East Asia and Pacific Region contributed consistent and unflagging support. We are especially indebted to Paul Collier, Jemal-ud-din Kassum, and Homi Kharas for their encouragement and their faith in the value of the study.

The study team was ably supported by the research and organizational skills of Soumya Chattopadhyay, Farhan Hameed, and Yifan Hu. Simon J. Evenett contributed to the initial phase of the project. The manuscript was expertly edited by Rachel Weaving, and Rebecca Sugui facilitated its production. Nicola Marrian and Janet H. Sasser of the World Bank's Office of the Publisher delivered yet again. We thank them all for adding value in many ways.

ACKNOWLEDGMENTS

This study has drawn on a number of commissioned background papers and firm surveys, other publications, and World Bank reports. The background papers provided many of the building blocks for the study, and we are thankful to the authors for their efforts. Those contributing were Garrick Blalock, Bijit Bora, Carles Boix, Herman Chein, Jason Conway, Cindy Fan, Robert Crandall, Richard F. Doner, Dieter Ernst, Paul Gertler, John Gilbert, Hal Hill, Trevor D. Heaver, Gary Jefferson, Masahiro Kawai, Martin Kenney, Pingyao Lai, Andrew Lawlor, Richard Lester, Robert Litan, Peter J. Lloyd, Robert E.B. Lucas, Minako Mori, Gregory W. Noble, Richard Rose, Howard Pack, John Ravenhill, Eisuke Sakakibara, Robert Scollay, Alan J. Scott, Edward Steinfeld, Timothy Sturgeon, Ken'ichi Takayasu, Sharon Yamakawa, and Yanyan Zhang.

The background papers and earlier drafts of this report were presented at seminars and workshops in Bangkok; Beijing; Cambridge, Mass.; Tokyo; and Washington, D.C. Valuable comments and contributions were provided, and we would like to thank all of those who participated in these seminars as moderators, discussants, and presenters. Specific thanks go to Ehtisham Ahmad, Rie Atachi, Luis Benveniste, Deepak Bhattasali, Peter Brimble, Paul Crampton, Dilip Das, David Dollar, Lewis Branscomb, Julian Chang, Richard N. Cooper, Dennis Encarnation, He Fan, Robert Feldman, Richard Freeman, Andrew Feltenstein, Bernard Hoekman, Ira A. Jackson, Gary Jefferson, Dale Jorgenson, Masahisa Fujita, Fan Gang, Yasheng Huang, Takatoshi Ito, Wang Jici, Masahiro Kawai, Fumio Kodama,

Jun Kurihara, Rajiv B. Lall, Xue Lan, Pisit Leeahtam, Frank Lichtenberg, Toby Linden, William Martin, Ashoka Mody, Jon D. Mills, John Montgomery, Shuzo Nakamura, Yoshino Naoyukio, Yumiko Okamoto, Arvind Panagariya, Mari Pangestu, Jay Rosengard, Anthony Saich, Kamal Saggi, Li Shantong, Gao Shiji, Ammar Siamwalla, Chris Thomas, Lu Tingjie, Masatsugu Tsuji, Shujiro Urata, Kerrin Vautier, David Weil, Liu Xielin, Jiang Xiaojuan, and Yu Yongding.

Many helpful suggestions and comments were also provided by Esra Bennathan and three anonymous referees who reviewed the entire manuscript. Last, but not least, we deeply appreciate the logistical support provided by the Bank's country offices in Beijing and Tokyo.

ABBREVIATIONS AND ACRONYMS

AFTA	ASEAN Free Trade Agreement
AMC	Asset Management Corporation
APEC	Asia Pacific Economic Cooperation
ASEAN	Association of South East Asian Nations
BOP	Balance of payments
CAMEL	Capital adequacy, asset quality, management, earnings, and liquidity
CCF	China-China-foreign
CEPT	Common Effective Preferential Tariff
CMI	Chiang Mai Initiative
CPN	Cross-border production network
EMEAP	Executives' Meeting of East Asia-Pacific Central Banks
EMS	Electronic manufacturing system
EU	European Union
FDI	Foreign direct investment
GDP	Gross domestic product
IBRA	Indonesian Bank Restructuring Agency
ICT	Information and communications technology
ISP	Internet service provider
KAMCO	Korean Asset Management Company
NAFTA	North American Free Trade Agreement
OBM	Original brand manufacturer
ODM	Original design manufacturer
OECD	Organisation for Economic Co-operation and Development

OEM	Original equipment manufacturer
PAYG	Pay-as-you-go
R&D	Research and development
SEACEN	South East Asian Central Banks
SEANZA	Southeast Asia, New Zealand, and Australia Group
TFT-LCD	Thin film transistor liquid crystal display
TIMSS-R	Third International Math and Science Study-Repeat
TOEFL	Test of English as a Foreign Language
TRIPS	Trade-Related Aspects of Intellectual Property Rights Agreement
WGIPC	Working Group on Intellectual Property Cooperation
WTO	World Trade Organization

CHAPTER 1

ECONOMIC CHANGES AND POLICY
IMPLICATIONS IN EAST ASIA

T he crisis of 1997–98 challenged the resilience of East Asian economies and raised a question mark over their ability to regain the momentum that characterized the East Asian "miracle."[1] Confidence gave way to nagging doubts, which prompted a wide-ranging search for answers.

This study seeks to identify the choices available to East Asian economies as they attempt to resume and sustain rapid growth in a changing, more competitive, and more integrated world. The study argues that revival will depend on retaining the strengths of the past (macroeconomic stability, openness to trade, high rates of saving and investment, and human capital development), overcoming the weaknesses of the present (in the financial sector, corporate governance, regulatory oversight, legal framework, exchange rate management, and social protection), and deriving much more of the impetus for growth from innovation than from factor accumulation.

The study focuses on the policy measures needed for this transformation. This chapter provides an introduction to economic conditions in the region, followed by an overview of issues examined in the volume. Chapter 2 discusses national reforms most suited to overcoming existing weaknesses, and chapter 3 extends the discussion to cooperation among countries as a means to strengthen the regional economy. Chapters 4 to 8 focus on the initiatives needed to foster the

---

1. East Asia is defined as China, Hong Kong (China), Indonesia, Japan, the Republic of Korea, Malaysia, the Philippines, Singapore, Taiwan (China), Thailand, and Vietnam.

capacity for innovation, and chapter 9 distills the key policy messages of the study.

FOUNDATIONS OF PAST SUCCESS

East Asia has achieved rates of economic growth unprecedented in recent economic history, and the determinants of that growth have been studied extensively.[2] The strengths of the East Asian model of growth are best appreciated by comparing East Asia with other developing regions (table 1.1). Macroeconomic stability provided an ideal launching pad; the rate of inflation through the 1980s and up to 1997 was lower in East Asia than in Latin America and the Caribbean, South Asia, and Sub-Saharan Africa. This stability was leveraged by a significantly more open economy, as measured by the share of trade in gross domestic product (GDP). Saving and investment rates were much higher, and the labor force was considerably more educated (as measured by enrollment rates in primary- and secondary-level education), facilitating industrialization.

As a result, East Asia proved to be the most attractive developing region for global investment, and, as its manufacturing capability has strengthened, so has its appeal to foreign investors. More than 17 percent of total foreign direct investment (FDI) worldwide between 1990 and 1997 was in East Asia (table 1.2). The fruits of the region's policies also are evident in the growth rates of GDP and progress in poverty reduction. East Asia achieved significant reductions in poverty over this period, with the number of people living on less than $1 a day (the official poverty line) falling almost two-thirds, from 720 mil-

---

2. A large literature chronicles East Asian development since the era of rapid growth commenced in the late 1960s. The literature ranges from individual country studies to subregional and regional cross-country studies. Much of the writing focuses on the factors leading to the emergence of export-oriented manufacturing sectors because this is where East Asia has excelled. World Bank (1993) offers an illuminating perspective on growth through the end of the 1980s. Other recent book-length publications examine cross-country development in the region: for example, Agarwal and others (2000) focus on policies dealing with industrial competitiveness, and Timmer (2000) focuses on the manufacturing sector. The East Asian crises spawned a torrent of publications on the causes of the crisis and on how countries have fared since. On these, see Haggard (2000), Noble and Ravenhill (2000), Stiglitz and Yusuf (2001), and Yu and Xu (2001). On Korea, see Emery (2001) and Smith (2000). On Indonesia, see Hill (2000b). Publications on China in the 1990s alone would fill a small library.

Table 1.1 Foundations of Economic Growth, by Region, Select Years, 1980s–90s

Indicator and time period	East Asia	Latin America and the Caribbean	South Asia	Sub-Saharan Africa
Inflation (percent)				
1980s	6.7	23.8	8.6	9.8
1990–97	5.6	25.7	9.2	17.9
Trade as a percentage of GDP				
1980s	107.0	26.1	20.2	54.4
1990–97	121.6	28.6	26.4	55.2
Gross domestic savings as a percentage of GDP				
1980s	31.5	22.9	16.8	18.2
1990–97	33.7	20.1	19.1	15.8
Gross fixed capital formation as a percentage of GDP				
1980s	28.2	20.2	19.6	19.9
1990–97	31.6	19.2	21.6	17.1
Gross enrollment rate (percent)[a]				
Primary, 1996	102.6	113.2	93.7	73.7
Secondary, 1996	74.9	59.0	43.9	25.6
Tertiary, 1997	30.5	19.5	6.5	3.6

Note: For 1980s and 1990–97, the figures show simple averages. Inflation is measured by the GDP deflator.

a. Data on gross enrollment rate for Taiwan, China, are missing.

Source: World Bank, *World Development Indicators* (various years).

Table 1.2 Investment, Growth, and Poverty Reduction, by Region, Select Years, 1980s–90s

Indicator and time period	East Asia	Latin America and the Caribbean	South Asia	Sub-Saharan Africa
Percentage of global FDI inflows[a]				
1980s	7.47	8.11	0.32	1.37
1990–97	17.14	9.65	0.65	1.15
Annual growth of GDP				
1980s	6.53	1.92	5.85	2.23
1990–97	6.76	3.33	5.21	1.94
Change in number of people living below $1 a day (millions)				
1987–98	−261.2[b]	2.9	−49.8	−84.5

Note: For 1980s and 1990–97, the figures show simple averages.

a. Excludes Hong Kong, China, and Taiwan, China.

b. 1985–96; includes the Lao People's Democratic Republic, Mongolia, Papua New Guinea, and Vietnam.

Source: World Bank, *World Development Indicators* (various years).

lion in 1975 to 210 million in 2002. This occurred largely because the rapidity of growth outweighed the modest increase in inequality (Warr 2002; World Bank, East Asia Region 2002).[3]

This impressive performance was interrupted by the crisis of 1997–98, with the poor, the less educated, and unskilled workers among the worst affected. Unemployment and underemployment rose significantly—in the Republic of Korea, from 2.5 percent in 1996 to 4.6 percent in late 1999 (after a high of 8.7 percent in early 1999); in Thailand, from 2.3 percent in early 1997 to 5.4 percent in 1999, despite the nascent economic recovery (World Bank 2000c); and in Indonesia, from 4.7 percent in 1997 to 5.5 percent in 1998. Although unemployment increased modestly in Indonesia, wages declined 34 percent in real terms in the formal urban sector and 40 percent in agriculture. By some estimates, the number of Indonesia's rural poor doubled in 1998, along with a sharp increase in extreme poverty (Dhanani and Islam 2002; "Indonesia: Poverty Reduction" 2002).[4] After the crisis, in Indonesia and to a lesser extent in Thailand, there was also a major shift from formal to informal employment and from the urban to the rural sector. Even in China, which largely avoided the negative effects of the crisis, poverty rose in its aftermath—from 210 million in 1996 to 219 million in 1999 (World Bank 2000c).

CURRENT WEAKNESSES

Many studies have examined the causes of the Asian crisis, and although different researchers assign different weights to the con-

3. Dollar and Kraay (2002) empirically trace the close relationship between growth and the decline in poverty. Others who have analyzed changes in global poverty, which is strongly influenced by the incidence of poverty in China and India, maintain that poverty must have declined much more than is suggested by the World Bank's estimates, highlighting the success of growth-enhancing policies in East and South Asia (see Bhalla 2002; Sala-i-Martin 2002). Bhalla's calculations point to a reduction in the incidence of poverty in East Asia from 31 percent in 1990 to 6 percent in 2000, whereas the World Bank's findings indicate that poverty fell from 27 percent in 1987 to 15 percent in 1998 (see Ravallion 2002 for an explanation of the differences between the two estimates).

4. Cline (2002) estimates that crises in emerging markets, starting with Mexico in 1995 and continuing with Argentina and Turkey in 2001, are responsible for pushing at least 40 million to 60 million people below the poverty line—and possibly as many as 100 million.

tributing factors, there is broad agreement on the principal causes (table 1.3).[5] The crisis revealed the inadequacy of corporate and financial institutions, exchange rate management and coordination, and social protection in several East Asian countries. It forced countries to incur large fiscal deficits in order to restore economic activity, and their continuing efforts to sustain economic activity, recapitalize banking systems, and restructure some corporate entities are creating budgetary pressures that will need to be dealt with through fiscal measures in the future.

Strong macroeconomic fundamentals were a hallmark of the successful East Asian economies. But by the middle of the 1990s some countries had become less watchful, and budget and current account deficits had begun to widen, most notably in Korea and Thailand (figure 1.1 shows current account deficits; chapter 2 presents budget deficits).

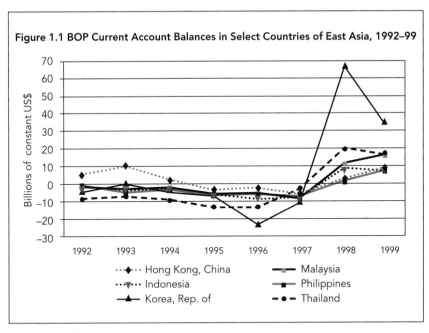

Figure 1.1 BOP Current Account Balances in Select Countries of East Asia, 1992–99

Note: BOP = balance of payments.
Source: World Bank, *World Development Indicators* (2001).

---

5. See Eichengreen (1999); Radelet and Sachs (1998a, 1998b), among others. For a political economy perspective, see Haggard (2000).

Table 1.3 Causes of the East Asian Crisis, 1997–98

Source	Cause or vulnerability
Radelet and Sachs (2000)	• General weaknesses in the Asian economies, especially poor financial, industrial, and exchange rate policies
	• Poor investment choices, resulting from the moral hazard of implicit guarantees, corruption, and anticipated bailouts
	• Financial panic, caused by weaknesses in the structure of international capital markets and early mismanagement
	• Exchange rate devaluations in Republic of Korea and Thailand that may have panicked investors
Eichengreen (1999)	• Modest macroeconomic imbalances: appreciation of real exchange rates and current account deficits
	• Serious banking sector problems
	• Mismanagement of the maturity structure of debt
Krugman (1998)	• Serious problems in the banking sector (crisis only incidentally about currencies)
	• Poor investment choices—office towers, auto plants—rather than excessive investment per se
	• "Herding" by investors, exacerbating overinvestment and overvaluation of assets
Kawai, Newfarmer, and Schmukler (2001)	• Burgeoning flows of private capital
	• Macroeconomic policies that allowed large inflows of short-term, unhedged capital to fuel a domestic credit boom
	• Newly liberalized but insufficiently regulated domestic financial markets with highly leveraged corporations
	• Mounting political uncertainty in Indonesia, Republic of Korea, and Thailand
Lindgren and others (2000)	• Financial and corporate sector governance that allowed excessive risk taking, as prudential regulations were inadequate or poorly enforced
	• Macroeconomic vulnerabilities
	• Formal and informal currency pegs, which discouraged lenders and borrowers from hedging
	• Capital inflows, which fueled rapid credit expansion, lowered the quality of credit and caused asset price inflation
	• Weak supervision of nonbank financial institutions
	• Highly leveraged corporate sectors, especially in the Republic of Korea and Thailand, and large unhedged short-term debt, which increased vulnerability to changes in market sentiment in general and to exchange and interest rate changes in particular

	• Excessively close relationships between governments, financial institutions, and borrowers, particularly in Indonesia and the Republic of Korea
	• Weak accounting standards, especially for loan valuation and disclosure practices, which hid problems from policymakers, supervisors, market participants, and international financial institutions
	• Inadequacies in assessing country risk on the part of the lenders
Yoshitomi and Shirai (2000)	• Massive inflows of short-term capital aided by unsophisticated financial systems, which financed excessive investments in real estate and some manufacturing industries
	• The coincidence of a sudden reversal of capital flows with a cyclical downturn
	• Twin currency and banking crises, which led to deterioration in the balance sheets of financial institutions and business enterprises

Source: E. Sakakibara and Yamakawa (2002).

Demand Management and Public Spending

Until recently, the dominant view was that high rates of investment (principally in export-oriented industry and supporting infrastructure)—financed by domestic savings and in combination with trade liberalization—were the keys to rapid economic expansion.[6] Growth in demand derived in large part from exports and domestic capital spending, while the mobilization of domestic resources minimized current account imbalances and foreign borrowing. East Asia followed this successful strategy, as is particularly clear in the case of high-technology exports.[7]

In the future, investment in export industries backed by high domestic saving will remain an important plank of East Asia's growth strategy. But East Asia's increasing share of world exports, plus the slowdown in export growth in 1998 and again in 2000–01, suggests that some countries will need to recalibrate their domestic saving, as Korea is already doing.[8] Rates of domestic saving as high as a third of GDP are less desirable when external demand weakens. And if exports will be expanding more modestly in the future, governments would be well advised to temper the incentives to invest heavily in a few subsectors of manufacturing exports. Slower growth in capacity in certain subsectors, such as in the fabrication of silicon wafers, might be warranted.[9] A more diversified mix of exports, including in-

---

6. Some observers question the gains from trade liberalization on theoretical grounds, on the basis of past experience, and with reference to the equivocal nature of empirical evidence (Deraniyagala and Fine 2001; Rodríguez and Rodrik 2000). However, some carefully specified tests in a panel-based framework, using data from 73 countries, reaffirm the positive long-term effects of trade liberalization on growth (Greenaway, Morgan, and Wright 2002). See also Irwin and Tervio (2002) regarding the positive relationship between the share of traded GDP and the level of incomes.

7. In 1999 close to one-third of East Asia's merchandise trade, both exports and imports, was in information and communications technology products—a larger share than in any other developing region (see Lall 2000b). Moreover, trade within East Asia generated the world's highest volume of exports in office and telecommunications equipment. Overall, Asia accounted for just under half of trade in these categories in 1999 and supplied three-fourths of U.S. information technology imports (Sidorenko and Findlay 2001).

8. In a few economies of the region, domestic savings have diminished because government savings have fallen (Y-H Kim 2001), but so have household savings, from 35 to 22 percent in Korea during 1998–2001. Elsewhere—for instance, in Japan—the concern about the ability of governments to deliver on future social security payments has led to a rise in precautionary savings.

9. By the end of 2002, 15 plants capable of manufacturing 300-millimeter silicon wafers were in operation (substantially augmenting industrial capacity based on plants producing 200-millimeter and smaller silicon wafers), with the number projected to reach 23 in 2003 and 40 in 2007, at which time the production capacity would be double the anticipated level of demand ("Chips on Monster Wafers" 2002).

novative and differentiated products, and a wider spectrum of trading partners would be safer bets (E. Sakakibara and Yamakawa 2002).[10]

To lessen the sometimes excessive dependence on the external sector, there may be scope for gradually raising private and public consumption—as with the tax breaks that have stimulated the use of credit cards in Korea, where cardholders spent $333 billion in 2001 compared to $48 billion in 1998.[11] If productivity can be increased throughout the economy, especially in the nontradable service sector, lower rates of investment need not retard growth.

In 1998–2002 governments in China, Japan, Korea, Malaysia, and Singapore used fiscal spending to sustain economic activity in the face of weakening demand. As measured by general government spending, the size of government in East Asia is about half that in countries in the Organisation for Economic Co-operation and Development (OECD).[12] Broadly conservative spending policies have limited the burden of public debt (Boix 2002). But as a result of recent reflationary spending, public investment in infrastructure, and attempts to restructure banks and clean up their balance sheets, the ratio of public sector debt to GDP has risen, which in turn has raised debt servicing costs; for the region as a whole, it climbed from about 28 percent in 1997 to 45 percent in 2001 (see Hemming, Mahfouz, and Schimmelpfennig [2002] on the limited reflationary effects of public spending plus the consequences for fiscal deficits). The true extent of public debt is much higher when the contingent liabilities associated with nonperforming loans by banks and with debts accumulated by state-owned enterprises are factored in. The heavy debt burden presages higher spending in the future, and hence the efficient use of public funds and effective management of public debt will remain a priority (Gooptu 2001; Green and Campos 2001).

Beyond this looms a larger issue. Do East Asian countries need to raise the level of state spending and transfers so as to provide the most vulnerable households with a stronger safety net and to enhance

---

10. The diminished reliance of Hong Kong, China, on exports to the United States and its increased export of services are a case in point.

11. Because of government incentives for households to use credit cards, almost 40 percent of all consumer transactions use credit cards, and household debt rose from 50 percent of GDP in 1997 to 71 percent in 2002, so clearly the trend will need to be contained (see "Doubts Grow" 2002, "South Korea: Burdened Banks" 2001, and "South Korea: Curbing Credit" 2002). A billion is 1,000 million.

12. General government spends 45 percent of GDP in the OECD countries as a group. Japan spends 31 percent.

the efficacy of automatic stabilizers?[13] Safety nets are inadequate in most of the region, and stabilizers barely have any effect, given the degree of openness, the pace of innovation, and the susceptibility to shocks.[14] Current levels of social spending as a share of GDP are relatively moderate, but it will be difficult to increase them substantially to finance higher transfers. Raising tax rates to finance unemployment insurance, for example, is problematic because of international fiscal competition, factor mobility, and the growth of e-business. Evidence from research also points to the deadweight costs of higher taxes, their negative effects on labor supply, and the apparent absence in the OECD countries of measurable gains in welfare following the post-1960 expansion in social spending (Tanzi and Schuknecht 2000).

Many of the region's economies need to rethink their tax and transfer policies, although several have private mechanisms that are worth sustaining for insuring against shocks. Nevertheless, if the region is to become even more open, and thus vulnerable to economic turbulence, welfare and political considerations argue for at least a minimum safety net for the groups most at risk. Moreover, an early decision should be made to take full advantage of East Asia's relatively youthful demographic structure to fund costly pension schemes and efficiently invest the resources mobilized (Atkinson 1999; Y-K Ng 2000).

Exchange Rate Management and Regional Coordination

In the years leading up to the crisis, East Asian countries implicitly pegged their currencies to the dollar, while ostensibly tying their rates to a basket of trading partner currencies (McKinnon 2000, 2001). When currencies came under speculative attack, the pegs could not be defended, resulting in steep losses of reserves and deep

---

13. Auerbach and Feenberg (2000) find that tax-linked automatic stabilization in the United States offsets about 8 percent of a shock. An equal effect follows from unemployment compensation and labor market response. Government size is seen to reduce output volatility in the OECD countries, with a 1 percent increase lessening volatility by 0.08 percent (Fatas and Mihov 2001). By comparison, the fiscal systems of East Asian economies provide virtually no automatic stabilization (Green and Campos 2001).

14. Reich (2002) argues that extraordinary dynamism, innovation, and urbanization of the leading industrial economies have worn away the protective institutional insulation between individuals and the economy, increasing the degree of risk.

devaluations of the baht, rupiah, and won.[15] To avoid a recurrence, several economies now officially maintain a flexible peg, some apparently with reference to a trade-weighted basket of currencies.[16]

Exchange rate fixity has its attractions, but for most East Asian economies, a flexible regime is advisable. One approach is to peg the rate to a basket of currencies such as the dollar, euro, renminbi, and yen and adjust the weights periodically. Other options short of a clean float are also feasible and, in conjunction with inflation and output targeting using a Taylor adjustment process, might be suitable for smaller, open economies.[17] Quite possibly, a single rule may not be suitable for all countries (as is apparent from the diversity of approaches adopted by East Asian economies during 2001–02; see Kawai 2002), and a pragmatic approach that is alert to changing circumstances and cross-country experience and has some flexibility has definite advantages given the current state of knowledge. Since the crisis, East Asian economies have been exploring mechanisms to guard against shocks or to lessen their impact through regional and bilateral currency swap arrangements amounting to $25 billion, buttressed by surveillance mechanisms (Henning 2002). They have complemented these attempts with other actions whose purpose is to reinforce institutional reforms through policies governing competition and investment and through actions on intellectual property rights. Several countries, such as Japan, Korea, and Singapore, are pursuing bilateral trade negotiations. There is a greater sense that trade with China could become an engine of growth for the region. In East Asian forums, there is also talk of coordinating macroeconomic and exchange rate policies and, in the distant future, arriving at a unified exchange rate so as to reap the benefits of exchange rate stability (E. Sakakibara and Yamakawa 2002).[18]

---

15. In defending the baht during mid-1997, the Central Bank of Thailand ran down its reserves from $30 billion to $6 billion within a matter of weeks.

16. The East Asian crisis showed that countries with a low ratio of reserves to short-term external liabilities were particularly at risk of speculative attack. In response, economies in the region accumulated large foreign exchange reserves amounting to $700 billion by running current account surpluses in 2002 (World Bank, East Asia Region 2002). Most also reduced their stock of short-term debt. The latter action is appropriate given the exposure of countries such as Korea. The former seems justified up to a point, but for lower-middle-income countries it represents an inefficient use of domestic resources given that a lower volume of short-term debt and greater reliance on exchange flexibility are alternative ways of achieving stability (Feldstein 2002).

17. See, for instance, Edwards and Levy-Yeyati (2002) on the apparent effectiveness of floating rates against trade shocks. Also see Edwards (2002).

18. Nicolas (2000) notes that the likelihood of East Asia arriving at a currency union in the near term is remote, but informal cooperation on informal exchange rates is possible. Bayoumi, Eichen-

Efforts at regional integration began many years ago, and regional organizations have proliferated, but many factors, including the heterogeneity of the countries involved, have hampered progress, which has been relatively meager (Bowles and MacLean 1996; Wesley 2001).[19] The crisis of 1997–98 and the downturn in 2001–02 have changed perceptions, and this may accelerate the process of integration, with the initiatives of the Association of South East Asian Nations (ASEAN) plus China, Japan, and Korea possible harbingers of future developments.[20]

If East Asia moves quickly toward integration, the initiatives with the highest medium-term payoffs for growth and stability are likely to be in the further coordination of trade and financial regulation. Special attention will need to be paid to the circumstances of the poorer countries that specialize in labor-intensive products. Once integration is more advanced, the coordination of policies governing competition would be an advantageous medium-term agenda.

Financial Development and Liberalization

East Asian governments have been tackling the problems of the banking industry piecemeal for close to two decades, while the costs of incomplete reform have continued to mount. The choices are not always attractive, but they can be defined and need to be made. The banking sector was at the epicenter of the Asian crisis, and its reform and recapitalization are necessary steps to a full recovery. In 1997 the problems stemmed from the deterioration in the financial balance sheets of already fragile banks (Dornbusch 2001b; Ito 2001). Banking sector problems were largely resolved in Korea and Malaysia during 2002,[21] but problems remain in China, Indonesia, and Japan.

---

green, and Mauro (2000) take the view that relative to the euro area, the Association of South East Asian Nations is still not politically or economically ready for a regional monetary arrangement.

19. Both Alesina, Angeloni, and Etro (2001) and Hughes-Hallett and Weymark (2002) suggest that where the heterogeneity of countries and policy preferences is significant, policy coordination is most feasible in smaller regional groupings where there is considerable common ground with respect to policy objectives.

20. The members of ASEAN are Brunei, Cambodia, Indonesia, Laos, Malaysia, Myanmar, the Philippines, Singapore, Thailand, and Vietnam.

21. By mid-2002 the percentage of nonperforming loans in bank portfolios declined to 2.3 in Korea, 10 in Malaysia, and to 11 in Thailand (World Bank, East Asia Region 2002; World Bank 2002e).

Banks are still the principal financial intermediaries in most of East Asia, and their reform and regulation are matters of priority.[22] Good regulatory practice calls for quick action to restore the viability of the banking system and to ensure that more funds are not channeled to inefficient or insolvent firms. Well-tested procedures exist for achieving this, including selecting the banks to be rescued, sequestering their nonperforming loans in asset management corporations, injecting equity, requiring adherence to CAMEL (capital adequacy, asset quality, management, earnings, and liquidity) regulations, and introducing organizational changes. Other banks need to be liquidated in a manner that minimizes damage to the economy, especially at the incipient stage of a recovery.[23]

Good rules in this area are hard to translate into action for many reasons, including the costs of cutting credit lines to firms that are having difficulty servicing their debts (this requires banks to take account of nonperforming loans by writing down their capital, forcing some into violation of capital adequacy requirements), willful regulatory forbearance, the absence of detailed and accurate information on the state of banks, political pressures arguing against closure, and the politically unpalatable budgetary costs of a full-scale cleanup. But permitting bad banks to continue functioning, possibly "gambling for redemption" by accumulating yet more nonperforming loans, only compounds the severity of the problem and squanders depositors' savings. Further delay is increasingly costly to the economy and regulators, who need to move quickly. Restructuring banks involves another set of choices. In some cases, the crisis enlarged the stake of governments in the banking industry (to 30 percent in Korea). Most of the recent research suggests that publicly owned banks are less efficient than privately held ones, so it would be advantageous to divest these assets. This would also entail scaling back industrial policy further, which is much overdue. Although consolidation has been under

---

22. Recent research assigns banks and the financial markets major roles in the growth process through their contribution to resource allocation, information gathering, and monitoring mechanisms, although in much of East Asia a long history of government-directed lending largely emasculated the capacity of banks to exercise a governance function over the corporate sector and delayed the widening of financial markets. Deregulation of banks was initiated in Korea in 1988 and in Taiwan, China, in the early 1990s (C-H Chang 2000; Kang 2000).

23. Both the concern about short-term damage to the economy and the threat of a sharp rise in unemployment have inhibited quick action in Japan. As the recession has lengthened, even otherwise viable firms are having difficulties and could be imperiled by measures to curtail bank lending to loss-making firms.

way for almost two years, several economies still have a large number of banks—Taiwan, China, has 53, and Hong Kong, China, has 145 ("Why Small Banks Survive" 2001). The presence of many smaller banks promotes competition and helps to serve different market niches with speed and flexibility, especially the needs of small and medium enterprises and of ethnic groups that might otherwise have limited access to the formal banking sector and do not always require a full range of banking services (see Calomiris [2002] for the proliferation of small banks in the United States). But smaller banks are less easy for regulators to monitor and could have difficulty competing with foreign banks once the banking sector is liberalized. For this reason, governments are promoting mergers so as to create banking entities capable of withstanding foreign competition.[24] At the same time, they are keen to ensure that the newly constituted entities do not become pliant appendages of existing industrial groups. The efficiency and productivity gains to banks from a government-orchestrated consolidation of the banking sector into an arbitrary number of groups have not been assessed as yet. And some research on OECD countries suggests that, in countries where financial development is at an early stage, bank consolidation could lead to or exacerbate greater concentration in product markets (Cetorelli 2001). This would be a matter of concern for Indonesia and Korea, for example.

Governments have not weighed the pros and cons of allowing foreign investors rather than local business groups to take over banks, assuming that such groups would most likely gain control if the banks were privatized. Foreign ownership is resisted on two counts: first, governments lose their leverage and ability to influence the allocative process, and, second, foreign-owned banks are less likely to service small enterprises. With governments rightly relinquishing industrial policy, the first concern should have less weight. The second deserves to be tested against the evidence.[25] Against the possible negative out-

---

24. Singapore's authorities have facilitated consolidation of the banking sector from seven to five banks in 1998. In 2001 another round of consolidation was leading to three banks, and eventually this may be whittled down to two ("Singapore Banking Mergers" 2001). An effort is under way in Taiwan, China, with 53 banks, to reduce their numbers through mergers ("Taiwan Acts" 2001). Malaysia has consolidated the original 58 banks into 10.

25. The findings of research on Latin America suggest that the fears are misplaced. Credit to the small and medium enterprise sectors usually does not diminish, and because foreign banks are more efficient, they can give rise to spillovers (Clarke and others 2001).

comes, governments need to weigh the advantages of technology transfers from foreign banks; the greater resilience of these banks, arising from their diversification across countries; and the extra oversight provided by regulators in their countries of origin, which are generally advanced economies with stronger regulatory organizations.

Restructuring the banking sector—through a combination of market forces and government guidance—must go hand in hand with achieving improved regulation equal to the challenges of globalization. Regulatory failure must surely have a prominent place among the causes of the crisis of 1997–98. Minimizing the risks of recurrence requires addressing financial market competition, ensuring adequate prudential regulation to offset asymmetric information, keeping systemic instability in check, and strengthening the legal system to support a rule-based market system and enforce bankruptcy laws. A regulatory system can take several forms, some more integrated than others, but all require skilled and motivated regulators, which most of East Asia lacks and needs to train (Carmichael 2001).

Industrial Organization. Alongside the reform of the financial sector and intertwined with it are market- and government-induced shifts in industrial organization. These are rendered more urgent by the persistent weakness of business profitability in most East Asian countries, which is reflected in low rates of fixed private investment (World Bank, East Asia Region 2002). For many years, lively debate has taken place over the merits of different models, with no clear winner emerging. However, the choices for policymakers have begun to crystallize. Some researchers believe that East Asia's future will depend on the emergence of world-class companies such as Samsung that can compete in global markets and create dynamic networks of affiliated suppliers.[26] At the other extreme is the Taiwanese model based on many small firms. Small and medium enterprises are increasingly viewed as one of the principal vehicles through which new ideas and technologies germinate and enter the industrial mainstream.

Research now appears to favor a mix of large internationally competitive firms and dynamic start-ups. The weight of evidence argues

---

26. Other East Asian companies are also carving out a place for themselves in regional and international markets. These include Huawei, Hyundai, ZTE, Haier, the leading Chinese producer of large consumer durables, and Galanz, the largest Chinese manufacturer of microwave ovens ("Haier Reaches Higher" 2002; Hart and Christensen 2002).

for government policy that creates a competitive environment with low entry barriers, so that an abundance of entrepreneurial, innovative firms can enter the market and, where opportunities permit, grow to a size that allows them to compete on a global stage.

The choice many governments face concerns the phasing in of such an open and competitive environment, with its exacting requirements for corporate control, corporate governance, institutions, and provision of business services. Enlarging the role of foreign investors and the scope for hostile takeovers, which are rare in East Asia, could stimulate competition. A few economies have accepted market-determined outcomes, recognizing from their experience in the 1990s the ineffectiveness of government-orchestrated industrial policy. Other governments still worry about the disruption a sudden move would cause if large firms were allowed to go out of business or be taken over and if the economy's "commanding heights" were occupied by foreign firms. These views are reinforced by the lobbying efforts of beleaguered firms and others for which protection helps to protect profit margins.

Governance. The issues of industrial organization and financial reform are enmeshed with those of governance at two levels. Public sector governance shapes the business environment through its effects on the transaction costs of firms, entry barriers, and the degree to which the rule of law is in place and practiced. Corporate governance affects the relations between firms and institutional investors and between company managers and boards of directors; it also affects the relative weights given to minority shareholder rights as against the claims of dominant shareholders and stakeholders. Both public sector and corporate governance depend on the openness of political activity; on the integrity, procedural efficiency, and enforcement capability of the legal system; and on the effectiveness of the media in inducing "socially acceptable" behavior.[27]

---

27. Research both on the costs of corruption and on the gains from instituting the rule of law is assembling a convincing case for measures that strengthen accountability and individual rights. While democracy has limited effects (if any) on growth, the rule of law is more likely to have positive consequences for growth and investment (Barro 2000; Tavares and Wacziarg 2001). Wei has shown that perceived corruption is negatively correlated with FDI (Wei 2000). On the role of the media in influencing corporate governance, see Dyck and Zingales (2002).

Since the crisis, standards of corporate governance in the region have received considerably more attention, with the shakeout of the corporate sector and the development of more choices for investors, greater demand for transparency, and a wider role for overseas corporations (Rajan and Zingales 2001). In particular, the practices being scrutinized are those that have sanctioned a regime of low profits, assigned a dominant weight to stakeholder interests while giving minority shareholders a limited voice, sheltered firms from hostile takeovers, and made it extremely difficult for creditors to liquidate insolvent firms so as to salvage some of their capital.

The stakeholder culture of the traditional East Asian business world is viewed as advantageous because it has inculcated a long-term perspective. It engenders employees' loyalty, providing a basis for investment in firm-specific human capital. In economies with weak public social security systems, companies give their employees conditional assurance of employment, a pension, and, occasionally, medical benefits. An abrupt withdrawal of these benefits would be a blow for workers and could disrupt labor relations.[28] These implicit guarantees provided by firms, in certain instances based on a tacit underlying contract with the state, have constrained corporate action and government readiness to pursue restructuring.

A shift to Anglo-Saxon rules of governance, which ascribe centrality to the profit motive in the interests of the shareholder, may not be possible or even desirable for East Asia. Nonetheless, the maturing of market institutions, by augmenting shareholder rights, could force companies to improve efficiency, raise earnings, and disclose balance sheet information with greater frequency to inform rather than conceal the true health of firms.[29]

Most East Asian countries do not yet have governance structures capable of monitoring the behavior of firms in the interests of shareholders. None of the banks, fiduciary investors, or pools of external

---

28. Labor unrest in Korea, as the government and creditors have sought to restructure chaebols such as Daewoo and Hyundai, has discouraged radical corporate reforms. Employees strongly resisted foreign takeovers of Thai banks, and intense labor unrest marked the immediate postwar period in Japan until the system of tenured employment was introduced. The pressure from the urban labor force in China's state sector has hampered the liquidation of loss-making Chinese state-owned enterprises.

29. On the relative merits of different approaches to governance, see Allen (2001) and Dore (2000).

directors, as currently constituted, could police corporate actions or assure better performance.[30] And the situation is not helped by the disarray over accounting conventions and unsatisfactory audits. Nonetheless, governance and auditing systems are improving in Singapore and Hong Kong, China, for example ("Asia's Best Companies" 2002). Over the longer term, globalization is likely to require a change in the nature of corporate governance, and countries must choose from among the institutional possibilities to arrive at a mix that enables shareholders to demand a higher level of accountability and performance without eroding too severely the stakeholder rights that have contributed to the stable work relations and effective internal labor markets of East Asian firms.

GLOBAL AND REGIONAL CHANGE

Many interrelated developments at the global and regional levels strongly suggest that the future will be quite different from the past. Global integration is increasing, facilitated by freer trade, which is yielding a much more competitive environment and challenging once protected domestic markets. At the regional level, the Japanese economy is no longer the driver it was in the past. China is emerging both as a strong competitor and as a promising market. The technological revolution continues apace, and the organization of production is being transformed by the rise of FDI and by the emergence of international production networks that bring together component suppliers, assemblers, supply chain managers, and buyers in dynamic relationships.

Countries (and firms) that are well integrated into international production networks and widely exposed to market trends abroad will be much better placed to exploit market opportunities than those that remain less integrated. But unless East Asia moves toward a technological and skill-intensive, rather than a factor-intensive, mode of manufacturing, a slower increase in value added will constrain growth in the future, a tendency that could be exacerbated by a gradual cessation in the expansion of the labor force in several countries. It is imperative that East Asia prepare to move up the value chain, relying more on productivity-enhancing innovations based on science and technology for its dominant source of growth.

---

30. Conger and Lawler (2001) note that, even in Anglo-Saxon economies, building effective boards has been a slow process, and boards often remain subservient to chief executive officers.

Global Economic Integration

The increasing synchronization of economic activities—most clearly seen in the correlation of movements in international capital markets, the financial shocks crowding recent history (82 worldwide between 1970 and 1996; Eichengreen and Rose 1998; World Bank 2000k), and the speed with which information technology has spread—points toward a much closer integration of national economies.[31]

While globalization increases opportunities by providing access to bigger and richer world markets, it also entails a cost for countries that are not prepared for its challenges. East Asian economies gained an early advantage through their readiness to promote freer trade, attract FDI, and encourage the diffusion of technology. Now their governments need to undertake extensive reform on the domestic front, closer regional coordination, and a proactive role in the international policy arena. Delay in coming to terms with globalization—by postponing measures to deregulate, raise the efficiency of the services sector, especially nontraded services, or integrate capital markets—may seem to buy time but is almost certain to be costly in the longer term. Although it is often tempting to take the path of least political resistance and to sidestep institutional or policy issues, these issues will only become more serious if they are put on hold.

Changes in the Economic Roles of Japan and China

Two important factors are shaping the economic landscape in East Asia: the economic performance and relationships of Japan with neighboring countries and the economy of China.

Japan. During the 1980s and early 1990s Japan was East Asia's axial economy.[32] After the Plaza Accord in 1985, the strong yen created an incentive for Japanese exporters to relocate the labor-intensive elements of their production processes to reliable locations with cheaper labor. The share of Japanese foreign direct investment flowing into

---

31. *The Economist* notes some of the disadvantages of economies being increasingly in step because once that happens an escape from a downturn becomes much harder ("Unfinished Recession" 2002).

32. For an illuminating discussion of Japan's involvement in East Asia, see Hatch and Yamamura (1996).

East Asia increased from 10 percent in 1991 to 50 percent in 1997. This investment boom, followed by the trading activities of Japanese companies, powerfully influenced development in the region. Japanese firms are continuing to move their production facilities out of Japan, especially in electronics, although aggregate FDI from Japan declined steadily between 1995 and 2000 (see table 1.4).[33] For example, in the automobile industry, Honda has plans to open a new plant in China for assembly, to open a new factory in Indonesia for parts, and to expand its current facilities in the Philippines.[34]

Uncertain economic prospects make Japan unlikely to propel East Asia forward as quickly as in the past. Japan's economy contracted 1.3 percent, and more than two-thirds of all Japanese companies posted losses in 2001 ("Japan's Bad Banks" 2002). Rising exports raised hopes in the early part of 2002, but these were not sustained, and real GDP declined again during the year ("Japan Growth Calculations" 2002). Lack of progress in restructuring Japan's corporations, strengthening its banks (where nonperforming loans reached 8.4 percent in the first quarter of 2002), addressing the overhang of gross public debt (150 percent of GDP in 2002), and improving profitability may hinder growth in the years ahead (IMF 2002, pp. 18–19; "Japan: Tackling NPLs" 2002).

Japan also became East Asia's principal creditor, particularly to Indonesia and Thailand (IMF 2002, p. 21). During the 1990s, however, the scale of lending by Japanese banks declined significantly in the region. As financial pressures on the banks mounted and the Japanese premium rose, Japanese banks began withdrawing from the region. At the peak of the crisis in 1995, the stock of East Asian loans outstanding from Japanese banks was $318 billion; after the crisis, in 2000, it stood at only $114 billion.

---

33. Aiwa, for instance, will close all its remaining factories in Japan and relocate them to Malaysia; Matsushita plans to downsize its factories in Japan and rely more on production in Guangzhou; Sony is shifting more of its semiconductor business to Thailand and starting to produce notebook personal computers in China instead of relying solely on production in Japan; and Canon is planning to shift production of low- to mid-level copiers from Japan to China (see Fuji Research Institute 2002).

34. See www.honda.com/news/2002/c020710_1.html, www.honda.com/news/2002/c020710_2. html, and www.honda.com/news/2002/c020710_4.html. In addition, Honda is planning a new factory in Guangzhou, mainly for exports (see "Industry Baffled" 2002).

Table 1.4 Destination of Foreign Direct Investment from Japan, Fiscal 1995–2000 (millions of U.S. dollars)

Destination	1995	1996	1997	1998	1999	2000
United States	22,193	22,005	20,769	10,316	22,296	12,136
East Asia						
China	4,473	2,510	1,987	1,065	751	995
Hong Kong, China	1,125	1,487	695	602	971	936
Indonesia	1,596	2,414	2,514	1,076	918	414
Korea, Rep. of	445	416	442	303	980	813
Malaysia	573	572	791	514	526	232
Philippines	718	559	524	379	617	458
Singapore	1,152	1,115	1,824	636	962	424
Taiwan, China	457	521	450	224	285	510
Thailand	1,224	1,403	1,867	1,371	816	931
Total East Asia	11,763	10,997	11,094	6,170	6,826	5,713

Source: JETRO (2000, 2001, 2002).

The rest of East Asia has already reduced its dependence on Japan not only as a source of bank loans but also as a destination for exports. By 2000 the U.S. market was the most important destination for exports from all East Asian economies (except for Indonesia, whose exports went principally to Japan). The European Union market is also more important than the Japanese market for most countries in the region. The exports from ASEAN countries to Japan dropped from near 30 percent in 1980 to 13 percent in 2000.[35]

Although the shift in export destinations will reduce the impact of Japan's slow growth on the rest of the region, Japan's progress remains very important. As Callen and McKibbin (2001) show, if Japan's productivity growth slows, the short-run impact would be minimal, but in the long run, all the East Asian economies would see significantly lower real GDP; Hong Kong (China), Malaysia, the Philippines, and Taiwan (China) would be the most affected. While some segments of the manufacturing sector in Japan such as autos and consumer electronics have continued to sustain productivity increases, nonmanufacturing productivity diminished in the 1990s and shows no signs of recovery (Sato 2002).

---

35. However, their exports to the European Union and the United States have remained fairly steady at around 15 and 19 percent (E. Sakakibara and Yamakawa 2002).

China. In view of the uncertain prospects of the Japanese economy, China could emerge as the regional locomotive over the longer term if it sustains its growth and continues down the path of openness. But for other East Asian economies over the medium run, China's emergence as an economic center and competitor sends mixed signals. Rising domestic demand in China presents opportunities for exporters from elsewhere in the region. But in world export markets, the ASEAN countries, in particular, may find themselves losing out to China. China's widening cost advantages in increasingly sophisticated products have implications not only for export competitiveness but also for the ability of other countries to continue attracting the foreign direct investment they need.

China's accession to the World Trade Organization will increase competition in certain export markets, for example clothing, but it also will require the opening of China's domestic market. In recent years, China has made impressive progress in liberalizing its trade regime, lowering the average tariff from 41 percent in 1992 to 15 percent in 2001 (E. Sakakibara and Yamakawa 2002).[36] Other East Asian countries should be able to increase their exports to China—a process that has already begun. Simulation results by Ianchovichina and Martin (2001) show that Japan and the newly industrializing countries stand to gain by China's accession to the World Trade Organization: exports to China could rise 83 percent for newly industrializing economies and 43 percent for Japan. During the decade of the 1990s, the percentage of East Asia's exports to China doubled to 10 percent, side by side with a decline in Japan's share (see "Big Lift" 2002; Brice 2002). This process has accelerated over the past three years, with sales of electronics products from ASEAN to China rising almost one-third ("Enough for Everyone" 2002). In 2000 China's two-way trade with Southeast Asia already amounted to $40 billion, with ASEAN running a favorable balance of $5 billion (see "Southeast Asia, China Challenge" 2002).

As China's economy and trade have expanded, many analysts have wondered if China will increasingly displace the exports of East Asian economies, including Japan, in world markets. China is now the dominant exporter in the developing world, partly because of its cost com-

---

36. Because of tariff exemptions and evasion, the effective tariff rate in China was already close to 3 percent in 2000 ("China Tax Troubles" 2001).

petitiveness, achieved through reforms, and partly because of the sheer size of its economy. Among developing countries, China has moved from tenth position overall in 1985 to first place in total manufactured exports, as well as resource-based and light-technology manufactures; it is now the fifth largest trading nation. Worldwide, China has ascended to third position in exports of medium-technology manufactures and fifth in exports of high-technology manufactures.[37]

China currently has absolute cost advantages in a range of manufacturing subsectors not just over Japan but also over the rest of the region. Its annual labor costs are lower in manufacturing in general and in sectors such as transport and electrical machinery (see table 1.5). In manufacturing, for example, Chinese workers earned an annual wage only one-third of that of Thai workers in 1997. Such a difference is likely to increase the competitive pressure on Thai producers—especially considering that more than 35 percent of Thailand's exports consist of low-technology products (World Bank 1998a, pp. 24–25). Wage differences in 1997 were even wider in transport and electrical machinery, with Chinese workers earning close to $800 annually versus $4,200 for Thai workers and $6,500 for Malaysian workers.

The degree to which China's export expansion threatens the rest of the region depends on the robustness of the "flying geese" pattern of development in East Asia.[38] During the 1990s China's expansion of exports to the United States came mostly at the expense of the newly industrializing economies, but the displacement took place mainly in production lines that the latter were abandoning—clothing, footwear, toys, and household products (Loungani 2000). Meanwhile, the ASEAN-4 countries increased their share of exports in the United States by moving into more capital- and technology-intensive products.[39] While China's comparative advantage in all labor-intensive in-

---

37. A significant portion of China's exports are the result of investment by multinational corporations, some of which have shifted production from elsewhere in East Asia to China, but much also comes from domestic firms (Lall 2000b).

38. The "flying geese" pattern of East Asian development was first hypothesized by Akamatsu Kaname in the 1930s, and it has since been adopted by numerous researchers. It refers to the process by which countries move up the product and technology ladder as they develop, leaving the rungs they vacate to be occupied by the economies of the nations following in their footsteps.

39. The ASEAN-4 consists of Indonesia, Malaysia, the Philippines, and Thailand.

Table 1.5 Annual Average Wages in Manufacturing, Select Years, 1985–97

Economy	Annual average wage (U.S. dollars)			Annual growth rate (percent)	
	1985	1993	1997	1985–97	1993–97
China	379	581	716	5.4	5.3
Thailand	—	2,242	2,104	—	−1.6
Malaysia	—	4,868	5,907	4.8	5.0
Philippines	1,431	2,999	3,880	8.7	6.7
		3,369			
New tigers[a]	—	—	4,006	—	4.4
Hong Kong, China	3,464	8,580	11,003	10.1	6.4
Korea, Rep. of	3,719	13,237	16,730	13.3	6.0
Singapore	—	—	20,043	—	—
Taiwan, China[b]	3,832	13,014	12,083	10.8	0.1
Mature tigers	—	—	15,215	—	—
East Asia[c]	—	—	19,220	—	—
Mexico	—	—	2,897	—	—

— Not available.

a. Excludes Indonesia.

b. Data for 1995 in 1997.

c. Excludes China and Indonesia.

Source: Lall and Albaladejo (2001).

dustries has been increasing, that of the ASEAN-4 in these industries has been decreasing. Of more concern to the other countries in the region is that China is increasing its comparative advantage in a growing number of capital-intensive industries relative to the ASEAN-4, even while it retains its competitive edge in low-technology items such as toys and garments (Brice 2002; "Burying the Competition" 2002; Lall 2000b).[40]

Much depends on the extent to which exports from China and other economies overlap. By and large, China's mix of exports differs from that of Japan and the newly industrializing economies but is similar to that of the ASEAN countries (Xu and Song 2000). Manufactured exports from China to the United States currently overlap most extensively with those from Indonesia and Thailand (see table 1.6); the overlap with other East Asian economies remains modest for

---

40. China may soon become a powerful competitor not just in the production of semiconductor chips but also in their design. This is because of China's large domestic demand for chips, its ample supply of skills, and the incentives being provided by the Chinese government (A. C. Chen and Woetzel 2002).

Table 1.6 Competition between Asian Economies and China in the U.S. Market, Select Years, 1990–2000
(percent of overlap with China's exports)

Economy	1990	1995	2000
Japan	3.0	8.3	16.3
Korea, Rep. of	24.0	27.1	37.5
Taiwan, China	26.7	38.7	48.5
Hong Kong, China	42.5	50.5	55.9
Singapore	14.8	19.2	35.8
Indonesia	85.3	85.5	82.8
Malaysia	37.1	38.9	48.7
Philippines	46.3	47.8	46.1
Thailand	42.2	56.3	65.4

Note: The degree of competition with China is calculated using a 10-digit international harmonized system.
Source: Kwan (2002b).

the time being (Kwan 2002a).[41] This provides breathing space for these economies, but, as the table shows, the overlap is growing for them too. The competition is bound to intensify in a number of product groups unless countries make determined efforts to diversify their mix of products, to raise the technological thresholds in existing product categories, and to increase their trade in services. For Western and East Asian firms that either manufacture locally or export consumer durables and items such as cosmetics and detergents to China, the pressure from their Chinese competitors is mounting.

China has placed heavy reliance on FDI for inward technology transfer, and changes in China's production of exports—and also in its imports—are closely correlated with changes in inflows of foreign direct investment. In the 1980s China's FDI inflows were mainly concentrated in labor-intensive industries, but in the early 1990s they shifted toward capital-intensive industries, and that trend is continuing. A high proportion of China's FDI inflows come from the European Union, Japan, and the United States, but some also originate in

---

41. Even at this level of disaggregation, the true extent of sophistication is not measured. For instance, Japan still makes television sets, which are classified as mid-tech products, but Japanese televisions tend to be more sophisticated than those produced in China. Therefore, these overlaps should be taken as an upper bound. The extent to which this overestimates the true overlap depends on the heterogeneity of the quality of products in the 10-digit classification of the international harmonized system.

the newly industrializing economies.[42] A fifth of Japanese firms are considering shifting their production and procurement to China over the medium term in order to take advantage of lower production costs to supply the expanding domestic market and to supply parts to major customers (Abe and Lee 2001; Kaburagi and others 2002).[43] And a significant share of recent flows are into industries producing flat-screen televisions, DVD players, LCD monitors, plasma display panels, laptop computers, and digital cameras, which will augment China's manufacturing capability in higher-technology areas (Kuroda 2002).

Now that China is emerging as the new magnet for such relocation, other economies, especially ASEAN-4, are having difficulty attracting the additional FDI inflows needed to upgrade their industries.[44] If China successfully transforms itself from the "factory of the world" to the "design laboratory of the world" by using direct investment by Japanese corporations in research and development facilities, the pressure on Southeast Asian economies will sharpen further (Jefferson and Kaifeng 2002). For the ASEAN nations, this could drasti-

---

42. For instance, AU Optronics and Chunghwa Picture Tubes, both based in Taiwan, China, have substantially increased their capacity to produce LCD monitors in China in recent years. AU Optronics plans to produce 600,000 modules by the end of 2002, and Chunghwa Picture Tubes plans to produce 200,000 modules in China (see Goldman Sachs Global Equity Research 2002).

43. More and more Japanese firms are procuring products from China, reflecting not only the relatively low cost but also the improved quality of Chinese products. Since 1990 Japan's imports from China have more than tripled in value to $54 billion, and China's share of Japan's imports rose to 14 percent in 2000, which is more than the share of the European Union (E. Sakakibara and Yamakawa 2002). The cost differential between Chinese and Japanese industries is strikingly apparent in the semiconductor industry. Chinese electrical engineers have wages that are one-tenth those of their Japanese counterparts. The cost of electricity and water in China is half and rental charges for land are 2 percent of those in Japan. Moreover, equipment can be used for 360 days a year versus 260 days in Japan (see "Japan/China Hollowing Out" 2002). Minolta, for instance, will cease production of cameras in Japan and Malaysia and will move its entire production capacity to Shanghai by the end of fiscal 2002. Similarly, Olympus plans to produce all of its digital cameras in China by the end of 2004 (Fuji Research Institute 2002). Japanese companies are not alone. Intel doubled its investment in semiconductor production in Shanghai, and U.S. producers of telecommunications network equipment see China as the only market with substantial growth potential over the medium term.

44. According to a worldwide survey conducted by AT Kearney in 2002, a third of the senior corporate executives polled assigned the highest preference to China as a destination for their FDI ("China Dream" 2002). Even though worldwide FDI flows fell in 2001—to $750 billion—China attracted $47 billion, an increase of 15 percent over 2000. And although a further dip in global FDI occurred in 2002, it is estimated that flows to China exceeded $50 billion (Mody 2002; World Bank, East Asia Region 2002). In recent years, China has also become a source of FDI mainly to secure supplies of natural resources but also to enter foreign markets (M. Y. Wang 2002; Wu and Chen 2001).

cally heighten the urgency of developing new and differentiated products and services.

Changes in the Organization of Production

Another important development is the ongoing transformation of the structure of world production in leading industries such as automobile parts and electronics. Lead firms now outsource virtually all their manufacturing operations. The deverticalization of firms and the slicing of the value chain have created geographically dispersed global production networks dominated by very large contract manufacturers with revenues of $56 billion in 2001. Most of these contract manufacturers are headquartered in the West but have specialized production facilities in East Asia, Europe, Latin America, and the United States. Original equipment manufacturers prefer to deal with them because of their size advantage and global reach.

International production networks now orchestrate perhaps as much as two-thirds of all trade in "commoditized" manufactures. They present East Asian firms with new challenges as well as market access and spillover benefits. Firms need to extract the highest returns from participation in production networks and to develop their own differentiated products in order to avoid being marginalized. It is by working through and around these networks that firms from the region are likely to realize their technological potential and find niche markets for differentiated products.

Changes in the Sources of Growth

For much of the past 30 years, growth in East Asia derived largely from high rates of capital accumulation, which also served as the vehicle for technological change, and from the increasing influx of young, educated workers (Quibria 2002). But as the proportion of the working-age population begins to decline, only a leap in East Asia's technological capability will permit the region to keep up its earlier pace of advance and to catch up rapidly with the industrial economies.[45]

---

45. See recent research summarized by Easterly and Levine (2001) and Felipe (2000).

Several countries in the region are finding that less and less profit can be squeezed out of existing product lines. Many manufactured products (even high-technology ones) have now become standardized commodities traded in intensely competitive markets, much like primary products. "Commoditized" manufactures offer relatively weak prospects for growth because their real prices are decreasing and they have become barely profitable despite their manufacturers' efforts to raise productivity.[46]

The hard disk drive industry epitomizes the problems facing segments of East Asia's electronics industry: formerly exotic high-tech products once earning high rents are being transformed into marginally profitable commodities attractive only for companies with highly specialized technological capability and hard-won market share ("Tide Turns" 2002). Between 1988 and 2002 the price per megabyte of hard disk drive fell from $11.54 to less than $0.15, side by side with a drastic reduction in the size of each unit and a miniaturization of individual components. These trends, in turn, have forced the industry to consolidate and to increase the capital intensity of production and research into areas such as microelectromechanical systems to reduce the size of storage devices (Vettiger and Binnig 2003). Companies such as Hewlett-Packard, IBM, Read-Rite, SCI Systems, and 3Com have closed their plants in Penang (Malaysia) and Singapore, and some, most recently IBM, have withdrawn from the production of conventional disk drives altogether. Those that remain, such as industry leader Seagate, have cut back on employment—from 29,000 to 5,500 jobs in Malaysia and from 40,000 to 18,000 in Thailand—and are struggling to sustain modest profits through a mix of technological improvement and relentless cost cutting.

IMPLICATIONS FOR DEVELOPMENT POLICY

There is no question that East Asia's past areas of strength—macroeconomic stability, openness to trade, and human capital development—will continue to provide the bedrock of development. At the same time, the most serious weaknesses of the present—financial fragility and

---

46. Prices of a wide range of items, including television sets, large consumer durables, personal computers, and equipment of all kinds, have been falling steadily. A 21-inch color television set that cost $400 in China 10 years ago now costs only $80 ("Burying the Competition" 2002).

inadequate corporate governance, regulatory oversight, exchange rate management, and social safety nets—must be dealt with.

The real challenge for the region arises from the fact that factor accumulation can no longer provide an adequate basis for future growth. Innovations are needed that enhance productivity. To nurture them will entail a significant break from the past. The major policy challenges relate to how East Asian countries will cultivate creativity within their economies.

Led by Japan, several of the East Asian economies have already established a track record of innovation. Most have been working on parts of their innovation systems for decades. But overall they still need to strengthen and fine-tune their innovation systems, to recognize fully the interrelatedness of the many parts (especially the increasing skill-intensive bias of technological change), to establish channels for regional and global collaboration, and to advance on a broader front.

In all the areas discussed next, a combination of public and private initiatives to stimulate innovation (rather than policies targeting specific industries) will be critical to success, both for firms individually and for economies as a whole.

Education

Innovative economic systems cannot function well without a highly educated work force. Primary education has played a key role in the development of economies in East Asia, and it will continue to do so. Basic education and disciplined work habits have leveraged the benefits of macroeconomic stability and economic openness. During the 1990s this was deepened by the spread of secondary and tertiary education in the region's middle- and upper-income countries. The investment in education, and the education infrastructure it brought into existence, was money well spent, yielding high private and social returns of between 15 and 20 percent (Temple 2001). It also provided a stepping-stone to a more innovative economy.

Today, both secondary- and tertiary-level education are still geared mainly toward the factor-intensive model that served the region so well in the past. For the future, secondary education acutely needs improvement. Schools need to equip students not only with basic technical skills but also with creative abilities that are internationally comparable. Research points especially to the need for more student participation, questioning, and debate, rather than pure teacher-led instruction, in the classroom. This calls for a change in approach to teaching more than an increase in spending per student, although in some cases the latter might also be required. There are many ways to pursue this, including spurring competition among schools, allowing teachers more autonomy, and introducing incentives for teachers.

In tertiary education, policymakers need to consider various trade-offs among different kinds of tertiary-level skills, between the quantity and quality of skills, and between international and domestic sources of skills. However, regardless of the choices, all countries can leverage their investments in scientific and technological skills through greater openness to ideas and international circulation of knowledge workers, alliances among research entities (whether institutes or firms), and effective adoption of information technology.[47]

Education policy in East Asia should also seek to nurture the business, professional, and entrepreneurial skills needed to fuel the development of service activities, which are rapidly becoming the backbone of the high-tech economy.[48] Except in Hong Kong (China), Japan, Singapore, and Taiwan (China), gaps in business skills are evident throughout the region. Even in Japan, legal, accounting, and financial skills fall far short of the levels in other OECD countries. East Asia did not feel the shortage of professionals in these fields when its economies still concentrated on manufacturing and served mainly as suppliers to major U.S. or European companies. But gaps in business skills are a handicap today, as these economies attempt to commercialize the findings of research and as firms seek to develop, design, and market new products independently, establish their own brand names, and package services with higher value added together with manufactured products so as to widen their profit margins.

---

47. On human development issues for East Asia, see Quibria (2002). On the importance of mobility among knowledge workers, see Lucas (2002) and Saxenian (1999).

48. Spurred by information technology, services in Hong Kong (China), Singapore, and Taiwan (China) account for 60 percent of GDP. The shares are closer to 40 percent in some of the other East Asian economies (Wirtz 2000).

Research and Development

In the more advanced economies of the region and in China, where market competition is becoming increasingly fierce, the quality of university research is of major concern. These economies produce enough graduates with science and technology degrees, but they need to improve the quality of their skills and place greater emphasis on research, on the depth of expertise in research centers, and on the rigorous evaluation of research. Heightening competition among universities in the allocation of funds and in faculty selection may help to improve the research output.

The distribution of research in science and technology is shifting among large companies, government research institutes, universities, and smaller start-up firms, without a clear trend emerging. Government research institutes often are inefficient users of research and development (R&D) resources; they can become isolated from the business sector and other centers of research, and they are often ineffectual in producing commercial innovations.[49] As to research in large corporations, universities, private research institutes, and small start-ups, the policy choices relate not to the steering of research activity, but to the scale of efforts to enable different types of institutions to participate fully and fruitfully in the process of innovation. This involves lowering the entry barriers to research, improving access to funding for R&D, increasing the protection of intellectual property rights in the middle- and higher-income countries that are more dependent on innovation, facilitating networking between researchers within and among countries, and making it both easier and more profitable to commercialize research findings.

Past experience, mainly in OECD countries, shows that, apart from market competition, tax incentives and direct subsidies are among the most effective policy instruments for promoting R&D.[50] The Korean government successfully supports private R&D by giving tax credits, allowing accelerated depreciation, and lowering im-

---

49. Even so, public research institutes in Taiwan, China, have been conspicuously effective in initiating a virtuous spiral of research commercialization and cluster formation.

50. Lerner (1999), looking at the Small Business Innovation Research Program in the United States, finds that firms receiving government funding in research grow significantly faster than firms not receiving government funding.

port tariffs. Similarly, the tax system of Taiwan, China, provides full deductibility for R&D expenses, allows accelerated depreciation, and encourages large firms to invest 0.5–1.5 percent of their sales in R&D. Most empirical studies of firms in the European Union and the United States find that such policies have significant positive effects, although the magnitude of the benefits varies by time, industry, and country (B. H. Hall and van Reene 1999). These results are buttressed by case studies from East Asia (UNDP 2001).

Information Technology and Productivity

The latter half of the 1990s saw an enormous surge in the growth of industries, exports, and innovations associated with information technology. Some observers have heralded this as the dawn of a "new economy" that promises higher rates of productivity growth in economies that embrace information technology to the full.[51]

In the United States, the rapid and systematic adoption of information technology–based activities is enabling businesses to raise productivity and sustain price competitiveness—in spite of persistent economic sluggishness in 2001–02, productivity in the United States rose 5.3 percent overall and more than 8 percent in manufacturing. In East Asia, policies and institutions that can widen the use of information technology, particularly in the services sector, thereby promoting productivity growth, deserve priority. They include a flexible regulatory environment that can promote Internet development through ease of use and access, rules governing the contestability of Internet-based applications, freedom of international exchange by way of the Internet, and privacy of Internet-based transactions.[52]

---

51. A study by the Conference Board estimates that industries using information technology contributed more than half of the 2.4 percent annual growth of productivity in the United States during 1995–99. In Europe the contribution was one-third of an annual average of 1.5 percent ("Europe's Scant Info-Tech Payoff" 2001). East Asia's growing automobile industry could reap large savings from business-to-business and business-to-consumer trading. The Economic Strategy Institute estimates that for the average $26,000 vehicle in the United States production costs could be lowered by $3,600, and business-to-consumer transactions could save an additional $1,000–$2,500 (Economic Strategy Institute 2001).

52. Some observers worry that regulations are walling off parts of the Internet through the application of copyright and antitrust laws, thus reducing the "innovation commons" and narrowing the positive spillover effects (Lessig 2001).

Dynamic Urban Clusters

International experience suggests that much of the innovation that enhances growth and expands trade is likely to occur in industrial clusters in a few major cities that have strong research capacity and a full suite of other amenities. Agglomeration economies in these major cities can feed the growth impulse generated by industrial clusters.

Clusters form as a result of multiple factors. Among these are policy measures that influence the entry of entrepreneurial firms; the availability of skills, infrastructure, and amenities; and the presence of institutions that have a significant role in innovation.

Experience suggests that it is not desirable for governments to frame industrial policies deliberately to build high-tech clusters. But some East Asian economies such as Japan, Singapore, and Taiwan (China) have successfully laid the groundwork for such clusters by combining local capacity with international linkages forged through trade, FDI, and the movement of knowledge workers. Other countries such as China, Korea, and Malaysia, each of which has a base of high-tech manufacturing industries, are attempting to induce clusters that fuse manufacturing capability with research and producer services. One approach involves investing heavily in transport and communications infrastructure, serviced land, and research facilities and providing incentives for high-tech industries to locate in the designated area. The scale of the required outlay makes it necessary to weigh the options—and potential returns—carefully.

Experience does suggest that an open urban milieu is vital for creativity, that linkages offering opportunities for collaboration with firms in other clusters can support innovation, and that the circulation of human capital from overseas is critical. An advantage East Asia enjoys over many other developing regions is a large diaspora of skilled workers participating in some of the leading North American clusters where they have acquired intangible capital, contacts, and financial wealth. As in Hong Kong (China), Singapore, and Taiwan (China), these individuals can be the nuclei for cluster development in East Asia—provided that the institutional environment is hospitable. However, although all these mediating factors can certainly help, the lifeblood of high-tech clusters is the continuing innovation of firms and the networking among them. In the absence of this stream of innovation, there can be a collection of firms, but not a dynamic cluster.

CONCLUSION

Rapid global and regional transformations point to a future quite different from the past. At the same time, an old imperative has become even more central: routinized technological progress in a stable macroeconomic framework is no longer just a prescription yielding increased market competitiveness; it has become an essential requirement for survival. As profit margins are eroded on lower-end products, technical innovation is the only path to capturing markets higher up in the value chain and creating new ones. In the face of ever increasing global competition, East Asian countries need public policy reforms—yielding lower business costs, improved governance, and better infrastructure and helping firms to pursue the goal of global reach—if they are to retain their existing advantages in world markets and generate the growth they need to lift their standard of living and eliminate the remaining poverty among their populations.

Defining, meshing, and enforcing the many different policies that are needed will be a challenge even for countries with a remarkable history of economic achievement. But East Asia enters the future with a head start over other regions, and there seems no reason why it cannot extend its record of unparalleled growth and become part of the industrial world.

CHAPTER 2

STRENGTHENING EAST ASIAN ECONOMIES: MACROECONOMIC STABILITY, CORPORATE AND FINANCIAL REFORM, AND THE RULE OF LAW

The years leading up to and since the crisis revealed basic weaknesses in the region's fiscal, corporate, and financial sectors that can affect the stability and pace of future growth. What are the underlying causes of these weaknesses? What efforts have been made since the crisis to ensure macroeconomic stability, restructure corporations and banks, and reform their governance? And what are the issues facing governments as they seek to strengthen the bases for future stability and growth?

This chapter reviews the steps being taken to promote macroeconomic stability and restructure industry and the financial sector, the constraints that stand in the way of progress, the ingredients of effective governance in the corporate and financial sectors, and the issues involved in building institutions to enforce the rules of a market system independently, efficiently, and fairly.

FISCAL POLICY FOR MACROECONOMIC STABILITY

For the past quarter century, the ability to maintain macroeconomic stability has been one of the most important determinants of differences in economic performance and welfare gains among developing countries (Rodrik 1999). Countries that neglected the fundamentals of macroeconomic management were more susceptible to domestic crises and to external shocks than those that did not. Inability to respond to these shocks with remedial policy actions can lead to a collapse in growth and to a rise in unemployment and social unrest that may further undermine stability.

For East Asian economies over the past decade, increasing openness has brought within reach more of the opportunities inherent in the global marketplace. It has stimulated growth by encouraging innovation, competition, and foreign direct investment. Higher incomes, and the increasing share in the economy of services, which are less prone than manufacturing to business fluctuations, have also reduced the vulnerability of large segments of the population.

Nevertheless, the risks of external shocks have risen in parallel with economic openness. As much of East Asia, and in particular China, has become a part of global production networks, there is a greater tendency for firms to move production facilities among countries in response to changes in the business environment. Significant numbers of people in East Asia, including members of the enlarged middle class, are still vulnerable to sudden crises and to the adverse consequences of shifts in the location of export production. The risks of external shocks worsen when domestic policy vigilance slackens. Deriving the full benefits of openness while containing the costs of domestic and external shocks and the associated social turbulence has come to occupy a central place in East Asian development policies.

Looking ahead, increasing economic openness and the broad trend toward greater political participation mean that East Asian economies urgently need to provide greater income security in the face of shocks and some means of smoothing income flows. For this and other reasons, social expenditures in East Asia are likely to grow as a share of national income. This calls for reforms to achieve more efficient management of public funds.

Balancing Efficiency and Social Protection

Before 1997–98 East Asia seemed relatively impervious to shocks and cycles despite its economic openness. The crisis revealed how exposed the region was to sudden shifts in the expectations of investors and how ill prepared it was to weather prolonged downturns. The poorest were especially hard hit, but so were urban workers employed in sectors like construction, banking, and finance.

Four factors now make it urgent for East Asian countries to strengthen private and public safety nets so that at least the more vulnerable segments of the population—whose numbers are still quite large—have basic coverage for old age and disability and so that the formal labor force has some protection against unemployment.

The first of these factors is rapid urbanization along with the spread of democracy. The germination of pluralistic political institutions has given a bigger and more educated urban labor force, nongovernmental organizations, and newly emergent interest groups a significant voice for the first time and a readiness to demand that the government provide a buffer in particular circumstances.[1]

Second, the crisis showed that although informal safety nets still exist in many countries, family-based arrangements are wearing thin. Family size is shrinking, and the proportion of nuclear urban families is increasing. These changes call for a new and more formal social compact between generations to supplement or entirely replace the implicit contracts grounded in family ties.

Third, populations are aging. Within the next two decades, the average age will increase quickly in most of East Asia, starting with Japan and followed by Singapore, the Republic of Korea, and China.[2] Japan's dramatic inversion of the demographic pyramid, which will greatly expand the numbers in older cohorts by 2030, presages what will happen in other East Asian countries where fertility rates have fallen steeply (figure 2.1).

Fourth, in several East Asian countries the corporate sector, with the tacit support of the state, has supplied the safety net for a core ur-

---

1. Iversen and Soskice (2001) associate the specialization of skills, which renders individuals more vulnerable to unemployment, with higher demand for social policies.

2. Penner, Sawhill, and Taylor (2000, p. 122) rightly note, "Through most of human history, few people retired. Prior to the nineteenth century, most people worked until they dropped, and if they were not dead when they dropped, they would often expect to be treated miserably." With lengthening life expectancies, many people can now anticipate a long retirement, even if the current trend toward earlier retirement is halted or partially reversed. This, coupled with changed attitudes regarding the responsibilities of the state, the spread of democracy, and the decline in family size, as well as some increase in the number of elderly people living alone, has increased the need for a pension system.

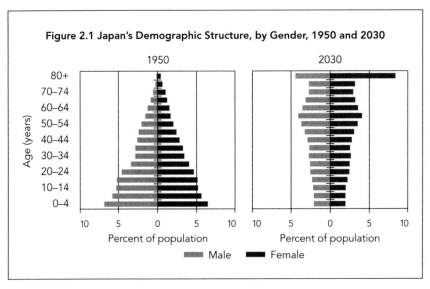

Figure 2.1 Japan's Demographic Structure, by Gender, 1950 and 2030

Source: United Nations Population Division (2000b, 2001).

ban work force. Although this corporate net is likely to persist, it is clearly shrinking, as companies in China, Japan, Korea, and Southeast Asia respond to competitive pressures by reorganizing to enhance flexibility and by cutting overheads, with tenured employment and benefits being fine-tuned or trimmed (Wise forthcoming). Magretta (2002, p. 7) notes, "As competition forces organizations to become more flexible and as technology enables organizations to work in new ways, they are less likely to provide structure and stability in people's lives."

Public programs seeking to bolster social welfare can have disincentive effects on investment and work input.[3] Moreover, financing these programs runs the risk of imposing deadweight losses from taxation and the misallocation of resources.[4] This underlies the negative relationship observed between the level of government expenditures and growth (Barro 1991; Engen and Skinner 1992).[5]

---

3. Gruber and Wise (2002) report evidence from analyses in 12 countries.

4. However, on balance, small open economies have proportionally bigger public sectors (Alesina and Wacziarg 1997).

5. Fölster and Henrekson (2001) support these findings, using panel data for a sample of high-income countries and correcting for the econometric shortcomings of earlier work.

To balance the twin goals of social stability and growth calls for clear purpose and careful design of public and private programs. Attention to the goals, scale, and design of programs can minimize the risk that higher levels of social spending will reduce a country's competitiveness in global markets. This may happen, for example, if government finances this spending through high payroll and other taxes, which then increase the cost of labor.[6] Equally, it may happen if government turns to borrowing on a scale that raises interest rates, crowding out private sector investment and increasing real exchange rates.[7]

Guidelines for Design of Safety Nets

Providing safety nets that meet the challenge of globalization and respond to both political change and demographic trends can contribute to income, growth, and welfare. Here it is worth identifying some key guidelines for the design of such systems.

First, a distinction should be made between unemployment-related schemes and others that are geared toward resource transfers and consumption smoothing. Unemployment schemes include unemployment insurance, unemployment assistance, unemployment insurance savings accounts, severance pay, and public works. Unemployment savings accounts are more a form of consumption smoothing than a form of insurance. The others have more of a redistributive role, although there is a risk that each can reduce the incentives to work, mainly assist workers in the formal sector, and do little to alleviate poverty. In principle, severance pay focuses largely on the sectors and firms that are affected and generates the fewest disincentives against job search. In the low- and middle-income countries, neither unemployment insurance nor severance pay is likely to be fiscally practicable except on a small and

---

6. Most industrializing countries, including those in East Asia, raise revenues through a motley collection of taxes that impose high deadweight costs rather than through the few, flat, broad-based taxes recommended by theory and best practice (G. S. Becker and Mulligan 1998). Very few studies have formally analyzed the effects of social security reform on labor-market outcomes. For Chile, Edwards and Edwards (2002) show that reform in the formal sector resulted in a modest increase in informal sector wages.

7. A country's integration into global capital markets tends to compound this pressure because it gives asset holders more opportunities to exit relatively less financially competitive markets. Rodrik (1997) notes that, in developing countries, the "capitalists" have better exit options than do workers and are most likely to close their plants and relocate as the costs of labor increase.

discriminatory scale and aimed at a slice of the formal urban work force. At higher levels of per capita income, mandatory severance pay might be practicable. This, plus public works projects, could prove to be the most cost-effective way for many East Asian countries to tackle the unemployment effects of shocks. Countries with the financial depth and regulatory capacity to handle broader schemes might well consider unemployment insurance savings accounts.

Second, the experience of Western countries and Japan argues for realism with respect to the scale of benefits—whether for unemployment compensation, health, or pensions. China's partial and recently instituted social security system confronts a projected deficit of $10 billion in 2005, rising steeply to $110 billion in 2010, unless reforms address the extent of coverage and the level of individual contributions, retirement age, and benefits (Pitsilis, von Emloh, and Wang 2002).[8] Singapore's Central Provident Fund exemplifies the difficulty of attaining a reasonable level of retirement benefits at an acceptable cost. This, the largest publicly run pension fund in Southeast Asia, embraces about 60 percent of the nation's work force and receives contributions from its members equal to 36 percent of their salaries. In spite of such funding, it can promise a salary replacement rate of only 35 percent. Less well-funded schemes in Malaysia and the Philippines have even lower replacement rates. A partial solution might be to expand the coverage (although coverage is already high in Singapore), defer the retirement age, and raise contributions. It would be more effective to invest pension fund resources so as to obtain higher returns. This will depend partly on financial market development and openness, as well as on lifting regulations that channel a substantial volume of pension fund resources into public sector projects where the returns can be low ("Southeast Asia: Public Pension Plans" 2002).

Third, a balance should be struck between public transfers to the young and the old for reasons of equity as well as efficiency. Higher transfers to the old often come at the cost of investment in the health and education of the young. Pension schemes should keep a close eye

---

8. The unemployment insurance scheme in China covered 100 million people and had assets of 20 billion yuan in 2001. Medicare reforms introduced in 2002 would affect 85 million people ("Quarterly Chronicle" 2002).

on these tradeoffs and minimize the incentives for early retirement (Blank 2002; Gruber and Wise 2001).

Fourth, to remain affordable, the public safety net has to be supplemented with measures that build up and safeguard the private safety net (on the political economy of reform and the privatization of pension schemes in Latin America, see Mesa-Lago and Müller 2002), notably investing privately managed funds in approved assets and mobilizing other household assets, such as the equity in housing, which can be tapped through reverse mortgages (Yusuf, Lee, and Kuchiki 2002).

Fifth, the public safety net must take account of the demographic transition in much of East Asia and how this affects dependency ratios. Although fully funded schemes have their merits, they may not provide adequate safeguards if economic growth slows in the future. As Lindeman (1996, p. 4) observes,

> Funded and pay-as-you-go (PAYG) retirement regimes share the same transition adjustments when large birth cohorts are followed by much smaller ones. In a PAYG regime, smaller successive cohorts may refuse to pay the higher contributions of payroll taxes necessary to support larger, previous cohorts at promised benefit levels, forcing the latter to work longer or accept lower consumption levels than they desire or accept. Assuming no major growth in the propensity to increase savings among smaller successive cohorts, in a funded regime, larger previous cohorts may find themselves trying to cash in assets whose value cannot be preserved at the levels needed to maintain desired or expected consumption in retirement. Either the nominal price of assets will fall as supply outstrips demand or demand-push inflation will erode the purchasing power of fixed price assets more than was expected.

To address the need to balance transfers between age groups, to build appropriate schemes, and to provide adequate transfers to the recipients, a PAYG system might be combined with an investment trust fund (Feldstein and Leibman 2000; Feldstein and Samwick 2001a, 2001b). This resembles the system being introduced for Chinese workers in the urban formal sector, which combines a defined-benefit PAYG portion with a defined-contribution system of individual accounts (Feldstein 1998; Zhao and Xu 2002).

However carefully it is designed, even a frugal safety net for the most vulnerable will largely be a public responsibility and will entail a gradual increase in the share of public expenditures devoted to transfers and public services and may require a greater tax effort by the state.[9] Projections by Heller (1999) suggest that Korea and Taiwan (China) will start to require substantial outlays between 2010 and 2025, with China, Hong Kong (China), and Malaysia being affected after 2025.

To conclude, a safety net only partly alleviates the instability arising from external macroeconomic shocks. To enable people to find and keep jobs in the face of long-term technological change, development of higher-order skills is the best policy (Kaufman and Segura-Ubriergo 2001). Moreover, the smaller is the increase in public revenues as a share of gross domestic product (GDP), the lower is the efficiency loss and the smaller is the erosion of incentives for workers and businesses.

Fiscal Issues and Trends

In the wake of the 1997–98 crisis, all East Asian countries except Indonesia have pursued expansionary fiscal policies in order to stimulate their economies. The financing of these programs and the costs of financial sector restructuring have raised their levels of public debt close to the world average of about 46 percent and above the average of advanced countries (figure 2.2). Much of the rise in public debt can be ascribed to reforms of the banking industry and public spending, most notably in Indonesia, Korea, Malaysia, and Thailand. Currency devaluations precipitated balance sheet losses on government books, and the restructuring of debts added to the aggregate burden of debt service valued in local currency.

Throughout the region, fiscal conditions have deteriorated since 1997. The budget surpluses of the early 1990s in Indonesia, Korea,

---

9. Boix (2002) considers the possible evolution of the public sector during the next 15 years by projecting the effects of factors such as economic development or modernization, trade openness, political regime, electoral turnout, and the interaction of political and economic variables on different measures of the size of the public sector. The results confirm that per capita income, size of the primary sector (for example, labor-intensive agriculture), and share of old-age population in a country are strongly correlated for most years. Economic development and trade openness positively affect the size of government. The size of the state is expected to grow with per capita income. Regardless of the political regime in place, the size of public revenues increases by around 10 percentage points from very low to medium levels of development and then by another 5 to 7 percentage points from medium to high levels of development.

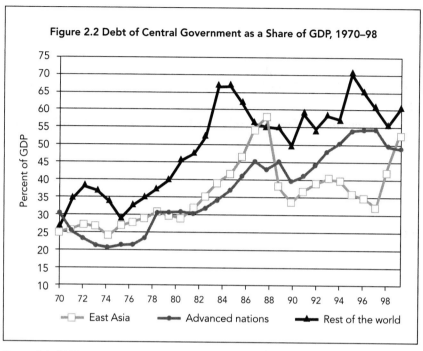

Figure 2.2 Debt of Central Government as a Share of GDP, 1970–98

Source: Boix (2002).

Malaysia, and Thailand have turned into deficits (figure 2.3). Between 1997 and 2000 public debt grew most rapidly in Indonesia (from about 38 percent of GDP to more than 100 percent) and in Thailand (from about 20 percent of GDP to 44 percent). In Malaysia it rose further from already high levels, pushed up by the sharp increases in domestic debt that resulted from financial sector bailouts. Overall deficits increased further in the Philippines and Vietnam, while the size of the surplus decreased in Singapore, which had consistently run an overall budget surplus for the preceding five years.[10] Large shares of these countries' public budgets are thus being used to cover interest payments on public debt, squeezing the ability of governments to spend on social sectors or on a safety net.

---

10. Budget deficits have also risen in China in large part because of government spending on public works programs. These are being financed through the sale of bonds, which in 2002 were estimated to amount to 5 percent of GDP ("China's President" 2002). See also "Philippines: Slowing Economy" (2002) on the rising budget deficit in 2002 and the still higher levels projected for 2003, "Thailand: Deeper in Debt" (2002) on similar tendencies in Thailand, and Koo (2002) on the worsening fiscal debt ratios for Korea since 1997.

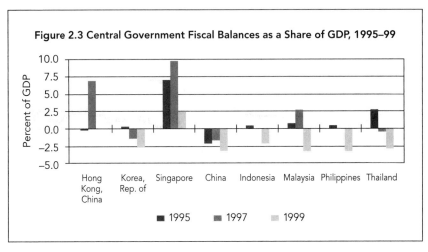

Figure 2.3 Central Government Fiscal Balances as a Share of GDP, 1995–99

Source: Asian Development Bank (2001).

Pattern of Government Spending

Compared with that in other countries, the public sector in East Asian countries has remained small over time. Except for Japan, the average East Asian public sector is only about half as large as the average public sector in the Organisation for Economic Co-operation and Development (OECD) countries and about one-third smaller than the average in other nations at similar levels of per capita income.

In the last half century, public sectors have expanded their share of economies across the world.[11] In the industrial world in the early 1950s, total current revenue of general government averaged 24 percent of GDP (figure 2.4).[12] By the mid-1970s it had risen to 36 percent, before stabilizing at around 44 percent in the early 1980s. The

---

11. Three broadly stated facts characterize the evolution of the public sector across the world during the twentieth century: first, its steady growth; second, persistent cross-national differences in its size; and third, rough stability in ranking among the nations of the world in terms of public revenue and spending. Except during times of war, government expenditures in Western countries during the nineteenth century rarely exceeded 10 percent of GDP. After 1914, because of wartime mobilization, the public sector grew substantially. It grew still further during the depression of the 1930s and World War II as governments took on larger responsibilities, nudged along by the spread of liberal thinking on economic policy and the role of the state (Blyth 2002). The strength of popular demand for welfare spending and government willingness to manage and insure against risks pushed spending even higher, from the 1950s and well into the 1980s (Ferguson 2001; Moss 2002).

12. This is an unweighted average for Australia, New Zealand, North America, and Western Europe.

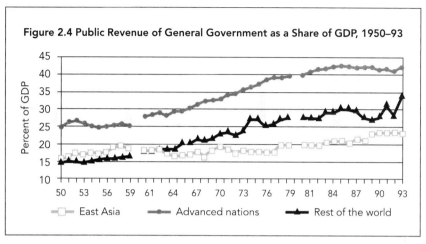

Figure 2.4 Public Revenue of General Government as a Share of GDP, 1950–93

Source: Boix (2002).

public sector has also expanded in developing countries, although less dramatically. East Asian public sectors have not grown as fast. Current general government revenues grew from about 15 percent of GDP in the 1950s to 20 percent in the early 1990s. Meanwhile, in the rest of the world, government revenue averaged 14 percent of GDP in 1950, reached 20 percent by the late 1960s, and then hovered around 27 percent from the late 1970s onward.

Except in Japan, governments in East Asia are substantially centralized, with about 85 percent of public expenditure controlled by the central government. Data on transfers, wages, and capital expenditure by central government can, therefore, be taken as a good proxy for the overall distribution of spending within the public sector (table 2.1).

The table confirms the small size of the public sector and the "welfare state" in East Asia. Government social expenditures are much smaller than would be expected, given these countries' level of economic development, demographic structure, degree of openness to trade, and political institutions.[13] Public pension systems, unemploy-

---

13. Theoretical literature on the larger size of the public sector in Western countries relative to East Asian nations suggests four possible factors underlying past trends and possibly future outcomes; Holsey and Borcherding (1997) and Lybeck (1988) provide extensive reviews. The "demand-side" explanation attributes this public sector growth either to social progress and demographic transformations or to different rates of productivity growth (and differences in the income elasticity of demand) in the public and private sectors. The "sociological" explanation links the size of the public sector to the structure of income distribution across society and to

Table 2.1 Distribution of Public Spending in East Asia, 1993–96

Indicator and country	General government			Central government			
	Total	Education	Social expenditure[a]	Total	Subsidies and transfers	Wages and salaries	Capital expenditure
Spending as a percentage of GDP							
Industrial nations[b]	45.0	5.3[c]	20.5	35.3	4.7	4.3	4.8
Japan	37.5	8.5	—	23.7	—	5.0	4.7
Korea, Rep. of	21.5	8.3	9.4	17.4	2.2	7.5	3.3
Singapore	16.9	2.6	6.4	—	4.9	0.5	2.4
Malaysia	—	4.9	9.8	21.4	6.3	1.0	4.0
Philippines	—	3.0	5.5	19.3	5.4	3.0	—
Thailand	—	1.1	5.5	18.9	5.1	4.3	3.3
Indonesia	—	2.5	3.9	15.8	2.4	3.0	0.6
Vietnam	20.3	—	5.4	—	—	2.8	—
China	13.6	—	6.7	8.0	0.7	2.0	—

— Not available.

Note: Averages are for 1993–96, except transfers and subsidies in Japan (where data are for 1990 only).

a. Includes expenditures on education (Heller 1999).

b. OECD countries excluding Japan.

c. Includes Japan (World Bank, World Development Indicators, various years).

Source: Boix (2002).

ment benefits, sickness-related payments, and public health care have remained extremely limited, at least until the late 1990s.[14] The shares of social welfare–related expenditures in East Asia are well below the share in OECD countries and smaller than that in Latin America (Heller 1999). In East Asia, Japan spends the most and Indonesia spends the least.[15]

There are three possible reasons for these relatively low levels of spending. First, the significantly lower level of revenue mobilization by central governments in East Asia has constrained spending.[16] Second, the prevailing family support systems in East Asia—and, possibly, limited trust in state guarantees—have held back the redistributive pressures that have enlarged the welfare state in Europe. Third, the relative weakness of labor movements in East Asia has made it difficult for them to place fiscal demands on the state. The European experience suggests that welfare states are created in slow steps, and it is only after many years of democratic and participatory governance that public programs are established and grow to maturity.

Whatever the reasons in East Asia, it seems inevitable that as these economies develop, age, and urbanize and as political participation increases, social spending will also increase. The possible adverse ef-

---

the level of mobilization and organization of different social and political groups. Hence, the expansion of the state is linked to its redistributive consequences. The "economic openness" explanation suggests that higher levels of trade systematically lead to a larger public sector across both developed and developing nations. Greater trade integration, coupled with high sectoral concentration in the economy, leads to growing risks associated with the international business cycle, which in turn puts pressure on policymakers to develop publicly financed compensatory mechanisms in favor of the exposed sectors. The "institutional" explanation attributes the growth in the size of the public sector to the effect of differences in the structures of government (such as bureaucracies, the legislative branch, or federalism) on the aggregation of citizen preferences.

14. On the provision of health coverage in Hong Kong (China), Malaysia, and Singapore, see Ramesh and Holliday (2001).

15. A significant proportion of public expenditure in Japan takes place at the local level. In 1997 the sum of social security and social services expenditure by all levels of the Japanese government was 19 percent of GDP. The very low figures of the remaining countries simply reflect the general absence of public pension programs and unemployment benefits and the low level of expenditure on public health. Thus in Korea, for which data are available for the sum of central and local governments, public spending on social security and welfare programs was 2.3 percent of GDP in 1997. The figures are not higher in the other countries.

16. The East Asian countries had successfully maintained fiscal discipline before the 1997 crisis, keeping government expenditures in line with government revenues. As a result, the size of the public sector has not grown as rapidly as in a typical advanced welfare state.

fects of higher spending can be mitigated only by making public spending more efficient, a subject we now address.

Efficient Management of Public Funds

In much of East Asia, the impression of fiscal discipline is sometimes more apparent than real. The fiscal situation is rendered fragile due to widespread use of off-budget accounts by governments and by the scale of contingent liabilities and quasi-fiscal operations resorted to by state financial institutions and state-owned enterprises.

Off-Budget Accounts. Government spending from off-budget accounts is difficult to quantify. Off-budget operations are substantial in Indonesia, Malaysia, and Vietnam and of concern in the Philippines, Thailand, and elsewhere in the region. In Indonesia, for instance, off-budget items in the mid-1990s, which included reforestation and development funds as well as pension and housing programs for public employees, fluctuated around 0.5 percent of GDP; another 0.5 percent of GDP consisted of educational fees (World Bank 1998b). In China off-budget funds (surtaxes, levies, and user charges) grew rapidly from about 2.6 percent of GDP in 1978 to more than 4 percent in 1996 and to perhaps 8–10 percent in subsequent budgets; most of these funds were in the hands of local governments.

To the extent that the public sector uses off-budget accounts, the fiscal deficits of general government are underreported. Off-budget operations jeopardize fiscal stability; they obscure information on the overall allocation of resources and often allow expenditures to bypass established procedures for assuring accountability. Aside from undermining fiscal discipline, the use of off-budget funds weakens a government's control over resource allocation by its agencies, which in turn have little incentive to adhere to overall budget discipline.

Chronic use of off-budget funds has severely compromised the predictability, transparency, and accountability that are the hallmarks of effective systems of expenditure management. In Korea the government recognized the extent of the problem and in 1999 began to minimize the use of off-budget funds and to simplify the complicated system of special accounts. By 2000 the 75 separate funds that existed at the end of 1999 had been consolidated and reduced to 55. The processes for monitoring funds and enhancing the coordination of funds and public finances were reviewed, and the system of special accounts was revised (Ahmad 2001). Korea has been moving toward a single treasury account, but vested interests continue to resist changes, making it harder to overcome obstacles as the economy recovers and the memory of the crisis recedes.

Contingent Liabilities. Contingent liabilities, emerging from past commitments based on law and contracts, are another major source of fiscal risk. The explicit contingent liabilities of a government can arise from guaranteed debts and other liabilities of state-owned enterprises and from the implied public financing needs of existing price support programs. Implicit contingent liabilities include government commitments arising from off-budget obligations, political announcements (such as Thailand's proposed Village Fund), public expectations, and pressures from interest groups that trigger financial support from the public sector if certain thresholds are crossed. Other sources of fiscal risk include the power sector and the pension system.[17]

Indonesia's experience with banking sector liabilities mirrors problems in other countries. Where deposit insurance exists (and is extended to all creditors, as in Indonesia) and the asset base is increasingly suspect, the incentives to undertake further risky lending are high (see also Caprio and Klingebiel 1997). In 2001 the Indonesian government faced a contingent liability of about Rp28 trillion on credits outstanding. Indonesia's largest contingent liabilities relate to the banking sector, resulting from the government's explicit guarantee on interbank claims and implicit commitment to recapitalize large state-owned banks and maintain a stable financial system.

In China the level of nonperforming loans in the banking system is probably higher than the official estimate of about 25 percent of GDP. This is partly because the new classification system conforming

---

17. Computations of budget-at-risk are under way in some countries in East Asia, at least for those contingent liabilities considered large and of high risk. In the case of state-enterprise borrowing, for instance, when the probability of loss in a project is deemed to be very small, the notional value of the government's commitment to the project that is being guaranteed can overstate the expected loss to the government. However, the government's exposure may be understated to the extent that it has provided explicit or implicit guarantees that can be called in the event that the project does not materialize. In that case, the resulting contingent liabilities of the government can exceed the direct notional exposure.

more closely to international standards is more exacting and partly because the experience of other countries indicates that banking crises reveal losses higher than estimated by supervisory agencies. The official estimate assumes a 30 percent loan loss rate. Based on experience in other countries, however, a more likely range is 60–90 percent (Krumm and Wong 2002). Contingent pension and social security liabilities amounting to almost $1 trillion should be added to the nonperforming loans ("China's President" 2002).

The Philippine government is exposed to the possible repercussions of obligations made by subnational governments to assume the nonguaranteed debts of state-owned or private enterprises and to cover business losses. Such obligations need to be managed carefully to prevent them from undermining efforts to restore and maintain sound and sustainable fiscal management.

To measure and control its contingent liabilities, a government needs to assess its exposure to loss from all forms of explicit and implicit financial commitments. Few governments relish this exercise, but the crisis nudged most countries in the region to begin such accounting. To contain contingent liabilities and manage fiscal risks, several countries in East Asia have launched monitoring programs on a more sustained basis. But the design of policies to hedge public fiscal risks in the budgeting process is at a nascent stage and will have to be undertaken over several years.[18]

Reform of Public Spending

Fiscal stability can be secured by taking measures in three areas: by strengthening public finances (especially by improving the management of expenditures and eliminating off-budget accounts), by im-

---

18. Contingent guarantees can be a treacherous policy tool if appropriate bounds are not established. Contingent guarantees can easily reduce discipline in the markets and lead to economic inefficiencies and, eventually, to high budgetary costs and economic disruption. Discipline is lost, in part, because those in receipt of the guarantees have fewer incentives to act diligently. Discipline is also lost because contingent liabilities typically are not valued for the expected payments that may occur and sometimes are not even recorded systematically. As such, because they do not require an immediate cash payment, they become a mechanism for deferring payments into the future. Although these future payments may never materialize because the risky events may not occur, experience shows that implied and explicit guarantees are often called; when that happens, they create budgetary stress. Moreover, contingent liabilities have a nonlinear payment schedule (Gooptu 2001).

proving the accounting for contingent liabilities, and by containing the growth of such liabilities. These actions would limit current and future budgetary imbalances and raise the efficiency of public spending. Efficient management of expenditures, together with some additional revenue effort, would make resources available for safety nets that are appropriate for highly open economies. Along with stronger fiscal fundamentals, improved safety nets would lessen the risk of shocks and minimize their adverse effects.

In the past, aggregate fiscal discipline was too often achieved at the expense of sectoral efficiency and operational effectiveness. During the crisis, some countries, such as Thailand, were able to maintain reasonable sectoral efficiency, which protected social expenditure and ensured that cuts fell on lower-priority items. But other countries tended to make arbitrary cuts with little regard for sectoral implications—resulting in a growing gap between stated government goals and the actual distribution of public spending.

With budgetary pressures likely to mount, fiscal reforms to accommodate a possible increase in transfers take on a new urgency. While more revenues will need to be raised, the goals of stability and growth could be served more effectively by reforming budgetary processes to enhance accountability, transparency, and efficiency in the use of public finances.

Some East Asian countries have adopted multiyear approaches to fiscal planning. Most countries still have a five-year plan, although seldom one that includes rigorous multiyear fiscal forecasts or detailed spending plans. The Philippines and Vietnam have introduced public investment programs, including more detailed forward estimates of capital expenditure. A few countries use a rigorous medium-term fiscal framework and a medium-term expenditure framework; here Malaysia, the Philippines, Thailand, and Vietnam are in the lead, although their budget reforms are by no means complete.

In most countries, however, the lack of a medium-term fiscal strategy and the single-year focus of the budget process imply that allocations for operating and maintaining completed projects are not treated systematically in budget planning. Where levels of investment were high before the economic crisis, as in Malaysia and Thailand, implying high levels of subsequent recurrent expenditure, this could be a cause for concern. The lack of a medium-term fiscal strategy also lessens the certainty of funding for ministries and departments over the medium term, restricting their ability to plan spending on multiyear projects.

Although no country in East Asia has a medium-term fiscal strategy, institutional reforms and capacity-building programs are under way in some, including Thailand and Vietnam, with a view to managing public expenditure programs on a multiyear basis in the future. This should help to maintain fiscal stability in an increasingly open environment.

Because of the demand for more effective financial accountability, most East Asian countries are implementing reforms of one kind or another. Many of these reforms rely on large outlays for information and communications technology hardware to support integrated financial management information systems (see chapter 8). However, the most promising reforms, particularly those in Malaysia and, to a lesser extent, in Thailand and Vietnam, start from a fundamental rethinking of the foundations of financial accountability, focusing first on the budget process and the control regime.[19]

The ongoing process of fiscal and administrative decentralization in several East Asian countries carries risks—overlapping expenditure provision, less efficient service delivery, and macroeconomic instability—if fiscal decentralization does not go hand in hand with functional assignment of responsibilities and if financial management capacity and financial accountability are not established at the local level. The rapid decentralization ongoing in countries such as Indonesia will need to be carefully orchestrated to avoid perverse results. Once some progress has been made with such structural reforms, the next step would be to computerize the systems of financial management and accountability.

---

19. China has recently begun moving treasury functions from the People's Bank of China to the new Treasury Department in the Ministry of Finance, building on the information infrastructure now available with the interbank real-time gross settlement system and permitting rapid information flows and relatively limited, but effective, control procedures. The specific reforms include (a) stepwise consolidation of government budget and extrabudgetary cash resources, including the adoption of a single treasury account for all levels of the general government, to ensure transparency in and effective control and monitoring of public finances; (b) development of an integrated government financial management information system to provide timely information on budgetary payments and execution; and (c) installation of cash and liquidity management and financial planning (cash forecasting) systems using internationally accepted standards.

ISSUES IN CORPORATE AND BANK RESTRUCTURING

East Asia's industrial firms came under severe pressure during the crisis of 1997–98. Banks were forced to cut credit lines because of liquidity constraints, the accumulation of nonperforming assets, and defaults, and highly leveraged corporations were unable to meet their debt obligations because their credit lines had dried up.

After the crisis, it was clear that restoring industrial capability would require substantial banking and corporate restructuring, including selling off the assets of nonviable firms and consolidating the debt of viable ones to give them some breathing space.[20] Countries have used several mechanisms for this purpose.

Many governments created asset management corporations (AMCs), which employed proven restructuring mechanisms to address simultaneously the immediate problems of industrial firms and banks in trouble, but with mixed results. An AMC can play the critical role of financial intermediary when the financial sector is in distress by handling the closures and liquidations of nonviable entities. AMCs in East Asia have bought bad loans from banks, bought equity in distressed corporations and banks, and taken control of entities in order to liquidate or restructure them. It is assumed that once market confidence is restored, an AMC will sell its assets back to the public and the financial sector. Several East Asian countries followed this strategy and created large AMCs with strict sunset clauses: the Indonesian Bank Restructuring Agency (IBRA), the Korea Deposit Insurance Corporation, Danaharta in Malaysia, and the Thailand Asset Management Corporation. China created a separate AMC for each of its four large government-owned banks ("China Banking Debt" 2001).[21] Japan relied mainly on existing government institutions to refinance its banks, but in 2002 it took the unusual step of having the

---

20. According to current private estimates, the total volume of nonperforming loans in East Asia, including those of Japanese banks, amounts to $2 trillion or 30 percent of regional GDP (Berger, Nast, and Raubach 2002).

21. China's four AMCs were set up in 1999 to restructure $400 billion in nonperforming assets. The four companies have since accumulated 3 trillion to 4 trillion renminbi in nonperforming loans.

Bank of Japan commit to purchase part of the equity portfolios of troubled commercial banks ("State Intervention" 2002).[22]

Governments also used mediation to create a level playing field for negotiations that were frequently based on the "London approach" pioneered by the Bank of England.[23] This approach requires voluntary involvement and consensus among parties. The basic idea is that the creditors and debtors should work together to resolve corporate distress and be willing to share the burden of loss resulting from any decision.[24]

Many governments also opted to fund incentive schemes to stimulate the restructuring effort. These took the form of blanket guarantees, insurance, or subsidies. For example, the Bank of Korea introduced a limited deposit insurance scheme in January 1997 and then in November extended the guarantee to all financial institutions, including coverage of their foreign liabilities. This was crucial in restoring confidence in the Korean economy (Chopra and others 2001).

As described in the following case studies of restructuring in Korea and Indonesia, the restructuring process has often been slowed down by governments' reluctance to make difficult decisions, by legal constraints imposed on AMCs and bank restructuring agreements, and, as in China, by difficulties AMCs face in disposing of loans.[25] In some countries, the creation of an AMC, as in Indonesia and Thailand, was not accompanied by the legal changes that would have permitted quick out-of-court settlements and empowered the AMC to implement the government's strategy most expeditiously.

---

22. On the halting progress made in Thailand, where the Thailand Asset Management Corporation had disposed of 40 percent of assets acquired by August 2002 relative to a target of 70 percent by the end of 2002, see "Thailand: Asset Management" (2002) and "Thailand: TAMC" (2002).

23. Stone (2000, p. 13) describes the basic principles of this approach as follows: "i) if a corporation is in trouble, banks keep credit facilities open and do not press for bankruptcy; ii) decisions about the debtor's future are made only on the basis of comprehensive information shared amongst all banks; iii) banks work together; iv) seniority of claim is recognized, but there is an element of shared pain."

24. The Corporate Debt Restructuring Advisory Committee in Thailand developed a set of principles for voluntary workouts based on the London approach (Mako 2001).

25. China's four AMCs have disposed of only a small share of the nonperforming loans acquired and recovered about 21 percent on average. According to a report prepared by economists in the Bank for International Settlements, the People's Bank of China stands to lose $23.2 billion loaned to the four AMCs ("On the Road" 2002).

Restructuring in Korea

In Korea the main goal of corporate restructuring was to reduce the debt-equity ratio of viable firms and to liquidate over-leveraged ones. To expedite restructuring, in February 1998 Korea relaxed its rules on foreign investment, layoffs, ownership by financial institutions, and mergers and acquisitions. Tax codes were changed to reduce the transaction costs on capital gains resulting from corporate restructuring. A major problem exposed by the crisis was cross-debt guarantees and interunit transactions across affiliates among large chaebols (conglomerates). The chaebols are now required to issue consolidated financial statements, and many interunit transactions are prohibited (Chopra and others 2001).

The primary body responsible for Korea's corporate restructuring effort was the Financial Supervisory Commission. The Financial Supervisory Commission allowed the largest firms to restructure themselves provided they produced capital structure improvement plans to be monitored by banks and the Fair Trade Commission. Many large chaebols were forced to restructure, and, in the process, close to one-half of the top 30 ceased to exist by 2002. Smaller chaebols were given the option of out-of-court workouts based on the London approach; they and their creditors signed corporate restructuring agreements that committed them to certain workout procedures (Chopra and others 2001). The smallest firms were supported through credit guarantees and short-term credit lines. The authorities also injected $50 billion into banks through recapitalization. The Korean Asset Management Company (KAMCO) was created to lead efforts to provide liquidity to banks and sell assets. By buying nonperforming loans from financial institutions in exchange for guaranteed government bonds, KAMCO gained managerial rights in corporations through debt-equity swaps and played a role in corporate restructuring. The agency is credited with fostering markets for secondary debt and for nonperforming loans.

The major test for Korea's restructuring effort came with the collapse of the Daewoo Corporation in 1999. Daewoo was the second largest Korean conglomerate and accounted for more than 10 percent of merchandise exports; at the time of its collapse, it had estimated liabilities of $73 billion and a debt-equity ratio of about 527. It was thought to be "too big to fail." Instead of letting it collapse completely, the government negotiated with the creditors to roll over the corporation's short-term debt in exchange for taking control of its restructuring. Many of the Daewoo affiliates were put under workout plans, and some were slated for sale. Progress on Daewoo restructuring has been slow, however, and only a few affiliates had been sold by 2002, the most notable being the acquisition of Daewoo Motor by General Motors.

Many Korean firms have found out-of-court settlements hard to achieve and have been forced into court receivership. With a few exceptions (such as the sale of Kia Motors to Hyundai), only a few have been successfully restructured or liquidated through a court process. During 2001–02, the government softened its stance on restructuring by propping up some Hyundai affiliates, such as Hyundai Engineering and Construction (World Bank, East Asia Region 2001).

Korea has made considerable headway in reforming its capital markets and strengthening corporate governance. The government has announced a plan to complete bank privatization over the next three years, and Chohung Bank, the country's oldest lender, is the latest state-controlled bank to be put up for auction ("Chohung Bank" 2002). The task going forward on corporate restructuring is to expedite the disposal of the remaining distressed firms, which requires greater reliance on court-supervised insolvency (World Bank, East Asia Region 2002).

Restructuring in Indonesia

At the time of the Asian crisis, Indonesian corporations owed an estimated $118 billion, and their foreign liabilities accounted for 60 percent of the country's total debt (Mako 2001). To resolve their distress, the government set up the Indonesian Bank Restructuring Agency and IBRA asset management credits, which were responsible for buying bad loans and managing the portfolios of closed banks. Simultaneously, the government also established an out-of-court restructuring framework under the auspices of the Jakarta Initiative Task Force to mediate negotiations between debtors, creditors, and the government.

Both of these initiatives had wide support, but they were not able to fulfill their mandates. The first problem was the weakness of creditor rights and the inability or unwillingness of Indonesian courts to enforce them. Although a new bankruptcy law went into effect in

1998, it was poorly implemented. Many cases emerged in 1998 where firms had created "phantom" creditors and used them to obtain the 75 percent creditor approval needed to gain acceptance of their restructuring plan. The courts were unable to take action against this practice, which made forced restructuring difficult and held up the resolution of cases.[26] To address the problem, Indonesia issued a presidential decree (PP-17) empowering IBRA to seize and sell assets. IBRA has avoided using this power, however, because of concerns about legal challenges and the large losses implicit in the low sale value of its portfolio. Many other issues remain, including taxation and regulatory rules to facilitate the restructuring and capacity building of courts and the IBRA.

Both Indonesia and Korea, as well as other countries in the region, need to further strengthen the corporate fundamentals of their respective economies.[27] Here the role of the legal system is likely to be crucial, as is discussed in the last section of this chapter. Despite some resistance to instituting the legalistic and rule-based environment characteristic of some of the advanced Western economies, such a regime may be necessary if economies in the region are to retain their competitive edge.[28]

FINANCIAL SECTOR REFORM

In the East Asian context, industrial reform calls for a change in financial sector governance and vice versa. Government direction of bank lending has been at the heart of the industrial policies of many economies in the region. And it has been largely responsible for the overhang of nonperforming assets in bank portfolios, ranging from 16 percent in Korea to more than 50 percent in Indonesia in 2001 (table 2.2).

---

26. Those cases that have been resolved by IBRA and the Jakarta Initiative Task Force are biased in favor of debtors rather than creditors, with much of the equity control staying with management on more lenient loan terms. Many creditors, including IBRA, are unwilling to accept the losses associated with liquidation and significant restructuring.

27. Indonesia's leading auto producer, Astra International, has begun taking restructuring initiatives (including debt restructuring) that, if successful, could trigger an upsurge of such efforts throughout industry ("Driving Change" 2002). The market responded favorably in December 2002 by pushing up Astra's share price.

28. East Asian capitalism continues to be seen as distinct from European and North American forms in that it is based more on social connections, paternal obligations, trust, and gift giving than on the rule of law (Rozman 2002).

Table 2.2 Nonperforming Loans in Crisis-Affected Countries, 1997–2001 (percentage of total loan amounts)

Country and indicator	1997, December	1998, December	1999, December	2000, December	2001 March	June	September	December	2002 March	June
Indonesia[a]										
Total	—	—	64.0	57.1	54.4	52.6	50.5	48.8	50.3	48.5
Total excluding transfers to Indonesia Bank Restructuring Agency	7.2	48.6	32.9	18.8	18.1	17.6	14.7	12.1	12.8	11.8
Korea, Rep. of										
Total[b]	8.0	16.1	20.5	17.5	17.0	15.3	14.2	11.9	10.6	9.7
Total excluding Korea Asset Management Company and Korea Deposit Insurance Corporation	5.9	10.4	14.9	10.4	9.6	8.0	7.3	5.4	5.1	4.2
Malaysia										
Total[c]	6.0	21.1	23.4	22.3	23.2	23.9	24.6	24.4	24.6	24.1
Total excluding Danaharta	—	18.6	16.6	15.3	16.2	17.1	16.9	16.6	16.0	15.6
Philippines										
Total[d]	4.7	10.4	12.5	15.1	16.6	17.0	17.9	17.3	18.0	18.1
Thailand										
Total[e]	—	45.0	41.5	26.9	26.7	28.9	29.3	29.6	29.7	29.8
Total excluding asset management corporations	—	45.0	39.1	19.5	19.2	13.9	14.1	11.5	11.4	11.3

— Not available.

a. Uses a "stringent" definition of nonperforming loans.

b. Uses forward looking criteria.

c. Includes commercial banks, finance companies, merchant banks, and Danaharta.

d. Refers to commercial banks.

e. Includes commercial banks, finance companies, and estimated nonperforming loans transferred to wholly owned private asset management corporations.

Source: World Bank, East Asia Region (2002).

There is widespread acceptance of the view that the region's governments should end the practices responsible for so much moral hazard. But the reforms proposed often conflict with the desire not to sever the ties between government and the banks. The tradeoff continues to pose a dilemma because if banks are no longer subject to direction from the government, the government's ability to restructure firms is reduced. This is the case with the chaebols in Korea. Similarly, government-sponsored industrial firms in Indonesia are likely to collapse if the government does not help them to restructure.

Notwithstanding the above, the need for regulatory reform cannot be denied. Weak regulation and supervision of banks were major contributors to the financial crisis in East Asia. When capital controls were liberalized, chaebols in Korea and financial companies in Thailand were allowed to accumulate a large volume of short-run dollar-dominated debt that was not covered by foreign exchange reserves.[29] Financial sector regulation and supervision in East Asia still lack clear and comprehensive goals, except in Hong Kong (China), Singapore, and Taiwan (China). This allows certain financial intermediaries and particular activities to escape effective regulation and supervision. In Korea, for instance, the merchant banks owned or controlled by chaebols were virtually unregulated before 1997 and thus engaged in much riskier borrowing and lending than commercial banks.

In Indonesia, regulation and supervision still lack adequate statutory authority, delineation of functions, and resources. In both Malaysia and Thailand, the ministry of finance is the licensing authority, and in the Philippines the central bank is in charge of licensing. Without autonomy in issuing and revoking licenses, regulatory and supervisory agencies are unable to shape the size, number, and quality of industries, and they cannot effectively restrain violations. Further, for lack of sufficient funding, information, and staff, they are unable to spot financial volatility in time to take corrective action.

Retaining qualified regulatory staff has been a problem for decades, and personnel are still paid too little across much of the region. The fundamental human resource constraint on functioning courts and regulatory agencies persists and needs recognition. Senior managers

---

29. The ratio of short-term debt to reserves in 1998 exceeded 100 percent in Indonesia, Korea, and Thailand (Arestis and Glickman 2002).

of agencies are typically appointed by government, and some even have to take personal liability for their supervisory actions, as in the Philippines (Mishkin 2001).

The experience of Western countries suggests that autonomous regulatory agencies are no panacea and remain susceptible to capture by interest groups. However, strengthening regulatory capacity and using it to enhance the functioning of the financial sector and the quality of appropriate governance are necessary while the legal system is being developed.

Financial Regulation and Supervision

An effective regulatory and supervisory framework has five key elements. First, regulatory and supervisory agencies must have clear and appropriately comprehensive goals. Traditional prudential supervision focuses on the quality of balance sheets and then determines whether financial institutions are complying with capital and disclosure requirements based on regulatory rules. This is becoming increasingly difficult, given that financial innovations can generate significant effects very quickly. Thus prudential supervision must now concern itself with the soundness of financial institutions' risk management practices (Mishkin 2000b).

Second, regulatory and supervisory agencies must have statutory authority and adequate resources for the defined mandate. Regulatory and supervisory agencies should be equally empowered to require information from firms, to assess the competence and probity of their senior personnel, and to act quickly and decisively against inappropriate behavior by them. Ideally, regulatory and supervisory agencies should be able to manage the entry and exit of firms by issuing and revoking licenses in an open, transparent way, with the senior managers of agencies enjoying legal protection in discharging their duties.

Third, regulatory and supervisory agencies must have enough funding, experienced professionals, and management expertise to implement their tasks. They should be able to offer staff competitive remuneration in order to attract high-quality personnel and to prevent bribery.

Fourth, they must be independent. Institutional and budgetary independence can shield against political interference and industry capture and enable prompt corrective action. The institutional independence of a regulatory and supervisory agency requires separation from government authority.[30] The agency's senior personnel need to be protected from arbitrary removal, and the rules for hiring, governing, and firing them need to be transparent and set out in an act of parliament. Budgetary independence requires an earmarked source of funding and the ability to allocate funding based on the agency's own internal priorities.[31]

Finally, they must be accountable. There are six criteria for a well-functioning accountability mechanism: the agency's legal basis; clear objectives; procedures for appointment, reappointment, and dismissal; override mechanisms; relationship with the executive branch, parliament, and the judiciary; and arrangements for transparency and for budgetary accountability (Quintyn and Taylor 2002).

Prudential Regulation

Protecting depositors is a major consideration in avoiding a run on a bank threatened by insolvency. The current methods of protecting depositors in much of Asia are informal rather than formal and specific. When the process is informal, governments often try to protect depositors too much. Explicit guarantees would limit government assistance, but they also might encourage excessive risk taking by banks, especially when prudential regulation is weak and contracts are difficult to enforce. Nevertheless, some form of protection for small depositors is desirable so as to instill confidence while minimizing moral hazard.

One approach to deposit insurance is to adopt the following features. Coverage should be only as great as needed to protect small depositors.[32] The insurance scheme should be privately managed with

---

30. It remains a controversial issue whether a regulatory or supervisory agency should be housed in a politically independent central bank (Abrams and Taylor 2000; Quintyn and Taylor 2002).

31. The funding could come from the general government budget, from the central bank, from the beneficiaries of regulation and supervision (financial institutions), or from combined sources. However, regulatory and supervisory agencies may trade off their dependence more or less in each situation (Abrams and Taylor 2000; Quintyn and Taylor 2002).

32. Of course, the ceiling will vary from country to country. The rule of thumb is that deposit guarantees of one to two times per capita GDP are more than enough to protect small depositors (World Bank 2001b).

mutual liabilities. Ex ante funding of deposit insurance should be avoided, unless legal and regulatory institutions are sufficiently developed to prevent exploitation and looting (World Bank 2001b). Efforts to protect depositors should not try to protect the banks' capital or to shore up industrial corporations that have borrowed particularly heavily from the banks. There is also no reason to protect large deposits of corporations, which should be able to take steps to protect themselves.

The core problems of prudential regulation are how to discourage financial intermediaries from making excessively risky loans and how to provision against bad loans. Regulators must ensure that all lending decisions by banks are made at arm's length and, in particular, that related transactions between banks and the individuals and companies owning them are strictly controlled or eliminated.

Even in the best of systems, as in many of the OECD countries, prudential regulators have difficulty keeping abreast of the increasingly sophisticated systems of the financial intermediaries themselves.[33] In most of East Asia, prudential oversight has fallen far short of these standards. Asian regulators could nonetheless accomplish a great deal simply by controlling and eliminating related lending—a task that is not technically difficult, as the experience of Chile, after its banking crisis in the early 1980s, attests. Korea is one of the few countries in East Asia to make progress in this regard. The Financial Supervisory Commission was created, consolidating the regulatory functions that were previously shared between the finance ministry and the central bank. Other countries, such as Indonesia, have yet to create an independent supervisory body to take over functions that are currently vested in the department of finance and the central bank (Kawai 2002b).

Prudential regulation cannot be separated from the broader issues of governance connected with the financial system. For example, if financial intermediaries are an integral part of a larger industrial conglomerate, oversight is likely to be particularly problematic; a bank owned by an industrial conglomerate or by central or provincial governments will be pressured to continue lending to affiliated firms or

---

33. On the problems encountered by the regulatory regime in Japan through much of the 1990s, including most critically the problem of forbearance, see Cargill and Parker (2001).

state-owned enterprises even when these entities are on the brink of insolvency.[34] The companies, in turn, will resist having the bank declare its loans to them to be nonperforming.

Put differently, an important potential role for any banking system is for the banks to monitor the performance of industrial corporations and to provide early warning when those corporations are heading for trouble. Banks that are owned by those same corporations or by governments are unlikely to perform such a role. Hence a move toward what many believe is the Japanese type of main bank system would be a retrogressive step for economies like Korea, Malaysia, and Taiwan (China) that do not have such a system.

Maintaining state ownership of banks is likely to result in financial inefficiency and to shore up the interventionist industrial policies of the past (La Porta, Lopez-de-Silanes, and Shleifer 2000). When the government directs banks to lend to certain industries and corporations, it is implicitly obliged to continue supporting the banks and the corporations if they run into difficulty. This, in turn, encourages both banks and corporations to undertake risky behavior. Such policies then also induce the government to protect the financial system from the system's own excesses (Cargill and Parker 2001). In Japan the actions and inactions of the government have created moral hazard situations, not the actions of the industrial conglomerates that may or may not control individual banks. In other parts of East Asia, such as China, Indonesia, Korea, Malaysia, and Vietnam, government actions have created moral hazard situations that have negatively influenced the behavior of both industrial corporations and banks.

Bank Consolidation and Recapitalization

How countries recover from the financial crisis will influence the long-term health of their financial systems and the capacity of these systems to contribute to growth in East Asia. Two features of the financial restructuring that has taken place are especially relevant.

The first is a big reduction in the number of financial intermediaries. Countries that were hard hit by the crisis and countries that avoided the worst, notably China, have closed down large numbers of

---

34. Backman (1999) provides some interesting details on such relationships in Southeast Asia.

nonbank financial institutions and consolidated many of the smaller banks into a few large entities. Thailand closed two-thirds of its finance companies in 1997; Korea reduced the number of banks from 26 to 17 in the three years beginning in late 1997 and reduced the number of merchant banks from 30 to 4; Indonesia closed 70 of its 237 banks and nationalized 12 others, with the intention of trimming the number down to 10–15 large banks; Malaysia has taken steps to consolidate its 21 banks, 25 finance companies, and 12 merchant banks into 10 financial groups led by anchor banks and expects eventually to halve this number ("Southeast Asia: Consolidating Banks" 2002). Singapore, in a first round of consolidation, reduced the number of large banks to five in 1998 and, in a second round begun in 2001, eventually expects to reduce the number to two (Kawai 2002b; "Singapore Banking Mergers" 2001).

In China the number of banks has begun to increase, and, what is more important, the reach of the private banks is likely to expand as China proceeds with a phased opening of its financial sector as part of the agreement reached in connection with entry into the World Trade Organization (WTO).[35] At the same time, China has closed many of its nonbank financial institutions, which provincial agencies had been using to circumvent the central government's control over direct bank lending. This could be a positive step, as provincial agencies generally favored lending to the inefficient state-owned enterprises under their jurisdiction.

The broad trend toward consolidation in the region could improve the governance of the financial sector. It may create stronger individual banks and financial groups and should simplify the task of prudential regulators as nonbank financial intermediaries are eliminated.

The second key feature of the restructuring is the role being played by governments, as discussed earlier in this chapter. In most cases, governments are forcing the closings and mergers, not the private sector acting on its own for commercial reasons. Although the changes create the potential for greater bank independence from government, better prudential oversight, more efficient allocation of financial resources, and increased efforts by banks to strengthen cor-

---

35. For details on how accession to the WTO is likely to affect China's financial system, see Lardy (2002).

porate governance, this potential may not be realized. Much depends on a government's reasons for retaining a high level of influence over banks. If they continue using the banks to restructure the economy along what they deem to be desirable paths—for example, further breakup of the chaebols in Korea, greater Bumiputra (Malay) ownership in Malaysia, or more loans to state enterprises in China—the possibility remains that initiatives will be diverted from their stated purpose.

The role of government also affects how banks are being recapitalized. Recapitalizing banks inevitably puts the government at the center of the process. As discussed, the government typically creates a separate agency to take over all or some portion of the nonperforming assets of banks that are insolvent or at substantial risk of becoming so. The government then injects capital into banks to bring them up to the standard required by the Bank for International Settlements to operate internationally.[36] The agency then sells the nonperforming assets at heavily discounted prices in an effort to recover at least some of the money that has been used to refinance the banks. In all of these cases, the effort strengthens the balance sheets of banks, although the degree of strengthening varies widely from one country to another, with Indonesia at one end of the spectrum of the countries hit by the financial crisis and Korea and Malaysia at the other.[37]

Recapitalization is needed not just in crisis-hit countries but also in China and Japan where banks face a worse situation than banks in some of the other countries. The absence of a crisis has meant that governments have been slow to deal with the full magnitude of the problem (Lincoln 2001; Norville 1998); banks have large amounts of nonperforming assets, still classified as performing assets, on their books, and they thus exist in a twilight zone where they are only formally solvent. The main question for these banks—and for the gov-

---

36. In Indonesia the government issued $68 billion in bonds, of which $45 billion went to recapitalize banks and $23 billion went to provide liquidity (Mako 2001, p. 15). In Korea the government injected an estimated $127 billion of public funds into financial institutions, putting the state in control of 30 percent of the financial sector ("Why Korea's Success" 2002). As a result of such measures, governments have attained control of large parts of the corporate and banking sectors in most crisis-affected countries. They now need to reduce their role by selling the stakes acquired out of necessity.

37. The Indonesian government's use of partially liquid recapitalization bonds, while notionally injecting capital, did not provide banks with the needed asset base.

ernments—is how the nonperforming assets will be removed from their books and the price that the government should exact for helping in this process. In the four countries most severely affected by the crisis, the remaining banks have been, or are being, recapitalized. But in China and Japan, recapitalization is moving much more slowly, and the banks must constantly seek guidance from the government. This has created a very cautious attitude toward making new loans to all but the safest of borrowers.

For the economies involved in restructuring their failed financial systems, the challenge is for government to complete the restructuring and then to adopt a more prudential role, relying on the rule of law to prevent abuses stemming from inefficient market structures and excessive market power. Such withdrawal will not be easy, and none of the governments facing this challenge has yet made much headway in this direction.

CORPORATE GOVERNANCE

The restructuring of distressed banks and firms is an immediate priority, but this must be followed up with a framework of corporate governance that would prevent the reemergence of past problems and allow financial markets to develop and perform their roles efficiently. Rules are needed to protect both creditors and investors who are not owner-managers of the firms in which they invest.[38] There would also need to be serious rethinking of the industrial policy regime that contributed to the stresses in the corporate and financial sectors.

Protecting Investors

The large body of corporate finance literature, most of it based on Western institutions and practices, is concerned with how to protect

---

38. As Tenev and Zhang (2002, pp. 127–28) observe, "The effectiveness of the modern corporate governance system rests ultimately on rigorous market tests of success or failure. Without a credible threat of failure in the form of loss of market share, bankruptcy, delisting, or hostile takeover, most instruments of corporate governance will remain unused or their effectiveness will be limited.... The strength of creditor rights in bankruptcy... underpins all other instruments that banks and other creditors have at their disposal to affect companies' behavior. Where these are weak, their role in corporate governance will remain limited."

investors from the predations of managers and how to ensure that investors get a return on their investment, especially in circumstances where the standards of financial reporting and auditing are low (Shleifer and Vishny 1997).[39] Without such assurances, it is difficult to develop capital markets, particularly stock markets, in areas where most participants are minority shareholders.

Through the 1990s most East Asian minority shareholders had few rights that were effectively protected by law or government regulation.[40] Companies were run by and for the controlling families, for the most part, and other shareholders could only hope to receive a part of the gains in corporate value that were being achieved (Backman 1999).[41] Economies other than Japan have almost all their corporations under such control (table 2.3). No more than 200–300 families control much of the national wealth in Thailand ("Thailand: Family Fortunes" 2002).

In Korea, families maintained control by cross-shareholding within a group of companies.[42] Among the top 5 and the top 30 chaebols, the controlling family, on average, held 15–17 percent of the outstanding shares of the group, while cross-shareholding within the group accounted for 40–45 percent of the shares in the early 1980s and a still high 33–35 percent by the mid-1990s (E. M. Kim 1997; Yoo and Lee 1997).

Korea is by no means an extreme case. In Hong Kong (China), Malaysia, Taiwan (China), and Thailand, however, the value of shares

---

39. In a survey by McKinsey and Company, Coombes and Watson (2000) show that investors were willing to pay a 20 percent premium for a well-governed Taiwanese company but a 27 percent premium for a well-governed Indonesian firm. The premium reflects the quality of financial information and the strictness of accounting practices.

40. In the few cases where minority shareholder rights were observed, those rights derived from political power, not from protections in the law.

41. Volpin (2002) concludes from his study of corporate governance in Italy that governance is likely to be poor when the leading executives of a company are also the controlling shareholders, when control is in the hands of a single major shareholder (a common phenomenon in Asia), and when those controlling a company own less than 50 percent of the firm's cash flow rights.

42. Most publicly traded firms worldwide are family controlled, including U.S. firms such as Ford and Wal-Mart (Burkart, Panunzi, and Shleifer 2002). When the cutoff point is moved from 10 to 20 percent, the share of firms in Korea under family control drops sharply. Korea has a somewhat different pattern of corporate governance than elsewhere in the region, with families effectively controlling firms through cross-ownership but with relatively little actual ownership. This creates strong incentives to appropriate minority shareholder value in various ways. The data suggest a similar situation in Taiwan, China.

Table 2.3 Control of Publicly Traded Companies in East Asia, 1996

Country and cutoff for voting rights of the largest shareholder	Number of corporations in the sample	Share of firms under ultimate control	Distribution of ultimate control			
			Family	State	Widely held financial	Widely held corporation
10% cutoff						
Hong Kong, China	330	99. 4	64. 7	3. 7	7. 1	23. 9
Indonesia	178	99. 4	68. 6	10. 2	3. 8	16. 8
Japan	1,240	58. 0	13. 1	1. 1	38. 5	5. 3
Korea, Rep. of	345	85. 7	67. 9	5. 1	3. 5	9. 2
Malaysia	238	99. 0	57. 5	18. 2	12. 1	11. 2
Philippines	120	98. 4	42. 1	3. 6	16. 8	35. 9
Singapore	221	98. 6	52. 0	23. 6	10. 8	12. 2
Taiwan, China	141	97. 1	65. 6	3. 0	10. 4	18. 1
Thailand	167	97. 9	56. 5	7. 5	12. 8	21. 1
20% cutoff						
Hong Kong, China	330	93. 1	66. 7	1. 4	5. 2	19. 8
Indonesia	178	94. 9	71. 5	8. 2	2. 0	13. 2
Japan	1,240	20. 2	9. 7	0. 8	6. 5	3. 2
Korea, Rep. of	345	56. 8	48. 4	1. 6	0. 7	6. 1
Malaysia	238	89. 6	67. 2	13. 4	2. 3	6. 7
Philippines	120	80. 9	44. 6	2. 1	7. 5	26. 7
Singapore	221	84. 5	55. 4	23. 5	4. 1	11. 5
Taiwan, China	141	73. 7	48. 2	2. 8	5. 3	17. 4
Thailand	167	93. 5	61. 6	8. 0	8. 6	15. 3

Note: The table reports the aggregate statistics on the distribution of ultimate control among five ownership groups. The ultimate control is studied at two cutoff levels—10 and 20 percent of voting rights—to show differences in the concentration of control in individual firms.

Source: Claessens and others (1999).

listed on stock exchanges has risen rapidly, enlarging the role of minority shareholders.

In China, until recently, the state itself was the majority shareholder in most listed companies; minority shareholders did not even have the right to select boards of directors or to hire and fire management. By 2000–01 only about 30 percent of the shares of listed companies were in private hands. Managers and boards of directors are still appointed by the state, and both managers and workers still identify with the state system and exercise a high degree of insider control over the workings of corporatized state-owned enterprises. Under these circumstances, the threat of hostile takeover is minimal, and both central and local governments are likely to step in to assist firms that are in trouble and faced with bankruptcy. Minority shareholders have virtually no scope in which to exercise their rights, and there are no institutional investors to take a lead in this regard, no company boards with independent directors willing to scrutinize performance and audits carefully, and no provision for class action suits. China's judicial system is weak, unsupportive of shareholder activism, and not yet disposed to enforce sound accounting practices, transparency, or disclosure ("Ally of the People" 2002; Tenev and Zhang 2002). However, China's Securities Regulatory Commission has recently taken steps to raise audit standards and have companies issue quarterly statements. In October 2002 it also announced preliminary regulations setting out the conditions under which buyers may take over listed companies, including those under state control ("China: M&A Potential" 2002).

In other countries, the barriers to effective corporate governance are less severe, but they remain serious. They run the gamut from protective cross-shareholdings and a corporate culture inimical to hostile takeovers, all the way to docile institutional investors, compliant auditors, and a chronic shortage of financial information.

Undoubtedly change is in the air, with local regulators and a growing pool of foreign investors taking the lead. Financial globalization has much to do with this, as does the shift by companies in Japan and Korea to financing from capital markets rather than from banks. Reforms in OECD countries are being faintly echoed; for example, Japan, Korea, and Taiwan (China) now require companies to issue consolidated accounts. The International Accounting Standards Board was constituted in 2001 to frame an acceptable set of rules for international business ("Accounting Standards Collaboration" 2002). Incidents of shareholder activism are occurring in Japan and Korea, and courts are gradually beginning to enforce laws affecting governance and to open the door to further legislation.[43]

Does this mean a new dawn for corporate governance standards in East Asia? Probably not for some time, mainly because an active market for corporate control will require governments to withdraw from an ownership role and to relinquish their tendency to manage the

---

43. By the late 1990s minority shareholders in both Japan and Korea had begun to voice their concerns, stung in part by the 1997–98 crisis (see "Day of the Shareholder" 2001 and "South Korea: Corporate Governance" 2002).

market. It will also require a framework of rules enforced by the court system. And, most important, it will require a mix of vigilant institutional and individual shareholders to work with regulators, auditors, and other market agencies to create an environment that gives incentives for better governance.[44]

Protecting Creditors

The crisis of 1997–98 revealed widespread weaknesses in the operation of bankruptcy laws and procedures in the worst-affected countries. Banks and other creditors, both foreign and domestic, found that existing laws often did little to protect them and did not provide reliable procedures for insolvent firms to work their way out of the crisis or be liquidated ("Southeast Asia: Bankruptcy Law" 2000).

Unlike the case with minority shareholder rights, however, efforts are being made to strengthen bankruptcy laws and procedures in the region. These efforts began in 1998 and are being spurred by the increasing presence of foreign investors in East Asian stock markets.[45]

Good bankruptcy legislation should improve the efficiency of the economic system by facilitating the exit of failed firms and paying off creditors in the process, while simultaneously giving firms that are viable over the long run an opportunity to restructure their finances and make other changes that will restore their economic health. Closing failed firms is important not only to eliminate business units that drain the country's resources but also to discourage other firms, not yet in trouble, from taking undue risks.[46] Good bankruptcy legis-

---

44. Piecemeal attempts to strengthen boards of directors, auditing standards, or an independent supervisory agency are unlikely to yield results. The U.S. experience with boards of directors cautions against expecting much from these bodies, irrespective of how they are staffed and whether incentives are used, such as stock ownership (or its absence), turnover of directors, or injunctions to exercise oversight through audit committees ("CEOs Weigh in" 2002; "Corporate Governance after Enron" 2002; "How to Fix Corporate Governance" 2002).

45. This presence is already sizable in Korea, where overseas investors hold more than a third of the equity of companies such as Samsung Electronics. Foreign investors are much quicker to criticize management and demand changes ("Investors Vent" 2002). The takeover or impending takeover of several major Korean companies is also encouraging a change in governance practices.

46. Cermele, Donato, and Mignanelli (2002) describe the costliness of bad debts for banks. They estimate that the costs of such debts for European banks during 1995–2000 amounted to 98 percent of profits.

lation is transparent, providing clear and sophisticated legal rules for dealing with a firm's insolvency. The legislation should also define precise guidelines for "procedure, proof, notification, time, and appeals" ("Southeast Asia: Bankruptcy Law" 2000).

If the legislation meets these criteria (and sometimes it does not, because of the inexperience of those drafting the laws), creditors and firms alike will know how to undertake a workout; this will reduce the ability of stakeholders to delay and distort the process. Long-delayed workouts typically reduce the value of assets, and one way to avoid this is to keep the procedures as simple as possible. Another way to shorten the process is to set time limits for the completion of its various components. Since the crisis, such time limits have been introduced in Indonesia, Korea, and Thailand.

Transparency involves not just good laws but also consistency in their application. In this respect, among the East Asian economies, Hong Kong, China, and Singapore have the best-developed legal infrastructure; Malaysia, too, has had a workable bankruptcy system for decades (Pistor and Wellons 1998). Indonesia, Korea, and Thailand have substantially changed their insolvency laws since the financial crisis, but in Indonesia and the Philippines the inconsistency and lack of credibility of the courts seriously undermine the transparency that the new laws are designed to achieve.[47]

Another problem with the administration of bankruptcy laws in East Asia is that the courts have little experience with corporate insolvency processes. Particularly where a firm is large and complex, inexperienced judges may find it difficult to determine the conditions under which a firm is allowed to continue operating while in the process of restructuring. Outright liquidation of the firm is less complex but still requires specific expertise. Thailand in 1999 established a separate bankruptcy court. But the Thailand Asset Management Corporation had not succeeded in forcing through liquidations by mid-

---

47. This discussion of bankruptcy legislation, including the paragraphs that follow, is based largely on Nam and Oh (2001). Joh (2001, pp. 16–17) notes that through 1997 formal bankruptcy procedures were rarely used in Korea: "Lengthy proceedings, often lasting several years, invited strategic and opportunistic debtor behavior, thus reducing bankruptcy alternatives for creditors. Although more than 17,000 insolvency cases were reported in 1997, only 490 were filed before the court. Of these only 38 liquidations were filed." Most recently, the government has signaled its intention of consolidating and strengthening the three separate existing bankruptcy codes (World Bank, East Asia Region 2002).

2002. Indonesia in 1998 revised its bankruptcy law (dating from 1911) and created four additional commercial courts, with 45 specially trained judges, to relieve the burden of insolvency cases on the existing courts ("Law Set to Push" 1998; "Thailand: Asset Management" 2002). However, by August 2002, IBRA had managed to dispose of only 17 percent of the $181 billion in assets acquired from the banks, with a recovery rate of 28 percent. Korea has a specialized division within each district court with responsibility for insolvency proceedings (Nam and Oh 2001, p. 53).[48]

When the executive branch of the government controls the workout or liquidation process, it is highly unlikely that the law will be consistently applied or the process will be transparent, although it may be fast. China has had bankruptcy legislation on the books since 1986, but only after 1997 did the government begin to liquidate and reorganize a large number of small- and medium-size enterprises. State-owned enterprises in particular were kept afloat even when they ran losses year after year and clearly were unable to repay their bank loans. When the government did decide to close some firms and to force the merger of others with more successful enterprises, the decisions were not made by the courts, nor were they made with due regard for the correct legal process. The executive branch of the government made the decisions using both economic and political criteria. Vietnam followed much the same approach when liquidating provincially owned firms in the early 1990s.

For bankruptcy laws, as for most legislation relating to corporate governance, enforcement is key. If the laws cannot be enforced, the legislation has little practical value, at least in the short run. Malaysia's courts have been generally effective in enforcing insolvency decisions, although not as effective as Singapore's. Korea, too, now has more effective enforcement mechanisms and is engaged in the restructuring and liquidation of some large conglomerates. Thailand, by contrast, had so many insolvency cases in the wake of the financial crisis that the courts were overwhelmed. In Indonesia bankruptcy enforcement has ranged from weak to nonexistent, which is not surpris-

---

48. Linnan (1999) examines the early and halting efforts made to implement the Indonesian bankruptcy legislation. In its first year of operation, this legislation had yielded few results. The few voluntary debt reorganizations that it prompted involved mainly debt rescheduling and little restructuring.

ing given the state of the legal system (Backman 1999; see also Nam and Oh 2001).

Industrial Policies and Corporate Governance

The enforcement of corporate governance laws in general and of bankruptcy laws in particular depends on more than the administrative capability of legal institutions. A major constraint on the enforcement of bankruptcy laws derives from the kinds of industrial policies that are pursued by many of the countries in the region, including Indonesia, Japan, Korea, Malaysia, and Taiwan (China). China and Vietnam also belong on this list, and their command economy background makes the problems especially intractable. In all these economies, the executive branch of the government targets certain sectors, and even individual firms, for development. To promote particular industries, governments not only ease their access to foreign exchange, where its availability is controlled, but also use other supportive measures such as favorable tax treatment and tariff protection. Most of all, governments use their power over banks to direct credit to these firms.[49] Governments enter into implicit contracts to support the large firms they have chosen to implement their industrial development goals.[50] With such arrangements, the implied support does not end when the firm gets into trouble. If firms are to carry out the government's wishes, they must also be reasonably sure that the government will help them if they fail.

A government wanting to shore up a troubled firm can always rely on tax-financed subsidies, but this can give rise to political difficulties; it is generally easier to instruct government-controlled banks to provide bridge finance. Industrial policies thus have also saddled East Asia's banking systems with nonperforming assets. Today the implication of industrial policy for bankruptcy processes is unavoidable: the executive branch is obliged to override the decisions of courts regarding the recovery of nonperforming assets for firms that have done the government's bidding.

---

49. Recently, the Philippine government announced a 1.6 billion peso ($31 million) package of incentives to help its garment exporters cope with the abolition of import quotas in the United States in 2005 and to compete with China after its accession to the World Trade Organization.
50. On some of the dealings between officials and chaebols, see Kirk (1999).

The experience of Korea illustrates the problem (A. O. Krueger and Yoo 2001). During its drive to develop heavy and chemical industries in the 1970s, the Korean government went to great lengths to ensure the development of certain industries and firms, including diverting large amounts of bank credit to them (E. M. Kim 1997). Many of the industries promoted were successful, but some were not, and the new Korean government of the early 1980s was forced to wrestle with the failures. In most cases, it decided to continue financing these industries while they were restructured and, often, put under new management. The process was handled not by the courts but by the executive branch of the government. In the 1980s and 1990s Korea began trying to move away from industrial targeting, but past commitments made it difficult for the government to relinquish all responsibilities, especially after the 1997–98 crisis.[51]

Largely because of the crisis, Korea elected a president, Kim Dae Jung, who had no personal or political obligations to the existing industrial arrangements and who expressed a strong desire to see the chaebol system restructured and dismantled.[52] He also had to find a way to recapitalze the banks, most of which were in trouble both because of the financial crisis and because of decades of often misconceived government direction.

To enforce its plans for industrial restructuring, the government relied on controlling the banks, which had been greatly enlarged following the crisis (Kirk 1999). Refinancing was made available only to those industrial firms that were prepared to implement the government's restructuring goals. Thus the effort to discontinue industrial policies in favor of a market economy, where all firms competed on a level playing field, appeared to relapse into the interventionist industrial regime of the past. However, after the crisis, the problem facing the government was systemic: how to handle the simultaneous bankruptcy of many banks and firms. The constraints on a government during such a crisis are much greater than those created by the failure

---

51. After peaking in the 1970s during the heavy and chemical industry drive (rising as high as 19 percent), the share of preferential loans from deposit money to total loans has been declining. During the latter half of the 1990s, preferential loans accounted for only a small share (2–3 percent) of total loans (A. O. Krueger and Yoo 2001).

52. On the direction proposed for restructuring the chaebol, see Akaba, Budde, and Choi (1998).

of a single firm. Letting Daewoo fail was a major step toward limiting moral hazard and signaled the right intention. It remains to be seen whether successor governments will be willing to let the market and the courts increasingly handle company workouts in the future. If the government does succeed in distancing itself from these decisions, the new laws pertaining to bankruptcy and minority shareholder rights will, with the support of the courts, eventually become meaningful.

Taiwan, China, has been trying to relinquish industrial targeting since at least the mid-1980s (Hsueh, Hsu, and Perkins 2001).[53] Here it has had one advantage over Korea in that many of its firms were quite small and not subject to micromanagement by government. Where the government of Taiwan, China, did pursue targeted industrial policies, it tended to rely mainly on state-owned enterprises supported by favored treatment from the largely state-owned banks. As the government has disengaged from targeted interventionist policies, the roles of corporate governance legislation and of the courts have taken on greater significance.

Malaysia has been more reluctant than Taiwan, China, to move away from targeted policies based less on sectoral and more on ethnic redistribution concerns arising from ethnic tensions that led to a serious outbreak of rioting in 1968. After the financial crisis, the executive branch made major efforts to restructure both the banks and some of the government-favored firms, which are owned mainly, but not exclusively, by newly wealthy Bumiputra businessmen. For smaller firms and more generally for Chinese-Malaysian firms, most of which do not receive assistance from the government, the bankruptcy laws and the courts are largely responsible for the workout or liquidation processes where needed.

In China and Vietnam, the executive branch of the government, at both national and provincial levels, is in charge of restructuring. The courts play little or no role.

Shifting away from discretionary intervention by the executive branch has a reasonably straightforward economic logic but is difficult to implement, especially where political considerations work against it. Not only do discretionary industrial policy interventions create opportunities for individual rent seeking, they also pave the

---

53. On the industrial policies of the pre-1986 period, see Wade (1990).

way for financing political campaigns and organizations. The experience of Korea in the 1980s also shows that the quality of government policy actions, such as the division of the Kukje Group, was influenced by noneconomic considerations that adversely affected the actions taken (Schopf 2001).[54] Few countries around the world have been able to create transparent and legal means for funding political campaigns. Discretionary government power over industry in East Asia has made raising funds for political purposes very easy (Kirk 1999). In most cases, politicians expect firms to contribute funds if they wish to participate in major government economic initiatives. In a few situations, including in Malaysia and in Taiwan, China, under the Kuomintang, the ruling party owns or controls firms that receive favored treatment in the awarding of government contracts. In such situations, reforming the economic system may also require a parallel reform of the political system and its financing, with emphasis on laws governing the disclosure of political financing (see Pinto-Duchinsky 2002 for an international review of political financing).

COMPETITION POLICY:
WHO DETERMINES MERGERS AND ACQUISITIONS?

Effective corporate governance would be hindered by the industrial concentration that is a legacy of past industrial policies. In much of East Asia, competition policy and the level of industrial concentration reflect a combination of market forces and direct government intervention designed to favor a particular form of industrial organization. The models of industrial development adopted by China, Malaysia, Vietnam, and, to a lesser degree, several other economies have been the Korean chaebols and the Japanese keiretsu, at least until the financial crisis of 1997–98. But from today's vantage point, the suitability of these models is in question. A major reorganization of industry is currently under way in much of the region, particularly in China and Korea.

---

54. Inefficient firms were often favored with credit in return for political support. Based on information obtained using the 1998 Korean Freedom of Information Act, Schopf (2001) calculates that during 1980–88 the government extracted $1.24 billion in bribes from the corporate sector.

In Europe and the United States, competition law is intended to discourage control or to thwart attempts by individual firms to dominate the market.[55] East Asia has competition laws with similar goals, but these have had little influence in most of the region—including Japan—until very recently. For governments as different as those of China, Korea, and Malaysia, the purpose of competition policy has historically been more to ensure that firms can compete internationally than to ensure fair competition in the domestic market. In fact, many countries in the region have given individual firms a monopoly in the domestic market for significant periods to make it possible for them to earn profits while gradually becoming competitive on the international scene.[56] Korea is now moving away from this approach because of its membership in the WTO and international pressure, but many other countries in the region have yet to do so.

Industrial Concentration

Concerns about the degree to which individual large firms or conglomerates control industry in a given country stem partly from concerns about economic efficiency. Experience in the United States shows that highly diversified conglomerates are usually less efficient and less profitable than less diversified firms.[57] The Kim Dae Jung government in Korea holds a similar view and has tried to correct the

---

55. The most recent well-known examples in the United States are the breakup of AT&T, the government's attempt to limit the monopoly powers of Microsoft (Fisher 2000), and the disallowing of a number of mergers in the telecommunications (for example, Worldcom and Sprint) and airline industries.

56. For many countries, the model of how to create internationally competitive firms, particularly in large-scale heavy and chemical industries, was first Japan and later Korea, which built up internationally recognized conglomerates such as Hitachi, Matsushita, and Toyota or Daewoo, Hyundai, and Samsung. For governments in China and Malaysia, for example, and to a lesser degree several other governments in the region, the prime task of competition policy was to create equally successful and internationally recognized national companies along the lines of the Korean chaebol and, to a lesser degree, the Japanese keiretsu.

57. Ravenscraft and Scherer (1987) show that in most cases conglomerate mergers during the 1960s to 1980s led to declining profit. Agrawal and Jaffe (2000) estimate that the long-term stock market returns to acquirers of firms were negative (see also Shleifer and Vishny 2001). Another issue is the efficiency of family ownership compared to other forms of ownership. Contrary to popular perception, Wiwattanakantang (2001), using detailed ownership data on Thai firms, finds that firms owned by a family are as efficient as foreign-owned firms. The reason for this is reduced agency cost.

perceived problem by forcing chaebols to concentrate on their core businesses.

Partly, too, these concerns relate to the desired concentration of political power, especially in countries such as Indonesia, Korea, and the Philippines. If a few families manage the destiny of a major segment of manufacturing, they also control the direction of the economy, who and how many people are hired, and which companies other than those directly controlled will be chosen to supply key inputs. They also have the resources to fund the political campaigns of their supporters and to withhold funding from their detractors. Through these levers, they can exercise a degree of political power that is widely felt to be incompatible with democratic government. In turn, this political power makes it possible for conglomerates to protect and perpetuate their economic dominance, despite the pressure of market forces that might otherwise erode their dominance.

High degrees of concentration also create "too big to fail" problems in addition to providing the basis for political influence through both votes and campaign contributions. This can take place in socialist countries as well, where large firms have advocates in the government through the classic socialist organization of ministries, which is then reflected in lobbying for resources within the government, including through pressures on the central bank. The political issue then is how to check such corporate power in various ways, including through regulation, the introduction of competition, competition policy, and transparency in business-government relations (including campaign contributions).

Between the 1960s and 1990s the concentration of production in industry varied widely among countries (table 2.4). In Korea and Malaysia most industries were dominated by a small number of firms. By contrast, in China sales were distributed much more evenly among firms.[58] In Taiwan, China, and the Philippines in 1995, after a period of economic liberalization, production was more concentrated than in China but was roughly comparable to patterns in the United States and Japan several decades ago.

---

58. The exception in China is the petroleum and natural gas sector, where fewer than four firms produced at least 60 percent of gross output.

Table 2.4 Concentration of Production, by Select Countries and Years in East Asia and the United States (percentage of sectors in different concentration bands)

Industry concentration ratio	United States, top 4		Japan, top 4	Korea, top 5	Taiwan, China, top 4	Malaysia, top 4,	Philippines, top 4		China, top 18–100,
	1963	1972	1963	1974	1976	1990[a]	1983	1995	1988
Number of sectors	417	183	512	205	131	22	31	31	39
Concentration ratio (percent)[b]									
80–100	12.2	6.0	5.6	26.9	10.7	18.2	25.8	9.7	5.1
60–80	9.1	13.7	7.8	17.9	12.2	40.9	41.9	16.1	5.1
40–60	19.6	26.8	27.9	27.3	24.4	31.8	16.1	29.0	7.7
20–40	39.3	34.9	25.4	21.9	35.2	4.5	16.1	35.5	17.9
0–20	19.8	18.6	33.3	6.0	17.5	4.5	0	9.7	64.1
Total	100.0	100.0	100.0	100.0	100.0	100.0	100.0	100.0	100.0

a. Concentration ratios adjusted for the level of import competition. These ratios probably more accurately reflect the level of competition; they show that the level of concentration is much lower if competitive imports are taken into account. Such figures were not readily available for the other countries.

b. The concentration percentages are based on the value of shipments by the top four firms as a percentage of total shipments in each industry for the United States, Japan, Republic of Korea, and Taiwan (China). The Philippine data refer to the share of output in each industry. The Chinese data are derived from Perkins (2002, table 4). They refer to the output produced by firms with more than 100 million yuan in gross output value, a number that varies by sector from 0 to 293 firms. The number of firms in the most concentrated sectors (with more than 60 percent of the output in that sector) ranges from 18 to 100 firms.

Sources: Caves and Uekusa (1976); De Vito (1995); Hill (forthcoming); Hsiao (1982); Yoo and Lee (1997).

What accounts for these patterns of concentration? In Korea under Park Chung Hee and the Philippines under Ferdinand Marcos, the high degrees of concentration reflected the government's use of directed credit and access to key inputs to assist a few large conglomerates or families. The Korean government also gave explicit monopolies over the domestic market for certain heavy industries, although these monopolies were temporary. China's industrial organization was not a product of market forces either. Industrial enterprises in China were a creation of the pre-1979 Soviet-style command economy with central planning. Enterprises were not really business organizations, but factory units under the active direct supervision of central and provincial government industrial bureaus. Once industrial reforms began in 1984, China attempted to turn these enterprises into truly independent business firms, with some, but limited, success. Chinese firms have tended to remain small relative to their international counterparts, partly because of local protectionism, which has limited the size of the market and led local governments to oppose mergers and acquisitions that would lead to the loss of local control over an enterprise. Lack of access to bank loans and to the stock market has further limited the size of firms; all but the largest state firms have had to rely mainly on internally generated funds for expansion (Steinfeld 2002).[59]

Taiwan, China, may be the closest to having an industrial structure dictated mainly by market forces.[60] The government did reserve certain industries for state-owned firms, but the share of the public sector has dwindled steadily as private firms have been permitted to enter sectors, such as petrochemicals, that had been reserved for the government's China Petroleum Corporation. The industrial organization of Taiwan, China, is difficult to interpret, however; numerous small firms are embedded in organizations that are led by larger firms and are not independent except in an accounting sense (Hsueh, Hsu, and Perkins 2001).[61]

---

59. Nolan (2002) shows that even the largest Chinese firms in sectors such as iron and steel are only a fraction as large as their major international counterparts.

60. Hong Kong, China, and Singapore have left decisions on industrial concentration almost entirely to the market, but the openness of these two economies means that industrial concentration ratios have little bearing on the level of domestic competition.

61. The same could be said of some small firms in Japan that serve as just-in-time suppliers to large companies.

Thus no example of industrial organization in Asia can reliably serve as a wholly market-determined model for others to follow.

Reorganization of Industry

All countries go through periods of organizational change in industry, whether through mergers and acquisitions or through the sale of subsidiaries. In the economies of Europe and North America, the process is left largely to market forces, which now include cross-national forces. The rules governing mergers and breakups are set by legislatures and are increasingly coordinated internationally and administered by legal systems. The role of the executive branch of government is confined largely to helping write the rules and to ensuring that the new arrangements do not unduly restrict competition.

In the reorganization of industry taking place in East Asia, the process of change is very different. Here, industrial organization is still governed as much by the actions of governments as by the efforts of firms themselves or by legal or regulatory systems. The activist role of government in industrial policy that flourished in the 1960s and 1970s is still very real today, although its goals have changed.

In the 1970s the goal of the Korean government was to support large conglomerates by putting them in charge of implementing the heavy and chemical industry drive. After 1997, and with the election of President Kim Dae Jung, the goal has been to restructure the conglomerates by forcing them to sell off subsidiaries that are unrelated to what the government considers to be their core businesses. In China, since the latter half of the 1990s, the government has been busy merging enterprises to form business groups (jituan).[62] The models that originally inspired these efforts, at least those sponsored by the government, were the conglomerates of Japan and Korea. After the financial crisis and the difficulties faced by the Korean chaebols, the ultimate goal of enterprise consolidation has begun to be reconsidered, but the mergers and acquisitions continue. Given the historical patterns, China's decision to create a more concentrated in-

---

62. By the end of 2000 there were some 6,027 of these groups, of which 2,655 were large enterprise groups, accounting for 57 percent of the assets of the industrial sector and 11 percent of urban employment. Less than two-thirds of them have majority state ownership, but the ones that do hold 92 percent of the total assets (China, National Bureau of Statistics 2000, 2001).

dustrial structure and Korea's decision to move in the opposite direction will probably lead to greater efficiency and competitiveness.

Vietnam has been following China, also inspired by the Japanese and Korean models, although its efforts have involved more the relabeling of government bureaus than the creation of truly independent large-scale firms. The functioning of the relabeled bureaus has not undergone much change and remains far from that of the independent conglomerates that the reorganizers had hoped to bring into existence.

Malaysia, since the 1980s, has struggled with how to create large Bumiputra business groups that can compete both internationally and with Malaysia's own Chinese-Malaysian companies. Initially, it created state-owned enterprises to produce steel, cement, and cars. Then these state enterprises were sold off, mainly to favored Bumiputra entrepreneurs, but the goal remained the same and had the backing of government-supported loans and other subsidies.[63]

In the Philippines concentration has declined, following the liberalization of a number of markets (Hill forthcoming). This decline can be seen clearly from the figures reported for 1983 and 1995 in table 2.4.

Should governments still be making decisions on industrial concentration and competition? In the early years of industrialization, it might have been desirable for governments to shape industrial organization. But after the experience of the past two decades, there is little reason for the executive branches of East Asian governments to continue doing so.

Governments appear to be trying to base their industrial merger and acquisition decisions primarily on economic and technical, not political or rent-seeking, criteria. But government leaders and bureaucrats, however well intentioned, generally lack the expertise and motivation of business people who have spent much of their lives engaged with the issues of technology, scale, and profitability in their particular industries. Given the right incentives and regulatory structure, which the government needs to provide, such expertise can be brought to bear effectively on the decisions to merge or divest based on market considerations. Even where governments have the technical competence—and many do not—decisions on whether to support or break

---

63. After the financial crisis, the government also took on the task of restructuring and consolidating the banking system.

up a large conglomerate are still likely to be heavily influenced by political considerations that undermine economic efficiency.

If government line ministries are not the ideal bodies to decide on industrial organization, what is the best choice? Prematurely leaving the matter to the market may perpetuate existing inefficient structures and allow individual companies to stifle competition by acquiring excessive control over their markets.

The remaining choices are either to set up a special regulatory agency with the technical expertise and power needed to make these decisions or—as in the United States—to create a group within the government to deal with competition policy and require it to bring cases before the judiciary, thus giving the judiciary final authority to decide whether a case has merit or not. The first of these approaches requires a regulatory body that is free from political manipulation and independent of the companies it regulates—a goal that few developed countries and perhaps no developing country has achieved. The other approach requires an independent and technically competent judicial system, a topic that is discussed next.

THE RULE OF LAW

The legal system is at the nub of many corporate and financial issues.[64] Relatively weak legal systems did not impede rapid growth in the past because domestic economies were relatively isolated from market forces. Today, if government is to cede its role to the workings of the market, market participants must be able to rely on an appropriate legal framework and on impersonal enforcement of the law. But in much of East Asia today both courts and regulatory agencies are very weak. The challenge of building a true market economy thus includes the difficult task of strengthening the courts, the regulators, or both, relative to the executive and legislative branches of government. This strengthening must be accomplished in countries with little experience with either independent judges or independent regulators.[65]

---

64. A substantial empirical literature, summarized and extended by Beck and others (2001), maintains that the efficacy of the legal system determines the effectiveness of the financial system in promoting growth.

65. With regard to some of the cultural and religious precepts that influence rights and legal traditions in East Asia, see Glenn (2000).

Historical Foundations of Judicial Systems

It is difficult to assess the ability of a judicial system to support efficient and equitable corporate and financial sector governance. But it is widely conceded that Hong Kong, China, and Singapore have the most effective legal systems in the region.

Hong Kong, China, and Singapore. Both Hong Kong, China, and Singapore were major commercial centers before they began building legal systems to serve more than the colonial power.

In Hong Kong, China, it was not until the 1970s that the government, seeing the increasing likelihood of reversion to Chinese control, embarked on a major effort to develop a legal system to provide a wide variety of rights to individuals in the colony.[66] By the end of the 1980s, Hong Kong, China, was graduating 150 or so lawyers a year, while simultaneously importing more lawyers from Britain and the United States. By the 1990s, prior to reversion, Hong Kong, China, was the one economy in Asia where the judiciary had nearly equal standing with the executive branch, and its citizens increasingly saw that system as protecting them as well as it protected the colonial power. Shortly after the colony reverted to China, the territory had roughly 5,000 lawyers of all types. Most of the smaller ethnic Chinese businesses still rely on informal mechanisms, built on the relationships of the past, to settle even major business disputes. Larger Chinese firms and the numerous multinational corporations headquartered in Hong Kong, China, however, do make extensive use of the legal system in commercial matters.

In Singapore, like in Hong Kong, China, the presence of many firms with foreign investment has been a source of demand for the legal system. By the 1950s and 1960s Singaporeans had gained a sense of ownership over and appreciation of the British law that they had inherited.[67] That said, Singapore's legal system today is not really independent of the executive branch of the government to a degree comparable to that in the United Kingdom or the United States. The

---

66. For a discussion of how the law has been applied in Hong Kong, China, since the territory's return to China, see A. H. Y. Chen (1999).

67. For a description of how Singaporean political activists used the law and the legal system to further their goals prior to independence, see K. Lee (1998).

main task of the courts was and is to implement the policies of the government, not to challenge them. In the economic sphere, this subordination may not matter a great deal, because the government generally does not use its discretionary powers to promote particular companies. In the settlement of business disputes, the courts are seen as impartial and are much more widely used than informal nonjudicial methods (Kamarul and Tomasic 1999).

Japan, Korea, and Taiwan (China). Qualitative appraisals suggest that the legal systems of Korea and Taiwan, China, are broadly similar to one another. Both originated in the German system introduced by the Japanese colonial administration. In both economies, the law was subordinate to decisions by the executive branch of government during the decades of authoritarian rule that ended in the late 1980s. Governments in both economies pursued industrial policies, although the degree to which they intervened differed. In the two legal systems, judges were more like civil servants, as they were in Japan. They were law school graduates who had passed an examination before receiving an additional year or two of formal training. Until recently, a high proportion were young and inexperienced and lacked stature.[68] In Korea before 1981 only 100 people a year were allowed to pass the examination to become lawyers, judges, and prosecutors. That number was subsequently raised to 300 a year and then to around 800 a year in the 1990s. Still, by 2000, the whole legal profession, including judges and prosecutors, numbered fewer than 7,000, only slightly more than in Hong Kong, China, with one-eighth of Korea's population.

The judges of Japan and Taiwan, China, have backgrounds similar to those of Korea, and their numbers on a per capita basis are similar.[69] Japan's judiciary, of course, has operated in the context of a dem-

---

68. This discussion and the paragraph that follows are based on exchanges with William Alford, of the Harvard Law School, who bears no responsibility for any errors in interpretation.

69. Japan, on whose model the systems of Korea and Taiwan, China, were built, was still producing only 1,000 lawyers, prosecutors, and judges a year by the late 1990s. As Lincoln (2001, p. 195) notes, "Unless government authorizes a dramatic increase in the number of lawyers and judges, a deluge of lawsuits initiated by private shareholders will clog the legal system." Japan is now making efforts to increase the number of graduating lawyers to 3,000 by 2010 and to establish graduate-level law programs by 2004. The small number of lawyers in Japan is misleading

ocratic society since the 1950s. In Korea and Taiwan, China, in the late 1980s, the advent of democracy ended the clear dominance of the executive over the judiciary. In Taiwan, China, this is evident in the behavior of the Council of Grand Justices, which, before 1987, took few, if any, steps to limit the inappropriate exercise of power by other branches of government. After 1987 the council not only supported private citizens who brought cases against the government based on the government's failure to comply with its own laws but also declared a number of laws unconstitutional (Cooney 1999).

The legal systems of Japan, Korea, and Taiwan (China) have yet to engage fully in overseeing and enforcing the rules of the market, although the framework for doing so is in place. These economies still rely on the many informal mechanisms that have been developed over the years to handle contract disputes and the like. Such informal mechanisms are increasingly inadequate for these complex modern economies.[70] The formal legal systems need to continue expanding, and the prestige and competence of their personnel need to be further strengthened.

China, Indonesia, the Philippines, and Vietnam. The weakest legal systems in East Asia are in China, Indonesia, the Philippines, and Vietnam; they are clearly not up to the task of overseeing and enforcing the rules of a market economy. In the medium term, the business community has little choice but to depend on the many informal mechanisms that substitute for a law-based system, while continuing to rely on discretionary government intervention in the economy where fundamental restructuring is required.

---

in some respects. Even though lawyers are the only ones hired to practice law, numerous professionals and judicial administrative personnel (patent agents and tax agents, among others) assist companies in legal matters. Companies may hire licensed attorneys, but many also hire people who studied law only at the undergraduate level. Given that there are about 36,000 university graduates from law departments (around 50,000 pass the bar exam in the United States each year), the number of trained legal personnel in Japan is not as small as the number of licensed attorneys suggests. See www.Asahi.com (www.asahi.com/edu/others/K200105 2600418.html and www.asahi.com/edu/lifelong/K2002012501067.html).

70. As the economy of Korea has become more complex, the business community has begun to complain that the legal system is too expensive and too inaccessible. Similar concerns have been voiced in Japan.

Both Indonesia and the Philippines have good laws on their books.[71] But it is widely perceived that judges in both countries can be influenced. A survey of Manila lawyers raised concern over the impartiality of judges, and similar concerns were expressed in the case of Indonesia (Backman 1999, p. 33; Bourchier 1999). The legal systems of China and Vietnam probably are a notch above those of Indonesia and the Philippines, but they perform little better, despite the lower level of corruption. China began restoring its legal system in the early 1980s. There are now shelves full of new laws designed to provide a legal framework for foreign investment and a market economy. In the 1980s, and even more so in the 1990s, the judiciary has been active in settling economic disputes, especially in the most advanced parts of the country. Among the larger firms in the major cities, formal contracts with suppliers are the norm, although disputes still rely mainly on informal negotiation for settlement. A survey conducted for the present study, covering 1,500 firms in five major cities, found that, on average, 12 percent of the disputes were resolved through the courts; the figure for Shanghai was 22 percent (Steinfeld 2002).

China's entry into the WTO will further reinforce the role of formal legal proceedings, but an enormous amount of work remains to be done simply to make Chinese laws compatible with WTO requirements. Enforcing those laws will be even more difficult.[72]

China has a plethora of conflicting rules and regulations created by many different authorities. The job of the courts is thus made much more difficult from the start, because they are supposed to adjudicate, but not interpret, the laws. When the courts do render decisions, enforcement is problematic; courts do not have primacy over ministries

---

71. With technical assistance from the International Monetary Fund and the Harvard Institute for International Development, Indonesia rewrote and legislated a long list of new financial laws, many of them more modern than those in much more advanced countries (Cole and Slade 1996). However, when the financial crisis hit in 1997–98, many of these laws made little difference. Prudential regulations designed to improve the banks' portfolios had been put in place in 1991–92, but little effort had been made to rein in the overseas borrowing that was the direct cause of the crisis. And in the immediate aftermath of the crisis, close ties between several of the worst-performing banks and the leaders of the government plus their family members and business associates ensured that the actions of regulators were overridden, whatever the law said. If the courts had been willing to intervene, they would have had little power to do so.

72. For a discussion of the impact of WTO accession on the legal system, see Kong (2000).

and other government organs, and many court rulings are simply ig-
nored (D. C. Clarke 1996; Lubman 1999). In addition, high-level officials can informally overrule both the courts and government organizations.

Reform of the Judicial System

The legal systems of many East Asian nations clearly are unable to support effective oversight of corporate and financial sector governance.
Not just China, Indonesia, the Philippines, and Vietnam, but virtually
all the region's economies, including Japan, need to reform their legal
systems. Can they achieve this goal over the next decade or so?

On the positive side, as their economies have become more complex, Japan, Korea, and Taiwan (China) have enhanced the capabilities of their judicial systems in the commercial arena. The same has
been happening in China, although from a much lower starting
point. In both Korea and Taiwan, China, the strengthening of democratic institutions has made it possible to begin creating a judiciary
with the power to curb government actions that violate the law as
well as to settle commercial disputes that do not involve the government. No comparable influence can yet be seen in Indonesia, the
Philippines, or Vietnam.

On the negative side, interventionist industrial policies continue to
provide a rationale for the executive branch of government to overrule the judiciary in China, Malaysia, and Vietnam. And in China and
Vietnam, the state's decision to retain a monopoly of power and to exercise that power with wide discretion throughout society clearly prevents the legal system from rendering and enforcing independent and
fair decisions.

Modes of Judicial Reform. Judicial efficiency is based on three factors: accuracy, speed, and costs.[73] Like many other judicial systems,
those in East Asia are plagued by problems such as long case completion times, high costs, and corruption. Judicial inefficiency is detrimental to the welfare of litigants and to general economic prosperity,
particularly if the cases are related to property and contracts. There

---

73. This section is based on Botero and others (2003).

are several common modes of judicial reform: increased funding, better incentives, and simpler and more flexible procedures. None of the proposals is without drawbacks; however, they do offer a menu of choices that, with suitable modifications, could be made to fit the needs of the countries in the region.

An increase in resources can make a difference in situations of severe and chronic underfunding, but otherwise its effects are only temporary. Increased resources come in many different forms, including more staff, more computerization, or fewer administrative duties for judges.

Limiting access to the courts could, in principle, reduce the caseload. But many studies in Latin America and the United States have found that limiting the number of filings seems to have little effect on efficiency, while raising concerns about fairness. Indeed, greater access could actually be more advantageous if it were associated with simpler procedures or fewer legal requirements.

The most effective reforms affect incentives. They include making judges more accountable, changing the incentives of lawyers and litigants, encouraging competition among courts, and providing alternative means of resolving disputes (Botero and others 2003). Judges can be made more accountable by introducing individual calendars and databases of cases to trace progress.[74] Other ways to improve case management include pretrial conferences and strict scheduling. These reforms give judges more leeway in determining how a case is handled, leading to more accountability.

The incentives of lawyers can be strengthened by raising standards for the legal profession, regulating attorneys' fees, and reforming the roles of subordinate judicial officials. Making lawyers compete with non-lawyers and self-representation can lead to more accountability and overall efficiency. In Japan 90 percent of the summary court cases do not involve lawyers (Botero and others 2003). Reducing the cost of legal help improves access to the judicial system. By the same token, more qualified legal professionals can expedite the legal process.

---

74. The individual calendar refers to the practice of assigning one judge to each case from beginning to end. This provides a way of metering the amount of time a judge takes in handling cases and serves as a benchmark for comparing performance. Judges feel more accountable for their cases, and their familiarity with the contents of the case can lead to more expeditious handling.

Another way to increase efficiency is to distribute the administrative tasks among subordinate judicial officials, since bribery may be easier where many administrative tasks are in the hands of one official. The incentives of litigants can be changed by shifting the burden of direct costs. In Singapore the vast majority of trials last only a single day because of the progressivity of fees after the first day. Making the loser pay would also reduce the load of cases.

Additional avenues to efficiency include competition among courts, the use of specialized courts, or alternative dispute resolution mechanisms. Allowing the courts to collect fees for their services would give them an incentive to provide better service. Specialized courts usually have streamlined procedures, and they offer an alternative forum for litigants. Small claims courts in many countries have been successful in reducing the time to disposition, while expanding access.

Judicial efficiency and access can also be improved by simplifying procedures and making them more flexible. This may include steps such as switching to oral proceedings, precourt agreements, mediation, or informal settlement. Instead of setting up another institution, some countries have tried to give the judiciary more leeway to adapt procedures, so as to allow experimentation and innovation and allow courts to adapt to local needs.[75]

Creation of an Independent Legal System. Creating legal systems that are competent, strong, and relatively independent of the executive branch of government will take a long time in many East Asian countries. But in the more advanced economies and polities of the region, that process is well under way. Not only in Hong Kong (China) and Singapore but also in Japan, Korea, and Taiwan (China), it is already possible to see an economic system that is governed by the rule of law.

---

75. New Zealand's tenancy and disputes tribunals have used some of these techniques to good effect. Before the inception of the tribunals, landlord-tenant disputes were slow, expensive, and complex. The tribunals now handle more than 41,000 disputes a year and settle most within 15 days and in a single hearing. They rely mostly on oral proceedings, and courts are not required to give formal technical legal explanations for their decisions. The judgment is open for appeal, but only 5 percent are in fact appealed.

Where the rule of law is weak, one option is to strengthen the formal regulatory system, governed by rules rather than by the discretionary judgment of the executive branch of government. Regulatory agencies would supplement or displace the courts in settling disputes and overseeing bankruptcies and mergers.[76] However, independent regulatory agencies have been difficult to establish, even in the most advanced economies, and in Asia they are generally the creatures of the executive branch of government. Particularly in the countries with authoritarian political regimes, the executive branch of government is generally closely tied to the large firms that the agencies are charged with regulating. Making governments adopt a more arm's-length relationship with big business has been a halting process. Democratization has helped in this regard in Korea and Taiwan, China, but in Japan it has had little impact for decades.

CONCLUSION

Macroeconomic stability helps both to lessen the risk of shocks and to reduce their adverse effects. It can be secured by strengthening public finances, by improving the accounting for contingent liabilities, and by containing the growth of such liabilities. These actions limit current and future budgetary imbalances and raise the efficiency of public expenditures. Better expenditure management together with some additional revenue effort—which is feasible given the relative smallness of the public revenues in most of East Asia—would make available the resources needed for safety nets in highly open economies. The reform of safety nets is urgent in much of East Asia. Even a frugal safety net for the most vulnerable segments of the population will require an increase in the share of public expenditures devoted to transfers and public services.

---

76. Such a shift in emphasis occurred in the United States at the end of the nineteenth century and continued into the twentieth. The belief was that regulatory agencies would administer fairer judgments than would the courts, because the courts' decisions could be subverted too easily, given the imbalance in power between the large corporations that, for the most part, were the source of the violations and the individuals and small companies that were their victims (Shleifer and Glaeser 2001).

The industrial and financial sectors of most of the economies of East Asia need restructuring. Insolvent firms with no prospects of recovery need to be liquidated, and the assets of viable firms need to be consolidated. If financial markets are to continue to develop in the region and to perform their roles efficiently, rules must protect investors who are not owner-managers of the firms. Much better bankruptcy legislation is needed, and it must be enforced efficiently and fairly. This is highly significant for the longer-term health of the banking systems in these economies, but it is only a first step toward protecting the rights of minority shareholders. Banks must also fundamentally change many of their past practices. They must be made more independent of government when it comes to deciding who does and does not receive loans. But they need more, not less, government involvement in the area of prudential oversight of bank loan portfolios.

Outside Hong Kong, China, and to a degree Singapore, the executive branch of the government has taken the lead in making decisions on industrial structure and in enforcing them through its command over banks. This has led both industrial firms and banks to rely on the government when they run into trouble—a situation that has created moral hazard, often in extreme forms. Today the challenge for most countries in the region remains to reduce or eliminate this interventionist role of government.

To move to a true market system requires a set of institutions that can enforce the rules of a market system independently, efficiently, and fairly. While striving to make their regulatory agencies more effective and independent, countries should put much more effort into establishing independent and efficient legal systems.

Creating the legal institutions of a modern market economy is a daunting task for any country. For those furthest behind in this regard, such as China, Indonesia, and Vietnam, the effort will certainly take decades. Japan, Korea, and Taiwan (China) already have the basic structure of a modern legal system and mainly need to increase the numbers and improve the competence of judicial and legal personnel and to rewrite some of the laws. At some point, the executive branch of government must be willing to give the judiciary enough power to overrule the decisions of the government itself. In all cases where this has occurred, except Hong Kong, China, the true independence of the judiciary has been preceded by the introduction of political democracy with competitive elections.

CHAPTER 3

REGIONAL COOPERATION IN EAST ASIA

A s the economies of East Asia become more interdependent, their efforts to achieve longer-term stability and growth are more likely to succeed if they can be coordinated. This chapter focuses on the likely future directions of regional cooperation in exchange rate and monetary policy, finance, trade, and areas such as investment.

Some joint responses to common problems are already evident. On the monetary and financial front, initiatives have ranged from ambitious proposals for an Asian monetary fund to the currency swap lines of the Chiang Mai Initiative.[1] The Association of South East Asian Nations (ASEAN) has established a surveillance procedure, based in the organization's secretariat in Jakarta, to encourage the coordination of macroeconomic and financial policies.[2] The ASEAN+3 countries are studying options for creating their own surveillance procedure.[3] Agreements on technical assistance and information sharing are almost too numerous to name.

The ASEAN Free Trade Agreement (AFTA) has been in effect among the five founding members since January 2002. ASEAN leaders are studying the feasibility of linking their economies with those

---

1. The Japanese government proposed an Asian monetary fund in the autumn of 1997 as part of the so-called Miyazawa Plan. The Chiang Mai Initiative was negotiated by members of the Association of South East Asian Nations with China, Japan, and Korea following their informal exchanges at the Asian Development Bank annual meeting in Chiang Mai in May 2000.

2. The members of ASEAN are Brunei, Cambodia, Indonesia, Laos, Malaysia, Myanmar, the Philippines, Singapore, Thailand, and Vietnam. The founding members (Indonesia, Malaysia, the Philippines, Singapore, and Thailand established the association in 1967) concentrated initially on political and security cooperation but turned their attention to the creation of a free trade area at the fourth ASEAN ministerial meeting in 1971.

3. ASEAN+3 countries are the members of ASEAN plus China, Japan, and Korea.

of China, Japan, and the Republic of Korea and are exploring initiatives to promote financial market development and foreign direct investment (FDI) from the Northeast Asian countries. Members of Asia Pacific Economic Cooperation (APEC) announced a clutch of negotiations and studies for bilateral free trade agreements at or following meetings of their economic leaders in 1999 and 2000.[4] The results included free trade agreements between Singapore and Japan and between Singapore and the United States and a study for a bilateral free trade agreement between Japan and Korea.[5] China has proposed establishing a free trade area with ASEAN within 10 years, leading Prime Minister Junichiro Koizumi of Japan to propose the creation of a Japan-ASEAN free trade agreement study group during his January 2002 visit to Southeast Asia.

THE CASE FOR REGIONAL COOPERATION

What problems cannot be solved by working through extant multilateral arrangements but instead would benefit from a regional approach? Why should economic problems be solved more efficiently, and opportunities exploited more fully, at the regional rather than the global level?

There are three rationales for a regional approach. First, negotiations at the regional level, involving a limited number of countries, may entail lower transaction costs and fewer large-number problems. Second, insofar as the members of a region have common histories, face common problems, adopt common policies, and share common understandings of their economic challenges, they should find it relatively easier to reach agreements.[6] Third, regional neighbors have a

---

4. APEC had 21 members at the time of writing: Australia, Brunei Darussalam, Canada, Chile, China, Hong Kong (China), Indonesia, Japan, Korea, Malaysia, Mexico, New Zealand, Papua New Guinea, Peru, the Philippines, Russia, Singapore, Taiwan (China), Thailand, the United States, and Vietnam.

5. On these studies and negotiations, see Findlay (2001), C. Kim (2001), and Scollay and Gilbert (2001). The agreement between Japan and Korea is expected to be concluded by 2005 ("Korea, Japan" 2002).

6. Fratianni and Pattison (2000) attribute the success of the Bank for International Settlements to the fact that, historically, it has been made up of a small number of (mainly European) members at similar stages of economic and financial development and with rather similar problems.

great incentive to reach agreements that promise to internalize externalities that spill over borders, insofar as those externalities are limited mainly to their geographic neighborhood. An example of such a problem is the Southeast Asian haze caused by Indonesian forest fires.[7]

Not all policy issues satisfy these criteria equally well; those that satisfy them most fully are the obvious candidates for regional initiatives.

EAST ASIAN PARTICULARITIES

Sifting through the options and evaluating their potential require identifying what is distinctive about the setting for cooperation in Asia. Five aspects stand out, each of which may pose particular problems for regional cooperation.

First, Asian economies are diverse in their levels of income and economic structures. Per capita incomes range from $1,430 in Laos to $25,170 in Japan in 1999 U.S. dollars at purchasing power parity. Market structures range from the concentrated, in Korea, to the relatively atomized, in Taiwan, China. Financial regulations range from the restrictive, in China, to the much less restrictive, in Hong Kong, China. The wide differences in development and in economic issues create obvious challenges for any attempt to agree on and cooperatively implement a coordinated set of solutions; these economies understandably have different attitudes toward issues ranging from infant-industry protection to intellectual property rights to international migration.

Second, East Asia has extensive trade and financial relations with other parts of the world. Harmonizing regional trade, monetary, and financial arrangements with those of other regions is therefore of exceptional importance. Less than a fourth of the exports of ASEAN countries go to other ASEAN countries; for ASEAN plus China, Japan, and Korea, that share is less than a third (table 3.1). In contrast, the comparable figures for the North American Free Trade Agreement (NAFTA) and the European Union are more than half

---

7. This case is analyzed by Lin and Rajan (2000). Financial contagion, which has a strong regional aspect, is a more controversial case in point (Glick and Rose 1999).

Table 3.1 Intraregional Trade, 1970–2000
(exports within a regional trading bloc as a percentage of total exports)

Regional trading bloc	1970	1980	1990	1996	1998	1999	2000
APEC	57.8	57.9	68.3	72.1	69.7	71.9	—
ASEAN	22.9	18.7	19.8	25.4	21.7	22.2	23.1
ASEAN+3	—	31.6	27.5	37.0	29.0	31.5	32.0
All East Asia[a]	—	33.8[b]	40.4[b]	50.4	43.0	44.8	46.3
Bangkok Agreement	2.7	3.7	3.7	5.3	5.1	5.3	—
European Union	59.5	60.8	65.9	61.4	57.0	62.6	62.1
NAFTA	36.0	33.6	41.4	47.6	51.7	54.6	54.9
Mercosur	9.4	11.6	8.9	22.7	25.0	20.5	—

— Not available.

Note: Exports within a bloc are the sum of exports by members of a trade bloc to other members of the bloc. Service exports are excluded. Although the blocs have been calculated back to 1970 on the basis of current membership, most of the blocs came into existence in later years.

a. Includes ASEAN plus China, Hong Kong (China), Japan, Korea, and Taiwan (China).

b. Does not include Taiwan, China.

Source: E. Sakakibara and Yamakawa (2002).

and nearly two-thirds, respectively.[8] For example, the United States is the single most important trading partner of many Asian countries and a significant source of foreign investment finance, as recognized in the establishment of APEC.[9] More generally, Asian regionalism is embedded in the larger multilateral system. The major economies are all members of the World Trade Organization (WTO) and of the Bretton Woods multilateral financial institutions.

Third, East Asia does not have a politically or economically dominant country to play the leading role in regional integration, a role that has been assumed by the United States in North America or

---

8. These ratios were 22 percent for ASEAN, 55 percent for NAFTA, and 63 percent for the European Union in 1999, according to E. Sakakibara and Yamakawa (2002). Whereas this ratio has been rising in the European Union and (especially) in NAFTA, it has not risen in ASEAN, reflecting the Asian crisis. As a measure of the effects of preferential trading arrangements, these summary statistics are likely to be biased, insofar as one would expect to observe higher ratios for larger regions that constitute a larger share of the world and its trade (Frankel 1997).

9. Japan remains the most important trading partner for a number of Asian countries, but its share in their imports and exports declined in the 1990s, reflecting Japan's economic slump. The United States accounted for 15–33 percent of the total exports of East Asian countries and 7–21 percent of their total imports at the end of the 1990s (Gilbert, Scollay, and Bora 2002). Europe is similarly an important and growing source of trade and, especially, finance. Awareness of these links has provided impetus to the meetings of European and Asian officials (Dent 2001).

shared by France and Germany in Europe. Although Japan played a major role in establishing the Pacific Economic Cooperation Council in 1980 and APEC in 1989 (Terada 2001), its economic and financial difficulties and its historical relations with other Asian countries prevent it from playing a more forceful role. In particular, the region's two largest economies, China and Japan, have a history of strained relations and have yet to agree on a common agenda.

Fourth, cooperation in Asia has been characterized by consensual decisionmaking and a preference for nonintervention in each other's national affairs (Harris 2000 refers to the result as "soft institutionalism"). This emphasis on consensus and collegiality imposes constraints on efforts to apply peer pressure for concerted action.

Fifth, East Asian economies are at special—and, in some sense, especially difficult—points in their individual histories. This is likely to be a major hurdle for regional cooperation. Japan has been embroiled in financial crisis and recession for more than a decade. China is navigating the winding path from plan to market; it is only now phasing in the liberalization measures to which it is bound as a new entrant to the WTO. The increase in China's medium- and high-tech exports is already placing intense competitive pressure on other economies in the region, even though the growth of its economy is simultaneously enlarging the market for goods from other East Asian countries.[10] Korea, while making good progress relative to other crisis-hit East Asian economies, is still cleaning up the detritus of the crisis and reforming its economic structure. Given the ongoing institutional changes in the region, there is a risk that regional arrangements designed for the circumstances of today may be ill suited to those of tomorrow.

These five features suggest that productive initiatives to deepen regional cooperation will have the following characteristics. They will be examples of "open regionalism" and will be designed not to dis-

10. See Lall and Albaladejo (2001) on the evolving pattern of East Asian exports and the competitive pressure exerted by China. Two-way trade between ASEAN and China rose from $8.6 billion in 1991 to over $40 billion in 2000. This amounted to 3 percent of ASEAN exports, and purchases from China equaled about 5 percent of the imports of the six ASEAN countries ("ASEAN and China Sign Deal" 2002). Trade between China and Korea reached $30 billion in 2000, and China is now Korea's third biggest trading partner ("South Korea/China, Deepening Ties" 2001).

rupt the economic and financial links with countries outside East Asia. They will be compatible with the participating countries' obligations to the WTO and the Bretton Woods institutions. They will take the form of what Europeans refer to as "variable geometry" or "reinforced cooperation"—that is, a series of overlapping arrangements in which countries opt into some agreements to cooperate, while opting out of others. And, given the recent Asian practice of noninterventionism, they are likely to be voluntary, unilateral, and incentive-compatible rather than enforced by sanctions, penalties, and fines.

East Asian countries will find it easier to cooperate on some policies than on others. All of them can benefit from currency stability, strong financial markets, and free trade. Regional arrangements affecting these issues are, therefore, more likely to be incentive-compatible and politically sustainable if pursued on a voluntary basis. In the future, they are also likely to gain from adherence to a regime of stronger intellectual property rights under the framework of the Trade-Related Aspects of Intellectual Property Rights (TRIPS) Agreement, the rationalization of policies toward direct foreign investment, and regional policy cooperation in areas such as competition policy.

COOPERATION ON EXCHANGE RATE AND MONETARY POLICY

Monetary and exchange rate policy is an area in which East Asian nations may be expected to cooperate. What form should such cooperation take? Should they maintain a collective system of common currency pegs against the dollar, the yen, or a basket of G-3 currencies, or are variable pegs a more robust alternative? Should they attempt to stabilize exchange rates symmetrically among themselves, similar to the exchange rate mechanism of the European Monetary System, as a stepping-stone toward regional monetary unification? Or should they pursue different monetary policy operating strategies and exchange rate arrangements while cooperating to limit the economic and monetary disturbances that are the underlying cause of exchange rate volatility?

Managed Exchange Rates

Since the East Asian crisis much attention has been focused on exchange rate policies and related mechanisms for lessening the risks of externally induced shocks. The region's economies have begun experimenting with alternative approaches to exchange rate management, and several have ceased pegging their currencies to the dollar and adopted a more flexible stance, either some version of the basket peg or a rule that more closely approximates a freer float (Kawai 2002a). Through the Chiang Mai Initiative, they have also entered into regional swap arrangements that would allow them to augment their now much enlarged reserves in the event of a crisis. Below we examine in more detail the directions of exchange rate management.

Currency Pegs. The rationale for pegging currencies is to avoid exchange rate fluctuations that can lead to financial instability and disrupt a country's growth and development strategies.[11] Exchange rate volatility is likely to be especially disruptive for countries that depend heavily on international trade and international production networks, as do most of those in East Asia. These features have prompted some researchers to argue for resurrecting Asia's currency pegs.[12] The importance of East Asia's exports to a variety of major markets (including Europe, Japan, and the United States) has led most of these authors to recommend pegging not to the U.S. dollar alone but to a basket composed of the three G-3 currencies.[13] In principle, this

---

11. The tendency for sudden depreciations to cause a mass exodus of international investors, creating financial distress among banks, firms, and governments with liabilities denominated in foreign currency, was evident in Indonesia and Thailand, and to a lesser extent other Asian countries, in 1997–98. The tendency for currency depreciation in one country to infect the rest of the region was similarly illustrated by the contagion that followed the initial devaluations (A. K. Rose 1998).

12. The "fear of floating" induced some East Asian countries to revert to de facto pegging after the crisis, at least during 1998–99 (McKinnon 2001; Y. C. Park and Song 2001). Since then, it appears that economies such as Indonesia, Korea, the Philippines, and Thailand are permitting their currencies to move in response to changing economic conditions, possibly with reference to a basket (Kawai 2002a).

13. Japanese firms tend to invoice in U.S. dollars even for trades with economies in East Asia. Since East Asia trades significantly with Japan and the United States, pegging to the U.S. dollar may have been justifiable, especially when the nominal anchor was needed (McKinnon 2000). Before the Asian crisis, many of the region's currencies were pegged to the dollar, whose appre-

would provide stability to effective exchange rates and, at the same time, flexibility to accommodate fluctuations in the yen-dollar exchange rate within a narrow band.

The argument against currency pegging for East Asia rests on the difficulty of sustaining currency pegs in a world where capital is highly mobile. The prerequisites for successful maintenance of currency pegs and bands are demanding. In the past, when growth of gross domestic product (GDP) and exports was regarded as paramount, there was deep and abiding support for subordinating other social goals to the imperative of exchange rate stability, which was seen to contribute to the growth of the exports that were, in turn, the engine of economic development. Today, however, Asian governments are pressed by their constituents to pursue an increasingly diverse range of social goals. These pressures cast doubt on commitments to defend the exchange rate under any and all circumstances and, in a world of highly mobile capital, the decline in policy credibility makes currency pegs increasingly fragile. From this point of view, it is no coincidence that most of the remaining peggers in Asia—China and Malaysia prominent among them—support their currencies with capital controls, which give the authorities some scope to balance the pursuit of exchange rate stability with the pursuit of other goals.[14]

Hong Kong, China, is the main exception. The reasons for its success in maintaining a pegged currency are readily apparent: its economy is unusually open;[15] it has exceptional wage, price, and labor market flexibility; and it has no contested multiparty elections to raise doubts about the future orientation of monetary policy. These exceptional conditions cast light, by their very absence, on what makes credible pegging difficult elsewhere in the region.[16]

---

ciation in the mid-1990s created problems for Asian competitiveness and helped to set the stage for the crisis. Ito, Ogawa, and Sasaki (1998), Williamson (1999), and a team of French and Japanese officials (see Kuroda and Kawai 2002) have all advanced variants of the argument that East Asian governments should agree on a system of collective basket pegs with weights on the dollar, the euro, and the yen. A symmetrical system like the European Monetary System in which each East Asian currency is pegged to the others via a multilateral parity grid, as proposed by Rhee and Moon (2002), has been the subject of less discussion, perhaps because it performs less well under a variety of economic shocks (McKibbin and Le 2002).

14. Malaysia imposed capital controls from 1998 to 2001 (with a substantial relaxation in 1999) in an effort to stabilize its exchange rate (Martinez 2002).

15. Gross exports—including re-exports—exceed gross national product.

16. The tendency to abandon soft pegs for either very hard pegs or greater exchange rate flexibility is not limited to Asia. A growing number of emerging market countries (including Argentina

A different concern is that pegging encourages the accumulation of unhedged exposures, if banks and firms take at face value the government's commitment to prevent the exchange rate from moving beyond prescribed limits and therefore do not hedge their liabilities denominated in foreign currency.[17] No currency peg lasts forever, and when it collapses, banks and firms suffer severe financial distress if their exposures are not hedged.

In the light of these considerations, neither a soft peg nor a currency board would appear to be appropriate for most East Asian economies. Pegging to a basket with fixed and uniform currency weights for all countries would be similarly disadvantageous. At the other extreme, however, a regime of free floating would impose large costs on traders and investors. A more viable policy might be for each country to peg to a basket of key currencies, define its own weights, and periodically vary the weights as circumstances change.

Chiang Mai Initiative. It is against this backdrop that in May 2000 the ASEAN+3 countries agreed to the Chiang Mai Initiative (CMI) of currency swaps and surveillance.[18]

---

and Venezuela) have accepted greater exchange rate flexibility, albeit reluctantly, while others (such as Ecuador and El Salvador, which, like Hong Kong, China, face unusual circumstances) have moved to the hardest of hard pegs by dollarizing. Fischer (2001), drawing on staff assessment of the International Monetary Fund (IMF) of the de facto exchange rate regime in member countries, shows that the proportion of countries with intermediate arrangements (neither hard pegs nor floats) was significantly lower in 1999 than in 1991 (34 percent versus 62 percent for all countries; 42 percent versus 64 percent for emerging markets).

17. Goldstein (1998) offers the classic statement of this view, which is directly inspired by the Asian crisis. As Lamfalussy (2000, p. 30) puts it, "There is little doubt that the pegging of East Asian currencies to the U.S. dollar played a significant role in the foregoing developments. It certainly blunted market participants' awareness of a potential foreign exchange risk—although I find it difficult to understand what appears to have been not just diminished awareness but its complete absence."

18. The CMI agreement was finalized in December 2000. It is a descendant of the Asian Swap Arrangement, established in 1977 by the five original ASEAN members and extended to the five other ASEAN members at the Darussalam ASEAN meeting of finance ministers in March 2000. That arrangement was transformed in May 2000 into the CMI, encompassing not just the 10 ASEAN countries but also China, Japan, and Korea. In announcing the initiative, the ministers declared their intention to cooperate in four areas: swap networks, regional surveillance, monitoring of capital flows, and training of personnel. Dedicated support lines are $1 billion each. The founding ASEAN members will contribute $150 million each, while every one of the new ASEAN members will contribute up to $60 million. Participants are eligible to borrow up to twice their maximum contribution. Swaps can be drawn for up to six months, with one six-month extension possible. These funds will be supplemented by a network of bilateral swap agreements among the 13 participating countries (some are in place, and others are still under negotiation). See ASEAN+3 Ministers (2000).

What are the goals of the CMI? Should it be seen as a first step to establishing a collective system of common currency pegs, in which the participating countries first create a mechanism for multilateral financial support and then establish the pegs? Or should it be seen as a mechanism for multilateral support to countries experiencing financial difficulties (including, but not limited to, those in the foreign exchange market) and as a means to ensure that major economic financial disturbances in any one country can be contained?

The structure of the CMI is compatible with both interpretations, and one answer is that it is too early to tell. The key difference between the swap lines of the CMI and the Asian Swap Arrangement that preceded them is that the new initiative allows countries to borrow reserves against local currencies, instead of having to offer U.S. treasury securities as collateral. This suggests that more finance will be available than previously. Although these swap lines are bilateral, the participating creditor countries will presumably coordinate the provision of funds through them.[19]

Another question concerns whether the initiative will make it possible to maintain a network of common currency pegs and whether such common pegs are even desirable, for the reasons stated above. The combined reserves of Indonesia, Korea, Malaysia, the Philippines, and Thailand rose by $100 billion between 1996 and mid-2002. Those of China and Taiwan, China, increased by $200 billion, so that by July 2002 the combined reserves of the seven economies net of gold holdings amounted to $714 billion. By comparison, the net outflow of capital from the region during 1997 was a little more than $100 billion (World Bank, East Asia Region 2002). Thus the additional liquidity to be made available to individual countries through the Chiang Mai Initiative—$28 billion in dedicated and bilateral swap lines (Kuroda and Kawai 2002)—is very small relative to the available

---

19. Up to 10 percent of the drawings available to a country can be provided for a limited period without its having entered into an IMF agreement. Subsequent disbursements will be linked to an IMF program and, therefore, to the government's success in meeting IMF conditions, thus meeting U.S. and IMF insistence that a regional support arrangement should not undercut the effectiveness of IMF conditionality. The IMF and the U.S. government both objected to the earlier Japanese proposal for an Asian monetary fund on these grounds. The Malaysian government objected to this linkage of support under the CMI to IMF conditionality, and in response the participating governments agreed to review the linkage after three years.

reserves and the potential liquidity of financial markets. They provide the authorities with only limited additional ammunition with which to fight off skeptical markets.[20]

Governments could conceivably commit more finance to the CMI, but they are likely to do so only if they can assure electorates that the resources would not be squandered. For this, the CMI will need to be accompanied by surveillance that is capable of anticipating and averting crises and by conditionality that leads to strong adjustment in the crisis country, which will reassure the markets and maximize the likelihood that the swaps will be promptly repaid.[21] Yet Asia has a tradition of nonintervention in the national affairs of other countries, which translates into a low-key approach to surveillance and conditionality.[22] This emphasis on consensus and informality is not obviously compatible with effective pressure for coordinated action. It made for a delay of more than a year in setting up the ASEAN surveillance process, since participants could not agree on how much sensitive economic data should be shared with their neighbors. Few details about peer reviews have been published, aside from their mention in official meeting statements. The ASEAN+3 countries are de-

---

20. Moreover, these amounts are miniscule relative to the amount of multilateral finance provided by the IMF and other official assistance when the Asian crisis destabilized exchange rates and financial systems. Thailand was promised $17.2 billion on August 20, 1997, Indonesia was promised $40 billion on November 5, 1997, and Korea was promised $57 billion on December 4, 1997.

21. Even in Europe, where the commitment to collective currency pegs was exceptionally firm, mutual surveillance and conditionality were not completely effective, leading to limits on the extent of support. Germany obtained an opt-out from the provision of the European Monetary System articles of agreement obliging it to intervene without limit in support of its partners, reflecting fears of the costs of unlimited interventions and the implication of unlimited support for its creditworthiness. Participants in the Asian Swap Arrangement, the precursor of the Chiang Mai Initiative, could also opt out of that arrangement.

22. Since 1998 ASEAN has conducted regional surveillance exercises whose purpose is to facilitate cooperation in the formulation of monetary, fiscal, and financial policies through information exchange, peer review, and recommendations for action at the regional and national levels. The surveillance process requires all members to provide the ASEAN surveillance coordinating unit, based in the ASEAN secretariat in Jakarta, with the same data that are supplied to the International Monetary Fund in conjunction with the IMF's Article IV consultations and program negotiations. The process was recently strengthened by the establishment of local surveillance units in some ASEAN countries. But the ASEAN way has tended to render surveillance a consensual and informal process, as Manzano (2001) puts it. However, CMI still requires significant drawings by member countries to be accompanied by IMF surveillance, contrary to its "ASEAN way" of nonintervention.

veloping a CMI surveillance procedure, but how it will deal with these issues remains to be seen.[23]

Currency Board and Monetary Union. If the East Asian countries decide not to establish a set of common basket pegs, what are their alternatives? One possibility is the more widespread adoption of currency board pegs, as used by Hong Kong, China. Proponents of this option argue that a currency board signals a stronger commitment to maintaining a stable exchange rate and to subordinating other goals of economic policy to the maintenance of the peg. But it is not obvious that such a commitment is credible. A currency board law, by itself, does not guarantee credibility, as the experience of Argentina has recently shown. The growing pressure on governments to spend on social goals poses no less of a challenge to the maintenance of a currency board than to the maintenance of a soft peg. Moreover, currency board pegs would not solve the problem of currency fluctuations within Asia unless all countries moved to currency boards simultaneously—which seems unlikely. Even more than an exchange rate band or zone, the currency board option creates the dilemma of what currency to peg to, since the link to the extraregional currency is especially tight. This, together with the existence of various commercial and financial links to other regions from different Asian countries, would make backing the board with the same outside currency, or even the same basket of currencies, very uncomfortable for at least some of the countries involved.

Going one step further to a monetary union would avoid intra-Asian exchange rate instability by eliminating intra-Asian exchange rates. This is at best a distant prospect, since monetary unification presupposes a willingness to contemplate political integration, in order to create political institutions that can undergird the regional central bank and hold it accountable for its actions.

---

23. The Chiang Mai statement of finance ministers announced a commitment to establish a "network of contact persons" to facilitate regional surveillance and the creation of a "well-coordinated economic and financial monitoring system in East Asia." The official statement issued at the fifth ASEAN meeting of finance ministers in Kuala Lumpur in April 2001 asserted that discussions were under way with the ASEAN+3 countries on how to enhance and extend the ASEAN surveillance procedure, and in Honolulu, in May 2001, these countries formed a study group on "enhancing the effectiveness of our economic reviews and policy dialogues" (Henning 2001, p. 16).

Going in the other direction—toward reimposing capital controls—would simplify the task of defending a regional system of currency pegs. But there is little appetite in the region for the reimposition of controls, the cases of China and Malaysia notwithstanding.[24] The low-income countries of the region continue to maintain them but generally regard them as transitional measures.

Inflation Targeting

Abandoning the exchange rate–centered approach to the conduct of monetary policy and allowing the currency to float, either freely or with management, creates the need for an alternative anchor for monetary policy.[25] The leading candidate here is inflation targeting. Inflation targeting is an operational strategy for monetary policy that needs five elements to succeed: (1) an institutionalized commitment to price stability as the primary goal of monetary policy, (2) mechanisms that render the central bank accountable for attaining its monetary policy goals and provide it with substantial autonomy to use selected instruments to achieve the desired outcomes, (3) public announcement of targets for inflation, (4) a policy of communicating to the public and the markets the rationale for the decisions made by the central bank, and (5) broad adherence to overall fiscal balance.

Institutionalizing the commitment to price stability lends credibility to that goal and gives the central bank the independence needed to pursue it. Mechanisms for accountability make this pursuit politically acceptable and impose costs on incompetent or opportunistic central banks. Announcing a target for inflation and articulating the basis for the central bank's decisions allow these mechanisms to operate.[26]

---

24. See, for example, the interview with Pridiyathorn Devakula, the then newly appointed governor of the Bank of Thailand, in *Far Eastern Economic Review* on July 26, 2001: "Yes, we have ruled out imposing capital controls. It's simple. Thailand is still a developing nation and a net borrower, and we have to be careful. Capital controls do not only prevent outflow of funds, but they prevent inflow of funds. So a capital-control policy would be very unwise if implemented; we still need inflow of funds. Not only now, but in the long-term future, we are still a developing country. That is the clear rationale—don't do it" ("A Little Sympathy" 2001).

25. See the papers in Gruen and Simon (2001).

26. In this context, it is important to distinguish *flexible* inflation targeting from *strict* inflation targeting. Strict inflation targeting means that only inflation enters the central bank's objective function; flexible inflation targeting means that there is also a positive weight on other vari-

Inflation targeting requires a central bank with enough independence to deflect political and economic pressures to favor other goals over the inflation target; this presupposes not just statutory independence for the central bank but also broad-based public support for its mandate. Effective inflation targeting also requires sound and stable macroeconomic and financial policies, because in a country with a chronic budget deficit or a weak and undercapitalized banking system, the central bank's commitment to pursue low inflation and disregard pressure to bail out banks and borrowers, public or private, will not be credible. Inflation targeting will not work, in other words, where the government relies, or may have to rely, on the inflation tax for revenue. Effective inflation targeting requires stable links between the central bank's instruments and policy outcomes—specifically, the ability to forecast inflation reliably and to influence inflation with conventional policy instruments. Finally, inflation targeting is unlikely to be attractive where changes in the exchange rate so destabilize balance sheets that the authorities simply cannot afford to let the exchange rate move.

A number of Asian countries—Korea, Thailand, and the Philippines among them—have moved toward inflation targeting and taken some of the needed institutional steps. Others, such as Indonesia, have announced their intention of doing so.

The experience of countries that have experimented with inflation targeting has not been without difficulties, but it has been positive in many respects: inflation has been moderate (and in the OECD countries, it fell after targets were announced [Johnson 2002]), and although exchange rates have fluctuated, they have not fluctuated so widely as to cause severe problems of overvaluation or financial distress.[27] At the same time, a greater degree of exchange rate flexibility has provided insulation from external disturbances along the lines promised by textbook models. For instance, when growth slowed in

---

ables, such as output, for example. Under flexible inflation targeting, the central bank does not attempt to return the actual inflation rate to its target immediately under all circumstances, for doing so would create undue volatility in interest rates and output. Rather, it eliminates discrepancies between actual and target inflation rates gradually over time based on some version of the Taylor Rule, since it is averse to sharp fluctuations in output (Croce and Khan 2000; Mishkin 2000a).

27. However, Y. C. Park and Song (2001) read the evidence from the two years immediately following the crisis as pointing to an attempt by the Bank of Korea to peg rates.

Korea in 2000–01, due mainly to a slump in the global electronics industry, the won depreciated, helping to insulate the Korean economy from the shock. With signs of recovery in the global electronics market in 2001–02, the currency recovered some of its lost ground.[28]

In the near future, inflation targeting is not likely to be appropriate for all Asian countries. For the more developed economies like Korea, Singapore, and Taiwan (China), inflation targeting is likely to be feasible and attractive. Inflation is not noticeably harder to forecast in these economies than in others that have successfully implemented this regime (Hoffmaister 2001). Financial markets are sufficiently well developed that there is already a stable relationship between the central bank's instruments and inflation. The adverse effects of exchange rate movements on balance sheets, while present, do not dominate all other effects of policy.

In less developed countries such as Cambodia, Laos, Myanmar, and Vietnam, such conditions are unlikely to prevail for some years. Foreign borrowing means foreign currency borrowing, magnifying the balance sheet effects. Financial systems are fragile, and budget deficits often remain a problem. If inflation targeting is not feasible, these countries may want to continue to peg and to support their pegs with capital controls.

Countries such as Indonesia, the Philippines, and Thailand do not clearly fall into either of these groups. In Indonesia, lingering financial weaknesses make it difficult for the central bank to commit credibly to an inflation target. In Thailand, inflation targeting with a heavy emphasis on the exchange rate has had a reasonable track record, but the central bank has come under periodic pressure from the government to disregard its inflation target and "go for growth." The Philippines has begun inflation targeting, after some hesitancy with regard to timing (Kongsamut 1999). Even if these countries are not yet fully in the inflation-targeting camp, there are grounds for thinking that they will be before long.

Even in Asian countries that are well placed to pursue inflation targeting, the regime must be implemented differently than in econ-

---

28. Coglin (2002) shows that Korea and other economies with similar monetary regimes were preferred by investors who saw them as outperforming countries with more rigid exchange rates that were, consequently, more vulnerable to external shocks.

omies that are less sensitive to fluctuations in trade and exchange rates. Targeting inflation does not allow the authorities to disregard movements in the exchange rate (or asset prices or output growth).[29] On the contrary, exchange rate fluctuations convey information about future inflation (as well as about the future evolution of other variables such as unemployment). A central bank seeking to minimize deviations in inflation (and perhaps also unemployment) from target levels will respond by adjusting policy when the exchange rate moves.

What is the role for regional cooperation here? In open economies, the availability of credits and swaps like those of the Chiang Mai Initiative could enhance the credibility of inflation targeting.[30] When inflation rises temporarily but output falls, a central bank may be reluctant to raise interest rates to defend its inflation target because doing so would aggravate the recession. The availability of foreign credits may resolve this dilemma—by financing intervention in the foreign exchange market that strengthens the exchange rate and facilitates the pursuit of the inflation target—without requiring the higher interest rates that are counterproductive from the point of view of the full employment target. Such assistance would be similar to that extended to support a peg or band, but it could be more limited, since there is less need to limit currency fluctuations under inflation targeting.

Hence regional cooperation, organized through the Chiang Mai Initiative, could play a constructive role in supporting a monetary policy using inflation targeting in East Asia. For that cooperation to be effective, of course, many of the same issues of surveillance and conditionality that arise in the context of schemes to peg exchange rates would need to be addressed. But those problems are likely to be less formidable than in the former context, since inflation targeting coupled with greater exchange flexibility requires fewer financial resources. Thus far Asian officials have been careful to avoid linking the Chiang Mai Initiative to any scheme for repegging exchange rates (E. Sakakibara and Yamakawa 2002). This suggests that they may, in fact, be thinking along similar lines.

---

29. The discussion here draws on Eichengreen (2001b).

30. In addition, agreeing on a common inflation target would be a small step in the direction of a common monetary standard, although it is no guarantee of exchange rate stability.

COOPERATION ON FINANCIAL POLICY

An expanding body of evidence indicates that policies to promote the growth of financial markets can make important contributions to the broader process of economic development (Levine 1997). Countries that have been unusually successful at cultivating financial institutions and markets have grown faster, while those that have had stunted financial development have been held back. Firms and sectors that would otherwise be credit-constrained, and are often hotbeds of organizational and technological change, are likely to be particular beneficiaries. A well-developed financial system allows small firms and start-ups to obtain external financing, households to smooth their consumption, and investors to hold diversified portfolios offering more attractive combinations of risk and return.[31]

Discussions of Asian monetary and financial policy tend to give less prominence to achieving financial development than to stabilizing exchange rates. Yet many consider that problems in the financial sector rendered the Thai crisis so disruptive and that the run on Indonesia's banks transformed the depreciation of the rupiah into a full-blown panic. Had banks been better supervised and financial markets better regulated, the fallout from these currency adjustments would have been less severe. And the literature suggests that output losses are up to two or three times as great when currency crises are allowed to become financial crises (Bordo and others 2001; Gupta, Mishra, and Sahay 2000; Kaminsky and Reinhart 1999; Mishkin 2001). If banks are strong and financial markets well regulated, the effects of currency adjustments that eliminate misalignments are more likely to be positive.

Similarly, the underdevelopment of East Asian securities markets—in particular, the bond markets that are the closest substitutes for bank credit—can be blamed for the exaggerated importance of bank finance, which turned out to be the weak link in the region's fi-

---

31. What kind of financial system is best is a subject of more controversy. Bank- and market-based systems have different strengths. Banks support small firms using known technologies that are engaged in incremental technical change, while securities markets are good at financing large projects and taking bets on radical new technologies (P. A. Hall and Soskice 2001). Recent evidence (for example, in Demirgüç-Kunt and Levine 1999) suggests that growth benefits from the presence of both bank- and market-based intermediation and, therefore, that countries should seek to develop both.

nancial armor. Securities markets are less amenable than banks to directed lending (since securities exchanges are more anonymous) and to the use of finance as an instrument of industrial policy (since securities markets are more decentralized and therefore difficult to guide). It follows that the development of decentralized, competitive, anonymous financial markets will strengthen market discipline and discourage governments from using finance to further nonfinancial ends, a practice not wholly compatible with financial opening and liberalization. Although bond markets flourish in all of the middle- and upper-income countries in East Asia, their scale remains limited. This is largely because of the long-standing reliance on bank financing, modest or negligible government deficits, and the limited role of domestic institutional investors in several economies.[32]

Today, with macroeconomic and currency stability largely restored, bond markets could expand if governments would continue to issue benchmark securities of different maturities regularly to establish a yield curve for the corporate sector and would put in place the missing pieces of institutional infrastructure (as Thailand is doing, for example) that will result in a thriving corporate bond market.

This involves a number of steps, the most important of which is creating liquidity through a network of primary dealers (in Thailand, for example, there is the Thai Bond Dealing Center) to serve as a vehicle for new issues and regular high-volume trading. Complementing the dealers are agencies that rate bond issues and real-time computerized settlement systems. These systems are well established in Hong Kong, China, and Singapore; in Thailand, the system is still paper based, with prices noted a few times each day. A bond market is incomplete without a secondary market that buttresses liquidity by permitting traders to refinance their inventory. Moreover, dealers need to be able to hedge against risks, for instance, by way of interest rate swaps. These institutions are still at an early stage of development, because regulations prevent institutional investors from undertaking certain kinds of trades and because other types of activities

---

32. Domestic debt securities outstanding as a proportion of GDP are 1.5 percent in Indonesia, 13 percent in Taiwan (China), 17 percent in Hong Kong (China), 23 percent in Singapore, and 32 percent in the Philippines; this contrasts with 60 percent in the United Kingdom, 93 percent in Germany, 137 percent in Japan, and 160 percent in the United States ("Asia Pacific: Bond Market (A)" 2001).

need to be induced deliberately through policy action (Becker and Pit-silis 2000; Hoschka 2001; World Bank and IMF 2001). Since 1997–98 activity in the corporate bond market has risen in Singapore, led by public sector enterprises such as Singtel, and in Malaysia, where firms have shown a preference for bond funds over bank borrowing. Bond market activity is also on the rise in China, although several concerns regarding issuance criteria, flexibility in pricing, and provisions for bankruptcy still need to be addressed ("China: Corporate Bond Market" 2002; "Southeast Asia: Attempts to Invigorate" 2002).

Until securities markets are well developed, banks will often remain too big and well connected to be allowed to fail. This fact does not go unnoticed by investors; indeed, in the first half of the 1990s, it encouraged relatively indiscriminate lending from foreign to local banks, which financed the accumulation in banking systems of dubious real estate loans (as in Thailand) and industrial commitments (as in Korea). Much of that foreign finance was short term, reflecting the absence of liquid markets in long-term debt instruments.[33] And when a shock to confidence caused this capital flow to reverse direction, the stability of entire national banking systems was placed at risk.[34]

To contain such threats to stability, prosperity, and growth, Asian countries have attempted to strengthen prudential supervision and regulation and to promote the development of their securities markets.[35] They have sought to apply market discipline to financial institutions, to remove implicit guarantees for domestic intermediaries, to open banking to foreign competition, and to strengthen their supervisory and regulatory agencies.

Promoting the development of financial markets entails the creation of a framework that facilitates transparency and strengthens

---

33. Also reflected were the artificial incentives of the Basle Capital Accord for short-term bank-to-bank lending, which reflected the assumption of the framers of the accord, which proved erroneous, that short-term loans were less risky because they were more liquid, justifying the application of lower capital charges.

34. Had the bond market instead mediated this money, it is argued, the result would have been different. In response to the shock to confidence, the prices of these assets and liabilities and not merely their quantities could have adjusted. Modest adjustments on several margins are easier to accommodate than major adjustment on one. Although the fall in bond and equity prices would not have been painless, it would not, in general, have threatened the stability of banking systems and financial markets as profoundly as did the liquidation of bank-to-bank loans.

35. A large literature (for example, Caprio and Honohan 2001) points to the most important measures needed to achieve these ends.

creditor rights (see chapter 2). It presupposes the prompt and effective dissemination of financial information by those issuing debt securities—something that can be facilitated by adopting securities market regulations requiring disclosure.[36] It also requires effective creditor rights—in the form of bankruptcy laws, restrictions on reorganization, laws mandating that secured creditors be paid first in the event of reorganization, and rules for whether management can remain in place following a reorganization (La Porta and others 1998).

Role for International Cooperation in the Development of Financial Markets

Does international cooperation—in particular, regional cooperation—have a role to play in stabilizing and developing financial markets in East Asia?

Financial stability is receiving a good deal of attention at the global level. The argument for international cooperation is that financial stability has the character of an international public good (Wyplosz 1999). Governments underinvest in financial stability in the absence of a commitment to internalize the cross-border externalities. For instance, without international agreement, regulators are reluctant to hold banks to expensive capital and liquidity requirements, since their banks then lose market share to less tightly regulated foreign competitors that provide the same services more cheaply. They also are reluctant to impose strict standards of disclosure of financial information as a prerequisite for listing an issuer's securities on a local exchange, since the latter then stands to lose business to exchanges that have less stringent requirements.

The Capital Accord of the Basle Committee of Banking Supervisors can be seen as an international response to the first of these problems, while the international standards of the International Organization of Securities Commissions, promulgated in cooperation with the International Monetary Fund and the Financial Stability Forum, can be seen as an international response to the second. The multilateral agencies have devoted considerable time and effort to promulgating standards and codes for sound financial practice, as-

---

36. In turn, this will limit the adverse selection and moral hazard that might otherwise stunt the growth of markets in these assets.

sessing the condition of national financial systems, and recommending corrective action. The Bank for International Settlements, which has taken on new Asian members, and the newly created Financial Stability Forum cover some of the same ground. The World Bank and IMF operate a joint Financial Sector Assessment Program. The IMF has spearheaded a global initiative to develop standards for data dissemination, bankruptcy and insolvency procedures, bank supervision, financial market and insurance regulation, corporate governance, and the like.

These multilateral initiatives notwithstanding, a case for regional cooperation can be made on several grounds. First, the structure of the global initiatives is not appropriate to the special circumstances of the region. The financial conditions that the IMF attached to its loans in 1997–98 were criticized for emphasizing the need to restructure and break up large industrial conglomerates and to discourage connected lending and for being insensitive to the role played by these arrangements in the Asian model of economic development. The international financial standards promulgated subsequently might also fall short of what East Asia needs. Asian countries might be better off designing such standards themselves.

Second, regional neighbors may share common problems, creating an incentive to pool their resources and devise a common solution. Many Asian economies share the problems of underdeveloped securities markets, bank-dominated financial markets, and inadequate financial transparency. To the extent that governments are aware of these common problems and have especially strong incentives to devise an effective policy response, the region is the obvious domain for organizing training programs and technical assistance and for promulgating common standards for supervision and regulation.

Third, the external effects of national financial problems may be mainly regional, giving regional neighbors special incentives to address their sources.[37] The transaction costs to be surmounted in arranging a cooperative response may be lower at the regional level, because the number of participating governments is smaller and the countries involved are more cohesive (reflecting similar historical ex-

---

37. The "wake-up call" hypothesis—that the Asian crisis was disproportionately felt within the region because its economies had structural similarities, creating both the fact and the perception that they had similar vulnerabilities—is consistent with this view.

periences, long-standing diplomatic relationships, or preexisting nonfinancial agreements).

To be compelling, the case for a regional initiative would need to be buttressed by specific illustrations of how distinct sets of Asian standards would differ from their global counterparts, by evidence that an Asian set of financial standards would not simply be more lax and thus more prone to financial excesses, and by the experience of regional entities and institutions.

The argument for a distinctive Asian approach is that Asia may wish to attain global standards of safety, stability, and efficiency in its own distinct ways. For example, Asian standards might include fewer and looser restrictions on portfolio concentrations. In many Asian countries, industrial development involves a prominent role for large conglomerates and industrial groups, which draw their external financing from a small number of closely allied banks. This development model implies that portfolio concentrations that are large by international standards may be a necessary corollary of economic development. But allowing claims on individual borrowers to constitute a larger share of individual bank portfolios, in turn, implies greater financial risk and the need for capital requirements that are higher than those required by the Basle Committee. In this example, a distinctive Asian approach to prudential supervision and regulation would not be more lax than that mandated by global financial standards. Looser restrictions in one area—portfolio concentration—could be offset by tighter restrictions in another—capital requirements. With the appropriate combination of measures, there is no reason why an Asian approach would necessarily be incompatible with the relevant global standards.

Such variations in regional practice may fall within the provisions of global standard-setting efforts. In the context of the current example, the proposed revision of the Basle Accord includes a provision along these lines; banks with large concentrations of risk to a single borrower or sector will be subject to an additional capital requirement or "granularity adjustment." Perhaps the Basle Committee's formulation of this tradeoff does not go far enough to satisfy Asian requirements. But its existence raises the question of whether separate regional financial standards are, in fact, needed.[38]

---

38. Indeed, concern has been voiced that the draft new Capital Accord (Basle II) could exacerbate financial instability because of the possibility of "capture" of regulators by large banks ("Banks Put Themselves" 2002).

Regional Initiatives for Financial Cooperation

ASEAN, APEC, and other Asian groupings of governments and central banks have undertaken various regional initiatives in financial cooperation. In 1999 ASEAN implemented a Finance Work Program to facilitate cooperation in the areas of insurance regulation, financial services liberalization, corporate governance, and capital market development. In practice, however, its main achievement—the adoption of the principles of the International Association of Insurance Supervisors as a minimum set of best practices—does not represent a departure from global standards.

APEC's economic leaders, prompted by the Asian crisis, pledged to cooperate in strengthening financial markets. In 2001 they agreed on collaborative initiatives to develop regional financial and capital markets and to support freer and more stable capital flows. Their initiatives include strengthening prudential supervision by training banking supervisors and securities regulators, reviewing the adequacy of bank supervisory regimes, strengthening disclosure standards, developing bond markets, and strengthening corporate governance.[39] However, in keeping with APEC's emphasis on institutional minimalism and voluntary action, concrete steps do not go beyond organizing seminars and training programs on these subjects. It is not clear that APEC can provide an effective mechanism for peer pressure and concerted action.

Other regional initiatives focusing on financial cooperation also serve mainly as forums for sharing information and expertise. The Manila Framework Group is designed to provide a means for regional cooperation in the pursuit of financial stability. However, with no permanent secretariat or funding of its own, it "does not appear to be strongly influential in the region" (E. Sakakibara and Yamakawa 2002). With 14 countries and representatives of the international financial institutions present, it has been unable to reach decisions quickly and functions mainly as a forum for the exchange of views.

EMEAP (Executives' Meeting of East Asia-Pacific Central Banks) has among its objectives regional surveillance, the exchange of information and views, and the promotion of financial market develop-

---

39. See www.apecsec.org.sg/fora/ activity (May 9, 2001).

ment.[40] Its activities include annual meetings of central bank governors, semiannual meetings of deputy governors, and three working groups concerned with bank supervision, financial markets, and payments and settlement systems. Its weaknesses include an irregular schedule of meetings and a lack of continuity. Like the Manila Framework Group, EMEAP has no secretariat; the responsibility for organizational matters, along with the meetings themselves, is rotated among the participating central banks.

The SEANZA (Southeast Asia, New Zealand, and Australia) Group grew out of a 1956 meeting of central bank governors from the Asia-Pacific region, where it was agreed that the central banks of the region should pool their resources in order to provide training courses for central bank staff. An offshoot—SEACEN (South East Asian Central Banks)—was established in the 1980s as a training and research organization. The SEANZA Forum of Banking Supervisors was established in 1984 to exchange information on issues and problems of common interest. More recently, special-purpose regulatory agencies have joined the central banks in this forum. But the inclusion of a number of smaller countries makes the forum unwieldy for regional cooperation. This creates the potential for ASEAN+3 to play a larger role in financial cooperation in the future.[41]

Perhaps because it is a relatively new and informal caucus, ASEAN+3 is notably absent from the efforts to coordinate financial policy. But the Chiang Mai Initiative, negotiated by ASEAN+3, could conceivably serve as a basis for cooperation in strengthening financial markets and promoting financial development.[42] The swaps and dedicated funds of the CMI could be used to encourage financial reform by providing conditional assistance for countries pursuing the relevant measures as well as emergency assistance for countries whose financial reforms are at risk of being derailed by a banking panic or a stock market crash. Even if the details of the surveillance process re-

---

40. EMEAP was organized in the early 1990s with leadership from Australia and Japan. Its members are the Southeast Asian and Australasian members of SEANZA: Australia, China, Hong Kong (China), Indonesia, Japan, Korea, Malaysia, New Zealand, the Philippines, Singapore, and Thailand.

41. On the basis of developments in the last few years, Stubbs (2002) contends that ASEAN+3 has the potential to become the dominant regional institution in East Asia.

42. For a proposal along these lines, see Eichengreen (2001a).

main to be worked out, CMI surveillance could provide a useful basis for dialogue and consensus building regarding essential reforms.

The fundamental mechanisms are already in place. The involvement of China, Japan, and Korea means that there is enough finance to provide meaningful incentives and, in principle, enough leverage for effective peer pressure. Such an arrangement could provide services, such as reserve management, clearing, and settlement, to member central banks. It could be a venue for the negotiation of common agreements on capital and liquidity requirements and regulatory processes intended to promote the stability of banking systems and the negotiation of standards for information disclosure, securities listing, and corporate governance designed to promote the development of regional financial markets. It would be a small step to create an ASEAN+3 financial institute or organization to offer technical assistance to national agencies seeking to strengthen prudential supervision and regulation. Such an institute could run training programs for bank inspectors, securities and exchange commissioners, and accountants, enlisting students from all of its members, exploiting economies of scale and scope, and encouraging the efficient pooling of knowledge and expertise.

The danger is that a mechanism for dialogue and consensus building that also entails credit lines (as is the case with the CMI) could be counterproductive unless the problems of exercising firm surveillance and applying forceful conditionality are solved first. This is because the promise of foreign support for countries experiencing a banking panic or a stock market crash that threatens their reforms would create moral hazard; it would lessen the pressure to push ahead with essential reforms that reduce the risk of such panics and crashes.

COOPERATION ON TRADE

Trade liberalization at the regional level may enhance a region's welfare, provided that the new rules create trade rather than simply divert it away from other countries. Geographically proximate countries trade disproportionately with one another. And negotiations limited to a set of regional neighbors may suffer less from the large-number problem that so complicates global negotiations.

But liberalization at the global level promises even greater welfare gains. Studies suggest that the more countries are included in a free trade arrangement, the greater are the gains; this is true both of Asia and more generally.[43] The World Trade Organization and the Doha round of global trade negotiations already exist. Global arrangements are more encompassing; they are less likely to give rise to trade diversion.

In addition, the global approach provides more scope for linkages conducive to greater liberalization. For example, if negotiations were conducted only among the other Asian countries, it is hard to imagine China making the same concessions on liberal access to its domestic financial system as it made in return for entry into the WTO. The question, then, is whether East Asian countries should pursue preferential trade arrangements at the regional level rather than simply participate in the existing multilateral process.

Regional trade arrangements do offer benefits. Intraregional trade in East Asia is substantial (table 3.1), and, more important, East Asian economies trade with each other more intensely when the size of their trade is taken into consideration (table 3.2).[44] Theory suggests that further liberalization within the region will create rather than divert trade. Most empirical studies of regional trade arrangements conclude that, in practice, these have created trade for members rather than diverted trade away from nonmembers of the arrangements.[45] Another benefit of regional trade arrangements is that they can encourage cooperation among participating countries on a variety of other political and economic issues. In Europe, for example, a regional free trade area created pressure for regional agreement on exchange rate stabilization, which, in turn, lent impetus to the process of monetary and financial integration, resulting in the euro area that exists today. In North America, NAFTA stimulated foreign

---

43. For a recent survey and contribution with a focus on Asia, see Scollay and Gilbert (2001).

44. The trade intensity index is used to measure the strength of bilateral trading relationships among members of a group. The trade intensity within ASEAN has not risen in recent years, unlike that in NAFTA and in the European Union (E. Sakakibara and Yamakawa 2002).

45. This tends to be the conclusion of empirical studies, including Frankel (1997) and Gilbert, Scollay, and Bora (2002), for ASEAN, APEC, and more generally. Most regional trade arrangements have been implemented in an environment of low and falling global tariffs, minimizing the scope for trade diversion. Trade diversion may dominate, however, for individual participating countries (see, for example, Fukase and Martin 2001).

Table 3.2 Trade Intensity in East Asia, 1998–2000

Economy	China	Hong Kong, China	Indonesia	Japan	Korea, Rep. of	Malaysia	Philippines	Singapore	Thailand	Taiwan, China	United States	European Union
China	n.a.	6.2	1.5	2.8	1.7	0.7	1.1	1.1	0.7	0.8	1.3	0.4
Hong Kong, China	11.1	n.a.	0.8	1.0	0.7	0.7	1.8	1.2	1.0	1.0	1.2	0.4
Indonesia	1.6	0.9	n.a.	3.8	3.0	2.5	2.4	5.7	2.0	2.0	0.8	0.4
Japan	1.8	1.6	2.3	n.a.	2.5	2.2	3.6	2.0	3.0	3.5	1.6	0.4
Korea, Rep. of	3.2	1.9	3.2	1.9	n.a.	2.1	3.9	1.5	1.3	2.3	1.1	0.4
Malaysia	0.9	1.4	2.9	2.1	1.4	n.a.	2.9	8.9	3.7	2.3	1.2	0.4
Philippines	0.5	1.5	0.7	2.6	1.3	3.5	n.a.	3.6	2.8	4.0	1.8	0.5
Singapore	1.2	1.8	4.3	1.3	1.5	14.0	4.4	n.a.	4.8	2.1	1.0	0.4
Thailand	1.2	1.6	3.7	2.7	0.8	3.2	2.9	4.6	n.a.	1.9	1.2	0.5
Taiwan, China	—	6.6	2.0	1.8	1.0	1.9	3.6	1.7	2.0	n.a.	1.4	0.4

n.a. Not applicable.

— Not available.

Note: Table reads as trade intensity of an economy in the left-hand column with an economy in the top (header) row. Some 2,000 import and export data were estimated. The trade intensity of country i to country j is calculated as $Iij = (X_{ij} / X_{iw}) / [(M_{jw} / M_{ww} - M_{iw})]$, where X is exports, M is imports, and subscripts i, j, and w indicate country i, country j, and the world, respectively. The higher the index, the more intensely these country pairs trade with each other.

Source: E. Sakakibara and Yamakawa (2002).

direct investment and production outsourcing by the United States, first in Canada and then in Mexico.

Regional trade arrangements have not obviously sapped the momentum of multilateral liberalization; if anything, the existence of the regional option has intensified the pressure on those engaged in multilateral trade negotiations to agree on mutually acceptable terms. Efforts to liberalize trade at the regional level have not obviously weakened Asia's commitment to the new WTO round.

Implications of Ongoing Changes in East Asian Trade

Asian countries are increasingly trading not just with one another but also with the rest of the world. What do the trends in trade imply for regional cooperation policy?

For many years, Asian trade followed the so-called flying geese model, in which other economies developed the same export industries that had been pioneered by Japan, while Japan shed its initial export industries and moved into the production of more technologically sophisticated goods. In this model, the case for regional free trade was not compelling; many of the principal markets of the export industries in question were outside the region, and countries acquired foreign technology as much via licensing as via FDI. To the extent that Japan and other East Asian countries specialized in rather different industries and products, a regional approach to trade liberalization threatened to produce more trade diversion than trade creation.

Since the 1980s, foreign investment by Japan in other parts of East Asia has been based on a pattern in which the lower value added activities of Japanese industry are outsourced to subsidiaries and partners in lower-wage Asian countries, and the products of those activities are increasingly used as inputs into production in Japan. Intra-ASEAN trade in manufactured products is heavily dominated by inter-company transfers of Japanese parts and components for regional assembly ("East Asia: ASEAN Plus 3 [A]" 2001). Hong Kong (China), Singapore, and other East Asian economies are now interacting with China in a similar manner. In this model, there is a strong case for regional trade liberalization as a way to boost foreign direct investment, since FDI designed to build regional supply chains is clearly more economical and attractive when trade within the region is free.

In the 1990s the major changes in the structure of Asia's trade arose from three sources: the stagnation of the Japanese economy and the increasing technological leadership of the United States, the emergence of China as an export powerhouse, and the continuing development of regional supply chains and production networks. Among these factors, the growing reliance of Asian producers on U.S. firms and markets for imported technology weakens the case for a regional trade arrangement; concentrating on intra-Asian trade opportunities might deflect producers' attention from the likely source of the most advanced technologies.[46]

But insofar as China increasingly competes directly, in a range of industries, with the low- and middle-income countries of East Asia, this strengthens the economic logic for regional initiatives, since it means that trade creation is likely to outweigh trade diversion. And production networks, in which components that are produced in some countries are inputs into final goods produced in others, thrive best in an environment of free and unrestricted trade. To the extent that they have a regional logic (because, among other things, transport costs decline with proximity), their development strengthens the case for a regional approach to liberalization.

On balance, therefore, current trends suggest that countries will benefit from the pursuit of regional preferential trading arrangements.

Regional Free Trade Initiatives

In 2000 the 10 ASEAN member states, together with China, Japan, and Korea, agreed to explore the creation of an East Asian free trade area and subsequently established a working group to study the possibility.[47]

Some years ago Prime Minister Zhu Rongji of China suggested that ASEAN and China explore the establishment of a free trade area, and an expert group, announced in 2001, was charged with analyzing the scope for it. Although concerns remain about the relative eco-

---

46. For example, a regional arrangement that favored trade in computer hardware among Korea, Singapore, and Taiwan (China), as opposed to encouraging these economies to expand their international division of labor vis-à-vis the United States, would not encourage technological dynamism.

47. ASEAN+3 is a caucus without a secretariat that meets at the invitation of ASEAN.

nomic weight of countries in the free trade area, the ASEAN countries signed a framework agreement with China on November 4, 2002, in Phnom Penh to create a free trade area by 2010 that would embrace a population of more than 1.7 billion ("ASEAN and China Sign Deal" 2002). At the same meeting, the Chinese premier proposed a joint study into a three-way free trade agreement involving China, Japan, and Korea ("East Asia: Trilateral FTA Proposal" 2002).

The members of APEC agreed in 1996 to free trade within the Asia-Pacific region by 2010 (2020 for the less developed members). Adopted in response to pressure from the United States, this initiative was criticized as unrealistically ambitious at the outset, and it lost momentum, partly as a result of the 1997–98 crisis. A limited initiative to pursue voluntary sectoral liberalization in nine industries similarly produced little. Faster progress was stymied by Japanese opposition to the liberalization of sensitive sectors at the 1998 APEC summit—opposition that other members found impossible to overcome, given the voluntary and consensual nature of APEC decisionmaking. Beyond the sensitivity of some sectors, the problem reflected an underlying lack of consensus about whether APEC should function like a Pacific Organisation for Economic Co-operation and Development (that is, whether it should be a minimalist forum designed to reinforce and coordinate the commitment of its members to their other agreements) or whether it should strive to become a free trade area in and of itself.

The Shanghai Accord, signed at the APEC leaders' October 2001 summit, seeks to bridge this gap. It is designed to solidify support for free trade by tempering the Bogor commitment and by acknowledging that trade liberalization and other reforms need to be carefully sequenced and that different countries, facing very different circumstances, will progress at different speeds. At the same time, it seeks to ratchet up the pressure for liberalization by strengthening the peer review process in which member countries review the voluntary trade liberalization agendas and achievements of their partners. Whether these initiatives will reinvigorate APEC's commitment to free trade remains to be seen.

Barriers to Further Regional Liberalization

Resistance from sectoral interests poses a major stumbling block to further regional liberalization. Resistance is most prominent in agriculture. Agricultural imports are politically sensitive not just in Japan but also in Korea and other high-income East Asian countries. Conversely, the ability to export agricultural products is essential to lower-income countries like Indonesia and Vietnam.[48] An East Asian free trade area would raise the net agricultural exports of ASEAN and China, while reducing those of Japan and Korea, with opposite welfare effects for agricultural producers in the two sets of countries (Cheong 2002).[49] Countries tend to tax agricultural exports during the early stages of their economic development and to subsidize them later, and agricultural trade liberalization is likely to be especially problematic for a region, like Asia, composed of countries at very different stages of economic development (Anderson 1995; Lindert 1992).[50]

The problem of sensitive sectors extends beyond agriculture. Reflecting this reality, ASEAN's Common Effective Preferential Tariff (CEPT) scheme permits members to exclude trade in a variety of so-called sensitive goods, as they continue to do (table 3.3).[51] While the

---

48. China could override the objections of its farmers producing tropical products in competition with Southeast Asian nations, when negotiating its bilateral free trade agreement with ASEAN (an agreement currently scheduled to be inaugurated in 2010). Dismissing objections is harder in multiparty democracies with contested elections and is likely to become harder if and when China moves in this direction.

49. Gross agricultural exports rise even in Japan and Korea in Cheong's simulations, but this response reflects the stimulus from freer trade to the production of processed foods, not to primary production. Hence, primary producers in these countries continue to be adversely affected by regional liberalization.

50. Western Europe faced this same dilemma when creating its free trade area in the 1960s and responded by essentially exempting trade in agricultural goods (by creating so-called green exchange rates and the common agricultural policy). But, there, the two proponents of the process—France and Germany—were in similar positions and had similar attitudes toward restricting trade in agricultural products. In East Asia, four of the principal drivers of integration—Japan and Korea, on the one hand; ASEAN and China, on the other—are in different positions and are likely to have rather different attitudes. None of this is to deny that the objections of farm interests could be overcome, but they could be overcome only with political costs to the proponents of regional integration.

51. The six founding members of ASEAN originally agreed to form an ASEAN free trade area and to establish a common effective preferential tariff in 1993. In 1995 they shortened the time frame for these previously agreed reductions in tariffs (from 15 to 10 years) and committed to expand the agreement to include not only commodities and manufactures but also services, intellectual property rights, investment, and nontariff barriers. In 1998 they agreed to accelerate the rate at which tariffs would fall to below 5 percent and set a target of zero tariffs on manufactured goods for 2003 (in the case of the original members). These initiatives built on the 1977 preferential trading arrangement, which had provided for preferential tariff rates on trade in basic commodities within the region.

Table 3.3 ASEAN's Common Effective Preferential Tariff Scheme

Country or grouping	Number of tariff line items in				
	Inclusion list	Temporary exclusion list	General exception list	Sensitive list	Total
Brunei Darassalam	6,276	0	202	14	6,478
Indonesia	7,158	25	65	4	7,248
Malaysia	8,859	218	53	83	9,130
Philippines	5,571	35	27	62	5,633
Singapore	5,739	11	109	0	5,859
Thailand	9,103	0	0	7	9,103
ASEAN-6					
Total number	42,706	289	456	170	43,451
Percentage	98.3	0.7	1.1	0.4	100.0
Cambodia	3,115	3,523	134	50	6,772
Laos	1,247	2,142	74	88	3,463
Myanmar	2,386	3,016	49	51	5,451
Vietnam	3,573	1,007	196	51	4,776
New members of ASEAN					
Total number	10,321	9,688	453	240	20,462
Percentage	50.4	47.4	2.2	1.2	100.0
ASEAN					
Total	53,027	9,977	909	410	63,913
Percentage	83.0	15.6	1.4	0.6	100.0

Source: ASEAN (1999–2000).

initial Asian free trade area program also required members to remove nontariff barriers progressively, it did not indicate how nontariff barriers affecting trade in products covered by the CEPT were to
be identified or eliminated.[52] In addition, the disruptions caused by
the Asian crisis led ASEAN members to agree on a protocol permitting countries to delay the transfer of products from the temporary
exclusion list, although at their meeting in mid-2002 ASEAN leaders
reaffirmed their commitment to removing trade barriers.

Progress on trade liberalization at the regional level reflects the fact
that countries in ASEAN are at very different levels of economic development and have very different views of the proper role of infant-
industry protection in their national development strategies. For ex-

---

52. Progress has been greatest in electrical and electronic goods, all of which are now in the inclusion lists of the six original signatories to the agreement. Average duties on these goods are
minimal. Less progress has been made in other sectors.

Table 3.4 Import Tariffs on All Products, Select Years, 1990–99 (percent)

Economy	1990	1996	1999
China	40.3	23.6	16.8[a]
Hong Kong, China	0.0	0.0	0.0
Indonesia	20.6	13.2	10.9
Korea, Rep. of	13.3	13.4	8.7
Malaysia	17.0[b]	8.7	7.1[a]
Philippines	27.8	14.3	10.1
Singapore	0.4	0.4	0.0
Taiwan, China	9.7	9.7	8.8
Thailand	39.8	23.1[c]	17.1
Vietnam	—	12.7[d]	15.1
Australia	14.2[b]	6.1	5.0
Japan	6.9[b]	5.9	5.2
Mexico	11.1	12.6	10.1
New Zealand	14.5[b]	7.2	3.8
Peru	26.0	16.3[d]	13.0
United States	6.3	5.8	4.8

— Not available.

Note: These figures are unweighted averages of tariff rates.

a. 1998.

b. 1989.

c. 1995.

d. 1994.

Source: World Bank (www1.worldbank.org/wbiep/trade/TR_Data.html).

ample, while AFTA's goal is to reduce tariffs to below 5 percent, Vietnam has until 2003 to bring its tariffs below 5 percent, Laos and Myanmar until 2005, and Cambodia until 2007. These countries have long exclusion lists of products deemed sensitive to tariff reduction ("East Asia: ASEAN Plus 3 [A]" 2001). And whereas the six founding members have already brought roughly 90 percent of the items in the inclusion list in line with the requirement, the comparable ratio for Vietnam is only 70 percent (tables 3.4 and 3.5).

NAFTA has shown that regional free trade can thrive even when the trading partners have very different economies and income levels. But income diversity is even greater in ASEAN than in NAFTA,[53]

---

53. Per capita incomes vary by less than a factor of 4 among the three NAFTA partners (from $8,000 in Mexico to $32,000 in the United States in 1999 at purchasing power parity), but by a factor of 15 within ASEAN.

and ASEAN countries are more diverse than the three NAFTA members in their development models and in the roles they see for foreign trade and investment in economic growth.

A further barrier to progress is that none of ASEAN's three largest export markets (the European Union, Japan, and the United States) is included in the ASEAN free trade area. For AFTA countries, less than one-fourth of the total trade occurs within the grouping. This pattern has encouraged free trade initiatives at the level of ASEAN plus China, the level of ASEAN+3 (the informal grouping including not just ASEAN but also China, Japan, and Korea), and the level of APEC (which includes not only China, Japan, and Korea but also the United States). Gilbert, Scollay, and Bora (2002) show that the benefits to the participants of APEC-wide free trade (encompassing economies on both sides of the Pacific) are larger than the benefits of ASEAN+3 free trade, which, in turn, are larger than the benefits of ASEAN free trade (table 3.6). In addition, given the importance to East Asia of trade with North America, the magnitude of the gains depends largely on the inclusion of the United States. As might be expected, the most-favored-nation approach is better than the preferential approach, especially given the substantial cost borne by nonmember countries. Consequently, world welfare is much lower under the preferential approach than under the most-favored-nation approach.

Except in the low-income members of AFTA, tariff levels in East Asia are already low compared to those of, say, Western Europe after World War II. This gives grounds for questioning whether further reductions can significantly stimulate growth. But historical experience, including that of Western Europe, suggests that the benefits of liberalization are not limited to those associated with the removal of barriers at the border. Deep integration, involving the harmonization of product standards, competition policies, and monetary policies, among others, appears to deliver significant additional productivity and growth, which could reinforce the structural reforms proposed in chapter 2. Europe's experience with the single market points in this direction. So does experience with NAFTA, another case where tariffs were already low when the free trade agreement was negotiated.

Table 3.5 Number of Tariff Lines of the Six Original ASEAN Signatories with a Tariff of 0–5 Percent

Country	Number of tariff lines in 2001				Percentage of total			
	0–5 percent	More than 5 percent	Other	Total	0–5 percent	More than 5 percent	Other	Total
Brunei Darassalam	6,1071	157	12	6,276	97.3	2.5	0.2	100.0
Indonesia	6,451	739	0	7,190	89.7	10.3	0.0	100.0
Malaysia	9,189	823	0	10,021	91.7	8.3	0.0	100.0
Philippines	5,040	530	40	5,610	89.9	9.5	0.7	100.0
Singapore	5,859	0	0	5,859	100.0	0.0	0.0	100.0
Thailand	8,195	908	1	9,104	90.0	10.0	0.0	100.0
Total	40,841	3,166	53	44,060	92.7	7.2	0.1	100.0

Source: ASEAN Secretariat (www.aseansec.rog/12021.htm).

Table 3.6 Welfare Gains from Trade Liberalization

Grouping	Japan–Rep. of Korea		Japan–Rep. of Korea–China		ASEAN+3		APEC most-favored nation treatment		APEC preferential treatment	
	Millions of U.S. dollars	Percent of GDP	Millions of U.S. dollars	Percent of GDP	Millions of U.S. dollars	Percent of GDP	Millions of U.S. dollars	Percent of GDP	Millions of U.S. dollars	Percent of GDP
Members	2,010.4	0.0	10,483.0	0.2	17,601.3	0.3	29,075.6	0.2	40,282.8	0.2
Nonmembers	-1,492.2	0.0	-6,349.1	0.0	-9,869.3	0.0	15,406.5	0.1	-11,989.1	-0.1
World	518.2	0.0	4,134.0	0.0	7,732.1	0.0	44,482.1	0.2	28,293.7	0.1

Source: Gilbert, Scollay, and Bora (2002).

Bilateral Initiatives

Challenges to an East Asian free trade area include the rapid growth of Chinese exports, competition with products from other Asian countries, and the resistance of Japan and Korea, both of which have protected agricultural markets and powerful farm lobbies.[54] Some of these obstacles might be overcome by approaching the problem not at the level of ASEAN+3 but at the level of ASEAN plus Japan or ASEAN plus China.

But if multilateral initiatives bear insufficient fruit, Asia will have to rely on a plethora of bilateral free trade agreements.[55] Singapore, for example, has entered into bilateral pacts with Australia, Japan, New Zealand, and the United States and is exploring a free trade agreement with Korea ("Seoul, Singapore" 2002; "Singapore in Free Trade Pact" 2002). This approach is controversial and may not lead to as efficient and rational a set of trade relations as more broadly based multilateral initiatives. It tends to give rise to hub-and-spoke arrangements in which the hubs have bilateral arrangements with a number of spokes, but the spokes have no bilateral arrangements among themselves. It has been argued that this approach tends to benefit the hubs, but not the spokes (Wonnacott 1996).[56] Subsequent research does suggest that such arrangements are likely to enhance welfare modestly: if implemented in an environment of low tariffs, they are unlikely to be a serious source of trade diversion and do not seem to diminish the participating countries' enthusiasm for multilateral initiatives.[57]

---

54. *Oxford Analytica* notes that Japan's powerful rice lobby is likely to clash with agricultural interests in other East Asian countries ("East Asia: ASEAN Plus 3 [A]" 2001).

55. In all, Scollay and Gilbert (2001) list 25 proposals in the APEC region during 1998–2001. Korea has completed its first bilateral trade agreement with Chile. Chile also plans to begin negotiations with Japan, New Zealand, and Singapore ("Chile/South Korea: Trade Treaty" 2002).

56. This may explain why some countries, such as Singapore, have taken aggressive steps to establish themselves as hubs.

57. Gilbert, Scollay, and Bora (2002) find limited effects on the participating countries, depending mainly on the induced change in the bilateral terms of trade and minimal spillovers to third countries. They find that bilateral free trade agreements with Japan and the United States offer the best prospect for significant welfare gains for other economies in the region. That the net effects, especially of bilateral free trade agreements that do not involve Japan and the United States, are small is hardly surprising, since in many cases the amount of trade involved is itself small. This conclusion is reinforced insofar as recent bilateral agreements exclude trade in the products of sensitive sectors and only gradually phase in free trade in services (which remain among the most highly protected).

Given all of the obstacles to trade liberalization at the regional level, why not conclude that Asian countries should concentrate on multilateral liberalization initiatives, especially now, in light of the agreement at Doha to proceed with a new trade round? If the goal in East Asia is trade liberalization in and of itself, then the priority should be to pursue multilateral negotiations, perhaps with regional negotiations as a fall-back option if the Doha round collapses and as an additional source of pressure on countries outside the region that might stand in the way of its success. In contrast, if the goal is not just trade liberalization but deep integration extending well beyond national borders into, say, monetary policy, competition policy, and product standards, then the regional approach to trade policy might have additional advantages. This raises the question of how committed Asian countries are to integration in other functional areas.

COOPERATION IN OTHER AREAS

Other areas in which a case may exist for East Asian regional cooperation include promoting foreign direct investment, strengthening intellectual property rights, and regulating international migration. Overall, the scope for cooperation in these new areas appears to be less than in trade, monetary policy, and finance, which have been the traditional focus of regional integration efforts.

Foreign Direct Investment

Foreign direct investment not only contributes directly to capital formation and employment but also conveys technological and organizational knowledge. It has contributed significantly to growth in China (especially the coastal regions), Hong Kong (China), Singapore, and other Asian economies.[58] More recently, FDI has begun enabling East Asia to upgrade the service activities that are likely to be among the principal growth sectors of the future. In fact, by 2000

---

58. Some countries, such as Korea, were traditionally relatively closed to inward FDI. After the Asian crisis, however, restrictions on inward FDI were relaxed, and foreign firms were able to purchase distressed enterprises at substantial discounts.

half of the entire stock of FDI in developing countries was in the services sector, twice the level in 1990 (UNCTAD 2002). FDI has started to reshape the industrial landscape, directly through mergers and acquisitions and indirectly through mergers of local banks and companies seeking to create internationally competitive units. Asia also contains one of the principal sources of its own FDI, namely Japan, as noted in chapter 1.

The steps needed to create a more hospitable environment for FDI are well known. Countries must eliminate local ownership requirements and other restrictions most common in the services sector,[59] streamline and simplify corporate taxation, remove obstacles to the repatriation of profits, and eliminate further restrictions on international payments. They should limit preferential investment subsidies for domestic producers, abolish operational requirements such as local content schemes, and lift restrictions on the access of foreign-owned enterprises to domestic finance. Where East Asian governments must approve FDI, they should ensure that proprietary commercial material does not leak. In addition, East Asian economies will need to press ahead with reforms of the type discussed in this study to enhance their attractiveness for investors, particularly by focusing on innovation systems and the supply of skills.[60]

Although much of what needs to be done can be done unilaterally, and through bilateral treaties, of which there were 2,100 by the end of 2001 (UNCTAD 2002), regional cooperation has a role. A code of commercial and technical requirements for foreign investors will be easier to assimilate if its core features are harmonized across countries. Extending national treatment to foreign producers will be more attractive politically when the home countries of those foreign producers do the same. If local ownership requirements can be defined as regional ones, it becomes possible for third-country investors to access Asian countries through Asian joint venture partners. Coopera-

---

59. Local ownership requirements were imposed in the hope that this kind of requirement would spur domestic linkages. However, the evidence increasingly suggests that wholly owned affiliates are more likely to develop local suppliers (Moran 2002). About 80–85 percent of the restrictions worldwide are in services industries (Sauvé 2002).

60. Recent empirical work by Noorbakhsh, Paloni, and Youssef (2001) shows that the availability of human capital is becoming an even greater attraction for foreign investors.

tion in limiting subsidies and other artificial incentives for inward FDI is also important, especially in light of the zero sum nature of such subsidization (Moran 2002).

Recognizing these arguments, ASEAN created the ASEAN investment area in 1998 with the goal of extending national treatment to all industries by the early twenty-first century. National treatment will be extended first to ASEAN investors, starting in 2003, and subsequently to investors from other parts of the world. At the meeting of economic ministers in Hanoi in September 2001, the deadline for achieving this goal was advanced from 2020 to 2010 for Brunei Darassalam, Indonesia, Malaysia, the Philippines, Singapore, and Thailand and to 2015 for the new ASEAN members. In principle, all exceptions to free entry and national treatment will be eliminated by these deadlines. As with AFTA, however, the Asian investment area agreement also features a temporary exclusion list and a sensitive list, enumerating industries that enjoy temporary waivers from these deadlines.

The idea of packaging together initiatives for liberalizing trade and investment follows from the rationales for freer trade and investment within the region, and the consequent benefits are themselves linked. For example, as noted, producers are more inclined to distribute the production of components within the region if there is free trade in those components and in the products into which they are assembled.[61]

The achievements of the ASEAN investment area are modest; they have included joint investment promotion seminars, joint investment promotion missions to Europe and the United States, and publications with titles like "Investing in ASEAN." Member countries have also completed individual action plans describing the voluntary steps they propose to take to facilitate the liberalization and promotion of investment, but these have not yet been released to the public.[62]

The difficulties of approaching investment liberalization at the level of ASEAN are also familiar: progress toward trade liberalization

---

61. Foreign subsidiaries facilitated entry by developing-country firms into production networks and diverse export markets, although mainly as second- and lower-tier suppliers of the less sophisticated parts and components (Ramstetter 1998).

62. See www.aseansec.org/view.asp?file=/economic/ov_inv.htm.

has been slow, and two of the largest markets for the association's exports and sources of inward foreign investment, Japan and Korea, are outside the grouping.

APEC, too, has sought to promote FDI. The Bogor Declaration set a deadline of 2010 not just for free trade but also for free investment flows in the Asia-Pacific region. APEC then established the Investment Experts' Group to develop a set of nonbinding principles for foreign investment and encouraged members to phase in national treatment for foreign and domestic investors by 2020.[63] Countries have proposed individual action plans, but there has been disappointingly little progress (Bora and Graham 1997).

Ironically, progress has been least where the case for it is most compelling—namely, in the policy on competition for inward FDI. Subsidies for FDI will distort the allocation of resources except in the limiting case where they are symmetrically offered by all potential recipients, in which case their main effect is a transfer from the receiving to the sending country. At the same time, FDI recipients face a prisoner's dilemma when contemplating the abolition of such incentives. Yet most individual action plans have failed to address the issue of disciplining the use of incentives.

To conclude, the circumstances in Asia are conducive mainly to voluntary, incentive-compatible forms of cooperation. This does not bode well for regional initiatives to attract foreign direct investment; the voluntary approach to cooperation, which renders principles for foreign investment nonbinding, seems to be problematic in areas, such as investment subsidies, that are nontransparent and difficult to monitor and where competition for foreign-owned plants tends to be viewed as a zero sum game.[64]

---

63. The group also issued the Osaka action agenda and the Manila action plan, which are intended to achieve free and open investment in the Asia-Pacific region through the liberalization of investment regimes, the provision of most-favored-nation and national treatment, and transparency (on these initiatives, see Bora and Graham 1997). It is not a coincidence that the deadlines for free foreign direct investment are the same for ASEAN and APEC; ASEAN has consciously sought to harmonize its initiatives with those of the larger grouping.

64. In contrast, trade liberalization is more likely to be viewed as a positive sum game.

Intellectual Property Rights

The strength of intellectual property rights in a country has important effects on the willingness of multinational firms to invest there and to transfer advanced technologies (Maskus 1998). It also affects the willingness of firms in high-income countries to license their technologies abroad (Yang and Maskus 2001a).

Intellectual property rights remain weak in some East Asian countries. In the past, Asian governments have not regarded the case for intellectual property rights as compelling.[65] But, as we note in chapter 4, the risk that locally produced, patented, and trademarked goods will be counterfeited deters potential foreign investors and strains relations with trading partners. Weak enforcement of intellectual property rights, including patent and trademark protections, may also slow the transition of Asian economies from importing technology to developing technology, as scientists and entrepreneurs are deterred from making market-oriented investments. Stronger protection of intellectual property has been shown to significantly increase developing countries' imports of high-technology products (Maskus and Penubarti 1997).

A case can be made for international cooperation in the design and administration of rules for patent and trademark registration—to minimize confusion, pool expertise, and maximize the attractions to investors and to assist countries in enforcement and training of judges (World Bank 2001d). This is what TRIPS is designed to achieve at the global level.[66]

To the extent that stronger harmonization of national policies is desirable, a case can also be made for regional cooperation. In 1995

---

65. As Adolf (2000) notes, for example, not only was it standard practice for the famous works of Balinese artists and sculptors to be copied, but those whose works were copied felt proud of the recognition. He argues that similar attitudes were traditionally evident in China and India.

66. The protection of intellectual property rights was brought to the international agenda through TRIPS, sponsored largely by the European Union, Japan, and the United States, which account for much of the global production of new knowledge. As the global trade in knowledge-intensive goods is expanding rapidly, it is no wonder that these countries have pushed for better protection of intellectual property rights around the world. TRIPS sets a baseline for intellectual property rights in the member economies of WTO. Specifically, it mandates national treatment and most-favored-nation treatment. For patents, it sets 20 years from the time of application as the minimum standard. Software is protected through copyright, which grants protection during the life of the creator plus 50 years (50 years in all for corporations). In addition, TRIPS offers dispute settlement through the WTO framework.

ASEAN members signed the Framework Agreement on Intellectual Property Cooperation, which identified certain priority areas: strengthening intellectual property legislation, improving administration and enforcement of existing laws, and promoting public and private sector awareness of intellectual property rights and protections. The following year they adopted an action program to implement activities identified in the framework agreement and subsequently established the Working Group on Intellectual Property Cooperation (WGIPC). ASEAN is now working to establish a regional trademark filing system as an initial step toward creating an ASEAN trademark system. Its Expert Group on Patents has recommended, and the WGIPC has endorsed, the idea of a regional patent filing system.

That ASEAN members are not moving faster reflects the wide differences among their economies. According to McCulloch, Winters, and Cirera (2001), strengthening intellectual property rights will, at least in the short run, likely benefit middle-income countries, while almost certainly hurting poorer economies.[67] Middle- and high-income countries tend to be developers of intellectual property, and they therefore benefit from strong protection of property rights. Low-income countries tend to use intellectual property developed elsewhere and therefore prefer weaker protections (see Pacon 1996).[68] While ASEAN recognizes the case for intellectual property rights protection and the need to harmonize its practices in this area with those of the TRIPS, the wide disparities in levels of income and economic development within the grouping pose obstacles to concerted action.

Competition Policy

A case can be made for cross-national cooperation in the design and administration of competition policies that, as yet, have been fully adopted by only three East Asian economies, Japan, Korea, and Tai-

---

67. One consideration is that once more countries such as India adhere to TRIPS by 2005, the option of importing low-cost drugs will diminish for low-income countries lacking pharmaceutical industries ("India: Patent Potential" 2002).

68. Recent disputes over patent protection and licensing fees for pharmaceuticals illustrate the point, which is a long-standing issue in the negotiations over TRIPS.

wan (China). Lloyd and others (2002) present two arguments for co-operation. First, harmonization will reduce the costs to firms of doing business in multiple jurisdictions. Uncertainty about what is permitted in different jurisdictions can deter firms considering new investments. When competing jurisdictions apply different standards, the deterrent effects of uncertainty are likely to be particularly strong for complex projects, like cross-border mergers and acquisitions, where delays in obtaining administrative approval can be lengthy. In Europe, when the centralization of competition policy at the European Union level relieved these concerns, transactions related to mergers and acquisitions grew explosively (see also Yusuf and Evenett 2002).

Second, without international cooperation, competition policies may be difficult to enforce and penalties difficult to administer when the offending entity resides outside a particular jurisdiction. A related concern is that competition policy may not be effective if the market is larger than the administrative jurisdiction. For example, when two national markets are linked by trade, a permissive policy against cartels in one country that allows producers to raise prices will tend to raise prices in the other country as well, despite the existence there of a less permissive policy against cartels (Levinson 1996).[69]

Since multinational production and investment in Asia involve much cross-border trade and input-output linkages, many of the benefits of a more effective competition policy are likely to be attained by harmonizing policy within the region.

In practice there are several obstacles to regional cooperation. One is the "generally... low level of appreciation of the benefits of greater competition" in East Asia, as claimed by Lloyd and others (2002, p. 33). Reflecting this fact, a number of East Asian countries, typically the less developed, do not even have comprehensive competition laws. Industrial policies that involve subsidies for infant industries and national champions are unlikely to be compatible with internationally harmonized competition laws. And the continuing prevalence of state-owned enterprises in some countries—enterprises that require protection from competition to survive and often receive it—creates further conflicts for those charged with designing and administering an internationally harmonized competition law.

---

69. It would also result in smuggling from the low-cost to the higher-cost producers.

Indeed, ASEAN has made only limited progress in this area. Although its 1998 Hanoi plan of action proposed to explore the case for a common competition policy, no concrete steps have yet been taken. APEC's 1995 action plan, for its part, committed members to introduce and enforce competition policies and laws so as to encourage the efficient operation of markets throughout the Asia-Pacific region. The main effect of the APEC initiative has thus been to raise consciousness of the issue among members rather than to change competition laws and policies.

Migration

Technical skills and unskilled labor are scarce in some countries and abundant in others. The same economic case that can be made for capital mobility can also be made for labor mobility.[70] In practice, migration tends to complement trade and foreign direct investment; overseas Chinese networks, for example, facilitate the establishment of trade relations and attendant investment flows (Rauch and Trindade 2002). Migration is a channel for acquiring information about foreign market conditions and a mechanism for importing technical and organizational knowledge (Saxenian 1999; see also chapter 6 for the role of diasporas in knowledge transfer).

The case for regional cooperation on migration issues is based on the observation that migratory flows are heavily intra-Asian. Japan reports nearly 300,000 resident foreigners, mainly from China, India, and Indonesia, while Korea records upwards of 60,000 (Lucas 2002; Manning 2002). Hong Kong, China, employs more than half a million migrant workers (excluding migrants from the mainland), including some 150,000 workers from the Philippines engaged mainly in household services. The International Organization for Migration estimates that as many as 450,000 Filipinos may be living elsewhere within Southeast Asia (International Organization for Migration 2000), while Kassim (1998) estimates a stock of more than 700,000 Indonesian workers in Malaysia alone. A number of other Asian economies, including Korea, Malaysia, and Singapore, are now prin-

---

70. Some of those who regard the effects of capital mobility as mixed may even be inclined to argue that the case for labor mobility is more compelling.

cipally countries of in-migration. Korea imports labor from Bangladesh, China, the Philippines, and Vietnam. As much as a fifth of the work force in Singapore commutes in, while the resident foreign population is nearly 17 percent of the total. In Malaysia in 1998, an estimated one-eighth of the labor force was foreign. Thailand remains both a sending and a receiving country, dispatching contract labor to Hong Kong (China), Malaysia, Singapore, and Taiwan (China) and receiving workers from Myanmar and Vietnam.

Many of these flows are of unskilled workers, individuals on fixed-term contracts organized by recruiters. In addition, Hong Kong (China), Japan, Singapore, and Taiwan (China) all send highly skilled individuals to work in the overseas branches of their companies. Foreign direct investment and skilled migration are clear complements in these cases. Much of the movement of skilled workers within East Asia has been to service direct investment, rendering such investments the principal determinant of migratory flows (Lucas 2002; Manning 2002).

Political sensitivities have prevented the issue of freer migration from being addressed systematically. The agreement creating the Asian investment area contains a provision obliging ASEAN members to undertake individual action plans to "promote the free flow of capital, skilled labor, professions, and technology among the member states." But neither ASEAN nor other regional groupings have yet sought to emulate Europe by creating an integrated market in labor.

CONCLUSION

Sound policies at the national level remain the most important way of ensuring that the benefits of Asia's growing interdependence outweigh the costs. But because international transactions involve more than one country, their efficient management often requires the international coordination of policies.[71] The main question is whether cooperative initiatives should be pursued regionally or globally; that

---

71. Strictly speaking, international coordination of policies is called for when such policies cause nonpecuniary spillovers—that is, when they have effects on neighboring countries that do not simply affect relative prices.

is, whether attempts to address these problems at the regional and global levels are substitutes or complements. Economic theory does not provide a clear answer, but studies of existing regional arrangements, such as the European Union and NAFTA, suggest that regional and global initiatives can be complementary.

Efforts in other parts of the world provide little guidance for regional cooperation in East Asia. These efforts have tended to start with trade and to move from there to factor market integration and finally to monetary and financial integration. In Europe, for example, the integration process has been undergirded by a desire for closer political integration and a willingness to build truly transnational institutions of economic management. It has also been driven by a desire to minimize intraregional disparities and insulate certain sectors from cross-border transactions.

In East Asia, priorities and goals are different: the motivation for economic regionalism is as much the desire to create a zone of monetary and financial stability as to create a free trade area. It is thus not clear whether the same progression—from trade integration to financial integration and from there to monetary integration—makes sense for East Asia. Moreover, in East Asia regional integration is driven by the desire to encourage the further development of regional production networks, not to reproduce all regional economies in the same image. Nor is there a European-style impulse for closer political integration.

East Asia also faces a unique set of circumstances—some would say obstacles—on the road to regional integration. But these can be surmounted if there is the political will.

CHAPTER 4

THE TRANSITION TO INNOVATIVE ECONOMIES IN EAST ASIA

Innovation has become vital for the future economic performance of much of East Asia. In today's intensely competitive, increasingly interdependent world, a necessary, although by no means sufficient, condition for rapid growth is the ability to harness technological knowledge creatively.[1] In this context, Baumol (2002, pp. 133–34) observes, "Per capita GDP [gross domestic product] has increased almost nine-fold in the United States since 1870 . . . nearly ninety percent of current U.S. GDP was contributed by innovation carried out since 1870. The total contribution of innovation is certainly greater than that, since pre-1870 innovations such as the steam engine and the railroad . . . still add to today's GDP."

INNOVATION SYSTEMS

An innovation system is a "set of institutions whose interactions determine innovative performance" (R. R. Nelson 2000, p. 12). Some of

---

1. Technological capability is a composite of the abilities to assimilate and adapt existing technologies and to devise new technologies (Dodgson 2000). Added to this is what Lall (2000a) calls technological mastery, which puts a country at the frontier of a particular field. Experience also shows that the scale of innovation is only a necessary, not a sufficient, condition for superior economic performance. For example, Japan in the 1990s was a highly innovative country, coming a close second to the United States in the number of patents registered. But Japan's high spending on research and development (3.2 percent of gross domestic product in 2000) and its remarkable facility for adding to the fund of industrial innovation no longer translate into economic growth.

these institutions might be deliberately created by government; others might arise spontaneously from social and market circumstances. Whereas in the past it might have been appropriate to think of autonomous national innovation systems (and indeed most innovation systems have strong national characteristics), today successful systems are distinguished by their openness and their links to innovation systems in other countries. The efficacy of the innovation process depends not only on the domestic environment but also on global connectedness.

Innovation systems are becoming central to growth in East Asia not only for countries that have achieved income parity with the industrial West, but also for middle-income and even some of the lower-income countries that are still in the catch-up phase. For the higher-income countries, close to or at the technological frontier, the growth potential inherent in the manufacturing and service industries in which they have acquired comparative advantage now rests on staying abreast of the latest technological developments elsewhere and producing a steady stream of innovations. With product cycles now measured in months rather than years, only a continuous flow of commercially successful innovations can assure the rents needed to sustain high levels of income.[2] Countries and firms in the lead cannot afford to ease the tempo of innovation because any successful product immediately attracts imitators that rapidly erode profitability.

For the middle- and lower-income countries of East Asia, intensifying regional competition, particularly from China, and global competition from South Asia and Latin America make it necessary to compete harder on the basis of price, quality, and speed of delivery. At the same time, they need to augment this by developing the capacity to introduce product and design innovations starting in the industries that are their mainstay, for example, garments, agro-processing, toys, footwear, small consumer electronics, and leather goods.

Innovative capability is a cumulative process requiring deep foundations. There is relatively little scope for leapfrogging. Each country

---

2. A product cycle—that is, the time elapsing between the introduction of a new product and the appearance of equivalent or nearly equal products—was nearly 33 years during 1870–1906. It fell to approximately 14 years during 1927–46 and to less than 3.5 years during 1967–86 and has since dropped even further, especially for dynamic industries such as electronics, where innovation in some components is being driven seemingly inexorably by Moore's law (Agarwal and Gort 2001).

must build skills, institutions, experience, tacit knowledge, local networks, and international collaborative arrangements from the ground up. In certain areas, such as silicon wafer fabrication, memory chips, and flat-screen displays, it is necessary to make very large investments in production capacity, so as not to miss a new generation of technology. The significance and intensity of the "innovations arms race" (to use Baumol's phrase) are inescapable. Firms that compete in international markets and are active in global production networks must now rely even more on innovation to survive. Baumol (2002, pp. 45–46) puts this succinctly:

> A firm that falls behind in its innovations for a substantial period of time can expect considerable erosion of its market, either because its product is considered inferior by customers or because its costs, and therefore its prices, are higher than those offered by its rivals for products of comparable quality. Consequently, no firm will in the long run dare to under-spend its competition systematically. Thus, one can expect an industry norm to emerge, with firms that engage in substantial R&D [research and development] outlays generally making sure that their R&D expenditures are up to the norm. That norm will constitute an equilibrium in the arms race, but one that is only temporary—a truce, not a full end to hostilities.

Thus continuous investment—drawing on domestic and foreign sources—in innovation capability and production facilities is becoming an imperative for countries seeking growth in a competitive, international trading environment, although it results in periodic excess capacity worldwide in some subsectors and concomitant price fluctuations that sweep away the weaker companies. This aspect of the innovation system has acquired even greater salience in recent years. A second dimension that differentiates the new innovation system is the centrality of collaboration among researchers and among firms because of the rising complexity of new technologies, which often require a fusion of several disciplines and large outlays on research, testing, certification, and building of both experimental and production facilities.

The initiatives of researchers and the efforts of firms depend, in turn, on the evolving market environment and the policy cues provided by public agencies. Thus the working of the innovation system is closely linked to the mix of policies and institutions—many domestic but also foreign ones. In several fields, going it alone is a recipe for failure, and even the largest companies now seek alliances with their competitors or the acquisition of new firms with promising technologies as a necessary means of achieving the requisite technological progress.

In this chapter, we first describe the forces determining the supply of innovations, followed by an examination of the organizational, macroeconomic, and institutional prerequisites for an innovation system.

WHAT FEEDS INNOVATION?

The key to innovation is human creativity. For a sufficient number of creative sparks to arise and produce positive economic outcomes, several inputs are needed: people with the appropriate world-class skills, expenditure on R&D, capital investment (including venture capital) that finances research and production facilities, and foreign direct investment (FDI).

Human Capital

During the past 25 years, research on East Asia consistently emphasized the role of human capital in promoting growth and frequently underlined the impressive contribution that national education policies made to the East Asian miracle (Crafts 2000; Temple 2001; World Bank 1993).[3] By moving quickly to provide virtually universal access to primary education, many East Asian economies created a work force that facilitated the emergence of a light manufacturing sector, often with the help of foreign capital seeking either market access or, more recently, ways of reducing production costs (Hanson and Feenstra 2001). And many countries have made impressive progress in extending access to secondary and tertiary education.

Now Japan, the leader in East Asia, is being joined by a few economies that are seeking to key their growth and competitiveness to innovation. China, the Republic of Korea, Singapore, and Taiwan (China) all produce large numbers of graduates with science and tech-

---

3. Bils and Klenow (2000), Easterly (2001), and Pritchett (2001) challenge this contention, finding a weak or nonexistent relationship between the level of schooling and growth. However, see chapter 5 on other research validating the role of education.

nology degrees, but they still need to improve the quality of their skills, deepen the expertise in research centers, and institute the rigorous screening of research. The number of researchers and the increase in R&D spending in East Asia have yet to translate into a steady flow of innovations comparable to that in the advanced economies of the West.

Improving the quality of secondary- and tertiary-level science and technology skills, to encourage creativity and enlarge the fund of research expertise, is a critical strand of innovation policy. A second strand is the augmentation of business, professional, and entrepreneurial skills. Chapter 5 discusses these in detail and provides an international perspective on developments in East Asia.

Research and Development Spending

R&D spending complements human capital in the innovation system. It directly enhances the capacity for innovation and facilitates the assimilation of process and product technologies from overseas. For latecomers, in particular, the absorption of process technology paves the way for incremental improvements in the manufacturing process. At a later stage, as R&D intensifies and deepens the capacity for innovation, countries can start creating product innovations for the local market as a prelude to tackling global markets.

Although relatively little attempt has been made thus far to estimate the returns from R&D spending in East Asia, the evidence from Western countries suggests that private returns are high: in the 20 to 50 percent range. For East Asian countries in the catch-up phase, the returns from R&D aimed at acquiring process technology and a modest degree of incremental innovation must be at least as high, if not higher.

In these countries, R&D contributes to productivity growth through various channels, including increasing the stock of knowledge, creating new scientific instruments and methodologies, training skilled staff and graduate students, forming networks, and stimulating social interactions (see Adams 1990; Griliches 1992; Hu 2001). At a more advanced stage of development, which China, Korea, Singapore, and Taiwan (China) are now approaching, countries can supplement applied R&D with basic research that broadens research capability, especially in the sphere of product innovation. Increases in the stock of knowledge and the development of new instruments and methods—heavily supported by basic research—are especially important in new and fast-growing high-technology areas. For example, in the United States, 11 percent of new products and 9 percent of new processes could not have been developed without basic research (Mansfield 1991).[4]

Most economies in East Asia invest much less than 1 percent of GDP in research and development, the exceptions being Japan, Korea, and Taiwan (China). Stimulating productive R&D spending is thus a challenge for these economies. In low- and middle-income countries, the amount spent on R&D depends on the strength of the rule of law and on the risk of expropriation (G. R. Clarke 2002).[5] The government is the main source of research funding in several East Asian countries, including China and Malaysia, and it provides nearly half such funding in most of the others, except Japan (where it accounts for 22 percent), Korea (where it is 18 percent), and Singapore (Dodgson 2000).[6] But the private share of research funding is rising (Chung 2001; Sato 2001).

The question of whether public R&D and private R&D are complements or substitutes has been studied extensively. David, Hall, and Toole (2000) find, on balance, that they are complements, and studies at the aggregate level show that government R&D positively affects private R&D.[7] For East Asian countries, there is little evidence, although a study based on data from high-technology firms in China suggests a significant positive relationship between public and private R&D (Hu 2001), and the weak linkages between corporate labs, government research institutes, and universities may be a brake on the productivity of research in Korea (Chung 2001).

Past experience, mainly in countries in the Organisation for Economic Co-operation and Development (OECD), shows that tax incentives and direct subsidies are among the most effective policy in-

---

4. Korea lags in fields such as biotechnology because of insufficient basic research.

5. Close to 90 percent of all research is still done in the industrial countries (Hill 2002).

6. Singapore's government has given research a priority and offers a variety of inducements (Hill 2002).

7. For example, public grants for R&D provided to finance research consortia through Israel's Magnet Program yielded respectable returns, measured by the number of new products and patents and bolstered private sector activity (Trajtenberg 2000).

struments for promoting R&D. Lerner (1999) finds that, in the United States, firms receiving government funding for research grow significantly faster than firms not receiving such funding. The Korean government successfully supports private R&D by giving tax credits, allowing accelerated depreciation, and lowering import tariffs. Similarly, the tax system of Taiwan, China, provides full deductibility for R&D expenses, allows accelerated depreciation, and encourages large firms to invest 0.5 to 1.5 percent of their sales in R&D. Most empirical studies of firms in the European Union and the United States show that such incentive policies have significant positive effects, although their magnitude varies by time, industry, and country (see B. H. Hall and van Reene 1999). These results are buttressed by case studies from East Asia (UNDP 2001).

Capital Investment

To fuel an innovation system calls for large investments in the physical infrastructure of research and in myriad specialized skills (see, for instance, "Seriously Big Science" 2002). But the investment does not end with the equipping of research facilities. The transition from innovation to production is a costly process involving many refinements to the product innovation and advances in process technology both in gearing for production and in learning from the experience of producing. Increasingly complex technology and shorter product cycles are raising the costs of equipment and demanding continuous investment in new expertise. They are also hastening the obsolescence of expensive equipment, software, and skills (see Jovanovic and Rousseau 2002). Some examples from the electronics industry can illustrate the scale of outlays required to remain at the cutting edge of technological change. Wafer fabrication, which is at the heart of chip making, is constantly in the throes of change, with producers moving to larger and larger wafer sizes to maximize the number of chips that can be etched. The most recent jump has been from 200-millimeter to 300-millimeter wafers, which raises yields 2.5 times. However, whereas the old fabrication factories cost between $1 billion and $1.5 billion, the new, larger establishments are priced at between $2.5 billion and $3.5 billion ("Chips on Monster Wafers" 2002).[8] Neverthe-

---

8. A billion is 1,000 million.

less, companies that are to remain in the technological race must invest in these monster facilities or risk falling behind in vital production knowledge and the associated incremental innovation that determines the productivity of such plants. An identical situation exists in the innovation and production of flat-screen displays. Here innovation in areas such as fusion glass, vapor deposition, and use of organic materials for diodes must go hand in hand with investment in new generations of multi-billion-dollar factories. No producer can risk skipping a generation because of the cumulative nature of technological knowledge and production expertise. Staying in the race and increasing market share mean taking large gambles. As Murtha, Lenway, and Hart (2001, pp. 184–85) observe with respect to Samsung, "Management decisions to expand production [in 1999] and to continue thin film transistor liquid crystal display (TFT-LCD) generational progressions in the face of the Asian financial crisis surprised industry observers. But it was consistent with the high-volume industry's early history of countermanding financial intuition in decisions to move ahead. This thrust Samsung and LG well ahead of more cautious producers in Japan." This story was repeated again in 2001, when Korean companies such as Hyundai, LG, and Samsung invested where Japanese and Taiwanese investors hesitated. As a result, in 2001 Korea's share of LCD flat-screen displays rose to nearly 48 percent, whereas Japan's slipped from 48 percent in 2000 to less than 25 percent in 2002 ("Flat Screen" 2002).

To afford the resources needed for innovation, production, and training thus calls for high levels of savings. East Asian countries are among the world's biggest savers, so a shortage of capital overall is not an immediate concern. However, it is notable that private fixed capital investment in several East Asian countries fell significantly between 1990–97 and 1998–2000 (see table 4.1), which could affect future competitiveness in the technology- and capital-intensive manufacturing sectors. In addition, the availability of risk capital may not be adequate for new and technologically dynamic start-up firms, an issue examined next.

Venture Capital

The supply of venture capital from public and private entities surged in East Asian economies during the 1990s, stimulated by develop-

Table 4.1 Nominal Fixed Investment as a Percentage of Nominal GDP, 1980–2000

Type of fixed investment and country	1980–89	1990–97	1998–2000
Private			
Malaysia	17.0	26.9	12.9
Philippines	17.2	18.0	14.9
Thailand	21.1	30.9	12.1
Korea, Rep. of	24.2	31.4	24.3
Public			
Malaysia	14.4	13.2	16.7
Philippines	8.7	5.4	6.3
Thailand	11.9	9.5	11.5
Korea, Rep. of	10.0	6.1	6.3

Source: World Bank, East Asia Region (2002).

ments in Silicon Valley and by euphoric business sentiments in East Asia. In 1999 the pool of funds raised reached $65.8 billion, with up to 78 percent being used to finance start-ups or the mezzanine (intermediate) expansion phase.

During 2000–02, the bursting of the Internet bubble slowed the growth of the venture capital market and generated pressure for market restructuring and policy adjustment. In several countries, notably China and Japan, there is now more venture capital than there are investment opportunities in a risk class that appeals to relatively cautious and frequently publicly managed venture capital funds.

East Asia's venture capital industry straddles four groups of economies: Japan and Korea; Hong Kong (China), Singapore, and Taiwan (China); China; and other developing Asian countries (Indonesia, Malaysia, Philippines, Thailand, and Vietnam; see Kenney, Han, and Tanaka 2002). Japan and Korea have a long history of abundant venture capital, mainly from the public sector or the banks. Japan's venture capital industry is the oldest, dating back to 1963. The three Southeast Asian economies have the most dynamic and viable venture capital industry, and among them Hong Kong, China, and Singapore export venture capital to other parts of Asia. For example, Hong Kong, China, exported more than 85 percent of its venture capital funds to other Asian countries in 1997–99, in particular to China, where venture capital financing accelerated substantially to between $700 million and more than $1 billion between 1994 and 1999. In the other Southeast Asian countries, the venture capital industry is taking off, but the volume of funds and investment remains fairly limited, and the environment for venture capital is constrained by an undeveloped industrial base, weak research capability, unstable political structures, and immature legal, accounting, and financial systems.

In Singapore, Taiwan (China), and the United States, venture capitalists concentrate their investments in high-technology and high-value-added sectors such as Internet-related services, computers, communications, electronics, or biomedical industries. Their close relationships to Silicon Valley have helped to direct investment to these areas. Venture capital in other countries still focuses on the more traditional and less innovative sectors, such as the manufacturing and energy sectors.

Government plays a much greater role in venture capital in East Asia than in the United States. Government is a major source of venture capital in China, Korea, Singapore, and the lower- and middle-income countries.[9] In Korea government funds have created or supported many large venture capital funds, and in 2001 the government invested more than $300 million to pull the venture capital market out of recession. In Singapore the government has committed more than $2 billion in venture capital; in China government and government-related organizations concentrated in a few major cities, such as Guangzhou, Shanghai, and Shenzen, supply more than 80 percent of venture capital investments; and in Malaysia the government provides more than 40 percent of venture capital funds each year (Kenney, Han, and Tanaka 2002). Government entities are a source of venture capital in other East Asian countries as well. In the mature venture capital markets, however, government funding is generally modest, although it has been used to support small business in the United States, and the government has been a source of venture capital in Germany as well.

Until the 1990s regulations often discouraged the entry of entrepreneurial firms and inhibited the activities of venture capitalists. In recent years, these regulations have been eased, but investors face difficulty in liquidating their investments. Successful venture capitalists are not permanent investors; they need an "exit" route to liquidate

---

9. In Taiwan, China, the leading industry, electronics, accounts for a quarter of GDP and owes its growth to active lobbying by the industry for government support, including the provision of public funds to supplement the resources of private venture capitalists.

their investments. A liquid and transparent equity market offers a desirable avenue for quick exits, and all East Asian countries have created new stock markets with easier listing requirements (in the 1980s, listing could take 10 years in Korea, and most small firms with any promise were purchased by the chaebols). Thus far, however, most of those markets still have small trading volumes, low liquidity, and little transparency and fail to offer a real exit path.[10]

In most of East Asia—Korea and Taiwan, China, being the exceptions—neither the increased supply of risk capital nor the developments in stock markets have yet resulted in a significant increase in the entry of new firms bringing new products or processes to the marketplace. Government agencies' over-regulation of venture capital and heavy involvement in its provision may have limited the contribution of venture capital to innovation. Public bureaucracies are rarely as effective as venture capitalists (and even the most experienced private and corporate venture capitalists can make the wrong bets ["Corporate Venture Investors" 2002]), and private venture capitalists in East Asia are often inexperienced, preferring to invest in relatively safe, traditional sectors (see also chapter 8). Public provision of venture capital does not seem to have much effect on high-tech employment, and it risks crowding out essential private venture capital (Wallsten 2000).[11] In addition, traditions of corporate governance, which place much of the authority in the hands of the company owner, generally limit the scope for substantive intervention by venture capitalists.

Foreign Direct Investment and Technology Transfer

Since the 1960s FDI has served as a source of capital for several East Asian economies and as a vehicle for technology transfer. In recent years, its role in building innovation systems has grown, as a result of

---

10. In China, for example, regulatory hurdles make it virtually impossible to exit by way of an initial public offering, and selling out to a multinational company often requires relationships that few venture capitalists have formed ("People's Republic of Capital" 2002). For a detailed analysis of the availability and use of venture capital in East Asia, see Kenney, Han, and Tanaka (2002). Public sector involvement also may be having a negative effect on the willingness of high-tech business incubators to take risks and pursue the most exciting possibilities (Harwit 2002).

11. However, in China, for example, the emergence of diverse venture capital funds is beginning to introduce some much-needed change. Both Beijing University and Tsinghua University have partnered with W. I. Harper from San Francisco to set up venture capital funds to invest in enterprises started by their academics.

spillover and production networking and, more directly, because of investment in R&D facilities by multinational companies. China has attracted the most interest because of the abundant supply of talented scientists, with companies such as Alcatel, General Electric, Intel, Matsushita, Microsoft, and Siemens all establishing large research centers that work closely with their home-based laboratories ("High-Tech in China" 2002).[12] Malaysia and Singapore have relied on technology transfer from multinational enterprises more than other economies in East Asia.[13] China has been encouraging and receiving a tremendous inflow of FDI since the 1990s with the total stock reaching $447 billion in 2001. On the whole, about 10 percent of the capital formation in East Asian economies during 1990–95 took the form of foreign direct investment. Although a substantial part of the FDI was of a horizontal nature and sought to establish assembly operations as an entrée to local markets, vertical FDI that develops a base of production through backward and forward linkages and exports to other countries continues to grow in significance, in association with the sharp rise in trade.

Although FDI helps to draw local companies into international production networks, opens market opportunities, and builds production expertise, some experience suggests that technology spillovers in the manufacturing sector from foreign firms to local ones may be modest and that, as in Indonesia (chapter 7), vertical transmission to related firms is far more likely than horizontal transmission.[14] However, other findings suggest that domestic firms do derive technological gains from FDI through various channels, although these may take time to filter through. For example, FDI into Chinese electronics and textile subsectors from OECD countries—but not from Hong Kong (China), Macau (China), and Taiwan (China)—initially appears to

---

12. In particular, the existence of multinational enterprises can greatly enhance the diffusion of knowledge, which is constrained by distance, in developing countries (Keller 2002). The additional effect of FDI is to encourage the entry of new firms, which intensifies competition in the domestic market. In the short run, this competition may lead to lower profits for domestic firms, but in the long run, it should lead to higher productivity for both foreign and domestic firms (Hu and Jefferson 2002).

13. For the experience of Malaysia and Singapore in the semiconductor industry, see Mathews and Cho (2000).

14. See Saggi (2002) for an overview of this literature. The causal link between FDI and the productivity gain of domestic firms is quite ambiguous, especially when a competition-enhancing effect is present that stems from the entry of a new firm.

shrink the market share and productivity of domestic firms, but the ones that survive take advantage of the spillovers, close the productivity gap, and emerge as strong competitors (Hu and Jefferson 2002). Many multinational enterprises offer on-the-job and other training to local workers. Local firms have the opportunity to observe multinational enterprises and to learn new ways of organizing production or new production processes. Moreover, in Singapore and Taiwan, China, the gradual congealing of local backward and forward linkages has allowed substantial know-how to flow between multinational enterprises and local firms. Such linkages can also foster the development of supporting industries, which, in turn, may lead to the emergence of high-tech clusters and to the circulation of skills in the "thick" labor markets that develop in them.

However, diffusion of technology through FDI is not automatic. An important mediating factor is the local supply of skills and R&D capability (Mody 2002; Nabeshima 2002b). This supply influences the volume of FDI, the sectors to which it flows, and the assimilation of technology by domestic industry. Without investment in basic skills and the constant upgrading of skills, host countries cannot hope to assimilate the technologies brought by FDI. Furthermore, both the absorption of technology and the development of new technologies in collaboration with foreign firms rest on the scale of domestic R&D and on the degree to which it moves domestic firms closer to the technology frontier.

ORGANIZING FOR INNOVATION

The flow of resources can influence the supply of innovation, but firms must still translate this innovation into products and process-related changes that add value in the marketplace. The remarkable achievements of leading European and U.S. high-tech firms owe much to their ability to introduce new business models and to devise organizational forms that have proven to be flexible, focused, efficient, and supportive of innovation.[15] Organizational diversity has en-

---

15. Among European firms, some of the organizational innovations introduced in the 1990s were the adoption of ISO 9000 rules, total quality management, team-centered activities, flatter hierarchies, and benchmarking (Cooke 2000, p. 69).

abled firms to respond quickly to competitive pressures, to develop and market innovations, and to adapt their internal practices so as to stimulate innovative activity. Virtually every one of the leading firms is distinguished not just by its range of products or services but also by distinctive organizational attributes that reinforce technological advances. For example, flatter hierarchies in many high-tech firms have promoted flexibility, diffusion of information, experimentation, and faster decisionmaking. The success of a firm as large as Microsoft depends on the suppleness of its organization. Dell's business model has also helped to transform the approach to selling a wide range of high-tech products.

In some parts of East Asia the business milieu and the nature of government direction have, by and large, discouraged organizational change, entrepreneurship, and the development of fresh business models. Family ownership and a patriarchal management structure have remained the norms. While quite nimble in seizing opportunities and changing direction, East Asian organizational models tend toward hierarchies that circumscribe initiative and innovation; employees are more likely to follow instructions than to show much enterprise. This has slowed the response to the problems revealed by the 1997–98 crisis. Not even leading firms such as ACER, Asustek, Legend, Quanta, or Samsung Electronics have introduced organizational changes comparable to their initiatives in process technologies and, in the case of Samsung, product technologies as well.[16]

Organizational conservatism and the lack of diversity in business models constrain entrepreneurial initiative with respect to developing and commercializing new findings. The tenacity of indigenous business cultures is bolstered in some economies by the efforts of government to manage markets, sheltering firms and discouraging organizational change, by way of mergers and acquisitions. Shortages of professional skills in areas such as management, financial planning, auditing, and consulting are another reason why East Asian businesses have been slow to evolve and experiment.

More is needed than exposure to global competition. New business models are needed that induce transnational R&D collaboration

---

16. Samsung remains a family-controlled conglomerate with a top-down hierarchy ("Samsung Tries" 2002).

and result in East Asian companies seeking a global presence comparable to what companies such as Sony have achieved and Haier, Hyundai, and Samsung are attempting to emulate. Commenting on the emergence of new firms in Korea, *The Economist* ("South Korea: Entrepreneurial Fresh Air" 2001, p. 60) observes,

> The new entrepreneurs face one big constraint that also affects old enterprises following their examples, a severe shortage of professional managers. Senior managers in old enterprises are used to working to orders from the top and they lack the innovative ideas required by the new culture. The problem is particularly acute for new enterprises that have been founded by engineers. After a few years, many of these engineers turned entrepreneurs want to concentrate on research in order to develop new products. But they find it virtually impossible to recruit a manager who can leave them free to do that.

Company Management of Research and Inter-firm Collaboration

A firm's organizational structure has implications for its innovativeness: structure determines how the firm manages its own research and, in large firms, how it guides innovation and quality control in suppliers and affiliates. For leading East Asian firms seeking to leverage research as a means to assure growth and enlarge market share, two objectives are paramount. One is research collaboration; the other is the productive management of the company's research assets.[17]

Although competition among firms has long been viewed as one of the principal drivers of innovation, more recently competitors are finding it expedient to cooperate in product or process development even while they continue to compete in the market. A company-centered and purely local approach to innovation is no longer the most productive—or even a viable—approach. Awareness of developments in key markets, the presence of sentinel firms or offices in major production or research hubs, and collective effort are often now the name of the game in successful innovation. Rigby and Zook (2002, p. 82) note that some of the fastest growing and most profitable industries are finding

---

17. An official of Japan's Ministry of Economy, Trade, and Industry has noted that Japanese companies have "lots of overlapping efforts, lots of projects, but no one could understand how they were doing . . . the management of [corporate R&D] has not been very effective" ("Japan Asks Why" 2002, pp. 1230–31).

open market innovation to be a critical new source of comparative advantage, an approach that uses tools such as licensing, joint ventures, and strategic alliances to bring the benefits of free trade to the flow of new ideas. For example, Tetra Pak, one of the world's leading makers of packaging systems, was only able to devise a novel lightweight rectangular container by working closely with companies specializing in paper and polymers and hospital sterilizing equipment. Overseas research laboratories and partnerships with other auto companies and component vendors have been responsible for saving General Motors millions of dollars. Software developed in India helped to design an auto platform for the North American market and was instrumental in facilitating the reverse engineering of a European platform for the Indian market (Green and Zimmerman 2002).

Innovations are springing up throughout the industrial world, and it is impossible to predict when and where they will occur. Therefore, firms need to take a regional, if not an international, approach to networking in pursuit of innovation and to design business models and a management process that bolster their chances of benefiting. Murtha, Lenway, and Hart (2001, p. 31) observe,

> Companies with affiliates in a country or region where an industry emerges have as good a shot as local companies at taking integral positions, provided their managers can fully leverage local organizational capabilities with global technological capabilities as these opportunities arise. In the successful companies, local managers functioned in peer networks as global managers. Local initiatives served as a primary means to go after global opportunities. Long-standing corporate research traditions in underlying technologies combined with strong local operations to establish these companies' stakes in the rapid accumulation of knowledge assets. Developing such a knowledge stake formed a necessary condition for successful physical asset deployments anywhere in the world, including at home.

As noted earlier, countries that are in the catch-up phase can obtain above-average results only by cutting costs or by offering improved or differentiated products. The pressures on them are more intense because their entry enlarges supplies and pushes down prices even faster. The collaborative approach is a way forward, but it must be backstopped by a steady and systematic accumulation of knowledge and capabilities in core areas. To quote Murtha, Lenway, and Hart (2001 p. 188) again,

This means entering [an] industry with current generation technology, achieving commercial yields, and running at efficient scale to build up the knowledge foundations necessary to seize a leadership position as the next generation emerges. The importance of individuals and teams grows as the pace of industry evolution from generation to generation increases. This occurs because during periods of generational transition, personal and unwritten knowledge accumulates more rapidly than knowledge that is written or embodied in fixed assets such as capital equipment and materials.

While external collaboration and outreach are some of the dimensions of research management at the company level, there are others as well. They embrace the substantive interaction of research with marketing, engineering, and production departments; personnel policies to permit the periodic rotation of employees from other parts of the company;[18] creation of a research ambience that balances detachment from day-to-day operations with awareness of commercial imperatives; development of a geographically dispersed portfolio of research centers drawing on talent in other countries; and efforts to nurture the research and design potential of affiliated firms.

Technology management skills are scarce in East Asia, as Dodgson (2000, pp. 244, 250) notes,

> Policies for training technology managers in Asia are generally variable in quality and commonly limited in scale; they often focus on inappropriate European and American models. For innovation policies to succeed, policymakers must learn to develop and change policies over time.... [In Indonesia, for example] perhaps the greatest problem is the lack of management capability as technology projects become more complex, which reflects the weak educational and R&D base of the country.[19]

An enabling business environment is a step toward the development of innovative industrial capability. Realizing the potential of the market environment depends to a considerable degree on entrepreneurship in the firm. Harryson (2002) suggests that within organizations themselves, ranging from mature firms to recent start-ups, a

---

18. In Japan this involves the internal labor market of firms and a regime based on rotating engineers from R&D to production to marketing. "The transfer of researchers is like breathing: both necessary and normal" (Malecki 2000, p. 192).

19. Hill (2002) notes other problems that affect the company-level research environment in Indonesia: the lack of program coordination across ministries, weakness in the rule of law, and ineffectual financial management.

number of entrepreneurial management skills can be vital for spurring innovation and providing strategic direction. These include the following from Harryson (2002, pp. 16–21):

First, the open sharing of ideas, technologies, and human resources should be common within business units. At Sony, for example, promotion criteria explicitly include the sharing of past mistakes.

Second, rewarding and promoting collective achievement are important. At Canon (one of the most innovative international firms), staff formulate corporate visions and ensure that various business units set goals that correspond with these visions.

Third, the ability to develop a new product prior to placement in the marketplace and willingness to take the risks associated with such development are fundamental to keeping companies dynamic. [Companies such as Intel and Sony are hard at work on the next-generation product even as the current-generation microprocessor or game console enters the market.]

Fourth, excessive employee specialization and corporate fragmentation inhibit cross-functional learning and technology transfer; the ability of personnel to rotate functions and develop an innate knowledge of overall company formation increases flexibility.

Fifth, in order to orient R&D toward the market, researchers and engineers can undergo training in sales and production, thereby attuning themselves to market needs.

Networked Clusters

Information, learning, competition, and other pressures that induce innovation can be stimulated by the clustering of firms in urban centers. Where clusters result in the emergence of networked arrangements, demand is further reinforced as leading firms pull up others and force them to keep pace, not the least through technical assistance and the sharing of tacit knowledge. Only certain kinds of clusters spur innovation, and these are the ones where competition among closely matched rivals and from new entrants with fresh ideas is toughest. These are also the clusters that are the most open to outside influence and have the widest range of global contacts. We take an in-depth look at various kinds of clusters and their dynamics in chapter 6. But above all, innovative clusters need a stable, open, and fair environment in order to flourish. We now discuss this aspect of the transition to innovative economies.

STABILITY, OPENNESS, INTELLECTUAL COLLABORATION, AND PROPERTY RIGHTS

The actions of companies that are the drivers of commercial innovation, and ultimately of growth, must be viewed in the wider context of macroeconomic policy and the variety of critical market and non-market institutions that contribute to innovation. A stable and open environment is the cornerstone of technological advance. Policies supporting openness promote innovation by way of trade, competition, foreign investment, the sharing of ideas, and the circulation of skilled workers within and among countries. In the earlier stages of development, these assist in the absorption of technology. As the process of catching up accelerates, an open economy is more likely to seek competitiveness through innovation. Although the experience of the past two decades suggests that the smaller open economies are more susceptible to shocks, there can be little doubt that, in today's world, technological progress demands openness, and the competitiveness it imparts is inseparable from economic resilience. Openness is also necessary for the formation of high-tech clusters, which have emerged as the wellspring of innovativeness. Writing on the significance of openness for Silicon Valley, Spence (1996, p. 187) remarks,

> If you consider Silicon Valley or any one of the many advanced centers of biomedical science in the United States, you find companies and universities interacting daily. You will find investors, venture capitalists, and entrepreneurs in constant contact. New companies are started and then taken public or purchased by larger companies. In biotechnology, many companies make marketing contracts with multinational pharmaceutical companies. Large companies increasingly enter into alliances with multinationals based outside the United States to develop new and expensive technologies. Even trying to close this system is difficult to imagine. If a serious attempt were made to do so, the required steps would substantially interdict the flow of scientific and technological information in the U.S. economy, within the scientific community, and between that group and the private sector. The openness of that complex system has been one of the most important contributors to the efficiency of the science and technology investment process.

The Role of Competition Policy and Industrial Organization in Generating Demand for Innovation

The supply of inputs is not enough to ensure that innovation will occur. Only competition—through openness to trade and FDI—can push firms to innovate as a matter of course and to see innovation as essential to their growth, if not survival. Competition policy, together with trade policy, provides an essential dose of dynamism and helps to build an innovative system equal to the challenge of globalization. The role of competition policy (and competition law) is straightforward: to encourage competitive pricing, facilitate entry by new firms, and pressure producers to innovate and improve their technical efficiency (which entails maximizing the output from given inputs).[20]

The entry of new firms into the market is one source of innovation. The emergence of a few dominant large firms is a second, and their size, market power, and deep pockets can underwrite the long-term commercial success of promising innovations. This is apparent from the experience of Lucky Goldstar and Samsung in Korea and, more recently, Haier, Huawei, Legend, and ZTE in China. Market contestability pressures large firms to sustain their competitiveness, which they do by innovating, augmenting their productivity, and modifying their business strategies in anticipation of changing market circumstances. In a globalizing world, the contestability of markets implies openness to competition from foreign firms in domestic markets. This is the flip side to the aggressive expansion overseas that the major domestic firms in the high-tech sectors of smaller economies need to survive and grow.[21]

In the U.S. software sector, competition law (antitrust policy) has held down the barriers to entry and accommodated the growth of firms, while attempting to maintain contestability (Mowery 1999). In most of East Asia, competition policy is much weaker, and only three

---

20. As Lloyd and others (2002) note, monopoly power can stimulate innovative activity by providing additional resources and promising additional profits to potential innovators. However, this is an argument for the protection of intellectual property on new processes and products, but not for the maintenance of monopolies in existing products, which is the problem that competition policy is intended to address.

21. A large, integrated domestic market is also a tremendous asset, something that assisted the development of the United States in the nineteenth century despite the country's maintenance of a protectionist trade regime. China's lack of such integration has until recently hampered firms and affected the pace of innovation-led growth (Young 2000).

economies have a comprehensive system in place—Japan, Korea, and Taiwan (China). Even where there are fewer and fewer barriers to entry, as in Korea and Malaysia, governments still seek to protect firms from foreign competition in imitation of the Japanese model of 1950–80. This approach seemed to deliver results in some cases, possibly because domestic competition and protection from foreign competition combined to allow the emergence of national champions, akin to NEC, Sony, and Toyota, capable of playing a global role, as Hyundai Motor and Samsung Electronics do now (Nelson 2000; M. Sakakibara and Porter 2001). But the small size of domestic markets in much of East Asia and the absence of a demanding local clientele do not provide the stimulus and sophisticated market feedback needed to prepare firms to compete internationally. Moreover, membership in the World Trade Organization makes it increasingly difficult for governments to protect specific sectors and for firms to enhance their profitability through price discrimination.

Trade barriers are coming down everywhere, and the luxury of a long spell of infant-industry protection, sheltered by tariff and nontariff barriers, is disappearing. Competition policy as practiced by countries in the region must now focus on accomplishing the following. First, it must focus on relaxing the remaining barriers to entry—and exit—of firms. Djankov and others (2000) find that entry barriers in most East Asian economies are high relative to those in OECD countries, reflecting governments' tendency to pursue industrial policies by targeting specific sectors. Barriers to exit are as important as barriers to entry. Efforts by governments to shore up failing enterprises stifle competition and divert valuable resources away from users with better prospects. Second, it must permit mergers and takeovers. Mergers and takeovers are relatively rare in East Asian economies, including Japan. Existing business conventions proscribing takeovers, reinforced by cross-shareholdings among firms and banks as well as by protective corporate alliances, have a deleterious effect on profitability. They lessen the pressure on a company to maximize profitability using all avenues at its disposal, including innovation, and restrict the options for growth through mergers—the road that has been taken by most of the large and dynamic new firms in the leading Western economies. Third, it must attempt a progressive harmonization of intercountry rules. This topic is discussed in chapter 3.

A long-standing debate about the merits of the different models of industrial organization for stimulating competition—and through it innovation—has not yielded a clear winner. However, the choices for policymakers have begun to crystallize.

Small and medium enterprises are increasingly viewed as the vehicles through which new ideas and technologies germinate and enter the industrial mainstream.[22] In particular, small new start-ups have had a role in pushing the information technology industry into a higher orbit. In the OECD countries, but also in Korea and Taiwan, China, more R&D is being concentrated in small start-up laboratories and companies. Some of these launch new technologies and are then taken over by bigger companies, while some upgrade their products and productivity, enter the export market, and become larger firms.

Large and highly diversified conglomerates, such as the Korean chaebols and some Japanese companies such as Hitachi and Mitsubishi, have suffered in the lean years following the crisis.[23] In fact, on closer examination, many of the Japanese keiretsu appear to be a loose collection of firms with weak links to a main bank and with no clear strategic objectives (Miwa and Ramseyer 2002). These groupings have proven difficult to manage.[24] Lacking a core competence and a strong shareholder orientation, their overall efficiency and profitability have been weak, and in recent years several have experienced difficulties. A few of the leading conglomerates, such as Samsung, continue to compete vigorously in export markets, in computer memory chips, mobile telecommunications, flat-screen displays, and consumer electronics, and they remain innovative and retain pockets of high manufacturing efficiency. Others such as Hyundai, once the largest company in Korea (but ranked sixth in 2002), have been partially dismantled.

---

22. However, the basic research that is the source of innovation is conducted largely in publicly financed laboratories (OECD 2001c).

23. Each of the top 30 groups in Korea has at least 20 affiliates. Since the crisis, 14 of the top 30 chaebols have been broken up, with the constituent parts either liquidated or absorbed by the surviving conglomerates ("Strategic Planning Perspectives" 2002).

24. The unsuccessful efforts of Chinese authorities to form business groups, starting in the early 1990s, were undertaken to reform state-owned enterprises. They did little more than recreate the earlier industrial bureaus in the guise of corporate systems, without subjecting them to market selection and rationalization (Keister 2000).

The dissatisfaction with large conglomerates does not extend to large enterprises per se. This is because size is evidently a source of international competitive strength: it is the basis for building a brand image, for penetrating overseas markets, and for creating an in-house capability for technological development across a broad front (see "Asia Learns Size Really Matters" 2001; "Why Tech's Heavyweights" 2002).[25] Some researchers believe that East Asia's future will depend on the emergence of world-class companies that can compete in global markets and create dynamic networks of affiliated suppliers.[26] In fact, the experience of the United States suggests that large companies such as Dell, General Electric, IBM, Intel, Microsoft, and Wal-Mart are a major source of innovation and competitive pressure. They generate significant spillovers and are able to weather the tough competitive environment of the global economy.

In sum, research now appears to favor a mix of large, internationally competitive firms and dynamic new start-ups. Conglomerates of the kind that evolved in Korea under government tutelage, although they were successful (with government support) in building an industrial base and penetrating overseas markets, have, on balance, not distinguished themselves from a business perspective since the mid-1990s, and they have been politically unpopular as well.[27] The attempts in Korea during 1998–2000 and currently ongoing in China to induce the consolidation of firms, although compensating for the absence of a market for mergers and acquisitions, are fraught with risks.[28]

---

25. Nolan (2002) believes that the absence of large firms in China comparable in size to the multinational corporations is a major handicap. However, within China local brands of computers, shampoos, soaps, laundry detergents, refrigerators, and air conditioners dominate the market. A few Chinese companies selling white goods (large consumer durables), mobile handsets, and computers are now venturing overseas—for example, Haier—and joining a handful of Taiwanese firms such as Quanta and TSMC. Techtronic, which is based in Hong Kong, China, has factories in Dongguan, and makes power tools and floor care appliances, has also established an international presence by acquiring Vax, a maker of vacuum cleaners, and Ryobi, a producer of corded power tools ("Techtronic Branding" 2001).

26. After an initial strong push during 1998–2000, the Korean authorities eased off on their efforts to dismantle the chaebols and limit the extent of ownership of banks ("Return of the Behemoths" 2001; "South Korea's Chaebol Counterattack" 2001). See also Nolan and Zhang (2002) on the prospects of large Chinese firms in fields such as petrochemicals and aerospace.

27. Until 1989 chaebol-affiliated groups in Korea had lower profits. Since then, the differences have disappeared, and affiliates have achieved somewhat higher growth rates (Choi and Cowing 1999).

28. The government-directed merger of LG Semicon with Hynix Semiconductor in 1999 saddled Hynix with an additional 12,400 billion won in debt that was a severe drag on Hynix

Since the weight of evidence argues for creating a competitive environment with low entry barriers, policy should enable an abundance of entrepreneurial, innovative firms to enter and, where market opportunities permit, to grow large enough to compete on a global stage.

The challenge facing many governments is to determine how best to phase in this open and competitive environment, with its exacting market for corporate control, corporate governance, institutions, and providers of services, especially venture capital. Enlarging the role of foreign investors and the scope for hostile takeovers—rare thus far in East Asia—could stimulate competition. A few governments have accepted market-determined outcomes, recognizing the futility of persisting with industrial policy and of attempting to engineer a specific kind of industrial organization.[29] Other governments still worry about the disruption that a sudden move would cause, the cost of exits (if even large firms are allowed to go under or be taken over), and the danger that foreign firms will occupy the economy's "commanding heights."

Intellectual Property Rights

Abraham Lincoln maintained that the patent system could encourage innovation because it added "the fuel of interest to the fire of genius." But for economies in the catch-up phase of development—such as the East Asian economies in the past quarter-century—the existence and enforcement of a regime protecting intellectual property had minimal consequences for innovation or the productivity of creative industries. Lerner (2002) demonstrates that changes in patent protection in the countries he studied (which already provided some protec-

---

during the lean period of 2001–02. Hynix's problems forced government-owned banks to step in and roll over the chip producer's debts, because the company was responsible in 2001 for 4 percent of Korea's exports and employed 18,000 workers. This assistance gave rise to loud protests from German and U.S. producers and their governments ("Hynix Tightens Its Belt" 2001; "Infineon's Head Gloomy" 2001).

29. Industrial policy was of questionable utility even in its heyday during the 1970s and 1980s and now is increasingly at odds in a world subject to the discipline of the World Trade Organization (Yusuf 2001). Noland and Pack (2002a) conclude that industrial policies during this period—for example, in Japan and Korea—had little positive effect on growth. See also Quibria (2002).

tion) did not have much effect on innovation. Moreover, recent work by Song (2002) on Korea suggests that the accelerating rate of patenting is a reflection of investment in R&D and the competition between large Korean chaebols and their foreign competitors. It has little to do with Korea's regime of intellectual property rights.

As we look ahead, however, the situation could change with the strength of intellectual property rights becoming far more relevant to the performance of East Asian countries in certain areas for three main reasons. First and foremost, as growth comes to depend much more on innovation and on maximizing the fruits of innovation, encouraging innovation in industries with large up-front research costs demands greater protection of property rights. The speed with which some products can be reverse engineered, especially chemicals and pharmaceuticals—products that are enormously expensive to develop —has led industrial countries to heighten their pressure for protection.[30] Moreover, the creative industries, whose share in East Asian economies is on the rise, suffer large losses because of rampant piracy. Thus support for the Trade-Related Aspects of Intellectual Property Rights (TRIPS) Agreement has solidified among the signatories of the World Trade Organization, even though not all countries stand to gain from the rules that will come into force by 2005, and some of the poorer countries (with limited manufacturing capacity) probably will lose by having less access to cheap generic drugs from abroad. A second, closely related, reason is that technology transfer through FDI, collaborative research, and licensing, which necessarily supplements domestic R&D, can be sustained only if foreign partners are assured of an adequate regime of intellectual property rights. Furthermore, in this technologically charged competitive environment, companies need patents and patent safeguards to negotiate the exchange of technology with their competitors and to have bargaining leverage if they are involved in the all-too-frequent litigation on patent infringement.

---

30. Each new therapeutic drug introduced into the U.S. market costs an average of $800 million to develop. So high are the financial and transaction costs (drugs take 10–15 years to develop) of introducing new drugs that patent protection is of particular significance (Henry and Lexchin 2002). A recent study suggests that were such protection to be eliminated for all current and future drugs, for every dollar that current consumers would gain from lower prices, future consumers would lose three dollars as a result of a decline in pharmaceutical innovation, which has contributed vastly to longevity and the quality of life. See Hughes, Moore, and Snyder (2002).

This might be less significant in subsectors in which product life cycles are short (Viren and Malkamaki 2002).

Third, the emergence and commercialization of the creative industries in many East Asian countries have generated increasing domestic support for rules that protect writers, musicians, producers of software, the movie industry, and other forms of entertainment. In China, for instance, pirated copies of music compact disks and movie DVDs are available at a fraction of the legal price within three to four days of release of the product. The same is true for software and games consoles such as PS2 and X-Box, whose motherboards are modified so that the consoles can play illegally copied games ("Mod Squad" 2002; "Pinch of Piracy" 2002). China's case is by no means exceptional; the problem is as acute in Hong Kong (China), Indonesia, Thailand, and elsewhere and extends to fashion accessories and other items. Without protection, creative efforts would be undersupplied; by assigning exclusive rights and protecting these rights—which has a cost—society can benefit from the increase in creative effort.

The design of protection for intellectual property rights must strike a balance between giving enough incentives to generate intellectual property and, at the same time, allowing the dissemination of new knowledge.[31] The very nature of knowledge calls for sharing information with the widest possible audience, especially since the marginal cost of doing so is close to zero. Granting exclusive rights to knowledge hinders this social objective. With this in mind, the protection of intellectual property typically grants only temporary rights to the owner, after which time the intellectual property is moved into the public domain.[32]

Safeguarding intellectual property rights has a complex effect on economic growth because of the interaction with other aspects of a country's institutional environment. For instance, the cost of protect-

---

31. For a comprehensive treatment of the overall aspects of intellectual property rights, see Maskus (2000). Poor protection of these rights gives rise to secrecy, and firms often choose not to patent in order to avoid the disclosure requirements. Not patenting is detrimental to society because, without the disclosure of information that it entails, the R&D efforts of firms have limited spillovers (Cohen, Nelson, and Walsh 2000).

32. Much controversy remains over the nature—long and narrow or short and broad—of patent protection that is most conducive to future innovation and also limits the negative consequences for consumer welfare (Gallini and Scotchmer 2002).

ing intellectual property rights (a rise in price due to the market power of the property owner) depends on how the market is structured. Granting a patent, copyright, or trademark does not necessarily create a monopoly in a given market; it merely creates some market power that allows firms to charge prices above marginal costs. The size of the markup that the firms are able to charge depends on the intensity of competition, including the ease of entry and exit in the market in which they are selling and, in the case of pharmaceuticals, the appearance of comparable drugs.

In accordance with the TRIPS, most economies in East Asia have either updated their laws on intellectual property rights or expect to be in compliance with TRIPS by 2005. By 2002 most were in compliance with the minimum standards of TRIPS. What should economies in East Asia do now?

Different regimes of intellectual property rights are likely to be appropriate for countries at different levels of development. A country will not enjoy the dynamic gains from protecting intellectual property rights if it lacks an adequate supply of human capital and supporting institutions such as a market in venture capital. Different means of protection are available, depending on the type of intellectual property in question. Here we discuss patent, copyright, and trademark protections, which we consider to be the most relevant for East Asia.[33]

Patents. Patent protection is granted if an invention is novel, nonobvious, and applicable to industrial use.[34] Since most new inventions originate and are patented in industrial countries, many developing countries see patent protection as something that prevents them from accessing and benefiting from new inventions, an impediment to upgrading their technological base. This belief has led in the past to rel-

---

33. Although the issues of plant variety and other areas of intellectual property rights are important, they tend to be sector-specific. In contrast, the issues surrounding patents, copyrights, and trademarks generally apply to all sectors of the economy, and thus we focus our attention on these.

34. TRIPS allow broad exclusion of subject matters from patent protection ostensibly to protect public order or morality, prevent environmental deterioration, and protect animal, human, or plant life, if and only if these exemptions do not lead to commercial exploitation (Maskus 2000). For instance, pharmaceutical products, if deemed necessary to address public health issues, may be excluded from patent protection.

Table 4.2 Length of Patent Protection at the End of 1997

Economy	Length of protection in years	Starting time	Notes
China	20	Application date	
Indonesia	14	Application date	Extension up to 5 years
Japan	20	Application date	25 years for pharmaceutical patents
Korea, Rep. of	20	Application date	25 years for pharmaceutical patents
Malaysia	15	Award date	Patents limited to no more than 20 years from application
Philippines	17	Award date	
Singapore	20	Application date	
Taiwan, China	20	Application date	25 years for pharmaceutical patents
Thailand	20	Application date	
United States	20	Application date	25 years for pharmaceutical patents

Source: Lerner (2000).

atively weak patent protection (see table 4.2). But as domestic firms strengthen their technological capabilities and compete on the basis of innovation, this is set to change (Maskus 2000).[35]

In the past, the laws protecting patents were relatively strong in the poorest countries. These countries, however, were not equipped to enforce patent rights, although patent infringement tended to be infrequent because the technological capability was, and remains, weak. Protection then tended to diminish as incomes rose, because the incentive to imitate foreign technologies strengthened. At a per capita income of around $2,000, patent protection started to climb again, regaining the level in low-income countries at a per capita income of $7,750. This also generally coincided with a high degree of openness (Y. Chen and Puttitanun 2002; Maskus 2000). As economies such as Japan, Korea, and Taiwan (China) have become richer, they have tended to strengthen patent laws and put resources into more rigorous enforcement (table 4.3).

In many subsectors, patent protection is not a significant means of capturing the benefits from innovation, and firms often eschew patenting in order to avoid disclosing new technologies. The lead time for product development and tacit knowledge coupled with

---

35. This is also seen in the evolution of intellectual property rights in the United States (Khan and Sokoloff 2001).

Table 4.3 Ginarte-Park Index of Patent Protection for East Asia, Various Years, 1960–90

Economy	1960	1965	1970	1975	1980	1985	1990
Brazil	1.64	1.64	1.64	1.51	1.85	1.85	1.85
Hong Kong, China	2.04	2.04	2.04	2.04	2.24	2.57	2.57
India	1.85	1.85	1.42	1.42	1.62	1.62	1.48
Indonesia	0.33	0.33	0.33	0.33	0.33	0.33	0.33
Japan	2.85	3.18	3.32	3.61	3.94	3.94	3.94
Korea, Rep. of	2.8	2.8	2.94	2.94	3.28	3.61	3.94
Malaysia	2.37	2.37	2.37	2.37	2.57	2.9	2.37
Philippines	2.19	2.52	2.67	2.67	2.67	2.67	2.67
Singapore	2.37	2.37	2.37	2.37	2.57	2.57	2.57
Thailand	1.51	1.51	1.51	1.51	1.85	1.85	1.85
United States	3.86	3.86	3.86	3.86	4.19	4.52	4.52

Note: The Ginarte-Park index ranges from 0 to 5, with 5 being the strongest protection of patents. The index is based on the letter of the laws concerning patent protection and does not consider the enforcement side of patent protection.
Source: Ginarte and Park (1997).

strong marketing capabilities and secrecy have been used successfully to appropriate the gains from new inventions. The situation differs in industries such as chemicals, pharmaceuticals, and certain complex electronics products.[36] Pharmaceutical firms rely heavily on patenting because their inventions can be easily imitated once the formula for a particular drug is determined (Kingston 2001; Maskus 2000).

The rising trend in the number of patents not just in Japan and the United States (more than 190,000 granted in 2002) but also in the emerging East Asian economies such as Korea and Taiwan, China, points to an increasing role for intellectual property rights. Part of the reason may be that patents not only give access to complementary technologies but also prevent copying and block rival patents on related inventions. In electronics and transport equipment, for example, firms seek patents so as not to be excluded from cross-licensing agreements and to enhance their bargaining power in such agreements.

This access to complementary technologies is crucial for industries with "complex" goods such as electronics, where a product incorporates numerous patentable components and parts that no one firm has

---

36. A survey of firms by Cohen, Nelson, and Walsh (2000) shows that the most cited reasons for not patenting new inventions are the ease of inventing around them (25 percent), inability to demonstrate novelty (32 percent), and need for disclosure (24 percent).

the resources to invest in entirely. Cohen, Nelson, and Walsh (2000) find that 55 percent of firms in "complex" product industries used patents as a source of cross-licensing opportunities, whereas only 10 percent of those in "discrete" industries cited this as the reason for patenting.

In economies with substantial technological capabilities that aspire to become front-runners in certain fields, patent protection needs strengthening.[37] Without such protection, their firms will have difficulty becoming "players" in global markets; by not having any patents to offer to other firms with complementary technology, they will be denied access to key technologies. In some cases, lack of, or even delay in, access is quite damaging, especially when product cycles are short (Kingston 2001).

For economies lagging behind in technological capabilities, Japan's patent system could be quite effective in promoting incremental innovation (Maskus and McDaniel 1999). Four key features of the pre-1988 Japanese patent system can foster the diffusion of knowledge and incremental innovation. First, the preference given to those who are first-to-file encourages patent applications even though the protection it offers is perceived to be weak. Second, eighteen months after the application is lodged, it is disclosed to the public, and anyone can file to oppose the application. The procedure for opposition gives incentives for firms to track and learn what other firms are doing, leading to a more rapid diffusion of new knowledge. Third, given that each patent contained only a single claim until the reform in 1988, other firms could and did "invent around" these patents (see Branstetter and Sakakibara [2001] for a discussion of the patent reform and its effect on the patenting activity in Japan). Fourth, incremental mechanical innovations that do not qualify for a regular patent—in either novelty or inventiveness—can still be protected through utility patents. The duration of protection for such innovations is much shorter than for patents. After the patent system was reformed to allow multiple claims, the applications for utility patents declined significantly (Maskus and McDaniel 1999; Okada and Asaba 1997). Each element of the Japanese patent system reinforced the others to stimulate diffusion and encourage incremental innovation.

---

37. It must be recognized that a patent system is costly to maintain and requires a huge effort from highly skilled people equipped with sophisticated data-access capabilities ("Search 500,000 Documents" 2002).

On the whole, the pre-1988 Japanese patent system—especially the early disclosure rule—contributed to the growth of the Japanese economy during that country's catch-up phase (Maskus and McDaniel 1999).[38] The Japanese system differs from the U.S. patent system, which features first-to-invent, confidentiality until grants,[39] and multiple claims. The U.S. system gives inventors more protection than the Japanese system at the expense of the wide diffusion of new knowledge, and aspects of this system might become more relevant once the capacity for innovation of East Asian countries has deepened substantially.

Copyright. Copyright protection is given to the expression of ideas, rather than, as in the case of patents, to new ideas themselves.[40] The lack of copyright protection typically gives rise to duplication of copyrighted materials and their unauthorized distribution. With today's technologies, duplication is generally a fairly low-cost and low-skill activity that shifts rents from copyright holders to copyright pirates.

Policymakers need to make a tradeoff between, on the one hand, the costs associated with displacing workers engaged in piracy and the potential increase in the consumer price of copyrighted materials and, on the other hand, the dynamic gains associated with greater access to a variety of copyrighted materials and the encouragement of creativity in the future.[41]

It is hard to argue that developing countries are disadvantaged in creating copyrightable materials (table 4.4). India has a thriving film industry in part because of adequate copyright protection (Maskus 2000). And whereas patent infringement typically requires substantial learning efforts, which can bring benefits to the domestic economy,

---

38. For a theoretical treatment of the issue of disclosure (pre-grant versus confidentiality until grant), see R. Aoki and Spiegel (2001). Mezzoleni and Nelson (1998) argue that Korea and Taiwan (China) benefit from lax protection, especially in electronics.

39. For those applying for international patent protection, the American Inventors' Protection Act of 1999 made the disclosure requirements similar to those of the Japanese system (R. Aoki and Spiegel 2001).

40. TRIPS specifies the minimum protection to be the life of the author plus 50 years; if the copyright is held by a corporation, the protection lasts 50 years (Maskus 2000).

41. A strengthening of copyright protection as conferred by the Sonny Bono Act in the United States in 1998 does not appear to have spurred the release of movies (Hui and Pong 2002). Moreover, excessive protection can slow the process of diffusion, thus retarding future innovation that builds on current findings.

Table 4.4 Book Titles Produced in East Asia, Late 1990s

Country	Year	Number of books
China	1996	110,283
Japan[a]	1998	65,513
Korea, Rep. of[a]	1999	36,425
Malaysia	1998	5,816
Philippines	1997	5,093
Singapore	1995	3,000
Thailand	1998	12,000
European Union[b]	1996	354,303
United States	1996	68,175
India	1997	57,386

a. New titles only.
b. The first 12 members of the European Union.
Source: International Publishers Association (www.ipa-uie.org/statistics/annual_book_prod.html); Maskus (2000).

the act of copyright piracy does not confer any learning for future capabilities.[42] As long as decompilation is permitted—thus allowing reverse engineering—this does not pose any difficulties for developing countries, except for the possible increase in the price of copyrighted versus illegally copied software.[43]

There does not appear to be a case for protecting copyrighted materials differently in developed and developing countries, at least under the law.[44] Of course, the ability of countries to enforce the law typically depends on their stage of development.

Trademarks. A trademark is an identifiable and unique mark associated with certain products. The benefits of protecting a trademark

---

42. One of the contentious issues in copyright protection is the treatment of software. The TRIPS agreement requires signatory countries to grant copyright protection to software. The United States is one of the few countries that offer patent protection for software. In recent years, the United States has seen a tremendous increase in software patents, including Internet-related patents that embody business models. Fewer than 100 Internet-related patents were issued prior to 1992. In 1999 alone the U.S. Patent and Trademark Office granted nearly 4,000 Internet-related patents. Some argue that the requirements for patent protection have been substantially lowered for patents regarding software (Hunt 2001).

43. The creation of software has two stages: writing a source code and compiling the source code into a binary file. A source code is often written in a high-level programming language, easily understandable by programmers. Compilation of the source code translates these instructions into what computers understand: a string of zeros and ones. Decompilation reverses this

are to reduce consumers' costs in searching for satisfactory products, ensure the quality of the products, and, for goods such as food, safeguard the health of consumers.

The protection of trademarks is especially important in East Asia, where economies need to move from offering low-cost products to offering differentiated products and extending their reach internationally through the creation of global brand images. Strengthening trademark protection by closing down the production and distribution of knockoffs (unlicensed imitations of trademarked products) raises concerns about the potential displacement of workers, as does copyright protection.

Are developing countries disadvantaged in creating brand images? To the extent that establishing a brand involves substantial costs in marketing, advertising, and quality controls, they may be at a disadvantage. But domestic firms do register for trademarks in East Asia, and in some countries applications by residents outnumber those by nonresidents by quite a wide margin (table 4.5). Maskus (2000) finds that many Chinese firms complain about the proliferation of knock-off products selling under their brand names, showing that, even at an early stage of national development, the creation and protection of a brand may be taken seriously.

University–Industry Links

An open environment with appropriate rights to intellectual property provides some of the economic and social conditions that can promote innovation. However, policies supportive of openness need to be supplemented by policies that deepen technological capability provided the requisite educational infrastructure is in place (a point discussed in chapter 5). Once university-based research gathers momentum— frequently with public funding—the volume of research and its use by industry depend on the institutions governing the interaction between

---

process and generates the source code from a binary file. Given the complexity of software today, decompilation is time-consuming and requires great effort to understand the underlying logic, akin to the reverse engineering of physical goods.

44. The "fair use" of materials for education and research is always an important issue in the copyright protection debate (Maskus 2000). For developing countries, liberal attitudes toward educational material such as textbooks may be warranted.

Table 4.5 Trademark Applications in East Asia, 1994 and 1999

Economy	1994			1999		
	Resident	Nonresident	Total	Resident	Nonresident	Total
China	117,186	25,431	142,617	140,620	24,508	165,128
Hong Kong, China	4,651	10,738	15,389	5,066	14,819	19,885
Indonesia[a]	15,696	10,485	26,181	16,251	11,938	28,189
Japan	152,708	20,151	172,859	104,252	17,609	121,861
Korea, Rep. of	56,319	16,262	72,581	71,262	16,070	87,332
Malaysia[b]	6,861	7,243	14,104	9,082	13,076	22,158
Philippines	—	—	—	4,913	5,157	10,070
Singapore	—	—	11,349	—	—	15,753
Thailand	8,955	6,907	15,862	13,601	8,838	22,439
United States	139,713	21,344	161,057	229,721	31,045	260,766

— Not available.

a. Data for 1994 and 1996.

b. Data for 1995 and 1997.

Source: World Intellectual Property Organization (1994, 1999).

universities and businesses. Some argue that universities should not have too close a relationship with industry, for fear that the needs of industry will dictate the research directions of universities, thereby undermining universities' autonomy, limiting the scale of basic research, and narrowing its compass. But underutilizing the fruits of university research is wasteful from a social standpoint.

Policymakers in different countries may want to resolve these tradeoffs in different ways. They have several pathways for encouraging business-relevant research in universities and for transferring intellectual property from universities to industry: licensing by universities, research collaboration between universities and industries, consulting by faculty members, and participation in business ventures. We deal with each of these in turn.

Licensing by Universities. In the United States, the Bayh-Dole Act of 1980 permitted universities to patent and offer exclusive licenses to their inventions and receive royalties to supplement their research budgets.[45] Although the act exerted only a limited influence on the

---

45. Massachusetts Institute of Technology (MIT) was granted 160 patents in 2001. It signed 77 licenses in 2001, generating about $20 million in royalty payments. MIT spends $10 million

volume of research or on the number of inventions, it stimulated an increase in licensing, which was already trending upward during the 1980s.[46] As it is, only a few licenses by universities generate substantial royalty incomes, and most of the licenses have been granted in software that was covered by copyright at the time (Mowery and others 1999).[47] Meanwhile, research has expanded, but for reasons largely other than the provisions of the act. For example, the rapid expansion in biomedical research can be traced to increases in federal support for such programs in the 1970s and to court decisions allowing the patenting of engineered molecules.[48] Both the University of California system and Stanford University saw an increase in invention disclosure and patent applications following passage of the act, although the ratio of patent grants to applications declined (Mowery and Ziedonis 2002).

How do Japanese universities fare in comparison? In 1994 Japanese academic institutions filed 129 patent applications, or only 0.04 percent of the total patent applications in Japan that year, while U.S. academic institutions filed 1.85 percent (1,862) of the total applications in the United States (Yoshihara and Tamai 1999). These statistics must be viewed through the lens of national practices. Because patent applications have relatively high transaction costs in Japan, universities there tend to transfer intellectual property rights to firms informally rather than formally. An estimate of such informal transfers suggests that 600–1,000 patents a year should be attributed to academic institutions or faculties (Kneller 1999). In exchange for intellectual property, firms give the universities grants and endowments, which are administratively less subject to government restrictions. Further, patents are not considered academic accomplishments in Japan (Yoshihara and Tamai 1999). All of these factors contribute to

---

annually on the administration of technology transfer, including the expenses of patent applications. That leaves only $10 million or so of additional funds available for research. On the face of it, the amounts involved are modest. However, the economic effects of MIT's research are enormous, through spin-offs and other avenues (www.mit.edu and personal comments by Richard Lester).

46. In 1980 there were only 25 technology licensing offices in the United States. By 1996 the number had increased to more than 200 (AUTM 1997).

47. Most successful licenses were nonexclusive.

48. Other developments to facilitate the transfer of technology from universities in the United States coincided with passage of the act (Mowery and others 1999).

the use of informal rather than formal mechanisms for the transfer of intellectual property rights from researchers to businesses in Japan.

Research Collaboration between Universities and Industries. Coauthorship between university faculties and industrial researchers has been rising in the United States. In 1981, 22 percent of industrial articles were coauthored in all the fields of engineering and science; by 1995, this figure had risen to 41 percent. Similar trends are apparent in Japan, where industry sources are submitting a growing number of articles to academic journals, and nearly two-thirds of these articles are written jointly with members of university faculties. Most of the collaboration takes place with faculty members from the leading national universities, with fewer collaborators from private universities. The most highly regarded of Japan's research universities are the national universities, especially the former imperial universities. Together, national universities account for 75 percent of the research and development budget of the Ministry of Education, Science, Sports, and Culture (Kneller 1999). Until recently, government R&D funds were allocated through general university funds, predetermined by the hierarchy of the national universities and independent of the actual performance of its R&D effort. However, following the reform of university funding practices, R&D resources are now being distributed with reference to the potential of projects ("Seven Former" 2002).

Consulting by Faculty Members. Especially for smaller firms, consulting by university faculty members is a valuable way to access technology that they may be able to incorporate in their business activities, without having to establish their own R&D units. Although such consulting is commonplace in the United States, it has only recently gained momentum in East Asia. In Japan it continues to be subject to restrictions, out of concern that faculty members may spend more time on outside activities than on teaching.[49] Such a diversion of energies could be a matter of concern for other East Asian countries at-

---

49. Until 1997, when the regulation was relaxed to allow certain types of activities such as R&D in the private sector, faculty members of national universities had few opportunities to engage in outside activities (Hashimoto 1999; Odagiri 1999).

tempting to expand the scale and quality of tertiary education. Thus incentives to strengthen university-business linkages will need to be tempered by the objectives of human resource development and the importance of augmenting the research skills of university graduates.

Participation by Universities in Business Ventures. Business ventures by entrepreneurial university researchers are beginning to catch on in countries such as Korea and Singapore. East Asian governments and universities may want to encourage this further, because entrepreneurial academics combine vision and creativity with focus and the capacity to think laterally (Birley 2002; "Building Scientific Networks" 2002). Research in the United States shows that the participation of academic scientists in business can facilitate the transformation of scientific discoveries into commercially viable products, especially in firms where innovative skills are complemented by good management.

What should universities in East Asia do to promote innovation in business? Over the medium run, they need to concentrate more on diffusing known technologies to firms that may benefit from them. This can be achieved through either consulting or coauthorship between university faculties and industry-based researchers. Industrial firms can also take more initiative in financing university-based labs—or, as Intel has done in the United States, "lablets"—to draw more scientists into research ("Corporate R&D" 2002). In the future, the spread of basic research and the development of advanced technology in universities could enable more East Asian countries to move beyond incremental innovation mainly in processes to embark on innovation in products and services. It remains to be seen whether universities in East Asia can join the ranks of the world's best research institutes. The evidence thus far suggests that this is a long road, even for universities in Japan.

ACHIEVEMENTS AND THE REMAINING AGENDA

A wide gap still needs to be closed before the innovative capability of East Asian economies, other than Japan, Korea, and Taiwan (China), catches up to that of the United States and the Western European countries. Clearly a modern innovation system is a construct that cannot be quickly cobbled together. Most East Asian countries have been working on parts of their innovation system for decades, but the more developed ones now need to recognize fully the interrelatedness of the many parts and to address on a broad front the supply issues, demand stimuli, and institutional prerequisites.

Intellectual property rights are receiving due recognition, but several countries have yet to appreciate their utility and to mobilize the apparatus to register and enforce them. Markets for technology also require more attention, again because the volume of technology transfer, not to mention the pace of innovation, rests on the dependability and policing of agreements between transacting parties.

In other respects, however, governments and companies in East Asia have been more proactive. Korea, Malaysia, and Taiwan (China) have created a large number of research institutes, and a few of these, such as the Industrial and Technology Research Institute in Taiwan, China, and the Korea Advanced Institute of Science and Technology, have proven highly effective.[50] Governments have also begun promoting R&D by providing tax incentives and research grants, although this has not always spurred genuine research, and spending on research in China is still modest (table 4.6). The creation of research consortia in Taiwan, China, has lent momentum to the development of the computer industry, as it has in Japan. Similarly, the setting up of science parks has attracted firms, although in most cases these have failed to give rise to high-tech activities. Most East Asian governments have sought to attract foreign direct investment, offering a range of inducements. But although they have drawn a large volume of capital to East Asia, the technological spillovers are still fairly limited, mainly because of the shortage of skills and innovation capability.

Several East Asian governments, in conjunction with the private sector, have moved quickly to provide risk capital for industry and to begin crafting stock market institutions to launch companies and enable venture capitalists to exit. These are early days, but little of the

---

50. Although many other government research establishments in Korea have a weak track record of performance.

Table 4.6 R&D Spending as a Percentage of GDP, Late 1990s

Country	Year	Spending as a share of GDP
Sweden	1997	3.85
Japan	1998	3.00
Korea, Rep. of	1997	2.89
United States	1997	2.60
Netherlands	1996	2.09
Taiwan, China	1997	1.92
United Kingdom	1998	1.60
Singapore	1997	1.47
China[a]	1997	0.65
Indonesia	1995	0.50
Thailand[b]	2001	0.16

a. Includes non-defense R&D spending only.
b. World Bank 2002e.
Source: National Science Foundation (2000, 2002).

venture capital has resulted in high-tech innovations in key sectors such as electronics, pharmaceuticals, and software.

Much investment has gone into transport and communications infrastructure, which has led to substantial advances in logistics and the level of information technology services. The ports and airports in Hong Kong (China), Inchon, Kuala Lumpur, Shanghai, and Singapore are among the most efficient in the world, with others throughout the region catching up.

Until recently, none of the East Asian economies except Hong Kong, China, and Singapore perceived the advantages of developing a competitive services sector to reinforce their strengths in manufacturing. Only now, and very slowly, is such competition being allowed. Few have accepted the benefits of introducing their own adaptation of the market for corporate control so as to quicken the pace of innovation and productivity growth. Although governments have been active in arranging mergers and creating industrial groups, they are still reluctant to let the market mediate the creation of world-class firms through mergers and takeovers regulated by competition policy. Similarly, progress toward expediting the exit of failing firms has been hesitant and ambivalent.

Over the coming decades, three sets of measures are likely to have the biggest effect on the productivity of innovation systems: those that affect the quality of secondary and higher-level training, those that bring together innovative firms in open, high-tech clusters that become part of international networks, and those that help the region to maximize the gains from information technology. These topics are addressed in the following chapters.

CHAPTER 5

EDUCATION FOR GROWTH

T he educational needs of East Asian countries vary with their level of development. They need to be reassessed now in the context of future aspirations. Until very recently, aside from Japan, all countries in the region could be characterized as passing through the imitative stages of development. During such a phase, the availability of sufficient numbers of workers with good technical skills is a critical requirement, and most of East Asia has been successful on this count. Now, however, a number of countries have reached the point where they aspire to compete at par with the developed countries, at least in a number of specific sectors. Other countries in the region are aiming to reach a similar point in the not too distant future. To realize such ambitions, these countries need to create the capacity for good tertiary education and to foster the creative abilities required for continuous technological innovation at or near the cutting edge.

This chapter reviews the current state of secondary and tertiary education in East Asia, discusses the changes needed to support growth in the future, and presents options for policymakers. It also examines lifelong learning in the context of a broader educational strategy for building dynamic societies.

SECONDARY EDUCATION

Economic growth is positively correlated with secondary education (Barro 1999, 2001; Godo 2002), and both its quantity and quality are important.[1] Analysis of export performance has placed considerable weight on the average years of schooling of East Asian work forces (Chuang 2000; Witte 2000; Wood and Berge 1997). This evidence is supported by empirical findings on the earnings of individual workers, which show that wages and labor market compensation increase as a result of policies that raise school enrollment rates (Duflo 2001).[2] The link between the quality of secondary education, as measured by scores on standardized tests, and economic growth has been demonstrated by Hanushek and Kimko (2000) and Hanushek (2002b).

Enrollment

Over the past four decades, countries in East Asia achieved an impressive expansion in secondary education; in the Republic of Korea and Malaysia secondary enrollment rates now exceed 90 percent. This is well in excess of rates in emerging economies in other regions. In 1970 the average education of the labor force was similar in East Asia and Latin America. Now it is more than nine years in East Asia compared to a little over five years in Latin America (Carnoy 2002).

However, there are countries in the region, such as Indonesia and Vietnam, with secondary enrollment rates still below 50 percent (figure 5.1). For them, expanding enrollment will continue to be a policy priority, requiring an increase in both public and private resources.

---

1. Even though vocational education has contributed to the development of East Asia and will continue to play an important role there, our focus is on general secondary education on the assumption that it has more to contribute to the development of higher-order skills, especially when technological change is rapid (see D. Krueger and Kumar 2002). For an overview of issues in vocational education, see Gill, Fluitman, and Dar (2000) and Gill and Ihm (2000). In Korea demand has already shifted away from vocational education and toward general secondary education, with parents increasingly preferring tertiary education for their children.

2. Positive returns to education are well supported in the microeconomic literature. For a survey of literature on the effect of education on wages in the United States, see Card and Krueger (1994). For similar analysis on Indonesia, see Bedi and Garg (2000). However, mixed findings are reported in macroeconomic research. For instance, Pritchett (2001) argues that the stock of human capital does not explain growth. Bils and Klenow (2000) question the relationship and test for reverse causality; they find that expected growth induces more education, not the reverse. Subsequent efforts have focused on reconciling the findings of micro and macro studies and reestablishing the links between education and growth by incorporating institutional differences (Chuang 2000), by considering the quality of education (Dessus 2001; Hanushek and Kimko 2000), and by using better data sets (de la Fuente and Domenech 2000; A. Krueger and Lindahl 1999, 2001). See Hanushek (2002b) for a discussion on quality of education and the long-run growth of an economy.

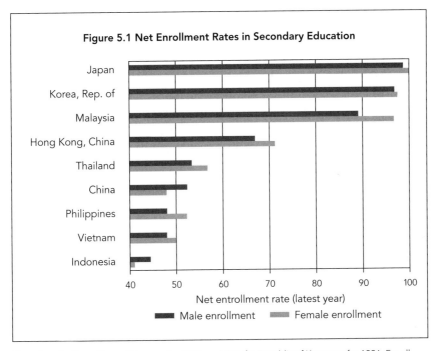

Figure 5.1 Net Enrollment Rates in Secondary Education

Net enrollment rate (latest year)

■ Male enrollment   ■ Female enrollment

Note: Data for Hong Kong, China, are for 1995, and data for Republic of Korea are for 1996. For all other economies, data are for 1998.
Source: World Bank, *World Development Indicators* (various years).

There are a number of successful examples from the region that can be emulated depending on circumstances. To increase enrollment in Thailand, the National Education Act of 1999 extended compulsory education from six to nine years and guaranteed 12 years of free education (Thailand, Ministry of Education 2000). To support the act, the government has been allocating 20 percent of the budget for education, which, as a share of gross domestic product (GDP), is comparable to spending in Korea (World Bank 2000i). If low enrollment rates reflect inadequate investments in schools and associated infrastructure, then evidence from Indonesia and Thailand supports the case for increased investment.[3]

---

3. In Indonesia 61,000 schools were constructed during 1973–78, increasing school enrollment rates of children ages 7 to 12 from about 70 percent in 1973 to over 80 percent in 1978 (Duflo 2001). In Thailand between 1995 and 1996, the number of lower secondary schools increased from 5,661 to 7,991 and the number of upper secondary schools increased from 2,049 to 2,817 (UNESCO 2001).

The schools need not be provided entirely by the state sector. Indeed, in certain East Asian economies—notably Indonesia, Japan, Korea, the Philippines, and Taiwan (China)—private schools have led the surge in secondary education (Mingat 1998; see table 5.1).[4] Moreover, the presence of private schools may well have other benefits. In the Philippines costs per pupil tend to be lower in private schools than in public schools both in secondary and tertiary education (UNESCO 2001). Private funding and management are more efficient than public funding and management in Indonesia (James, King, and Suryadi 1996). In addition, adults who attended private schools as students tend to earn higher wages after controlling for selection bias (Bedi and Garg 2000). In Thailand the cost of teaching students in private institutions is 25–35 percent less per student than the cost in public institutions, although the extent of the resulting quality differential is unknown (World Bank 2000i). Similarly in Korea the ratio of expenditure per pupil for private to public upper secondary schools was 0.58 in 1997. The gap between the cost per pupil has widened since 1987, when the ratio was 0.73 (OECD 1998).

Quality

Two dimensions of educational quality are relevant to the discussion. The first relates to the thoroughness of basic education and is often proxied by students' scores on national and international tests, typically in mathematics and science. The second dimension, of more recent interest, relates to cognitive ability as reflected in the ability to think creatively. In most countries in East Asia, attention is now shifting to this second aspect of educational quality, as economies seek to become more innovative in an increasingly open and competitive environment. We discuss the two dimensions in turn.

Test Scores. Educational performance varies considerably among the East Asian economies, as measured by scores on international tests in mathematics and science. Based on results from the Third International

---

4. In Indonesia 33 and 54 percent of students at lower and upper secondary levels, respectively, are enrolled in private schools; in Korea the respective enrollments are 24 and 59 percent. In the Philippines, 32 percent of middle school students are enrolled in private schools (UNESCO 2001).

Table 5.1 Total Spending on Education as a Percentage of GDP in East Asia, 1998

Economy	Public	Private
China	2.29[a]	1.10[b]
Hong Kong, China	4.20[c]	1.10[c]
Indonesia	1.43	2.20[d]
Japan	3.48	1.15
Korea, Rep. of	4.07	2.99
Malaysia	4.62[e]	0.11[a]
Philippines	3.20	2.88[f]
Singapore	3.07[d]	0.50[b]
Thailand	4.70	0.30[b]

a. 1996.
b. 1990.
c. 2001.
d. 1995.
e. 1997.
f. 1994.

Sources: World Bank *World Development Indicators* (various years); World Bank, EDSTATS; OECD Education database; Hong Kong, China, Education and Manpower Bureau.

Math and Science Study-Repeat (TIMSS-R), Hong Kong (China), Korea, Japan, Singapore, and Taiwan (China) occupied the top five spots in mathematics among the 38 countries that participated in the test in 1998 (see table 5.2). Malaysia followed these high-performing countries, scoring above the United States. Thailand scored a little lower than the international average, followed by Indonesia and the Philippines, with scores substantially lower than the international average.

In science, Taiwan, China, led the field, followed closely by Japan, Korea, and Singapore. The only upper- or middle-income East Asian economy not in the top five was Hong Kong, China, which ranked fifteenth in science. The rankings of Indonesia, Malaysia, the Philippines, and Thailand in science roughly mirrored their rankings in math. Thus there are five relatively high-scoring economies—Hong Kong (China), Japan, Korea, Singapore, and Taiwan, China—with others (Indonesia, the Philippines, and Thailand) struggling to reach the international average and Malaysia in between the two groups and trying to move up.

The priority for countries where test scores are low is to find ways to overcome the weaknesses in basic education. Here we report the results of research undertaken for this study on the determinants of

Table 5.2 Quality of Secondary Education, by Country Rankings, 1998

Economy	Rank	Average score
Math		
Singapore[a]	1	604
Korea, Rep. of[a]	2	587
Taiwan, China[a]	3	585
Hong Kong, China[a]	4	582
Japan[a]	5	579
Malaysia[a]	16	519
United States[a]	19	502
International average	n.a.	487
Thailand[b]	27	467
Indonesia[b]	34	403
Philippines[b]	36	345
Science		
Taiwan, China[a]	1	569
Singapore[a]	2	568
Japan[a]	4	550
Korea, Rep. of[a]	5	549
Hong Kong, China[a]	15	530
United States[a]	18	515
Malaysia	22	492
International average	n.a.	488
Thailand	24	482
Indonesia[b]	32	435
Philippines[b]	36	345

n.a. Not applicable.

Note: The United States is included for reference purposes. The ranking is based on 38 economies that participated in TIMSS-R.

a. Significantly higher than the international average.

b. Significantly lower than the international average.

Sources: Martin and others (1999); Mullis and others (1999).

student achievement using scores from the TIMSS-R database, which provides one of the few internationally comparable data sets available on education outcomes. The research uses an education production function approach and focuses on variation within countries rather than between countries (Nabeshima 2002a; Woessmann 2001). The analysis is based on extensive information on students' innate abilities, home resources, and family backgrounds, along with teacher and school characteristics.[5] This information is gathered by

---

5. Students' innate ability is captured by their response to the survey question, "How well do you usually do in math/science?" Even though we are not sure whether students answer this

surveys conducted as part of TIMSS-R. Such information is typically lacking in other studies of student achievement, and it provides fresh insight into the factors influencing student achievement.

The results suggest that after controlling for student ability and home resources, class size has little effect on test scores in a number of East Asian countries (tables 5.3 and 5.4).[6] The research also shows that teacher autonomy has minimal influence on test scores (Nabeshima 2002a). In the analysis, autonomy is represented by the ability of math and science teachers to choose textbooks, course content, or both. The hypothesis is that teachers with a high degree of autonomy are able to choose textbooks and pedagogies best suited to improving students' understanding. The results indicate that teacher autonomy improves student achievement in math in Indonesia, Malaysia, and the Philippines. In science, Malaysia is the only country in which teacher autonomy has a significant positive effect.

The research findings on teacher autonomy are highly dependent on the inclusion or exclusion of other variables in the specification. However, the results for the basic variables (gender, innate ability, and home resources) are stable, of expected sign, and significant. This suggests that various combinations of factors, such as the combination of quality of teachers and autonomy, may be more important than individual factors alone.[7]

The analysis does find that teachers' qualifications are, in general, important to student achievement, especially in science.[8] This is consistent with research in the United States, which suggests that performance improves in classes where teachers set high standards and grade accordingly (Figlio and Lucas 2000; "What Makes Sally Learn"

---

question truthfully, the results across different specifications indicate that the response to this question is a good predictor of student performance. Home resources are measured by the number of books at home, parents' educational background, and the presence of other educational materials. Family background reflects household composition (living with a single parent, number of siblings, and the like).

6. However, smaller classes do benefit math students in Hong Kong, China.

7. A case study from Chile shows that student achievement improved when teacher autonomy was coupled with autonomy in the hiring of teachers (Vegas 2002).

8. These results contrast with the findings of Hanushek and Luque (2002) that teacher quality has relatively few positive effects. The difference may be attributed to the definition of teachers' qualifications. Nabeshima (2002a) uses the qualification defined by the education authority in each economy, whereas Hanushek and Luque (2002) use the possession of a bachelor's degree as the qualification.

Table 5.3 Determinants of Math Performance in East Asia and the United States

Indicator	Hong Kong, China	Indonesia	Japan	Korea, Rep. of	Malaysia	Philippines	Singapore	Thailand	Taiwan, China	United States
Boy	4.21	14***	−6.58***	−2.24	−4.99***	1.42	−19.29***	11.19***	−1.79	4.01
	(2.63)	(3.84)	(2.45)	(2.34)	(1.94)	(3.86)	(2.72)	(3.19)	(2.4)	(2.7)
Low home resources	0.05	−10.34**		−34.4***	−14.82***	−3.71	1.98	−10.9***	−32.07***	−35.83***
	(3.04)	(4.48)		(5.1)	(2.35)	(4.5)	(5.82)	(3.57)	(4.71)	(7.12)
High home resources	8.50	−9.98		20.23***	31.79***	−2.50	−6.84	26.17**	25.37***	28.5***
	(7.36)	(12.03)		(2.83)	(4.13)	(9.17)	(6.82)	(10.6)	(4.22)	(3.38)
Teacher is qualified	30.79***	−3.64	15.9**	12.73**	−3.53	−75.09***	109.51***	8.44	−8.63**	
	(5.79)	(7.35)	(7.22)	(5.71)	(2.57)	(23.46)	(15.01)	(8.94)	(3.87)	
Class	−15.32***	14.1***	4.91	1.21	−3.99***	28.37***	87.58***	−4.34*	−12.43***	1.89***
	(2.36)	(2.03)	(12.53)	(0.76)	(0.82)	(6.12)	(10.28)	(2.33)	(1.9)	(0.48)
City	34.74***	72.38***	6.44	15.14**	30.91***	73.3***		30.81***	28.61***	−30.49***
	(9.75)	(16.52)	(5.26)	(6.93)	(2.76)	(23.1)		(10.15)	(7.51)	(5.22)
Auto1	29.01	−58.14*	1.39	−4.75	49.7***	−227.45***		73.99***	−4.17	−12.72
	(19.24)	(30.13)	(5.33)	(6.52)	(6.34)	(55.42)		(15.59)	(7.48)	(8.11)
Auto2	−4.94	34.54	−30.26**	−9.77	−23.06***	−38.93		72.48*	10.28	−36.17
	(20.53)	(25.83)	(13.73)	(6.04)	(6.04)	(44.06)		(40.43)	(6.3)	(24.42)
Auto3		293.2***		−2.04	56.61***	110.88***		19.37	3.19	−14.6**
		(27.09)		(5.16)	(6.93)	(27.44)		(24.32)	(6.66)	(7.16)

*** Significant at 1 percent. ** Significant at 5 percent. * Significant at 10 percent.

Note: "Low home resources" and "high home resources" are dummies with "medium home resources" as the reference point. These dummies were constructed by TIMSS using availability of educational materials at home and parent's education. "Teacher is qualified" is a dummy based on whether teachers in each economy meet country-specific qualification criteria. auto1 is a dummy variable for "cannot choose textbook but can choose content," auto2 is for "can choose textbook but not content," and auto3 is for "can choose textbook and content." The table includes only select variables of interest. The actual specification includes more variables, including student family structure, self-assessment, peer effect, aspiration, homework policies, and so forth.

Source: Nabeshima (2002a).

Table 5.4 Determinants of Science Performance in East Asia and the United States

Indicator	Hong Kong, China	Indonesia	Japan	Korea, Rep. of	Malaysia	Philippines	Singapore	Thailand	Taiwan, China	United States
Boy	8.31***	33.01***	3.14	11.44***	14.44***	2.57	-2.53	17.78***	10.7***	16.46***
	(2.98)	(3.17)	(2.54)	(2.73)	(2.19)	(4.55)	(2.57)	(2.73)	(2.18)	(3.68)
Low home resources	-0.38	-1.09		-37.19***	-21.35***	1.55	19.26***	-0.54	-24.61***	-31.15***
	(3.37)	(3.52)		(5.27)	(2.58)	(5.18)	(4.21)	(2.86)	(4.09)	(8.6)
High home resources	26.12***	4.46		29.06***	35.69***	-1.47	12.37	20.65***	23.98***	25.24***
	(8.3)	(11.14)		(3.34)	(5)	(11.77)	(7.71)	(7.39)	(3.73)	(4.48)
Teacher is qualified	13.14***	82.36***	3.17	4.02	14.94***	59.54***	-714.52***	9.02**	8.10	
	(4.83)	(20.68)	(4.52)	(5.36)	(3.02)	(11.02)	(64.44)	(4.47)	(6.83)	
Class	-9.97	24.12***	5.98**	1.03	-4.95***	-12.17***	232.81***	-3.54***	-10.67***	1.48
	(6.27)	(5.45)	(2.79)	(0.88)	(1.79)	(3.92)	(25.05)	(0.88)	(2.14)	(1.07)
City	19.54	-61.66*	-21.81***	-9.97	14.65***	49.47**		29.92***	20.87***	-12.65
	(13.8)	(32.05)	(5.97)	(7.95)	(3.3)	(20.98)		(8.39)	(7.14)	(9.09)
Auto1	40.67*	-252.35***	4.60	-4.10	3.76	-258.13***		18.34*	-5.23	-7.01
	(24.62)	(42.72)	(5.22)	(6.3)	(7.07)	(31.78)		(10.15)	(6.71)	(21.34)
Auto2	-139.13***		-13.40	0.80	8.45	142.7***		15.96	0.31	73.4***
	(32.55)		(12.52)	(8.43)	(6.75)	(23.62)		(16.69)	(5.77)	(24.46)
Auto3		-52.76	11.31	-0.69	47.24***			-20.15**	2.28	-11.29
		(46.65)	(12.87)	(6.73)	(6.56)			(10.27)	(6.45)	(12.87)

*** Significant at 1 percent.

** Significant at 5 percent.

* Significant at 10 percent.

Note: See table 5.3 for the definition of variables.

Source: Nabeshima (2002a).

2001, p. 38). The analysis also confirms that students perform better when their home environment both supports studying and demands excellence at school.[9]

In sum, as far as raising test scores is concerned, evidence from research using the TIMSS-R database suggests that teacher ability and home environment are the determining variables, while class size and teacher autonomy do not seem to be particularly relevant instruments. This conclusion is not surprising given that the East Asian countries that rank high on test scores are focusing on teacher ability and home environment rather than on class size and teacher autonomy.

Cognitive Ability. Even in the East Asian countries ranking high on test scores, there is a growing concern that secondary students are not being sufficiently equipped to think critically and creatively. This inability becomes a major handicap at the tertiary level of education. Educational specialists such as Mok and Morris (2001) characterize secondary classroom teaching in the region as embracing a "whole-class instructional style," using terms such as "mechanical" and "rote" learning to describe the pedagogical approach. Parents and governments in Japan, Korea, and Singapore all express worries about this aspect of upper secondary schooling (J. Lee 2001).[10] Reflecting such worries, policymakers in these countries are searching for ways to foster creativity in secondary education in order to provide the foundation for innovative research at the tertiary level.

---

9. The importance of family and home resources for student achievement is well documented. For recent studies on this issue, see Hanushek and Luque (2002) and Nabeshima (2002a). See also Ermisch and Fancesconi (2001) on the United Kingdom; Lee and Barro (1997) on a cross-sectional analysis of countries; and Liu, Hammitt, and Lin (2000) on Taiwan, China. Parents in Korea spend as much as 25 percent of their income to support their children's education through private tutoring, preparatory schools, and supplementary educational materials (J. Lee 2001).

10. An extreme opinion from Korea states, "After years of churning out students who top the world in math and science skills, Korea's schools are falling apart. Record numbers of children are dropping out, the teen suicide rate is soaring, and stressed-out students are becoming increasingly violent in the classroom. A recent survey on behalf of the National Assembly found that 65 percent of Koreans believe that the education system is in crisis. Families are so desperate to shield their children from the harsh classroom environment that they are leaving their homeland altogether in what has become known as education emigration" ("Lessons in Learning" 2002, p. 53).

Improving Cognitive Abilities

There is not much by way of definitive research findings to aid these efforts. Indeed, there is not even much consensus on how to measure student creativity. More often than not, the lack of dynamism in tertiary education and innovation in industry is attributed in part to a presumed lack of critical thinking in the pool of secondary school graduates. We discuss first some initiatives in pedagogical reform in the region and review measures that have been tried across the world to foster critical thinking and enhance cognitive ability. These include experiments with smaller class size, decentralization and more teacher autonomy, better teacher compensation, competition among schools, and the use of information and communications technology (ICT) in teaching. In a subsequent section we examine the state of tertiary education in the region.

Pedagogical Reform. A leading advocate of pedagogical reform, Hong Kong, China, introduced a target-oriented curriculum in the early 1990s. This emphasized "pupil activity, self-regulation, and pupil-centeredness, with much more cooperative and other group work" (Mok and Morris 2001, p. 458), small classes, greater autonomy for teachers, and higher expectations for performance, among other elements (Hong Kong, China, Education and Manpower Bureau 2001). To effect these changes, more resources were provided to schools, and further teacher training was made available—all supported by a strong commitment from the educational authorities. Mok and Morris (2001), looking at mathematics teaching after the reform, find that small but tangible steps had been taken, moving teaching away from the teacher-dominated or teacher-as-virtuoso pedagogical model.[11] Even so, teachers reportedly had great difficulty translating the rhetoric of a target-oriented curriculum into reality in the classroom (Dimmock and Walker 1998).

In Japan, where the school system is often characterized as rigid and uniform, reform is under way to stress the interests of individual

---

11. They conclude that the target-oriented curriculum "may have contributed to the adaptation of the nature of pedagogy used in mathematics classrooms, specifically the extensive incidence of group work over three years, the decline in the extent of pupil non-participation, and the increase in pupils answering teachers' questions" (Mok and Morris 2001, p. 467).

students rather than a uniform curriculum. A new subject, known as integrated learning, was introduced in 2002. What is unique about this subject is that, contrary to past practice, the Ministry of Education initially provided little guidance on how to teach it, allowing teachers significant latitude. The only specific guideline was that this class should be used to foster the ability to think, learn, and explore independently and creatively. The Ministry of Education ultimately published guidebooks on how to teach the integrated learning classes because many teachers and local school boards did not know how to approach such courses (Cave 2001; Muta 2000).

Teacher Autonomy and Decentralization. The current state of thinking on this subject is that teachers should be granted more autonomy in the classroom and in their choice of teaching materials and course content, but that this is not sufficient by itself. It should be accompanied by decentralization of authority allowing individual secondary schools to hire and promote teachers and determine compensation to some extent, so as to attract the most talented teachers. Decentralization involves moving away from central government dictates or tight control by regional or local authorities over the employment conditions of teachers. To be sure, these authorities retain an interest in ensuring that certain minimum standards are met.[12] Nevertheless, the tendency to micro manage school staffing and class content should be avoided.[13]

Most empirical studies regarding the effectiveness of decentralization are from Latin American countries where decentralization of education has been actively pursued since the 1990s. Jiménez and Sawada (1999) find that decentralization in El Salvador led to improvements in language skills and a reduction in student absences, primarily by making schools more accountable to local communities. Eskeland and Filmer (2002), investigating the effects of decentralization in Argenti-

12. For instance, countries can offer national tests to assess student achievement, as implemented in the Philippines (National Secondary Achievement Test) and in Korea (National Assessment of Scholastic Achievement). In terms of school quality, the Office for National Education Standards in Thailand goes so far as to evaluate every school and to publicize the ratings (UNESCO 2001).

13. Chapman (2000) discusses the effects of decentralization on quality of education, and Woessmann (2001) examines the relationship between institutional arrangement and student achievement.

na, find that more school autonomy is closely related to higher student achievement. There are a number of studies on decentralization in Chile, where the implementation of decentralization is widely viewed as successful (see Parry 1997; Vegas 2002).

However, the degree of improvement expected in the quality of education thus far has not been realized. One reason could be that the introduction of decentralization measures does not necessarily lead to implementation, as pointed out by E. M. King, Ozler, and Rawlings (1999). Another confounding issue is that decentralization is often introduced for political rather than educational reasons. In such cases, it is not surprising that there is little change in the learning environment. Moreover, shifting authority and responsibilities to local school administrators with inadequate experience and training will not yield the intended results. In her analysis of Thai educational reforms after the financial crisis, Witte (2000) speculates that the desire to build consensus around national educational policy initiatives came at the price of vagueness, which allowed teachers and officials to interpret rules as they liked. In Hong Kong, China, in 1991, the government announced the School Management Initiative, which resembles school-based management in the United States (Dimmock and Walker 1998). Despite evidence that standards of teaching improve and teachers have more flexibility in their use of resources following decentralization, student scores have not improved.

In most economies in East Asia, teacher autonomy has not as yet significantly changed the way teachers behave in the classroom. Table 5.5 depicts differences in the use of teaching methods by teachers with different degrees of autonomy. The TIMSS data set contains information on 25 teaching methods and three degrees of teacher autonomy, as measured by the ability of teachers to choose their textbooks, content, or both. In most countries, the teachers who had a choice of textbooks, content, or both chose roughly the same teaching methods as teachers who had no choice. The most significant impact of autonomy is seen in science teaching in the United States, where teachers who were allowed to choose both the content and the textbook employed seven teaching methods different from those employed by teachers with no autonomy. In other cases, even where teachers have been granted more autonomy, the learning and teaching environment has not changed enough to promote diverse styles

Table 5.5 Differences in Teaching Methods among Teachers with Different Degrees of Discretion and Autonomy

Economy	Math			Science		
	Can choose content but not textbook	Can choose textbook but not content	Can choose textbook and content	Can choose content but not textbook	Can choose textbook but not content	Can choose textbook and content
Hong Kong, China	0	0	0	0	0	0
Indonesia	1	0	2	2	1	1
Japan	1	1	2	0	0	0
Korea, Rep. of	0	0	0	0	0	0
Malaysia	2	3	2	1	0	1
Philippines	0	2	1	1	1	1
Singapore	—	—	—	—	—	—
Thailand	1	0	0	1	0	1
Taiwan, China	1	1	3	0	1	0
United States	1	2	1	3	2	7

— Not available.

Note: The number indicates the counts of statistically different responses given by teachers with partial and full autonomy compared to responses from teachers with no autonomy. The table is based on 25 different teaching methods or styles recorded in the TIMSS survey. Data for Singapore are not available because very few teachers have autonomy.

Source: Nabeshima (2002a), based on TIMSS data.

of teaching. This result confirms the findings of recent studies in East Asia, which suggest that even where schools and teachers have been granted discretion by policy or law, classroom teaching style has changed little (Nabeshima 2002a).

Decentralization clearly poses complex issues regarding the responsibilities to be delegated to the local level. Existing research suggests that decentralization of finance typically increases inequity in both access to and quality of education. Giving local autonomy to teachers alone does not seem to affect classroom conduct. The complexity of education systems means that several factors, including teacher qualification, community involvement, and school management, interact with one another to determine student achievement. Further research has been recommended to assess the kind of decentralization that would most effectively deliver the desired results (Glewwe 2002).

Teachers in much of East Asia may well lack incentives to deviate from preexisting norms of pedagogy and face little pressure from schools and parents to do so. They may also lack knowledge about alternatives. Decentralization needs to be accompanied by proper training for both administrators and teachers if it is to achieve its intended goals (Chapman 2000). Without such reform, teachers are likely to follow templates or frameworks laid down by authorities that may be either too rigid to allow autonomy or too vague to indicate priorities.

Competition. Increasing competition for teacher talent and for students is another initiative that has been experimented with to improve the quality of education. Competition would allow students to choose among existing private and public schools. Benchmarks would be needed to enable families, administrators, and public officials to evaluate the performance of both teachers and schools. The benchmarks would have to address many dimensions of performance if they are to inform parents (who "hire" schools) and administrators (who hire "teachers"). Experience from the United States suggests that competition between public and private schools offering similar types of secondary education enhances student achievement and induces a shift away from private school attendance (Hoxby 2000); it also improves teacher quality in public schools (Hanushek and Rivkin 2001).

Similarly in the United Kingdom, after the introduction of school choice (among other reform initiatives), student achievement improved dramatically without increasing the level of education spending (Glennerster 2002). Finally, the Shinagawa Board of Education in Tokyo introduced the school choice system for public elementary schools in April 2000 and has plans to expand it to lower secondary schools (Muta 2000).[14]

The competition facing public schools is intense in the presence of established private schools.[15] Under such circumstances, either the freedom of public schools to differentiate themselves from others will improve student achievement or fears about private sector "cherry picking" will come to the fore. Some governments may choose to provide direct support to families, supplying funds to use at the secondary schools of their choice.[16]

Teacher Quality. A motivation behind the push for decentralization and more competition among schools is the desire to recruit better-qualified teachers, while maintaining their motivation and quality over time.[17] To achieve this, teachers' pay must compete with the pay

14. Since upper secondary schooling in Japan is not compulsory, there is a significant degree of competition and sorting among schools, especially in urban areas.

15. Care must be given to the distinction between private and public schools. For example, although private upper secondary schools in Korea are well established, they are not private schools in the usual sense. Decisions on curriculum and tuition are made by the government, and the allocation of students is randomized across public and private schools. As a result, competition among schools is nonexistent. J. Lee (2001) views this lack of competition as one of the factors contributing to the poor performance of upper secondary education in Korea.

16. Using data from the Milwaukee Parental Choice Program in the United States, Rouse (1998) finds a modest increase in the performance of students who participated in the program compared to students who did not. However, Levin (1998) questions whether voucher systems are more efficient and equitable than the current U.S. system. See Ladd (2002) and Neal (2002) for a review of voucher schemes.

17. The current sentiment in the United States is that teacher quality is lower than it used to be and lower than quality in other professions. Lakdawalla (2001) finds that the relative human capital possessed by teachers compared to other workers has been declining throughout the twentieth century, mainly due to skill-biased technological change outside the teaching profession. That is, workers in other occupations have been accumulating more education faster than teachers have. This is especially true for teachers in primary schools, where general knowledge is taught. Strauss and others (2000) find that average SAT scores of students who intend to pursue an education major are around the thirty-fifth percentile in Pennsylvania. In addition, the passing score for standardized tests in Pennsylvania and other states that use the same test as part of their certification requirement is around the twenty-fifth percentile. Because of this low requirement, the passing rate is better than 95 percent for all applicants (Strauss and others 2000). Angrist and Lavy (2001) find that in-service training for teachers leads to better student performance, pointing to the importance of providing in-service training to refresh teaching skills.

Table 5.6 Relative Pay of Teachers

Economy	Teacher pay in U.S. dollars[a]			Ratio of pay to per capita GDP		
	Starting	15 year	Maximum	Starting	15 year	Maximum
United States	27,643	40,072	47,908	0.77	1.12	1.34
Japan	22,670	42,820	54,663	0.86	1.62	2.07
China	2,835	2,952	3,595	0.85	0.88	1.11
Hong Kong, China[b]	20,973	40,289	57,786	1.07	2.06	2.96
Indonesia	1,357	2,148	4,093	0.49	0.77	1.47
Korea, Rep. of	26,148	43,800	69,666	1.48	2.48	3.94
Malaysia	11,784	18,632	25,775	1.54	2.43	3.36
Philippines	10,409	11,491	12,374	2.80	3.10	3.34
Thailand	5,756	14,145	26,977	1.00	2.47	4.71
Taiwan, China[b]	15,060	22,590	30,120	1.12	1.68	2.24

a. At purchasing power parity.
b. 1992.
Sources: F. H. Nelson (1994); OECD (2002).

they could earn from other occupations (OECD 2002). This will be a challenge where the teacher population is aging and teachers are facing worsening working conditions as a result of both low pay and heavier workloads (Liang 2001; Santiago 2001; see also "World Teacher Crisis Looms" 2002).[18]

However, the evidence linking teachers' compensation to student achievement is mixed. Within East Asia, Malaysia and the Philippines offer the most generous wages to teachers (table 5.6), yet their students do not perform as well as those from other economies. Lavy (2002) finds that an incentive-based pay system does indeed lead to better student achievement in the United States, and Kingdon and Teal (2002) report that, in India, higher teacher pay has a positive effect on student achievement.[19] In contrast, Hanushek, Kain, and

18. Research in the United States shows that better-performing teachers tend to leave teaching for other jobs, attracted by the wage premium of as much as 40 percent in other professions (Temin 2002). This may be attributed to the growing opportunities available for women in the workplace. In the past, when occupations were segregated along gender lines, women had limited choice. However, when alternative occupations began to materialize, many highly qualified teachers and potential teachers were able to choose these occupations rather than teaching.

19. Their interpretation of the results differs from that of others. They argue that there are two different interpretations of the relationship between higher pay and higher student performance. One way of interpreting this relationship is to say that higher wages attract higher-quality teachers, which leads to higher achievement by students. A second way of interpreting this relationship is to point to the efficiency wage argument. That is, at higher wages, teachers will exert more effort not to lose their attractive jobs even if monitoring teacher effort is hard. Their results confirm the latter argument.

Rivkin (1999) find no relationship between teacher salaries and student achievement. Higher salaries do seem to affect the mobility of teachers among schools (Loeb and Page 2000).

Schools seem to have difficulty retaining well-qualified teachers once they are hired (Santiago 2001), but the reasons why many teachers leave the profession continue to be debated. Stinebrickner (2002) shows that for young, female teachers in the United States, the decision has more to do with the responsibilities of bearing children and raising a family than with the job itself. Half those who had left teaching were now earning less than when they were teachers. Stinebrickner also finds that higher wages can slow the exit rate of these young, female teachers, if they enable individuals to pay for day care services.

In principle, offering performance-based incentives to teachers could reduce attrition. However, this approach faces a number of obstacles. The first is the difficulty of measuring output. Measuring only easily observable achievements such as test scores can lead teachers to "teach to the test" (Jacob 2002). Further, students' overall performance is not determined by a single teacher, but by many teachers in different subjects. Incentives administered at the central level do not function as well as incentives administered at the local level by administrators who are well trained and well informed.[20] Nonetheless, private schools in the United States routinely use merit pay, suggesting that merit pay has some utility (Ballou 2001).[21]

Information and Communications Technology. Increasingly, policies in East Asia require adopting ICT in the classroom. Educators and policymakers perceive that familiarity with new technology should be part of the regular curriculum and that the adoption of new technology in the classroom may itself improve the quality of education.[22] For

---

20. See Chapman (2002) for the future demands placed on school management in Asia.

21. Ballou and Podgursky (1998) argue that the advantage of private schools lies precisely in the flexibility they have with regard to pay and hiring decisions. Kingdon and Teal (2002) find that hiring and remuneration practices differ between public and private schools in India. They find that neither type of school differentiates pay by the educational level of teachers. However, public schools seem to consider the experience of teachers much more than do private schools, whereas private schools pay more for teachers with preservice training.

22. Another potentially beneficial use of information and communications technology in education is distance learning, especially in countries such as Indonesia and the Philippines, with

instance, the relative ease of accessing vast amounts of information through the Internet, the presentation of materials using multimedia, and collaboration with other individuals, possibly located quite far from the school, can improve the classroom experience and ultimately may lead to improvements in cognitive skills.

Guided by these beliefs, schools in East Asia have been investing heavily in ICT for educational use. Hong Kong, China, mandated that each school must have a minimum number of computers connected to the Internet by the start of the 2001–02 school year (Hong Kong, China, Education and Manpower Bureau 2001). In Japan almost all schools have computers, and half of them have Internet connections (Japan, Ministry of Education 2000).[23] Between 1997 and 2000 Korea invested $1.48 billion to install computers, and Taiwan, China, is pushing to achieve universal computer and Internet access at the lower secondary level and above (Korea, Ministry of Education 2001; Taiwan, China, Ministry of Education 1999).[24]

To make the best use of such new technology requires additional investment in teacher training. However, that is easier said than done. All teachers in Hong Kong, China, had completed basic training in information technology by the start of the 2001–02 school year (Hong Kong, China, Education and Manpower Bureau 2001). And experience from Singapore shows that, even after training in the use of information technology was made compulsory in 1986, teachers still felt inexperienced and lacking in the skills they needed to integrate information technology in the classroom (P. Wang and Chan 1995).[25]

Furthermore, in order to improve the quality of education in the classroom, policymakers need to change the curriculum to accommo-

---

their many islands, and China, with its vast inland areas. The scope for distance learning is larger in tertiary education and lifelong learning than in secondary education.

23. As of March 1999 the Internet was used in 27 percent of primary, 43 percent of lower secondary, and 64 percent of upper secondary schools in Japan (OECD 2000a).

24. A billion is 1,000 million.

25. Reflecting this, Singapore has put teacher training as the centerpiece for the Masterplan for Information Technology in Education (1997–2002), providing teachers with 30–50 hours of core information technology training (Shanmugaratnam 2002). In the United States, teacher training in relevant software and applications is seldom offered when hardware is installed (Cuban 2001).

date the adoption of information and communications technology.[26] Wenglinsky (1998) finds that the impact of computers depends more on how teachers use them in the classroom than on the intensity of their use. In the United States, the adoption of ICT in the classroom has been successful when it has been associated with extensive teacher training and a change in curriculum ("Wired Schools" 2000).[27] Similarly, Hong Kong, China, mandates that 25 percent of classroom activities should be delivered with the active use of ICT (Hong Kong, China, Education and Manpower Bureau 2001). Taiwan, China, has mandated at least one hour of computer class per student per week (Taiwan, China, Ministry of Education 1999).

To date, however, there have been few systematic studies documenting the effect of investment in ICT on cognitive ability. A survey administered to a random sample of 4,700 students and 2,200 teachers in primary and secondary schools and junior colleges in Singapore reports that 82 percent of the students felt that information technology had increased their knowledge, 77 percent felt that it had improved their learning, and 77 percent felt that they had been encouraged to learn beyond the curriculum (Shanmugaratnam 2002). Among the teachers, 68 percent felt that information technology had encouraged more active student participation in class.

Problems with the effective integration of information technology into teaching have been much more widely reported. Angrist and Lavy (2002) find that teachers do not alter instructional methods significantly and do not receive training until after new computers arrive. Cuban (2001) finds in a study in California that most teachers were using the newly acquired machines mainly for administrative tasks (recording grades and preparing classes) rather than integrating them into the classroom. In the European Union, both the investment in computers and the number of teachers with adequate train-

---

26. The question remains as to whether the advance in technology is the cause of or merely a vehicle for a change in curriculum (Cuban 2001). Malaysia has taken the second position in implementing its Smart School Initiative. According to the Malaysia Ministry of Education, the main aim of this effort is to make learning more student-centered, supplemented by heavy investment in information and communications technology.

27. For the majority of elementary and secondary schools in the United States, however, the adoption of information and communications technology is low, and by and large teachers have not changed the way they communicate with parents and the way they teach ("Technology and You" 2002).

ing to use ICT effectively in the classroom are lagging behind investment in other regions ("Europe's Low-Tech Schools" 2002).[28] Furthermore, like other "new" technologies in the past (radio, film, and television), teachers tend to use computers as a tool to supplement their current teaching style rather than to transform their techniques. When these new technologies became available, many educators believed that they would transform the way students learn. For instance, in 1922, Thomas Edison proclaimed, "The motion picture is destined to revolutionize our educational system and . . . in a few years it will supplant largely, if not entirely, the use of textbooks" (as quoted in "Pass the Chalk" 2002). But, by and large, textbooks are still widely used, and learning at school has changed little (Cuban 2001).

The broad lesson from these studies is clear: investing in computer hardware is a first step, but changing classroom conduct by effectively harnessing such investments is essential to success.[29] This is not meant to imply that the use of computers does not affect student learning at all. On the contrary, the numerous success stories from around the world suggest otherwise. The question is how ICT should be integrated and how classroom conduct could be changed to take full advantage of the new technology.[30]

Conclusion. The state of secondary education varies considerably across East Asia. Some countries still need to concentrate on expanding enrollment. Others need to concentrate on acquiring the basics of good teaching to enhance technical skills as measured by performance on standardized tests. While all countries should be thinking about fostering the creative abilities of students, the challenge is most immediate for the advanced economies getting ready to compete with global leaders in specific technologies. For them, equipping second-

---

28. In the United States, only 8 percent of the spending allocated for technology adoption in schools was earmarked for teacher training ("Wired Schools" 2000).

29. There are signs that students' behavior changes after computers are introduced in the classroom. In Korea students are starting to question teachers more often than before, suggesting a gradual shift from rote learning to more active participation by students ("Wired Schools, Wired Nations" 2001).

30. Explicitly recognizing that ongoing integration of information technology in the classroom tends to support the existing curriculum, the Second Singapore Masterplan of Information Technology in Education will "seek to integrate information technology into the design of a more flexible and dynamic curriculum" (Shanmugaratnam 2002).

ary school graduates to conduct innovative research at the tertiary level is necessary in order to support economic competitiveness at the cutting edge. At the same time, both the capacity and the quality of tertiary education need to be enhanced to benefit from the creativity of the student pool. We now discuss the state of tertiary education in East Asia and assess its relative strengths and weaknesses.

TERTIARY EDUCATION

An adequate supply of well-trained and creative science and engineering graduates and an environment conducive to world-class research are essential components of economic growth in the future (World Bank 2002a).[31] Science and engineering talent offers the means to assimilate technology and propels innovation in newer industries, such as ICT or biotechnology, while energizing older industries (manufacturing) and emerging sectors such as services (OECD 2001f). Moreover, higher education provides intellectual access to the multitude of new ICT technologies evolving daily; as the use of ICT grows, the demand for skills also rises (Bresnahan and others 2002; OECD 2001f).[32]

University and college education is becoming widespread among the younger generations in leading countries of the Organisation for Economic Co-operation and Development (OECD). In the United States, nearly four-fifths of young adults 24–35 years old have been exposed to at least some tertiary education (World Bank various years). Among economies in East Asia, Korea is the front-runner, with a gross enrollment rate close to 70 percent. Gross tertiary enrollment rates are above or about 40 percent in Hong Kong (China), Japan, Korea, and Singapore, but much lower elsewhere (figure 5.2).

In 1997, just under 1 million students in Asia graduated from institutions of higher education with science and engineering degrees (table 5.7; National Science Foundation 2000).[33] Countries with an

---

31. Even if expatriates and nationals trained abroad continue to provide cutting-edge knowledge, locally trained workers inevitably will supply the bulk of higher-level skills.

32. In fact, the rate of return to tertiary education is higher than in the past, and it has risen over the past three decades relative to primary and secondary education (Carnoy 2002).

33. On aggregate in Japan, Korea, and Taiwan (China), about 24 percent of all 24-year-olds graduated with university degrees in 1997. In China, Indonesia, and Malaysia, the share was about 2.7 percent.

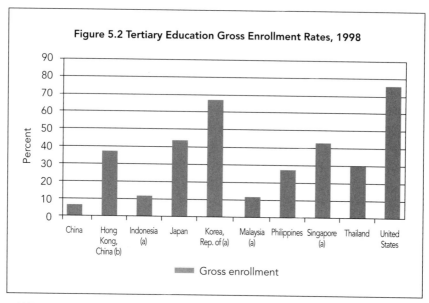

Figure 5.2 Tertiary Education Gross Enrollment Rates, 1998

a. 1997.

b. 2001.

Sources: World Bank, *World Development Indicators* (various years); Hong Kong, China, Education and Manpower Bureau.

established research and development presence, such as Korea, have large numbers of graduates in the core fields of science. As a result, three Asian nations are among the top 11 countries granted patents by the U.S. Patent and Trademark Office (table 5.8).

Over time, other East Asian countries should aim to increase their tertiary-level enrollment in line with emerging demand for various specialties. Enrollment can be expanded by encouraging private education rather than relying solely on an increase in government outlays.[34] Since individuals capture many of the gains from tertiary education, the justification for public funding is diminished.[35] However, university research, especially basic research, is thought to generate spillovers to society in general, justifying state intervention (OECD

34. Expanding tertiary enrollment through the use of public expenditures alone can lead to fewer resources for each institution. This problem arises when governments cannot discriminate among universities in the level of funding and are forced to equalize spending ("Education Shibboleth" 2002).

35. Among OECD countries, the private rate of return to tertiary education is highest in the United Kingdom (17 and 15 percent for males and females, respectively). The average for countries in the sample is 11 percent (OECD 2002).

2001a). In East Asia private institutions have been providing 70 percent or more of tertiary education in Japan, Korea, and Taiwan (China) since the mid-1990s, and in Malaysia, 25 percent of students enroll in private schools, typically run in cooperation with foreign universities (Neville 1998; Tilak 2001). China has more than 800 private institutes of higher education. However, the Ministry of Education recognizes only a few of them as degree-granting institutions (World Bank 2000e). To accommodate the increase in demand for tertiary education, China will need to rely more on private institutions in order to achieve an enrollment ratio of 15 percent by 2005 (Dahlman and Aubert 2001).Where capital markets are imperfect and individuals have difficulty funding their own education, public assistance in the form of financial aid, scholarships, loans, and other means may be warranted.

Quality of Tertiary Education

As in secondary education, the quality of higher-level training is uneven in East Asia. Universities in Korea are producing many graduates who necessitate further large investments by the government and industry in postgraduate training (L. Kim 1995, quoted in Tilak 2001), forcing reliance on graduates educated abroad. Complaints have been voiced about college education in China. Cao and Suttmeier's obser-

Table 5.7 Bachelor's and Science and Engineering Degrees of the 24-Year-Old Population in 1999 or Most Recent Year

Region or economy	Year	All bachelor's degrees	Total science and engineering	Engineering	Natural sciences	Social sciences
China	1999	440,935	322,769	195,354	59,804	67,611
Hong Kong, China	1998	11,362	5,425	1,822	2,370	1,233
Indonesia	1999	144,314	97,095	20,644	10,711	65,740
Japan	2001	532,436	350,535	103,440	32,718	214,377
Korea, Rep. of	2000	204,390	91,296	45,145	29,527	16,624
Malaysia	1998	10,511	4,760	877	1,685	2,198
Singapore	1996	5,599	5,599	1,676	2,103	1,820
Taiwan, China	2000	87,421	34,722	16,638	12,911	5,173
Thailand	1998	119,288	31,168	10,878	10,296	9,994

Source: National Science Foundation (2002, app. table 2-18).

Table 5.8 Countries That Registered Patents in the United States, 1996 and 2000

	1996			2000	
Country	Number of patents	Rank	Country	Number of patents	Rank
Japan	24,058	1	Japan	32,924	1
Germany	7,124	2	Germany	10,822	2
France	3,016	3	Taiwan, China	5,806	3
United Kingdom	2,674	4	France	4,173	4
Canada	2,639	5	United Kingdom	4,090	5
Taiwan, China	2,419	6	Canada	3,925	6
Korea, Rep. of	1,567	7	Korea, Rep. of	3,472	7
Sweden	971	10	Switzerland	1,458	10
Hong Kong, China	247	—	Hong Kong, China	548	—
Singapore	97	—	Singapore	242	—
China	48	—	China	163	—
Malaysia	24	—	Malaysia	47	—
Thailand	11	—	Thailand	30	—
Philippines	4	—	Philippines	12	—
United States	69,424[a]		United States	97,016[b]	
Total	121,806[c]		Total	176,087[c]	

— Not available.

a. 57 percent of total.

b. 55 percent of total.

c. 100 percent.

Source: U.S. Patent and Trademarks Office.

vation has widespread resonance in the region: "China's graduate education has problems to overcome. Admission is tough, while graduation is easy. Almost all the enrolled students get their degrees so that there is no incentive to study hard. . . . Graduate students seem to lack the passion for science which is necessary for a successful research career" (Cao and Suttmeier 2001, p. 982). In China the quality of research is affected by the caliber of many senior scientists trained during the years of the Cultural Revolution. Although they had little opportunity to improve their skills, these scientists now dominate research in certain fields.[36] In order to assess these claims, we report on a number of measures that reflect the quality and strength of tertiary education.

---

36. The echo effect of past training and emigration of skilled researchers on the current capabilities of the individuals leading science laboratories has also been felt in India ("Missing Generation" 2002).

Rankings of Universities. Few attempts have been made to rank major universities worldwide based on the quality of their research. A study comparing 200 universities worldwide with respect to the volume of research in economics places only two East Asian universities in the top 100: the Hong Kong University of Science and Technology ranks thirty-seventh, and the Chinese University of Hong Kong ranks eighty-fourth (Kalaitzidakis, Mamuneas, and Stengos 2001). Seoul National University, Korea's leading tertiary-level institution, is ranked one hundred and forty-fourth. In a ranking of research papers in economics from universities in East Asia, the top 10 slots are dominated by universities from Hong Kong, China, and Japan, with the first and second positions occupied by universities from Hong Kong, China (Jin and Yau 1999). Only Seoul National University is in the top 10, and none of the universities from China or from the members of the Association of South East Asian Nations, other than Singapore, is included in the top-rated group (table 5.9).

Share of Scholarly Publications. Assessing the quality of research skills is difficult; the few available indicators are all subjective and flawed to some extent. One of these is the share of the world's scholarly publications. In the 1990s the publication rate of scientific papers from China, Hong Kong (China), Korea, Singapore, and Taiwan (China) almost doubled (World Bank 2000e).[37] Still, only 15 percent of the world's papers were published in all of Asia in 1991–98 (figure 5.3). Moreover, the relatively small number of significant papers published in the region is linked to the paucity of carefully refereed, world-class journals in countries such as China and Korea. In the life sciences, for example, no Chinese journal equals or exceeds the best Indian journal (Cao and Suttmeier 2001; Lim 1999).[38] Limited access to the latest international journals and modest English language skills

---

37. On the rising volume of papers from China in recent years, see also "High-Tech in China" (2002).

38. In other rankings, especially of science and technology schools in Asia, five campuses of the Indian Institutes of Technology rank among the top 10 (www.asiaweek.com/asiaweek/features/universities2000/scitech/sci.overall.html). However, for the reasons cited in note 36, India's global ranking with respect to the number and quality of papers published in peer-reviewed journals has slipped substantially.

Table 5.9 Rankings of East Asian Universities by Research Productivity in Economics

Ranking and source	University	Economy
Kalaitzidakis, Mamuneas, and Stengos (2001)		
37	Hong Kong University of Science and Technology	Hong Kong, China
84	Chinese University	Hong Kong, China
105	Osaka University	Japan
116	University of Tsukuba	Japan
136	Tokyo University	Japan
144	Seoul National University	Korea, Rep. of
156	Singapore National	Singapore
164	University of Hong Kong	Hong Kong, China
176	Soongsil University	Korea, Rep. of
178	Tohoku University	Japan
179	Ewha University	Korea, Rep. of
181	National Taiwan	Taiwan, China
183	Kyoto University	Japan
195	Hitotsubashi University	Japan
Jin and Yau (1999)		
1	Hong Kong University of Science and Technology	Hong Kong, China
2	Chinese University	Hong Kong, China
3	Tokyo University	Japan
4	National Taiwan	Taiwan, China
5	Singapore National	Singapore
6	University of Tsukuba	Japan
7	University of Hong Kong	Hong Kong, China
8	Seoul National	Korea, Rep. of
9	City University	Hong Kong, China
10	Osaka University	Japan

Note: The ranking is out of 200 universities worldwide. The rank of an institution is determined by the adjusted page counts of papers published in the top 30 journals in economics in 1995–99. Rankings by Jin and Yau (1999) are for Asian universities. Their rankings are based on adjusted pages published in the top 36 economics journals from 1990 to 1996.
Sources: Jin and Yau (1999); Kalaitzidakis, Mamuneas, and Stengos (2001).

are additional handicaps. In addition, public universities in East Asia spend up to 80 percent of their budgets on personnel and student maintenance costs, leaving few resources for maintaining and upgrading research facilities (World Bank 2000k). In Japan, there is concern that the research output of Japanese universities is low for an advanced country, and reforms are under way to address the probable causes ("Japan: Education Reforms (A)" 2002).

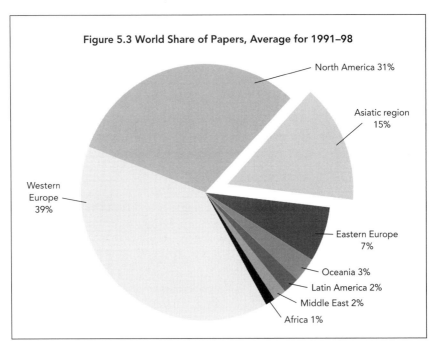

Figure 5.3 World Share of Papers, Average for 1991–98

North America 31%

Asiatic region 15%

Western Europe 39%

Eastern Europe 7%

Oceania 3%

Latin America 2%

Middle East 2%

Africa 1%

Note: Percentages are rounded to nearest whole number. South Africa (0.73 percent) and North Africa (0.44 percent) have been combined.
Source: Gálvez and others (2000).

Citations. One measure of the impact of research is the rate at which research publications are cited.[39] Here East Asia fares poorly overall (table 5.10), although some economies approach the international average rate of citation in a few specific fields. In the late 1990s, China, for example, received close to the average number of citations in agricultural science (9 percent below the average); Hong Kong, China, did the same in plant and animal science (7 percent below the average); and Japan received close to the average number of citations in material science, physics, chemistry, agricultural science, and space science (between 3 and 9 percent below the average). Korean papers tended to be cited much less often than papers from the other countries listed in the table, but the trend is rising, suggesting that Korean research is improving somewhat. Korean researchers wrote only a handful of "high-

39. Undoubtedly, this measure is biased toward native English speakers. However, researchers from other countries, including Israel, have a significant number of citations, so there is no reason to believe that researchers in East Asian economies cannot do the same.

Table 5.10 Relative Impact of Scientific Papers from Select Countries, 1996–2000

Country	Count of relative impact compared to world average 1996–2000[a]
United Kingdom	18[b]
Switzerland	18[b]
Sweden	15
Germany	17
Finland	13
Israel	10
Hong Kong, China	3[c]
Taiwan, China	1[b]
China	0
Japan	0
Korea, Rep. of[a]	0

a. Count of relative impact is a sum of fields in which countries received more than the world average number of citations out of 22 broad categories.

b. 1995–99.

c. 1995–99; includes microbiology, which received exactly the same number of citations as the world average.

Source: Various issues of in-cites (2000, 2001) at in-cites.com/research/.

impact" papers before 1994, but since 1994 (except in 1995), the number of high-impact papers has been greater than 10.[40]

China, Japan, Korea, and Taiwan (China) produce papers in similar fields, including chemistry, engineering, materials science, and physics. The notable exception is Hong Kong, China, which produces research in fields such as economics and business and the social sciences (table 5.11). In recent years, output from Korea has increased dramatically and now surpasses that of Taiwan, China, and other neighbors. Another notable feature of Korean research is that 10 percent (or 2.5 times the world average share) of papers are in materials science.

Doctorates and Researchers. An encouraging development during the 1990s was the rise in the number of students earning doctorates

---

40. High-impact papers are the 200 most cited papers in each of the categories in each year (see in-cites.com/countries/skorea.html). Even so, this number remains small compared to the 255 high-impact papers from Japan and the 2,875 high-impact papers from the United States (see in-cites.com/countries/japan1.html).

Table 5.11 Top Five Fields in Select Countries, Ranked by Share of World Output

Country	Field
China	Materials science, physics, mathematics, chemistry, engineering
Hong Kong, China	Economics and business, computer science, engineering, mathematics, social sciences
Japan	Materials science, physics, pharmacology, chemistry, biology and biochemistry
Korea, Rep. of	Materials science, engineering, physics, computer science, chemistry
Taiwan, China	Computer science, engineering, materials science, physics, pharmacology

Source: Various issues of *in-cites* (2000, 2001) at in-cites.com/research/.

from East Asian universities. In 1997 more than 18,500 people received doctoral degrees in science and engineering within East Asia, reflecting a 12 percent average annual increase since 1993.[41] Meanwhile, the number of degrees earned in the United States by students from these countries peaked at 6,900 in 1996 and declined in 1997 (National Science Foundation 2000, sec. 4-3).

Another positive trend is the number of instances of scientific collaboration with researchers from other Asian countries, as measured by coauthorship of scientific articles (table 5.12). For China, this figure rose from 16 to 35 percent of the country's internationally coauthored papers, and for Singapore it rose from 19 to 37 percent. Japan continued to show little evidence of collaboration with researchers from elsewhere in Asia,[42] and the collaboration rates of Korea and Taiwan, China, have changed little since the mid-1980s, both remaining in the 20 percent range.[43]

One reason for the limited incidence of intraregional partnering might be weaknesses in English speaking and writing skills. This is reflected in the low scores on the Test of English as a Foreign Language

---

41. Inadequate financial support for graduate students in China remains a problem. Students are highly dependent on their academic sponsors in the faculty, and this may stifle the creativity of their graduate-level research (Cao and Suttmeier 2001).

42. The Japanese higher education system is geared more toward importing ideas from around the world (aided by excellent translation services) rather than exchanging ideas globally (Kawaguchi and Lander 1997).

43. Korea seems to follow technological developments in Japan more closely than does Taiwan, China. Hu and Jaffe (2001) find that Korean firms cite Japanese patents more frequently than Taiwanese firms do, and Korean firms tend to be technologically similar to Japanese firms. This similarity can also be seen from table 5.11.

Table 5.12 Instances of Intra-Asian Research Collaboration and Number of Internationally Coauthored Articles, Two Periods, 1986–97

Economy	1986–88		1995–97	
	Instances of collaboration	Number of coauthored articles	Instances of collaboration	Number of coauthored articles
Japan	1,009	8,259	3,308	21,608
China	415	2,626	2,808	7,982
Hong Kong, China	83	333	1,235	2,694
Korea, Rep. of	191	686	1,139	3,892
Taiwan, China	157	754	599	2,813
Singapore	62	318	423	1,147
Thailand	134	493	381	976
Indonesia	57	215	277	631
Malaysia	70	249	270	554
Philippines	96	247	219	454

Source: National Science Foundation (2000).

(TOEFL) for countries in East Asia relative to others (table 5.13).[44] In 2000, on average, students from East Asia did worse on TOEFL than did students from other countries, the Philippines and Singapore (where education is conducted in English) being the exceptions.

Improving Tertiary Education

This review suggests that tertiary education in East Asia does need attention if it is to support the growth of innovative economies. Increasing the capacity for research, providing incentives for innovative research, and ensuring that complementary skills are available are important priorities in the medium run.

Research Capacity. Increasing the supply of innovative domestic research, assuming there is a demand to be met, involves a dynamic relationship among three factors: the quality of undergraduate education, the capacity for postgraduate research, and the quality of postgraduate research. If both the quality of undergraduate education

---

44. Selection bias may be driving the results. For example, Vietnam does relatively well on TOEFL, but this may be because only the most able take the test, while more people with varying abilities and educational background take the TOEFL in Japan and Korea, lowering their average relative to other countries.

Table 5.13 Average Scores on TOEFL Computer-Based Test, July 1999–June 2000

Economy	Number of test takers	Average score
China	14,539	211
Hong Kong, China	4,546	205
India	10,288	246
Indonesia	8,935	203
Japan	21,636	188
Korea, Rep. of	18,839	200
Malaysia	2,692	219
Philippines	9,690	234
Singapore	831	252
Taiwan, China	10,178	193
Thailand	4,072	194
Vietnam	1,289	200
Brazil	8,144	224
Mexico	7,479	228
France	10,546	229
Germany	11,380	249
Israel	2,342	235
Turkey	10,430	213

Note: The maximum score is 300. A score of 280 corresponds to the ninety-sixth percentile; 260 corresponds to the eighty-third percentile; 240 corresponds to the sixty-sixth percentile; 220 corresponds to the forty-ninth percentile; 200 corresponds to the thirty-fourth percentile; and 180 corresponds to the twenty-second percentile. TOEFL (Test of English as a Foreign Language) is also offered in the traditional paper-based format. However, more and more countries are moving toward computer-based methods of testing. In China, India, Japan, Republic of Korea, Taiwan (China), and Thailand, a substantial number of tests are taken on paper.
Source: Educational Testing Service (2000–01).

and the capacity for postgraduate research in a country are low, the immediate priority is to focus on improving the quality of undergraduate education. The first few cohorts of well-prepared undergraduates would best be encouraged to obtain graduate education at good institutions abroad. This period would be used to scale up the capacity for postgraduate education within the country, a process that would be helped by a subset of the returning students. For this strategy to pay off, the quality of domestic graduate education would need to be made comparable to that available abroad.

We can illustrate this transition using a very crude indicator—the proportion of the pool of undergraduate students in a country who are pursuing graduate education in the United States, as shown in

Table 5.14 Percentage of Graduate Students Studying in the United States from Pool of Undergraduate Students in the Economy

Economy	Percentage studying in the United States
China	8.9
Hong Kong, China	17.4
Indonesia	2.4
Japan	1.7
Korea, Rep. of	9.3
Malaysia	20.8
Singapore	18.6
Taiwan, China	19.6
Thailand	8.2
India	3.4

Note: The numerators are the number of graduate students in all fields from these economies studying in the United States in the 1998–99 academic year. The denominators are tertiary education enrollment in these economies.

Sources: National Science Foundation (2002); Institute of International Education, Open Doors (2002).

table 5.14.[45] The proportions are very low for Indonesia and Japan. Inferring from other facts about the two economies, it is reasonable to assume that in Indonesia the quality of undergraduate education is low, few students are being sent abroad for training, and the quality of postgraduate research is also low. By contrast, Japan has good undergraduate education and sufficient domestic capacity for graduate training—it does not need to send large numbers of students abroad. One can also infer that Japanese students find the quality of domestic postgraduate education to be high enough that they are not motivated to seek it elsewhere.[46]

---

45. This is a crude indicator because it ignores a number of confounding factors (affordability, language skills, government policy) that could affect the ability of students to obtain an education in the United States. It also ignores other destinations for higher education that might be more popular in some countries.

46. For instance, 2,632 Japanese students received a doctoral degree in science and engineering in Japan as opposed to 77 in the United States in 1975. In 1998 the number was 6,575 in Japan and 152 in the United States. Compare this to Taiwan, China, where, of all the doctoral degrees awarded to Taiwanese in 1981, only 49 were awarded domestically, while 444 were awarded in the United States. In 1999 the number of degrees awarded in Taiwan, China, increased to 734, closing the gap with the number of degrees awarded in the United States (892). See National Science Foundation (2002, app. table 2-41).

Hong Kong (China), Malaysia, Singapore, and Taiwan (China) have proportions on the high side. It could be argued that this reflects good undergraduate education (sufficient to ensure admission abroad) and limited domestic capacity for graduate education because of the size of the economies (Hong Kong, China, and Singapore), excess demand (Taiwan, China), or lack of investment (Malaysia). Not much can be inferred about the quality of domestic postgraduate training.

China, Korea, and Thailand represent the intermediate case. For China and Thailand one can speculate that the quality of undergraduate education is good or reaching acceptable levels, domestic capacity for graduate education is limited, and governments are sending students abroad under a planned program. For Korea one can argue that domestic capacity has increased sufficiently so that the proportion of students studying abroad is lower than in the past. Whether the quality of graduate training in Korea is as good as it should be cannot be inferred from this evidence. If it is not, a large proportion of the domestically produced graduates will be unable to contribute to the development of an innovative economy in Korea.

Promoting Innovative Research. The reforms in secondary education seek to ensure that students moving into tertiary education have the creative abilities to support an innovative economy. Equally important is the need to create an environment that supports innovative research at the tertiary level. To achieve this goal, high-quality research universities with world-class graduate and postgraduate programs and adequate incentives for professors to publish are essential. In developing countries, high-quality universities that focus on basic research tend to be public universities. Public funding of such research is warranted because of the potentially large spillover benefits to society (World Bank 2000e). The significance of university research is reflected in the recent interest in university-business linkages discussed at length in chapter 4. Universities must contribute their share to producing research that entrepreneurs can commercialize, and governments need to facilitate such a role.[47] The Japanese

---

47. See Stern, Porter, and Furman (2000), who find that a country with a higher share of research and development in the education sector produces more patents.

government is moving in this direction, pledging to more than double the number of ventures originating from universities over the next three years ("Innovation Takes Off" 2002).

One promising mechanism for universities to nurture creativity and flexibility is through academic exchanges or joint programs, as some East Asian and Western universities already have done.[48] The establishment of branches of well-known Western universities is another avenue. For instance, Singapore has encouraged the opening of satellite campuses by foreign graduate schools, including INSEAD, Massachusetts Institute of Technology, Wharton School, and University of Chicago ("Enter the Foreigners" 2000). Most national governments are eager to support transnational educational exchanges, which both enhance their countries' own capacity for higher education and reduce the outflow of students. To encourage such exchanges, Hong Kong, China, known for its laissez-faire approach to most aspects of economic activity, places few restrictions on foreign education providers; government agencies do not interfere with the quality, content, or the cost of such services.[49] By comparison, the Malaysian government places many limitations on foreign providers to make sure that the education offered conforms to national goals (McBurnie and Ziguras 2001).

Complementary Skills. The gains from invention usually depend not only on technical novelty but also on design, distribution, and marketing (Teece 1986) and on the entrepreneurship to tie these together effectively. To shape a resilient, competitive East Asia, college graduates specializing in accounting, law, management, information technology, and finance are as important as graduates in science and engineering (Pack 2002).

Higher education in East Asia is lagging on this front, sometimes not in terms of quantity but in terms of quality. The international ranking of business degrees reveals that only Hong Kong University of Science and Technology (ranked fifty-ninth) appears in the top 60 ("Financial Times MBA" 2003). For the executive master's of business

---

48. For instance, the number of academic exchange agreements between Japanese and foreign universities increased from 763 to 3,023 between 1984 and 1994 (Kawaguchi and Lander 1997).

49. Government regulation is concerned with the dissemination to consumers of accurate and detailed information about course offerings.

arts program, the Chinese University of Hong Kong (ranked twenti-eth) and China Europe International Business School (ranked forty-second) are the only two programs among the top 50 ("Financial Times EMBA" 2002). Even in Japan, where higher education is well established and well regarded, only 18 universities offer master's pro-grams in business, and of these only two are national universities (University of Tsukuba and Hitotsubashi University).[50] Singapore opened the Singapore Management University in August 2000.[51] As we argue in other chapters, to thrive, businesses—particularly innova-tive firms—need good governance, strong institutions, and developed infrastructures. These requirements call for highly educated people in various fields (World Bank 2000e).

Alongside the reforms in secondary and tertiary education, East Asian countries would do well to capture the benefits of self-directed lifelong learning. We discuss this aspect of education in an innovative society in the following section.

LIFELONG LEARNING

One consequence of East Asia's drive to move out of volume produc-tion of commoditized components and into newer technologies is the need to retrain a large number of workers. This and several other de-velopments have sparked interest in lifelong learning in East Asia and around the world: (1) knowledge has become even more important in many economic activities, (2) rapid technological advance has created a constant need for workers to upgrade their skills, (3) rapid growth in producer services has created demand for more highly qualified workers (OECD 2000c, 2001a), (4) the crisis of 1997–98 put large numbers of less educated people out of work, so as part of a social safety net, many economies are considering how lifelong learning can alleviate the costs associated with unemployment, and (5) in aging so-cieties, such as Japan's, retraining the elderly for productive employ-

---

50. See Nikkei Net (campus.nikkei.co.jp/mba/besines/index.html). Hitotsubashi University of-fers courses in English to accommodate faculties and students from around the world, especially from Asia. This is one of the six professional schools certified by the Ministry of Education in Japan ("School Daze" 2002).

51. Singapore, Ministry of Education (www1.moe.edu.sg/tertiarye.html).

ment is seen as a crucial means to lessen some of the anticipated fiscal burden of pensions.

The issue of aging is quite important for many economies in East Asia, especially for China, Japan, and Korea, which are facing declining fertility and mortality rates. In Japan the retiree population (65 years and older) was almost 15 percent of the total population in 1995; it will be 32 percent by 2050. Similarly, in Korea, the proportion of elderly will increase from 6 percent in 1995 to 25 percent in 2050.[52] The aging is so rapid that even with immigration, keeping the support ratio at current levels will be a challenge. Either the level of support will need to be lowered or the retirement age will need to be raised.[53] China is facing a similar scenario. Currently, the proportion of elderly is only 6 percent of the total population, but this is projected to reach 16 percent by 2030 and 23 percent by 2050 (Yi and George 2000).[54] The proportion of persons 80 years and older will be more than 10 percent in Hong Kong (China), Japan, and Singapore by 2050. Even though the proportion will not be as high in China, the absolute numbers will be large—99 million elderly by 2050. Given these projections, it is reasonable to assume that the retirement age will have to be raised further in the future, especially in Northeast Asia. This will add to the future demand for lifelong learning, which is already high because of continuing technological change.

Thus even though lifelong learning has been a part of education policy in many countries in the past, it has gained significance in recent years. Lifelong integrated learning was first introduced in Japan in the 1960s to augment the school-centered education system and to retrain adult workers (OECD 2000c). Increasingly, people perceive learning as a broader process than traditional school-based education. New institutions are emerging to take advantage of advances in technology, and existing institutions are beginning to accommodate the demand for lifelong learning (World Bank 2002c).

---

52. This projection assumes no immigration to Japan and Korea and assumes medium fertility and mortality rates (United Nations Population Division 2000a).

53. To keep the current ratio of working-age persons to elderly person at 4.8, Japan would need to raise the retirement age to 77 years. To keep the current ratio of 12.6, Korea would need to raise the retirement age to 82 years.

54. This is based on the assumption that life expectancy in China will improve from 68.4 years in 1990 to 78.8 years in 2050. This is a conservative assumption, given that life expectancy in Japan was more than 80 years in 1995.

Three issues deserve the most attention. The first is how to acknowledge or certify informal training, including relevant work experience. For adults who have completed secondary but not tertiary education and have worked for a long time, the opportunity cost of obtaining a college degree is quite high.[55] By receiving credits for their accumulated work experience, these individuals can greatly shorten the time spent in a tertiary-level program, thus reducing both the opportunity costs and the direct costs of obtaining a degree (OECD 2000c).[56]

The second issue is how to make this certification transferable across different educational and learning institutions. Not everyone would wish to or be able to obtain a degree during one continuous period of time or at the same place. To address this issue, some means of transferring past credits needs to be instituted (OECD 2000c). This is even more true for distance learning, since many students are interested only in participating in specific modules rather than in earning a degree (Bray 2002). Japan has introduced a "credit accumulation system" through which university degrees are conferred on the basis of total credits earned at one or more institutions (Itoh 2002).[57]

The third issue is how to harness ICT effectively and innovatively in the context of lifelong learning. Current integration of ICT in schools has not delivered the much hoped for improvements in student achievement. However, in the context of lifelong learning, especially in distance learning, ICT may widen the opportunities for individuals who would further their learning if appropriate infrastructure were in place.

A better certification of skills accumulated through work experience, coupled with the transportability of such certification across different educational entities, could increase the benefits of lifelong learning, raise the returns to such efforts, and reduce both the opportunity costs and the direct costs of acquiring additional skills (OECD 2001a).

---

55. For instance, the direct private cost of tertiary education is estimated at 20 million won, while the opportunity cost (forgone income) is estimated at about 42 million won (OECD 1998).

56. The National Institute for Academic Degrees in Japan grants degrees to qualified graduates of nonuniversity institutions (Itoh 2002).

57. Korea also introduced the Educational Credit Bank System in 1996 (Kang 1999; OECD 1998).

ICT and Lifelong Learning

As in mainstream secondary and tertiary education, many countries perceive that ICT can play a beneficial role in expanding the reach of lifelong learning programs. Most countries in East Asia have begun offering distance learning courses. Distance learning allows people to participate from virtually anywhere and, depending on the nature of interaction, possibly at any time. This flexibility is a great attraction, especially for people living in remote areas. Distance learning can accommodate a large number of students without adding to the costs of physical infrastructure, and it offers a relatively low-cost means of expanding education for the older population (OECD 2001a; see table 5.15).

The Korean National Open University, established in 1972, enrolls more than 200,000 students. It is open to adults as well as high school graduates and uses ICT to meet the large increase in demand for tertiary education among working adults (OECD 2000c). The Japanese University of the Air was established in 1985 with 62,000 students (OECD 2001a).

Table 5.15 Distance Tertiary Education in East Asia

	Enrollment		Unit cost as a percentage of on-campus unit cost
Institution or country	Number of students	As a percentage of total tertiary students	
Universitas Terbuka, Indonesia	170,000	18	13
University of the Air, Japan	68,000	4	13
Open Learning Institute, Hong Kong, China	20,000	21	—
Open University, Thailand	180,000	37	40
Korea National Open University, Korea, Rep. of	208,935	13	—
China	1,422,900	24	25–40
Universiti Sains, Malaysia	5,500	3	73
Indira Gandhi National Open University, India	182,000	11	40
Open University, Sri Lanka	16,400	32	—
Open University, United Kingdom	154,200	8	39–47

— Not available.

Source: World Bank (2002c).

Table 5.16 Development Costs of Materials per Student Learning-Hour in the United Kingdom, 1996

Medium	Cost (British pounds)	Ratio to print cost
Print	500	1
Audio	17,000	34
CD-ROM	20,000	40
Radio	27,000	54
Video	84,000	168
Television	125,000	250

Source: Adapted from Bray (2002).

Although promising, the early experience with distance learning cautions against exaggerated expectations. Even though the marginal cost of providing the service to additional learners is minimal, the cost of developing such programs is high (table 5.16). In particular, the up-front cost of developing the materials to be used is much higher than that of producing traditional books. And the basic ICT infrastructure must be laid down before any significant gains can be realized. Furthermore, dropout rates can be quite high, suggesting that only highly motivated people actually see such programs through to the end.[58] To alleviate the high dropout rate, there should be some means of interaction between learners and teachers. This is especially important for students from disadvantaged backgrounds for whom family and community support may be lacking (World Bank 2002c). In addition, Brown and Liedholm (2002) find that students learn significantly less well in "virtual" classes than in regular, live classes. These findings suggest that policymakers need to evaluate the effectiveness of distance learning, from the standpoint of both the cost and the quality of learning.

Directions in Lifelong Learning

Two lessons emerge quite clearly from global experience. The first is that educational systems need to be more flexible to accommodate more diverse student bodies. Rapid advances in technology and

---

58. For instance, the dropout rate is 50 percent at Sukhothai Thammathirat Open University in Thailand, 30 percent at China Radio and Television University, and 50 percent at Korea Air and Correspondence University (Bray 2002).

changes in external environments mean that individuals need to update their skills and knowledge continuously. Not all students will follow the traditional linear educational path. Nor does learning occur only through formal education; much can occur elsewhere through on-the-job training and work experience. More and more people are engaging in learning activities in multiple settings across time. In order to facilitate such learning, a system of credit recognition and transfers among different institutes is needed.

Second, the public sector alone cannot finance a sustainable system of lifelong learning. This is especially true for East Asia, which has achieved universal primary education and is rapidly increasing the coverage of secondary and tertiary education. Much of this expansion was achieved by private schools, especially for tertiary education. Given that the private return to higher education is significant and accrues mostly to individuals, individuals need to help finance their continuing education. However, some public involvement is called for on equity grounds and as a safety net in the face of technical change. Because retraining programs are quite heterogeneous and fairly new, evidence on their effectiveness and efficiency is quite sparse. Private training programs tend to be more effective, with rates of return in the range of 10–20 percent; for public training programs the rate of return barely approaches 10 percent. However, private training programs tend to focus on more educated workers, biasing results upward. The less educated workers who are more likely to lose their job are the ones who need retraining, yet would be neglected by the private sector. This is the justification for public provision of training as a part of the safety net (OECD 2001a).

CONCLUSION

This chapter underscores the fundamental significance of secondary- and tertiary-level education for development through innovation. It emphasizes the need to shift the focus of education and research toward creativity and quality in order to enable economies in the region to compete with global leaders in an increasing number of areas.

To achieve these goals, East Asian countries will need to employ a combination of measures: (1) increase the resource allocation to create the educational infrastructure needed to support future growth, (2) encourage experimentation at the secondary school level to improve cognitive abilities, (3) increase the capacity for research and provide incentives to promote innovative research through collaboration with industry and international institutions, (4) continue using reputable foreign universities to train outstanding students as long as necessary, while creating an environment that will make it attractive for these students to return, (5) ensure an adequate supply of complementary skills needed to support technological entrepreneurship and commercialization of research, and (6) benefit from the demand and motivation for self-improvement in a time of rapid change and increasing life spans by providing the infrastructure for lifelong learning.

CHAPTER 6

MAKING CLUSTERS INNOVATIVE

A s noted in chapter 4, a virtuous circle of steady technological advances most often occurs in localized high-technology clusters embedded in large, established metropolitan areas that generate significant agglomeration economies. Clusters form as a result of the entry and growth of entrepreneurial and innovative firms. Among the factors that influence the process are the availability of skills, infrastructure, amenities, and the presence of institutions that promote innovation and induce networking.

Innovative clusters are a local phenomenon, but their long-term dynamism rests on their becoming part of a global network of similar clusters and participating in the circulation of human capital among them. Policy actions, among other forces, also affect the openness of urban centers to the flow of capital, ideas, and talent from abroad. Such openness, as well as the ability to tap the diaspora of East Asian knowledge workers in countries of the Organisation for Economic Co-operation and Development (OECD), is critical to the emergence of innovative clusters in East Asia. Moreover, the success of these clusters ultimately depends on technological interaction between local and foreign firms abetted by the circulation of skilled workers bringing ideas, technology transfer, and access to foreign markets.

This chapter is divided into five sections. The first describes the main features of clusters and how they can play pivotal roles in innovation systems. The second briefly reviews the literature on agglomeration economies with a bearing on East Asia and explores why clusters derive leverage from such externalities. The third ties these factors to the emergence of high-tech clusters in East Asia. The fourth examines specific country experiences to draw lessons for poli-cy choices. The last section reviews the contribution made to cluster development and innovativeness by the international circulation of knowledge workers and suggests how East Asian countries could tap more fully the international pool of skills.

THE WHAT AND WHY OF CLUSTERS

East Asian economies have demonstrated a strong comparative ad-vantage in high-tech products, mostly manufactured in industrial parks in major urban areas. This comparative advantage has hitherto been mainly in product assembly, with most of the upstream research and design being done in the industrial countries and with many of the inputs being imported from these countries for assembly.

Even downstream activities of this kind provide valuable learning in manufacturing and can stimulate incremental process innovation, but the real rewards come from being at the innovative frontier—de-signing, developing, and introducing products or services that are new. This must be the longer-run goal of the industrializing East Asian economies.

More than a decade ago, Krugman (1991) observed, "The most striking feature of the geography of economic activity is . . . concen-tration."[1] A growing body of empirical research has since shown that the dynamism and growth of a modern, knowledge-intensive econo-my come from industrial and service activities that are clustered in a few choice urban venues. As Porter and Stern (2001, pp. 29–30) note in the following passage:

> Clusters offer potential advantages in perceiving both the need and the opportunity for innovation. Equally important, however, are the flexibility and capacity clusters can provide to act rapidly to turn new ideas into real-ity. A company within a cluster can often more rapidly source the new components, services, machinery, and other elements necessary to imple-

---

1. In this context, the specific location of particular activities has much to do with accident and history, "from the concentration of most U.S. manufacture of wind instruments in the tiny town of Elkhart, Indiana, of carpet manufacturing in Dalton, Georgia, and the locking-in of transitory advantages responsible for autos in Detroit and chips in Silicon Valley" (Krugman 1991, pp. 5, 9–10, 60).

ment innovations. Local suppliers and partners can and do get involved in the innovation process, especially when participants are located nearby. Reinforcing these advantages for innovation is the sheer pressure—competitive pressure, peer pressure, customer pressure, and constant comparison—that is inherent within a cluster.[2]

When competitiveness and economic advance are keyed to incessant technological change that shortens product cycles, the clustering of economic agents has manifold advantages.[3] First, a dense and multifaceted labor market that serves as a clearinghouse for a mix of workers with specialized skills is advantageous for both firms and job seekers. For firms, it reduces hiring and screening costs. For job seekers, it lessens the costs arising from acquiring, processing, and acting on information about relevant jobs because many jobs are gathered in one place. Also workers are more exposed to incentives to look for better jobs, while employers are less inclined to engage in costly labor-hoarding practices. "Thick" labor markets also socialize individuals into cluster-specific habits and aptitudes, thus reducing the per capita costs of providing training.[4]

Second, in many new high-tech industries where technology is still evolving, the mutual proximity of firms is important in preventing costs from spiraling out of control (Scott 1988). In these industries the input-output structure and relationships between firms and their suppliers tend to be fluid, and the resulting smallness of scale, variability of content, need to integrate design and manufacturing, and need to readjust inter-firm business transactions frequently result in high costs per unit of distance. In addition, where the nature, com-

---

2. See also Porter (1998a, 1998b). Michael Ruettgers, chief executive officer of the data storage devices company EMC, has remarked that staying ahead in the unforgivingly competitive information technology business requires constantly anticipating new product demand by talking to customers and determining their needs, maintaining close awareness of what rivals are doing, and always having the next-generation product ready for trial, even as the current generation is being shipped. In his words, "The defining characteristic [of EMC] is a sense of urgency. This primes us to seize opportunities that are just emerging" (Hemp 2001, p. 136). Staying a step ahead of the competition and relentlessly pushing the limits of microprocessor technologies are how Intel has maintained its lead ("Billion Gamble" 2002) and how IBM has remained the technological leader in the contract chip production business ("IBM on Target" 2002; "Kelly Puts" 2002).

3. These have been especially apparent in the aerospace, automobile, computer, and telecommunications industries and in the financial sector (Beaudry and Swann 2001).

4. See Dumais and Glaeser (1997), whose research on clusters in the United States using data for 1972–92 gives primacy to the role of labor markets.

plexity, and scale of transactions are unpredictable over time, the proximity of many specialized producers reduces the risks of any failure to establish prompt inter-firm contact. Best (2001, pp. 53, 77) points out,

> Inter-firm networking has evolved with a shift from price-led to product-led competition. This entails integration of manufacturing and new product development. But rapid new product development is not simply adding a product; increasingly it involves a whole group of specialist companies operating at different links along the product chain or nodes in the value networks. . . . Intel [for example] depends upon and reinforces an industrial district constituted by multiple design nodes. Intel not only partners with a vast array of specialist producers and research institutions; Intel draws upon an extended industrial high-tech district with an extraordinary capacity to conduct experiments, carry out innovations, and conduct research.

Third, where technological change is rapid, competitive pressure stimulates innovation. However, clustering also induces firms to engage in reciprocal exchanges outside the sphere of market relations (OECD 2001c). These untraded interdependencies are represented by flows of certain kinds of business information or knowledge spillovers, which is why spatial clustering is most noticeable in industries in which much new knowledge is being created (Audretsch and Feldman 1994). Untraded interdependencies are ubiquitous and fruitful in clusters marked by finely differentiated social divisions of labor (especially where habits of mutual collaboration mitigate the trust-dissolving qualities of more aggressive forms of market competition). They underpin many small-scale processes of learning and innovation, whose cumulative effects can strengthen local competitive advantages.

Fourth, clustering can significantly benefit business alliances and organizations. The presence of many different producers in one place facilitates the establishment of formal associations. Such associations can assist by way of advice or information, or they may offer regulatory services, as do those that promulgate fiduciary norms of business relations or arbitrate certain kinds of commercial disputes. Equally, clustering promotes the development of distinctive business cultures in particular places, thus helping the constituent firms to communicate with and understand one another. The nature of the business culture—particularly the openness to new ideas, the flexibility of business arrangements permitting easy entry of firms, and the richness of social capital—sets the pace of technological advance and the emergence of business models relevant to the times (Saxenian 1994).

Fifth, as is often the case, when the provision of infrastructure entails high fixed costs, significant savings per user can be obtained by spreading the consumption of infrastructure services over many individuals in one place. This feature reinforces locational concentration because large clusters of firms and workers make it possible to construct disproportionately dense and rich infrastructures, with many positive effects on local competitive advantage. Important components of the infrastructural environment of many highly developed regions today—above and beyond such customary items as roads, bridges, and utilities—are the various kinds of information technology and industrial service centers, such as applied research laboratories, innovation search providers, systems integration and back-office services, legal, accounting, and consulting firms, and worker education and training agencies (Bresnahan, Brynjolfsson, and Hitt 2002).

Last, but not least, the demands of interaction between individuals and firms and the emphasis on lean manufacturing and e-business with minimum inventory—within an attractive physical environment well supplied with social amenities[5]—affect geographic location and investment in the local transport infrastructure.[6] Singapore has supported cluster development by sparing no effort in building world-class facilities in transport and in information and communications technology that permit ease of travel and communications, be they local or foreign, electronic or face-to-face. That the city-state has done so without compromising the quality of its environment compounds its other advantages.

---

5. Consumption activities are an all-important hinge of the urban center, and the ability of cities to cater to the consumption needs of sophisticated and demanding consumers is a key to their success (Glaeser, Kolko, and Saiz 2000).

6. High-tech clusters rely on a large and continuous volume of market intelligence, so that innovation and speed of response are keyed to opportunities as they arise. Hence the quality of information technology and communication facilities is of paramount concern. Such clusters also purvey time-sensitive items, which need efficient logistics to ensure their prompt, dependable delivery to far-flung markets. For this reason, clusters located in China's coastal cities have an edge over those located inland and, in particular, the ones in the Shanghai-Suzhou and Pearl River Delta urban regions ("China: Pearl River" 2002; "New Workshop" 2002). Hummels, Ishii, and Yi (2001) and Abernathy and others (2001) stress the increasing time-sensitivity of many items with a relatively short shelf life, including computers.

HOW URBAN AGGLOMERATION BENEFITS CLUSTERS

Through networking among the economic participants, a cluster deepens and elaborates the urban agglomeration effects closely correlated with the productivity of cities.[7] Other things being equal, agglomeration effects derive from the existence of increasing returns, communications externalities, lower transaction and search costs, and higher returns to human capital as the stock of such capital in an urban location rises. Furthermore, the greater economic stability inherent in a large economy and the effect of a decline in transport costs perversely encourage clustering rather than dispersion of firms (Fujita and Thisse 2002; Quigley 1998). As Fujita and Thisse (2002, p. 18) observe,

> [L]ow transport costs with sufficient product differentiation push economic agents toward agglomeration. The reason is that product differentiation relaxes price competition and consequently allows firms to attract more consumers when they are clustered than when any firm chooses to stand alone.

Agglomeration effects, in turn, are usually broken down into so-called localization economies (efficiencies resulting from the clustering of firms in a given subsector) and urbanization economies (efficiencies resulting from the agglomeration of many different kinds of activities in a given region).[8] Localization and urbanization economies are statistically convenient concepts that make it possible to estimate the benefits arising from traded and untraded interdependencies, learning effects, local labor market processes, infrastructural services, and other specific kinds of externalities.

The relative significance of localization versus urbanization economies for the industrial productivity of cities has been much debated, but for high-tech clusters in large, generally polycentric urban areas, both are likely to be of equal importance. A successful cluster needs the specialized research and design skills and the production capabili-

---

7. Glaeser (1997) observes that cities give individuals manifold possibilities to learn from one another. High-tech clusters take this process several steps further by creating and motivating opportunities for interaction.

8. Glaeser, Kalla, and Scheinkman (1992) find that urbanization effects are more important in U.S. urban areas, while Beardsell and Henderson (1999), in their study of the computer industry in the United States, identify mainly localization effects for single-plant firms operating in cities with a high average level of education.

ties that are associated with localization effects; it also needs the industrial breadth, stimulus, opportunities, and cross-disciplinary knowledge that are provided by a large, multifaceted metropolitan region.[9]

Research on urban development in the industrial countries indicates that the size of cities, the concentration of mutually dependent activities, the scale of the labor catchment area, and the effectiveness of urban transport facilities have positive effects on productivity (Cervero 2001; Prudhomme and Lee 1999).[10] A further indicator of the power of agglomeration economies generated by large and diversified cities is the clustering of Internet commercial domain names in Los Angeles, New York, and San Francisco. In spite of the costliness of conducting business in these cities, it still suits the producers of Internet content to cluster together, although in some instances the knowledge spillovers of significance for software producers might be related to marketing and not to technology. Rumors of the death of distance and the dispersion of new industries are clearly premature ("How Location Clusters" 2002; Zook 1999).

A growing body of work examines the quantitative effects of agglomeration on productive efficiency in low- and middle-income countries. Early work found strong evidence for the existence of agglomeration economies and suggested that localization economies play a dominant part in this regard, while urbanization economies, although present, tend to be weaker (Henderson 1986, 1988).

Several recent econometric studies also underscore the positive effects of agglomeration (see also Henderson and Juncoro 1996; Richardson 1993). In the Republic of Korea, Henderson, Lee, and

---

9. A study by De Lucio, Herce, and Goicolea (2002) of Spanish firms during 1978–92 pinpoints the spillover effects of knowledge sharing in specialized industries. The metropolitan region of Kansai in Japan is an example of a networked polycentric system encompassing the prefectures of Hyogo, Kyoto, Nara, Osaka, Shiga, and Wakayama (Batten 1995). A cautionary note on the scale of agglomeration effects is desirable: an analysis of 216 large firms in the United Kingdom during 1979–90 does not find large agglomeration economies or technological spillovers (Geroski and Samiei 1998).

10. Although congestion costs and rising land rent can affect the livability and competitiveness of large cities, U.S. experience over a 300-year period from 1690 to 1990 suggests that larger cities have an edge. They derive significant agglomeration economies from the ease of coordinating market transactions among geographically concentrated buyers and sellers, thus lowering costs and enabling the bigger cities to maintain their growth rates and their rankings in the national hierarchy of cities (S. Kim 2000). In their modeling of cities in France and Japan, Eaton and Eckstein (1997) suggest that larger cities have not only a greater concentration of skills but also higher wages and higher rental costs.

Lee (2001) find significant localization economies in every manufacturing industry, which suggests spillover effects between firms in the same industry. Moreover, they find strong urbanization economies in the high-technology industries and some evidence of urbanization economies in the machinery-electrical industries, suggesting that the diversity of local industries enhances the environment for local information. In particular, industries undergoing rapid technological development benefit more from diverse local environments where producers can learn from firms and researchers outside their own industry (Henderson, Lee, and Lee 2001). Other research on Korea has also uncovered evidence of positive localization and urbanization economies for manufacturing industries; specifically, if employment in any sector in any region were to double, the gross output per worker would increase 3 percent and value added per worker would rise almost 8 percent (Y. J. Lee and Zang 1998).

Analysis of productivity in Chinese industries complements these findings from Korea and buttresses earlier research showing that large and medium-size cities yield better industrial returns than small cities because agglomeration can increase efficiency (Zhou 1988).[11] An increase of 100,000 in the nonagricultural population raises labor productivity by 58 yuan. Technical efficiency is especially high in large industrial cities such as Beijing, Guangzhou, Shanghai, Shenyang, and Wuhan and in the special economic zones of Shenzhen and Zhuhai (Charnes, Cooper, and Li 1989; Sueyoshi 1992). This lends further credence to research suggesting that restrictions on rural to urban migration might have slowed the growth of gross domestic product (GDP) by constraining the majority of Chinese cities from reaching an optimal size (Au and Henderson 2002). Findings for India, too, show that productivity increases with city size (C. M. Becker, Williamson, and Mills 1992; Mills and Becker 1986); for example, cities of 1 million inhabitants are found to be one and a half times more productive than cities of 10,000 inhabitants (Shukla 1996).

Although clusters in general gain from a mix of urbanization and localization economies, for high-tech clusters, the urbanization effects

---

11. Y. Chen (1996) shows that the effect of agglomeration on productivity is positive and high for the machinery industry and lower for less technology-intensive industries, such as food manufacturing.

The two main features of this cluster are its hierarchical, structured, subcontracting system and the coexistence of firms with complementary skills and capabilities. Manufacturers take orders from trading companies and wholesalers and then subcontract out several stages of the production process to first-tier suppliers for metalworking and processing. The first-tier suppliers, in turn, subcontract some work, such as polishing, to second-tier firms before shipment.

In China the Datang sock and stocking clusters in Zhejiang Province provide a vivid example of inter-firm links. Here, more than 10,000 households in 120 villages in and near Datang have become China's biggest center of sock and stocking production (Wang 2001). Unlike industrial agglomerations in cities, these enterprises are rural and family based. Each enterprise specializes in a particular aspect of the production system, covering manufacturing, machinery, marketing, and services, and this networked organization is considered the primary reason for the success of the small firms (Dun and Cai 2000). The division of labor and face-to-face networking in the system enable enterprises to respond quickly to market signals to raise efficiency and minimize risks and costs. This system is locally embedded, as inter-firm linkages depend heavily on trust and social capital.

The local government has fostered the cluster by providing technological information and market facilities. Many of the local officials run their own firms, so they take an active interest in the cluster's development. Local government has established marketplaces for inputs and promulgated market regulations and environmental regulations. The government also has organized an industrial association for the local sock and stocking industry and a private enterprise association.

Clusters in the Pearl River Delta are the backbone of China's export-oriented light manufacturing industry. Their products range from information technology–related products, personal computers, shoes, and small electronics to garments. They emerged around major state-owned enterprises and are a prime example of clustering driven by overseas investment (Wang and Tong forthcoming). The Pearl River Delta accounts for about 3 percent of China's population, but 9 percent of GDP and a third of China's total exports in 2001. Special areas such as the Shenzhen special economic zones became major destinations of foreign direct investment (FDI) because of tax

incentives provided by the government and the low costs of labor and land. In time, local supply networks evolved to cover more stages in the value chain until final assembly was moved to the Pearl River Delta. By 2001 more than 30 percent of exports from the delta were high-tech products, the region was attracting a quarter of total FDI, and it had begun moving away from a light-manufacturing base toward higher-tech activities that will challenge the clusters to the north ("China: Pearl River" 2002).

High-Tech Clusters. East Asia has a few innovative or proto high-tech innovation-driven clusters at early stages of the life cycle with the capacity to become the equals of mature clusters in Boston, Munich, or San Jose (OECD 2001c). Among the leading examples are Kyoto and Tokyo in Japan, Singapore, Hong Kong (China), Taipei/Hsinchu Park in Taiwan (China), and Shanghai in China. Several—such as Hsinchu Park, Daeduck (Korea); Zhangjiang (China); and Jurong, Woodlands, and Tampines (all three in Singapore)—started out as science parks, created in the belief that they would spur regional development.[15] By examining these leading East Asian clusters, it is possible to see the emergence of innovation capability in the region and to delineate policies that could speed the maturation of innovative clusters.

The Tokyo metropolitan region is at the core of the Japanese economy, providing the headquarters for most of Japan's leading firms and serving as the nation's financial center. Tokyo hosts several interlinked clusters, including electronics, engineering, entertainment, finance, and information technology.

Why Tokyo, and why such a proliferation of high-tech clusters? First, the strengths of the Japanese innovation system come together in the Tokyo area. Some of the most prestigious universities and research facilities and a number of leading companies with their own production and research infrastructure are located there. The concentration of banks and other service providers supports the entertainment, information technology, and manufacturing industries. Over time, Tokyo has accumulated a huge amount of intangible capi-

---

15. The view that science parks can serve as the nuclei of clusters emanates from the OECD countries. The United Kingdom, for instance, founded the first park, in Cambridge in 1972. By 1992 the number in the United Kingdom had risen to 42 (Westhead and Batstone 1998).

tal, including research and production skills; social capital, deriving from business associations and networks among researchers as well as among firms that are part of supply networks; and relationships among firms and service providers such as banks.[16] The base of knowledge is very large, and because the Tokyo-based clusters are at the leading edge of innovation, they both observe and closely interact with key clusters in other OECD countries. The accumulated expertise in diverse areas and the long history of successful innovation set the stage for continuing innovation. Buttressing these are the agglomeration economies of a large city, which provides a big and sophisticated market in which to introduce new products and services.[17] In addition, Tokyo, well equipped with institutions for imparting skills, offers companies an extraordinarily deep labor market.

Although Tokyo is vast and thickly populated, it is a relatively well-run city with excellent transport and communications infrastructure that is more than adequate for the needs of modern industry and capable of linking the city with the hinterland in the Kanto Plain and overseas.[18] Tokyo also offers a rich variety of social amenities in a cultural milieu hospitable to the coexistence of tradition and avant-garde modernity and to experimentation within an established order. This cultural environment is responsible for Japan's remarkable succession of contributions to the design of consumer products, video games, and entertainment, such as the internationally popular *Pokemon* (Gibson 2001). Tokyo's variegated neighborhoods, with their low incidence of crime and vibrant street life, offer the urban environment preferred by the types of workers who are decisive to the success of high-tech clusters. Living costs in the core metropolitan areas of Tokyo are high, as is congestion,[19] but these negatives are outweighed

---

16. Ohmae (2002, p. 76) observes, "During the 1970s and 1980s, the hidden key to Japanese success was the existence of two regions—Otaku in Tokyo and Higashi Osaka in Osaka prefecture—where thousands of manufacturers of high-quality precision mechanical and electronic components were clustered together. Major companies with international brand names like Sony and Toshiba have depended on them for their success."

17. The launch and success of NTT DoCoMo's wireless i-mode service are one example (Ratliff 2002).

18. One index of such international interconnectedness is the number of overseas flights. By this count, Tokyo is one of four top-ranked world cities (Taylor and Walker 2001).

19. Both of these erode the productivity advantages of large cities, especially for the manufacturing industry.

by the other advantages of agglomeration for clusters whose lifeblood is knowledge.

Nearly a quarter of a million researchers work in Japanese universities, almost twice as many as in U.S. universities ("Kyoto" 2002). In all, the number of researchers, including those in the social sciences, was 733,000 in 1999 (Sato 2001). Many of the most prestigious universities are in the Tokyo area, with the result that the base of skills available to clusters is unparalleled. To this must be added a large contingent of Japanese nationals who have trained overseas and returned to Tokyo to work. The international operations of Japanese companies have added to local capabilities by creating close connections with the leading centers of research in Europe and the United States. They have done this by investing in production and research facilities, by allying themselves with foreign companies, and by establishing links with research centers and permitting Japanese researchers to visit and collaborate with foreign scholars.

Kyoto, with its proximity to Osaka, has the advantages of being part of an agglomeration not too different in diversity and industrial depth from Tokyo, so that the urbanization economies are almost equally substantial.[20] Kyoto University and several others in the area are comparable in caliber to the leading universities in Tokyo, as are many of the specialized research institutes. Over time, they have established professional ties with high-tech clusters in the West. Osaka, being the second most important urban center in Japan, also has a concentration of service providers that lend valuable support to innovative firms in the surrounding industrial clusters.

Kyoto has an unusually attractive cultural ambience conducive to creative activity and the pursuit of knowledge. As a consequence, some of Japan's most promising and innovative firms have set up their research or production facilities in and around the city center. They range from major companies such as Kyocera (ceramic packages for semiconductors), Rohm (custom chips), and Nintendo (computer games) to smaller firms such as NIDEC (micro motors) and Omron (control components; see "Japan's High-Tech Hope" 1999).

---

20. The Kansai Plain around Osaka rivals the Kanto Plain around Tokyo.

Why Some Well-Endowed Science Centers
Have Not Become High-Tech Clusters

Comparing the clusters in Kyoto and Tokyo with the teaching and research facilities in the Tsukuba Science City 70 kilometers from Tokyo and in Daeduck, in Taejon, Korea, helps to highlight the key features of a world-class innovative cluster.[21]

Both Daeduck and Tsukuba are primarily scientific research centers brought into existence by government policy and the investment of public as well as some private resources. They have remained largely as research facilities, and they have generated little of the social-network capital or spillovers that lead to the growth of high-tech production and exports.[22]

Five factors help to explain why these well-endowed science centers have not developed into full-fledged, innovative clusters. First, their dearth of cultural and social amenities limits the attractions of these highly specialized locations for knowledge workers from within the country and, even more so, from overseas. And neither center is linked closely with clusters elsewhere, in Silicon Valley, the United Kingdom, or the Nordic countries, for example. This has resulted in a degree of intellectual isolation that can stifle innovation.

Second, both centers are somewhat remote from locations supplying financial, entrepreneurial, and managerial services. This, combined with the paucity of social capital and spillovers, has discouraged the entry of firms producing goods or services for national or global markets.[23] Even though many private firms have established facilities in Tsukuba, these have been mainly for research, not manufacturing (Castells and Hall 1994). Emphasis on science alone can be a drawback. In the successful high-tech clusters, the interplay of research,

---

21. Tsukuba was the most ambitious among the many high-tech industrial complexes created following the issuance of Japan's Technopolis Development Plan in 1975.

22. Tsukuba hosts 46 public research institutes, 4 universities, and 350 laboratories owned by private firms. The public facilities employ 8,500 researchers, and private laboratories employ another 4,500 workers. In all, Tsukuba absorbs 40 percent of the national research budget. Daeduck is home to 14,000 researchers who work in 49 research laboratories and 4 universities. Despite the scarcity of social-network capital or spillovers, by 1999 strong support from public institutes and the city of Taejon had induced 219 spin-offs (Oh 2002).

23. Castells and Hall (1994) observe that interaction among public and private institutes is largely absent in Tsukuba, leading to lack of joint research efforts and spin-offs.

production, and the testing of ideas by market forces has been a source of both tension and stimulus. These clusters are marked by the continual entry of firms launched by entrepreneurs with access to finance from relational networks and, increasingly, venture capitalists, as well as investment houses. These firms are often vehicles for innovation and the launch of new products.[24]

Third, specialized science centers lacking both a major research-oriented university and a major high-tech firm will have difficulty acquiring the type of reputation that draws in talented people and stimulates a start-up culture.[25] Moreover, without such firms, the spillovers from research will likely be captured by other centers with strong business role models.

A fourth and related factor is that the urbanization economies that are imparted by a broad industrial system are available in science parks only in a highly attenuated form. These economies include, in particular, services that support a start-up culture expediting the establishment of firms, their takeover by bigger companies, or their growth by way of initial public offerings (chapter 4).

Finally, a focus on basic research is effective only up to a point; applied work and development shaped by market realities are also needed.

Japan's high-tech clusters and science centers provide a lens for viewing other prospective high-tech clusters in East Asia. We now offer a brief assessment of these other clusters in order to bring the dynamics of cluster formation and growth into sharper focus.

Hsinchu Park outside Taipei generates a tenth of GDP in Taiwan, China ("When the Best Brains" 2001). The park grew out of combined efforts by government and the business community to create a Silicon Valley using as a nucleus a major and well-financed research facility, the Industrial and Technology Research Institute, established in 1970.

Hsinchu Park's successful imitation of the U.S. model owed something to the large output of local tertiary education institutions. But it

---

24. As mentioned in chapter 4, most firms are responsible for a single innovation; hence, continuing innovation depends on ease of entry. This, in turn, is facilitated by the availability of risk capital and the management and marketing skills needed to achieve commercial success.

25. Stanford University and the University of California, Berkeley, produced the talent that was responsible for firms such as Cisco, Excite, Google, Oracle, Sun Microsytems, and Yahoo.

also owed much to the growth of high-tech manufacturing in Taiwan, China, in the 1970s and 1980s. The government's targeting of broad areas of industrial development, supported by FDI, built up production skills and inculcated a taste for innovation among producers exposed to the sharp edge of international competition (Hsueh, Hsu, and Perkins 2001). Direct foreign investment in Hsinchu Park initiated links with U.S. firms and began a process of technology transfer, but the expanding diaspora of Taiwanese researchers and entrepreneurs in Silicon Valley was responsible for the virtuous spiral of high-tech development.

Government incentives lured back a trickle of researchers from the United States.[26] They brought into existence a network that spanned the Pacific and that, with the added inducement of Taiwanese manufacturing expertise in the Taipei area, created a new cluster with innovative capabilities comparable to those of Silicon Valley, albeit on a narrower front. Business skills and risk capital followed the researchers, and the deregulation of domestic markets enlarged the opportunities for innovative firms. While public agencies primed the pump, homegrown and U.S.-based venture capitalists augmented the resources available to start-up firms, which served as the centers of innovation, particularly in the electronics industry (Mathews and Cho 2000; Saxenian and Hsu 2001).

Singapore also gained recognition in the 1980s as an East Asian tiger because of its competitiveness in light manufacturing industries. By dint of the government's investment in skills and its efforts to attract multinational corporations, Singapore moved into higher-tech activities and, by the late 1990s, had become a major center of chip fabrication, assembly, and testing, employing more than 20,000 workers in that industry (Mathews 1999). Singapore's efficient transport facilities further reinforce its advantages in high-tech manufacturing. Service providers located in Singapore, catering to the needs of export-oriented industry, have accumulated expertise and acquired a reputation sufficient to make Singapore the second major center for services in the Southeast Asian region.

---

26. These incentives included tax exemptions and the provision of loans at low interest rates. A National Experimental High School was set up in 1983 for the children of Chinese returnees whose Chinese language skills were inadequate (Hsueh, Hsu, and Perkins 2001).

Again in a manner similar to that of Hong Kong, China, the Singapore authorities first used policy incentives and training schemes to establish a manufacturing base, largely with the help of FDI. Aside from government incentives overseas, investors were drawn in by the location, political stability, low labor costs, and the efficiency and customer service orientation of public administrative agencies.

As in the case of Hong Kong, China, the inflow of skilled expatriates as well as the reflux of Singaporeans trained abroad contributed enormously to the growth of the high-tech cluster. The number of professional or skilled foreigners rose from 60,000 in 1996 to 80,000 in 2000, and about 40 percent of Singapore's 4,000 research scientists are expatriates (Yeung 2001).

Singapore differs from Hong Kong, China, with respect to the initiative and entrepreneurship of its government agencies, such as the Economic Development Board, in enhancing the domestic capability to sustain both a service and a high-tech manufacturing sector (Mathews and Cho 2000). The government is relying not just on an ambitious program to expand science, technology, and business skills but also on alliances with foreign firms and universities, a large infusion of venture capital into biotechnology and electronics, and the ability to attract foreign knowledge workers and others from the Southeast Asian diaspora ("Can Money Turn" 2002).

Shanghai-Suzhou, in China, has an incomparably wide base of industrial activities and a hinterland of 159 million people—attributes that made it a natural focus of government efforts to create clusters in high-tech manufacturing and, eventually, in business services (Yeung 2001). National policies reinforced by municipal actions have made Shanghai, and the nearby municipalities of Kunshan and Suzhou, the second most important destination for foreign investment in China after Guangdong Province. FDI is enlarging the Shanghai region's stake in high-tech industry and enlivening domestic R&D.[27] Among the leading Chinese cities, firms from Shanghai have the highest ratio

---

27. On factors leading to Shanghai's development in the 1980s and 1990s, see Yusuf and Wu (1997). Kunshan is known as "Little Taiwan" because of the concentration of investment from Taiwan, China. Suzhou's industrial parks, one set up by Singaporean investors, have attracted a vast amount of foreign direct investment, in part because land is cheaper than in Shanghai, but Shanghai's transport facilities are only 50 kilometers away ("New Frontier" 2001). The Shanghai municipal authorities hope to overtake Beijing and Tianjin by 2010 and become the leading center of technology in China, the leading financial center, and a focus of logistics activities.

of new product sales to total sales (Jefferson and Kaifeng 2002). Science parks are creating proto clusters of firms engaged in electronics, biotechnology, information technology, and telecommunications, although these firms have yet to perfect networking arrangements that encourage traffic in ideas and allow the innovativeness of a few firms to stimulate innovation by the rest.[28]

Physical facilities and the basic financial infrastructure are in place, thanks to policy efforts and massive outlays of resources. The commitment of municipal authorities and foreign investors has contributed to the emergence of parks where biopharmaceutical, electronic, and computer equipment firms are aggressively adopting strategies grounded in the pursuit of innovation.[29] Many of the firms in these parks have been founded by returning Chinese or by Taiwanese investors or are collaborative ventures with multinational corporations. They tend to have links with companies outside China and to participate in existing networks of production. Not only has the Shanghai municipal government provided tax incentives, but it also has invested heavily in communications and transport infrastructure, commercial real estate, and housing to maximize the agglomeration economies (Yusuf and Wu 2002). The municipality has also attempted to encourage networking between researchers and firms (with some success), provided business consulting services, and sought to reduce the entry barriers for new firms.[30]

A survey of 1,500 firms conducted for this study in five Chinese cities shows that more than half the firms participate in business associations that include their suppliers and customers. These firms, mostly drawn from high-tech sectors, are much more likely to seek membership in associations in Shanghai, with its more evolved industrial clusters, than, for instance, in Guangzhou or Tianjin (Steinfeld 2002). Four-fifths of the survey respondents indicated that business associations are effective vehicles for gaining access to market infor-

---

28. Although their attempt to imitate Singapore has only partially succeeded, science parks in Suzhou have been attracting a flood of capital into high-tech manufacturing.

29. Three major semiconductor plants have been established in Zhangjiang, and the park has attracted pharmaceutical companies such as Bayer ("APEC in Shanghai" 2001).

30. See the findings of Lawlor and others (2002), based on a survey of firms in Zhanjiang Park in Shanghai's Pudong District and Zhougguancun Park in Beijing. On the policy measures to develop high-tech industry, see Segal (2003).

mation. Foreign investors have been attracted by urban living conditions and the ready availability of skilled workers. The coming of major multinational corporations such as Alcatel, Nokia, and Philips has begun to draw affiliated suppliers with the potential to create dynamic networking arrangements ("New Frontier" 2001).

Even so, the Shanghai area is still short of intangible assets, business services, and accumulated research experience (on the importance of such R&D capital, see Murtha, Lenway, and Hart 2001 and Parente and Prescott 2000). It has yet to show significant capability for innovation. Shanghai's clusters lack the technological mastery and creativity that differentiate the leading clusters from others. To achieve these is likely to require a steady upgrading of human resources and a deepening of skills in service sectors in particular locations to create the desirable critical mass. Beyond that, acquiring innovative capability comparable to that of the most dynamic clusters in the West calls for interaction and integration with those clusters, as well as for steps to attract more high-caliber Chinese professionals from abroad and more foreign knowledge workers.

Beijing is only slightly less populous than Shanghai—14 million as against 17 million people—and it has a stronger university system. It also has the advantages that derive from being the seat of central government, including good logistics and industrial breadth, although Shanghai is the more industrialized of the two. Relative to firms in Shanghai, however, firms in Beijing are not as innovative, as measured by new products and processes. Networking among firms and the formation of clusters have been less coherent and productive than in Shanghai, and the returns from R&D have been smaller (Jefferson and Kaifeng 2002). A survey of Zhongguancun Science Park indicates that many firms were established by university researchers and returning expatriates (Jefferson and Kaifeng 2002). Most firms locate in the park to take advantage of tax breaks and the supply of skilled workers. However, the benefits of agglomeration are not effectively harnessed, in large part because municipal policies do not motivate or reinforce the formation of clusters, and only a limited supply of venture capital is as yet available (Lawlor and others 2002).

The successful electronics industry in Malaysia, accounting for half of the country's total exports and employing a quarter of the manufacturing labor force, is a composite of three regional clusters, of which Penang is the largest and possesses the most advanced technology and management capacities (Best 2001; Mathews and Cho 2000).

A cluster-based development strategy is one of the key elements underlying Penang's success. Initiated by the state-owned Penang Development Cooperation founded in 1969, Penang's regional policies successfully attracted many of the world's leading electronic companies and encouraged these multinational corporations to upgrade the technological capacities and base of skills in the cluster. Penang started in the early 1970s with relatively low-wage, labor-intensive industries, such as assembly, packaging, and testing of semiconductors managed by foreign-based multinational corporations, and gradually developed a low-cost, high-volume, and increasingly automated world-class manufacturing center specializing in electronic components.

The tremendous growth in Malaysia's electronics industry has come mainly from expanding the volume of output rather than adding value. The essential reason is that the industry lacks the technology and innovation capacities to design and manufacture higher-return products. Even in Penang, the limited R&D by multinational corporations focuses mainly on small, short-term, and applied projects. There are only 10,000 scientists and engineers per million population in Penang—much lower than the ratio of 25,000 per million population in Hong Kong, China, and Singapore—in spite of the state government's emphasis on training and infrastructure through Vendor Partnership and other programs. This has been supplemented by the efforts of companies such as Motorola and Intel, which founded the Intel Design Center and Intel University. However, for Penang to compete effectively with Singapore or other high-tech centers emerging in the region will require substantial upgrading of skills; the proliferation of successful homegrown firms such as Eng, Globertronics, Trans Capital Holdings, and UNICO; and the deepening of both local and international networking.

Service Clusters

Most East Asian economies—led by Hong Kong, China—are becoming more service intensive as rising incomes are shifting demand toward services. Reinforcing this trend are the greater specialization and outsourcing of services by firms and the widening opportunities for trade in services such as marketing, distribution, after-sales service, finance, insurance, and real estate, all stimulated by information technology–based reductions in transaction costs (Wirtz 2000). Such opportunities have induced a large flow of FDI into services (Hanson and Feenstra 2001).

Against this background, the rise of information technology, the global financial industry, and the scope for e-business activities have enhanced the viability of service-only clusters, among which London and New York offer two leading examples. By networking with clusters in East Asia, service-only clusters are globalizing the provision of legal, accounting, and financial services (figure 6.1).

Service clusters are noteworthy for the support they provide to manufacturing clusters (both nearby and far removed).[31] London, for example, provides services for the high-tech manufacturing cluster that has emerged in the vicinity of the M4 motorway and exports services to clusters throughout the world. In Detroit, engineering services support the transport industry, while in Houston, engineering and computer services provide vital inputs to the petroleum industry. The information technology and biotechnology clusters around Washington, D.C., result from spillovers from federal research centers, particularly the National Institutes of Health; the entrepreneurial initiatives of former federal employees; and the demand for information technology services from the government, which accounts for a third of metropolitan GDP (Feldman 2001). Similarly, New York's entertainment-centered Silicon Alley depends on the metropolitan region's agglomeration economies and on close links to the Manhattan-based service cluster.

Even more so than manufacturing clusters, service clusters depend on knowledge workers for whom the physical, social, and cultural amenities offered by major cities are especially attractive, underscoring the role of particular urbanization effects in cluster formation.

In East Asia, Hong Kong, China, is a service cluster, while Singapore is a mixed cluster, with high-tech manufacturing coexisting and

---

31. The three principal information technology services in the United States are computer services; engineering and architectural services; and information, management, and public relations. Together, these account for one-third of high-tech sector employment and have strong links with manufacturing (Markusen and others 2001).

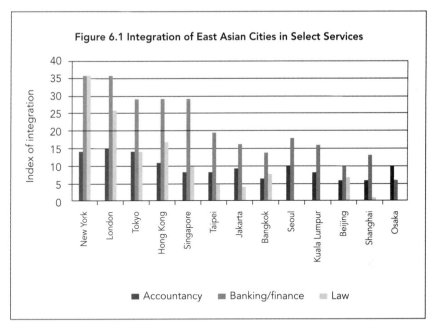

Figure 6.1 Integration of East Asian Cities in Select Services

■ Accountancy   ■ Banking/finance   ▨ Law

Note: The index of integration is based on an ordinal scale of 0–3, reflecting the extent of the integration (0 = least integrated, 3 = most integrated) of the firm's offices at a particular location to the other office locations of the same firm. The data are as reported in Globalization and World Cities Study Group and Network (2001) and also published in the reference cited. The columns in the chart denote the sum of scores for select transnational firms in each service. The data set comprises 5 accountancy firms, 14 banking or finance firms, and 16 law firms with operations and establishments in New York or London and also in the group of East Asian service locations. Hence, maximum value for accountancy is 15, for banking/finance is 42, and for law is 48.
Source: Globalization and World Cities Study Group and Network collected the data in 2001. Data Set 6 is available at http://www.lboro.ac.uk/gawc/datasets/da6.html.

drawing on the city's financial core. Hong Kong, China, is a center for services in the region and a linchpin of the international financial system. Its business services cluster—the most efficient in the region—supplies financial, legal, engineering, design, information technology, marketing, finishing, supply management, production-related, and other services, not only to the myriad manufacturing enterprises in China's Pearl River Delta area—many of which moved from Hong Kong, China, in search of lower costs—but also to producers in surrounding countries as well (Berger and Lester 1997). Most of the firms in Hong Kong, China, even the very small ones, employ the majority of their workers outside Hong Kong, China, mostly in Guangdong, which accounts for 40 percent of China's man-ufactured exports (Enright and others 1997, pp. 11–13).

Hong Kong, China, which started as a low- and medium-tech manufacturing cluster, began to specialize in business services in the 1980s. The growth of the service sector accelerated with the flow of FDI, attracted by the location, quality of governance, and supply of workers with some English language skills.[32] Even in the early stages, some FDI went into services. With the opening of China in 1979, op-erations shifted to industrial zones in Guangdong Province, and both local and foreign investors perceived the advantages of specializing in services to complement the burgeoning manufacturing strength of the South China region. The efficiency of trading services provided by Hong Kong, China, is such that when Chinese exports are routed through Hong Kong, China, buyers save, on average, 16 percent of the value of the exports (Feenstra, Hanson, and Lin 2002).

This process has been supported by public investment, which helped to build the basic infrastructure, especially worker housing. Liberal government policies pulled in local private investors and FDI into real estate, transport and communications, logistics, and other areas of im-portance for the urban service sector. The completion of a state-of-the-art airport at Chap Lap Kok—rated the world's leading airport in 2001—has augmented the quality of Hong Kong's infrastructure, and the cyberport inaugurated in October 2001 could become an addition-al source of strength (although its utility has been debated).

Business services require a high level of skills, only some of which were at hand locally; thus the Hong Kong, China, cluster has de-pended on a large infusion of professionals from abroad and now also from mainland China.

POLICIES FOR CLUSTERS

The preconditions for transforming industrial clusters into truly in-novative ones with the requisite long-term dynamism are quite exact-ing. Apart from geographic location and physical ambience, the sup-

---

32. The supply of engineers and skilled workers remains a draw for manufacturers of higher value added products (Lau and Green 2001). However, English language skills have eroded since 1997, threatening the lead of Hong Kong over Shanghai.

ply of skilled workers, industrial breadth, market institutions, infrastructure, and social as well as cultural amenities are all needed to attain the critical mass of intangible human, social, and physical capital required to make an innovative high-technology cluster.

Happenstance and market forces clearly constitute a large part of the story underlying the most successful innovative clusters, but experience shows that policies matter as well. In countries attempting to build innovative clusters in short order, they are likely to dominate the play of market forces (Hsueh, Hsu, and Perkins 2001; Krugman 1991; Mathews and Cho 2000). Assuming that the basic macroeconomic, political, and sectoral environment is favorable, public policies can play an instrumental role in several ways that impinge directly on the dynamics of firms, the supply of intangible capital, and their innovativeness.

Development policy in East Asia has traditionally focused on macroeconomic and industrial issues, such as export promotion, sectoral targeting, macroeconomic stability, and education. Attempts to develop clusters have generally taken the form of conventional urban planning approaches, large localized infrastructure projects, fiscal regimes, and financial assistance (science parks, special economic zones, export-processing zones, and so on).

But although these constitute one set of desirable initiatives, they alone are insufficient. An approach that encompasses the planning, organizational, and social capital aspects of cluster development is likely to yield better results. Even relatively sophisticated regional development schemes, such as Japan's Technopolis Program or Malaysia's Multimedia Corridor, would undoubtedly be much enhanced by such an approach.

Macro Policies as Instigators

With the benefit of hindsight, it is clear that leading industrial clusters in OECD economies, Singapore, and Taiwan (China) owe their existence to government actions. In the United States, for example, government spending on defense-related research and production, as well as on infrastructure, strongly influenced the success of initiatives taken by John Wallace Sterling, president of Stanford University, to set up a science park adjacent to the university. Government spending also provided the incentives for the start-ups linked with firms such as Fairchild. Silicon Glen in Scotland was the outgrowth of government efforts to attract information technology firms, as was Silicon Fen near Cambridge, England, albeit to a lesser extent. The Finnish government enabled Nokia to become the leading supplier of mobile phones and the hub of a telecommunications cluster by adopting the standard known as global system for mobile telecommunications and providing a regulatory environment conducive to development. The Finnish government also allocated nearly half a billion euros through the National Technology Agency (Tekes) to assist cooperation among scientists, industry, users, and financiers.[33] Although not directly targeted for cluster development, these resources encouraged networking and start-ups stemming from a few key firms (Richards 2001). Apart from channeling resources into research, university development, and infrastructure, governments, especially in the United Kingdom and the United States, were also major sources of stable demand for high-tech products.

Research on science parks in the United Kingdom has indicated that, by offering favorable and flexible lease terms, science parks could remove a barrier for start-up firms (Wallsten 2000). Once a park has achieved success, firms are willing to pay a premium to locate there so as to leverage off its reputation. However, Wallsten finds that creating science parks has no effect on country-level high-tech employment (see also Westhead and Batstone 1998).

The findings of surveys conducted for this study suggest that science parks in Beijing and Shanghai have, on balance, enhanced the productivity of R&D by firms. Concessions typically include standard "economic development tools," such as tax exemptions, subsidies, and zoning regulation compromises, in the effort to attract new investors (Wolman and Spitzley 1996). Used judiciously with a close eye to anticipated economic returns, they can produce results, as in Hsinchu Park near Taipei, the Pudong New Area, or Israel's Magnet Program and Binational Industrial Research and Development Fund (de Fontenay and Carmel 2001).

---

33. A billion is 1,000 million.

Focusing on individual firms and banking on spillovers to generate a self-sustaining spiral fail to address many facets of cluster formation.[34] Concessions tailored to individual firms rarely trigger an endogenous process leading to the formation of a cluster with significant growth potential. Likewise, public provision of venture capital, widely practiced in East Asian countries, has not yet had much effect on high-tech employment, and it risks crowding out essential private venture capital (Wallsten 2000). Firm-specific concessions have the additional drawback of encouraging predatory rent-seeking behavior.

Local-level measures often have uncertain outcomes because institutional and administrative competence is lacking. Such competence is necessary to cultivate competitive advantages in appropriate ways, especially in urban areas starting from relatively low levels of competitiveness.

A Framework for Action

What can central governments and local authorities do to ensure supplies of the types of public goods that support cluster formation? These public goods include many-faceted services such as network initiation, maintenance, and strategic programming, together with related investments in social and physical infrastructure designed to sustain a regional learning economy. The precise interventions that must be envisaged in pursuit of public goods like these are enormously disparate, and they must be tailored to the specificities of local context. However, three general categories of relevant public action can be identified at this stage.

Network Governance Operations. Probably the most difficult task in cluster development is to initiate the industrial network dynamics without which all other interventions are likely to be stillborn. The active cooperation of significant groups of firms and business associations is essential here, as are intermediation activities in which desig-

---

34. There have been some rare successes, however, such as the Taiwan Semiconductor Manufacturing Company founded by the Taiwanese authorities in 1987.

nated agents or brokers assume responsibility for animating the entire process.[35]

At a minimum, two sets of actions should be undertaken in this regard: the first of these involves (1) drawing up a strategic audit or critical inventory of the resources currently available to the putative network and the forms of interaction, if any, that already exist; (2) identifying particular market niches and proposals for contesting these niches through a systematic effort to develop and market differentiated products; and (3) encouraging deeper inter-firm transactional engagements and search for commercially useful forms of collaborative interaction, for example, in the areas of technology sharing, industrial design, supplier relations, and other forms of joint venturing (Izushi 1999).

The second set of actions is especially problematic in the sense that viable market niches need to be cultivated carefully over time and cannot be identified easily in advance of at least preliminary efforts at production and marketing. Hence this action needs to be approached in an open-ended, bottom-up manner, allowing the many different experiences of the evolving network to be pooled, analyzed, and followed up or abandoned, as the situation demands. An important principle here is to avoid, as far as possible, head-to-head competition with producers in more established agglomerations, for these producers will most likely have acquired first-mover advantages and a level of industrial performance that later entrants will always find hard to match.

Public Goods and Services for Urban Clusters. Once a clustered system begins to develop in earnest, specific kinds of public goods and services are needed to sustain the process. Among the more critical of these are cluster-specific technological information and labor training services. In the context of pure market relationships, private firms typically will underinvest in these services because it is so difficult for

---

35. The University of California, Davis, is a leading wine research center because of public investment supported by industry associations. The area hosts nearly 700 wineries and thousands of independent grape growers, who in turn are supported by a huge industry composed of firms supplying everything from grape stock to harvesting equipment as well as firms that do marketing and public relations and issue the numerous publications aimed at consumer and trade audiences (Porter 1998b).

any single party to appropriate the fruits of private outlays on them. Technological information is notoriously leaky, and workers always take their training with them when they switch jobs. An obvious response to problems like these is to provide a significant nexus of relevant services as local public goods.

Similarly, many firms, especially if they are small, are unable to equip themselves to efficiently handle software development, data analysis, marketing, export promotion, payroll preparation, and so on. In less developed parts of the world, entrepreneurial responses to these gaps in the production system may be deficient. Public agencies or local associations can often provide these inputs cost-effectively, either by direct subsidy or on a regional cost-sharing basis. Brusco (1992) calls the outputs of such agencies "real services" to distinguish them from the financial subsidies and tax breaks that otherwise often pass for regional development policy measures.

For more than a century, Japanese prefecture governments have taken the lead in setting up testing and research centers for development and dissemination of ceramic textiles and chemical and food products (Yamawaki 2001). Many trade associations also sponsor such facilities and serve as clearinghouses for information. Dutch flower-grower cooperatives are responsible for the auction, handling, and research facilities that are the source of the industry's competitive advantage. In Massachusetts manufacturers of medical devices have formed MassMedic to work with the U.S. Food and Drug Administration to streamline the approval process for medical equipment. As Porter (1998b) notes, this benefits the medical devices cluster, but it also helps to sustain the pace of competition.

Steering Problems. Clusters are constituted as intricate social mosaics of firms, workers, and institutional structures in dense geographic interdependent concentrations. If we take a snapshot of a given system at any one time, we are likely to see less a condition of static equilibrium than a moment in a historical process of adjustment, whose inbuilt structure is the result of all its past development. A peculiarity of evolutionary structures of this sort is their propensity to become locked into a narrow set of developmental paths, which sometimes lead to increasingly dysfunctional outcomes (P. A. David 1985). Once such a lock-in occurs, any readjustment of the main directions of regional economic change can be achieved (if at all) only at high cost.

The point here is that well-designed and prudently managed coordinating services can be extremely helpful in promoting socially desirable growth paths and in helping to foresee, deal with, and head off crises in the local system.[36] One possible institutional framework within which to provide such services is a common forum, in which potential problems can be brought forward and discussed and in which appropriate lines of remedial action can be hammered out.

Burgeoning industrial networks, too, will often benefit from the establishment of governance structures in order to maintain cooperative relations, to streamline inter-firm links (for example, by means of just-in-time processing activities), or to engage in joint marketing or product promotion (including, for example, the establishment and control of regional trademarks or quality standards). This is a sphere of activity in which appropriate prompting by public authorities can often galvanize producers to set up useful self-regulating associations. Measures to ensure that establishments owned by multinational corporations engage in effective forms of technology transfer and provide other positive spillovers may also figure under this rubric.

Finally, the institutions designated to serve these management functions need not necessarily be local government agencies. Depending on local conditions, traditions, and political sensibilities, there is no reason, in principle, why they cannot also take the form of civil associations (involving, for example, industrial alliances and associations, labor unions, or community groups), private-public partnerships, or indeed any other type of organization with the legitimacy and requisite social powers to carry out collective decisionmaking and action.

INTANGIBLE ASSETS: THE DIASPORA AND INTERNATIONAL KNOWLEDGE WORKERS

East Asia's high-tech clusters are built on domestic innovative capacity, but to draw abreast of and compete with the technologically ad-

---

36. Avoidance of coordination failures has been associated with past development successes in East Asia (Okazaki 2001).

vanced countries on the basis of innovation will require a substantial augmentation of the local pool of researchers, entrepreneurs, intermediaries, and business service suppliers. FDI in the form of joint ventures or subsidiaries leads to the diffusion of knowledge within a company, primarily through the transfer of skilled workers, but produces few spillovers (Globerman 2000). The real gains for East Asian economies lie in attracting back, temporarily or permanently, skilled nationals who are working outside the region. Attracting other experienced professionals to work in East Asian economies will also assist the development of technology.

What overseas human capital is potentially available to East Asian clusters? And what policies can be used to influence the supply of human capital and the circulation of knowledge from abroad?

East Asia's Diaspora of Skills

Attracting workers who have trained in the leading research centers abroad and acquired experience as well as contacts in some of the principal overseas high-tech clusters is the most expeditious approach. A large percentage of the potential candidates are likely to be found in North America. During the past two decades, the United States hosted more than half of all East Asian college students studying abroad, including a high percentage of the very brightest. This was and is related to the size, quality, and reputation of the U.S. university system, the availability of financial support, and the prospect of job opportunities after graduation (table 6.1).[37] The United Kingdom had the second largest contingent, followed by Germany, although only a very small number of East Asians were residing in these two countries.

Students from Hong Kong (China), Malaysia, and Singapore are well spread among Australia, Canada, the United Kingdom, and the United States.[38] In contrast, Taiwanese, Indonesian, Japanese, and Thai college students study mainly in the United States, while large

---

37. This section is based on Lucas (2002). In 1996 three-fourths of the 10,000 foreign doctoral students in the United States were supported primarily by their universities (OECD 2001d).

38. Data on the number of students from Hong Kong, China, studying in Canada show wide variations during the 1990s, apparently as a result of the large number of naturalizations (Skeldon 1997).

Table 6.1 Stock of International Students in the United States in a Given Year, 1981–2000

Economy	1981	1990	1995	2000
China	2,770	33,390	39,400	54,466
Japan	13,500	29,840	45,280	46,872
Taiwan, China	19,460	30,960	36,410	29,234
Korea, Rep. of	6,150	21,710	33,600	41,191
Hong Kong, China	9,660	11,230	12,940	7,545
Malaysia	6,010	14,110	13,620	9,074
Indonesia	3,250	9,390	11,870	11,300
Thailand	6,550	—	10,890	10,983

— Not available.

Source: Institute for International Education, Open Doors (various years) and www.opendoorsweb.org/Lead%20Stories/international_tuds.htm.

numbers of students from China and Korea travel to both Japan and the United States.[39]

Technical progress and technology transfer through clusters depend to a large extent on the role of scientists and engineers (Eaton and Kortum 2000). Of the East Asian–born college graduates who were employed in the United States in 1997, 23 percent were in science or engineering, with about 45 percent of these designated as engineers. The largest absolute number of scientists and engineers came from China, the Philippines, and Taiwan, China (mainly engineers), although even more came from India (table 6.2). The portion of East Asian scientists and engineers actually working in science and engineering occupations was much greater, at 56 percent, than those of foreign- or U.S.-born scientists and engineers (48 and 41 percent, respectively).

Permanent settlement in both Australia and Canada is subject to a skill-based point system (introduced by Australia in 1997), with the result that immigrants to both countries tend to be highly skilled (OECD 2001d). Australian data suggest that a greater proportion of Asian settlers are professionals relative to those from other parts of

---

39. In addition, the United Nations Educational, Scientific, and Cultural Organization reports some 8,500 Japanese and 6,500 Korean college students in China in 1993–94, although it is not clear how many of these were in Taiwan, China.

Table 6.2 Foreign-Born and U.S.-Born Scientists and Engineers in the United States, by Employment Status and Major Occupational Group, 1997 (thousands of persons)

Economy	Total	Employed						Not employed
		Computer scientists	Life scientists	Physical scientists	Social scientists	Engineers	Other	
East Asia	467.8	71.4	16.6	16.8	6.6	88.0	207.7	60.7
India	188.5	33.8	7.8	6.8	3.1	37.2	77.9	21.9
Other South Asia	32.9	4.5	—	—	—	6.2	22.2	—
Other Asia	112.9	13.5	2.9	3.4	2.5	24.9	52.6	13.1
Other foreign	713.9	63.4	25.4	24.1	22.2	95.3	461.4	117.4
United States	11,014.7	852.8	269.0	233.7	314.6	1,122.8	6,489.8	1,732.0
China	102.0	20.5	8.0	7.4	1.7	22.0	26.7	15.7
Hong Kong, China	35.0	7.6	—	—	—	7.0	20.4	—
Indonesia	6.7	—	—	—	—	—	6.7	—
Japan	37.9	—	—	—	—	5.0	32.9	—
Korea, Rep. of	53.5	5.4	2.0	—	—	7.7	28.5	9.9
Malaysia	7.1	2.1	—	—	—	—	5.0	—
Philippines	93.1	5.1	—	—	—	12.4	63.9	11.7
Taiwan, China	70.8	16.0	1.9	2.0	—	14.3	28.6	8.0
Thailand	8.1	—	—	—	—	—	8.1	—
Vietnam	45.5	9.3	—	—	—	13.1	23.1	—
Other East Asia	8.1	—	—	—	—	—	8.1	—

— Not available.

Source: National Science Foundation (1997, 2001b).

Table 6.3 Arrivals of Australian Settlers, by Occupation, 1996–97

| Economy | Total | | Occupation of those employed (percent) | | | | |
	Number	Percent employed	Managers and administrators	Professionals	Paraprofessionals	Others	Total
Total	85,752	52.5	13.6	27.7	6.3	52.4	100.0
Asia	32,084	51.4	18.7	32.7	5.2	43.3	100.0
India	2,681	55.6	9.7	50.0	4.5	35.8	100.0
China	7,761	59.0	16.8	39.0	7.0	37.2	100.0
Hong Kong, China	3,894	53.3	29.7	42.7	5.1	22.6	100.0
Indonesia	1,750	41.0	49.4	13.0	1.9	35.7	100.0
Philippines	2,808	44.1	5.4	21.8	12.2	60.6	100.0
Taiwan, China	2,177	42.4	63.0	21.3	1.1	14.6	100.0

Source: Iredale (2000, table 2).

the world (table 6.3).[40] In 1996–97 some 56 percent of the employed Asian settlers in Australia were in highly skilled occupations (managers and administrators, professionals, or paraprofessionals), compared with only 42 percent of non-Asian settlers.

The large-scale inflows of skilled workers to the United States commenced with the Hart-Cellar Act of 1965, which allowed immigration of people with scarce skills. This coincided with the growth of new industries in Silicon Valley (Saxenian and Hsu 2001). With respect to the departure of people with tertiary education as of 1990, Malaysia had the highest brain drain, followed by Korea (Carrington and Detragiache 1998). The brain drain in both of these countries is likely to have declined during the 1990s, as the college-educated base of workers expanded and a migration transition occurred. From China, the departure of tertiary-educated people accelerated in the 1990s. In all, close to 400,000 Chinese students went abroad between 1978 and 1999, 54 percent of them to the United States (OECD 2001d).[41] From Taiwan, China, the emigration rate of college-educated people was far greater; by 1990 almost 10 percent of all such persons and 20 percent of science and technology graduates were emigrating (OECD 2001d). From the Philippines, too, there has been a significant departure of people with both secondary and tertiary education. During the 1990s the United States attracted 650,000 people from emerging economies on professional employment visas alone. Currently, close to 40 percent of all foreign-born adults have some college education, and a fifth of all those working in the information technology sector are foreign born.

The OECD estimates may be biased downward by the inclusion of migration only from the largest source countries and by the omission of all short-term and many illegal migrants ("When the Best Brains" 2001). The figures most likely also understate the skills of migrants and their spouses, some of whom have high qualifications and work experience (Iredale 2000). In fact, more recent estimates for China

---

40. The absolute flow of Asian permanent settlers into Australia is fairly small relative to flows into Canada and the United States, although it is large relative to Australia's population. Annually in 1990–98, an additional 36,000 people from Asia were, on average, admitted on temporary permits.

41. See also www.chinanews.com.cn/2001-08.20.

alone suggest that 200,000 science and technology workers emigrated permanently between 1978 and 1999 (OECD 2001d).[42]

The circulation of scientific and engineering workers assumes additional importance from the perspective of future knowledge transfer when one takes into account the likelihood that it is often the brightest people who move and that most of them move to a few high-tech clusters (OECD 2001d).

Creating Social Networks

By creating a large reservoir of talent in the OECD countries, the departure of highly skilled people can also benefit those who stay in East Asia and promote the development of high-tech clusters. Whether these benefits are realized will depend on a mix of public policies to lure knowledge workers back from abroad, initiatives by private firms, and influence exerted by international social networks ("Tug of War" 2000).

What is the nature of international social networks, and what role do they play in promoting remittances, capital flows, foreign trade, and technology transfer? Since the 1970s, the Chinese diaspora has played a substantial role in East Asian development. More recently, the Indian diaspora has begun contributing to the growth of information technology in India ("In India, a Bit of California" 2000). In contrast, a Filipino, Malaysian, or Vietnamese diaspora is mentioned much less often.

A plethora of ethnic-based associations among East Asian professionals in the United States contributes to cluster development in China, Korea, and Taiwan (China). Such networks were initially local, providing immigrants with labor market information, professional contacts, and a safety net. Saxenian (1999, p. 21) notes, "As their communities grew during the 1970s and 1980s, these immigrants responded to the sense of professional and social exclusion by organizing collectively,"[43] and

---

42. About 15 percent of India's software engineers emigrate each year—the annual output of trained software specialists is 178,000. As a result, two-fifths of all Indian software developers now work in the United States ("Sub-Continental Drift" 2000).

43. "Many of these associations have become important forums for cross-generational investment and mentoring as well.... Individuals within these networks often invest individually or jointly... acting as 'angel' investors who are more accessible to immigrants than the mainstream venture capital community" (Saxenian 1999, p. 32).

It is a community of U.S. educated engineers who have built a social and economic bridge linking the Silicon Valley and Hsinchu Park economies. These highly skilled Taiwanese immigrants are distinguished from the broader Chinese diaspora by shared professional as well as ethnic identities and by their deep integration into the technical communities of both technology regions.[44]

In Silicon Valley, Chinese and Indian immigrants form the largest groups and are the best organized, although more recently Filipino, Japanese, Korean, and Singaporean organizations have also appeared. As the networks evolve, they will be better able to incorporate tacit knowledge into their learning processes and to expand their international activities.

One key international role of such networks is the transmission of information. For instance, the Chinese Institute of Engineers, founded in 1979 by a small group of engineers from Taiwan, China, working in Silicon Valley, organizes an annual seminar in collaboration with their counterpart organization in Taiwan, China, and provides consultative services to the government of Taiwan, China. Other far less formal transmission mechanisms also exist.

Saxenian (1999, p. 62) argues that Asian-born, U.S.-based engineers and scientists play a key role in stimulating investment and trade by acting as middlemen in the high-tech world:

> Silicon Valley remains the center of new product definition and design and development of leading-edge technologies, whereas Taiwan [China] offers world-class manufacturing, flexible development and integration, and access to key customers and markets in China and Southeast Asia.... However, these economic gains from specialization and trade would not be possible without the underlying social structures and institutions provided by the community of Taiwanese engineers, which ensures continuous flows of information between the two regions.

By enhancing the credibility of information, networks established by emigrants promote capital flows and trade as well as technology transfers (Kapur 2001).

They stimulate capital flows in other ways as well. Emigrants may be more ready than others to invest in their own countries of origin, because they are better placed to evaluate investment opportunities

---

44. See also Saxenian and Hsu (2001); Hsueh, Hsu, and Perkins (2001).

and retain contacts to facilitate this process.[45] Emigrants may also encourage foreigners to invest in their country of origin. Indeed, successful direct investment frequently demands a local facilitating partner. Emigrants are well placed to identify trustworthy and competent partners. Moreover, returned migrants, known to the foreign investor, may even take on the role of local counterpart.[46] In addition, exposure to nationals from a particular country may alter perceptions about doing business with that person's country, again encouraging foreign investment.[47]

Networks can be especially effective in channeling international capital flows to dynamic industries, in which information commands the highest premium. As Saxenian (1999, pp. 54–55) observes,

> The scarce resource in this new environment is the ability to locate foreign partners quickly and to manage complex business relationships across cultural and linguistic boundaries. This is particularly a challenge in high-technology industries in which products, markets, and technologies are continually being redefined—and where product cycles are routinely shorter than nine months.

Given the importance of high-technology industries in East Asia, the role of international networks in stimulating investments assumes special importance.

The magnitude of network effects on international capital flows remains to be estimated, although the diaspora clearly plays a role in promoting foreign investment in both China and Taiwan, China. In China, after the introduction of Deng Xiaoping's "open door" policy initiative in 1978, there was a steady but moderate inflow of foreign direct investment. This accelerated sharply after 1992, rising from $11.97 billion in 1991 to $62.4 billion in 2000. By 2000, 38 percent of the accumulated foreign direct investment in China came from Hong Kong, China, and Macao, China; and a further 5.6 percent came

---

45. Close to 800 firms in Silicon Valley in 1999 were headed by a chief executive of Indian extraction, and since the mid-1990s wealthy Indian professionals and business people have begun investing in India ("In India, a Bit of California" 2000).

46. Saxenian (1999, pp. 62–63) offers a case study of Hewlett-Packard in India.

47. Kapur (2001, p. 16) describes the mentoring role that TIE (a group of Indian information technology entrepreneurs and professionals) has played by boosting "confidence of overseas investors about India's potential despite India's innumerable problems."

from Taiwan, China.[48] The investments in China originating from the diaspora are by highly skilled, entrepreneurial emigrants whose families left China during the 1930s through the early 1950s (Gambe 2000).

The role of the Chinese diaspora in providing finance has led some observers to suggest that their influence has also been vital in promoting economic reform within China (Lever-Tracy, Ip, and Tracy 1996). Both in China and throughout Southeast Asia, in the transnational activities of the Chinese diaspora, "kinship ties are extremely important, and family control over firms is the rule" (Weidenbaum and Hughes 1996, p. 53). In other words, "The massive cross-investments among these nations are evidence of a new but poorly understood economic power... the bamboo network" (Weidenbaum and Hughes 1996, p. 8).

Throughout the 1990s, there was a steady two-way flow of knowledge workers, entrepreneurs, and capital between Silicon Valley and the Hsinchu-Taipei region in Taiwan, China. Saxenian (1999, p. 61) quotes one Taiwanese investor as saying, "When we invest we are also helping bring entrepreneurs back to Taiwan [China]. It is relationship building."

Chinese- and Indian-run firms remain relatively small in Silicon Valley, with an average of 21 employees in 1998 (Saxenian 1999, p. 24).[49] However, they accounted for a quarter of all companies in the cluster, generated $16.8 billion in sales, and employed more than 50,000 workers. These firms are becoming important contributors to the trading relationships that are critical to the growth of high-tech clusters.

Rauch and Trindade (2002) provide evidence of this relationship between migration and trade in their examination of the global patterns of bilateral trade in 1980 and in 1990. They find that ethnic Chinese networks in Southeast Asia significantly increase bilateral

---

48. The share from Hong Kong, China, and Macao, China, would have been 47 percent if the foreign direct investment channeled through the Virgin Islands had been included (Lai 2002). The figures are from Li and Li (1999) and China, National Bureau of Statistics (2001). Foreign investments arriving from Hong Kong, China, do not necessarily originate there.

49. Saxenian characterizes the relationships between Silicon Valley and the Bangalore-Hyderabad nexus in India as more arm's length than is the link with Taiwan, China. Nonetheless, Indian immigrants in the United States have become significant sources of venture capital for software start-ups in India as well.

trade. Rauch and Watson (2002) draw attention to the part played by network intermediaries drawn from the diaspora, who help to match demand for differentiated products with supplies, actual or potential, from East Asia. Migrations of highly skilled workers may play a more critical role in trade expansion than do other migrations because they augment the number of such network entrepreneurs (Rauch and Watson 2002; Saxenian 1999).[50]

Saxenian (1999, p. 60) notes, "This transnational community [of Taiwan-born, U.S.-based professionals] has accelerated the upgrading of Taiwan's technological infrastructure by transferring technical know-how and organizational models as well as by forging closer ties with Silicon Valley. . . . Management practices in Hsinchu companies are more like those of Silicon Valley than of the traditional family-firm model that dominates older industries in Taiwan [China]." By 2000 the number returning to Taiwan, China, with a Ph.D. degree had risen to 4,108, as against just 27 in 1983. This circulation has been facilitated by the more than 70 companies based in Hsinchu Park that maintain offices in Silicon Valley (OECD 2001d).

Migrants transfer technology through informal channels such as visits and communications as well as return migration. More formal contacts through associations and international meetings offer another channel. For example, in 1999 Singapore was chosen as the venue for the permanent secretariat of the World Chinese Entrepreneurs' Convention, which meets biennially. The Chinese Institute of Engineers and the Indus Entrepreneur are examples of other associations that have helped to establish links among overseas professionals.

---

50. Head and Reis (1998), in their examination of the links between the bilateral patterns of Canadian trade and the origins of Canadian immigrants, find that skilled migrants have a larger impact on trade than unskilled migrants. The elasticity of response of trade to skill-based migration (independent immigrants) proves significantly greater than the response to family-based, refugee, or business immigrants, and the import response proves largest for immigrants from East Asia. Combining these two additive effects, the estimates suggest that "East Asian independent immigrants have an export elasticity of 0.29 and an import elasticity of 0.74." In other words, a doubling of skilled immigration into Canada from East Asia is estimated to be associated with a 74 percent increase in Canadian imports from East Asia.

Stimulating the Circulation of Human Capital

East Asia needs to maximize the circulation of skills, with nationals who leave to acquire skills and experience in the industrial countries returning periodically, if not permanently, to apply and share their expertise and learning in their country of origin. In addition, East Asia should seek to attract more leading foreign knowledge workers for short or long periods by providing open and technologically dynamic environments.

Surveys conducted in the United States during the 1990s show that of the foreign Ph.D. graduates in science and technology from American universities, 47 percent remained in the United States. The lowest rates of return to origin were among graduates from India (21 percent) and China (12 percent), but the numbers were larger for Japan (87 percent) and Korea (89 percent), suggesting that preferences can shift over time and with the level of development (Finn 1997). Of the 22,000 Chinese who earned doctorates in the United States during 1986–98, more than half indicated that they had no immediate plans to return to China (Cao and Suttmeier 2001).[51]

The factors involved in return migration and the policies that governments have adopted to encourage return vary considerably from country to country. During the 1960s both Korea and Taiwan, China, experienced a low return rate of students graduating from U.S. universities, and governments reacted by initiating programs to encourage a reversal of the brain drain, with considerable success. Indeed, by the late 1980s in Korea there were even complaints about a glut of graduates with a Ph.D. degree from a U.S. university (Yoon 1992).[52]

Encouraging Repatriation

Efforts to encourage repatriation have been coordinated by the Ministry of Science and Technology in Korea and by the National Youth Commission in Taiwan, China. In both contexts, government support

---

51. Of the 300 most eminent Chinese life scientists overseas, only 5 returned to China, and these were not from among the top fifth.

52. However, in both Korea and Taiwan, China, it remains unclear how many of those who returned were attracted by government measures rather than the rapid economic development that was widening opportunities and greatly improving living standards.

for development of research centers and high-tech clusters has played a key role.

In Korea the initiative began in 1966 with establishment of the Korea Institute for Science and Technology, followed by several other R&D institutes and engineering schools concentrated in the Seoul Science Park and Daeduck Science Town. Within the Korean public research institutes, repatriates have been offered premium salaries, although this has aroused resentment among locally recruited staff (Yoon 1992).

In Taiwan, China, too, the government set out "to improve and strengthen the institutions of higher learning" and to support facilities such as the Hsinchu Science Park (S. L. Chang 1992, p. 38). Such facilities have succeeded in attracting repatriates: "In 1996, 82 companies in the Hsinchu Science Park (or 42 percent of the total) were started by returnees from the United States, primarily from Silicon Valley, and there were 2,563 returnees working in the park alone" (Saxenian 1999, p. 58).[53] The National Youth Commission in Taiwan, China, has also offered some financial incentives to returnees, in the form of travel subsidies and assistance with job placement and business investments (obtaining loans, production locations, and facilities).

Perhaps equally important, both the Ministry of Science and Technology in Korea and the National Youth Commission in Taiwan, China, have been instrumental in promoting contact between scientists and engineers at home and abroad. The Korean government has subsidized and supported professional associations of Korean scientists in Canada, China, Europe, Japan, and the United States. The Monte Jade Science and Technology Association is a private organization dedicated to promoting business cooperation, investment, and technology transfer between Chinese engineers in the San Francisco Bay Area and Taiwan, China.

The government of China has been less concerned with networking issues than with attempts to induce the return of nationals. Missions have, however, been set up to stay in touch with students abroad, with cadres on campus liaising with consuls.

---

53. Yoon (1992) reports 908 repatriates employed in public R&D institutes in Korea between 1968 and 1989.

Engelsberg (1995) reports that by 1992 some 100,000 self-financed students had left China, most to study in the United States, and almost none had returned. Moreover, the Chinese Academy of Science sent more than 7,500 of its personnel as visiting scholars and graduate students from 1978 to 1991, about half of whom had returned by 1991. In response, the Chinese government introduced a series of incentives to return, including a new service center for returnees set up in 1989, allocations for housing, duty-free purchases of computers and automobiles, and offers of return airfares for self-financed students.

China's creation of the National Science Fund for Distinguished Scientists in 1994 enabled the authorities to improve the financial inducements to promising researchers under the age of 45. These awards augment salaries that generally are quite low. A large donation from Li Ka-Shing—the Hong Kong, China, billionaire—helped to launch the Cheung Kong Scholar Program to endow academic positions in universities—more than 600 positions had been financed by the end of 2000. The Chinese Academy of Social Sciences' Knowledge Innovation Initiative offers returning scholars generous grants and housing subsidies. Some universities such as one in Nanjing have also been prepared to set up new laboratories to entice leading scientists to return. Clearly these are significant steps; however, given the mobility of the most talented individuals, the attractiveness of the work environment, facilities, and salaries might need to be substantially improved.

Side by side with the emigration and reflux of nationals is the increase in foreign knowledge workers who are willing to seek employment in East Asian clusters. China alone attracted 210,000 mainly short-term migrants between 1978 and 1991, increasing to 614,000 in 1992–99. Most of these were engaged in foreign investment operations, but a rising percentage provided scientific expertise. Large numbers of foreign professionals are employed in the high-tech clusters in Hong Kong, China, and Singapore. Indonesia also hosts a sizable community of itinerant foreign professionals not necessarily engaged in industrial clusters.[54] These statistics point to East Asia's new and growing access to the pool of global skills.

---

54. The number of professional expatriates in Indonesia in 1997 was estimated at 48,410 (Iredale 2000).

CONCLUSION

Should current trends persist, the innovation systems of East Asian countries will evolve within a few large polycentric metropolitan areas that are rich in agglomeration economies. These innovation systems will feed the manufacturing and service clusters that will spur growth as technology becomes the arbiter of economic performance. The increasing salience of business services among high-tech industries and the symbiosis between such services and manufacturing make it likely that clustering will demand an open urban milieu well stocked with amenities.

The significance of agglomeration effects and their role in inducing high-tech clusters are still poorly understood. And the design of policies that can give rise to innovative clusters is also very much an art form, even though the workings of the principal ingredients are well known. Experience suggests it is undesirable for governments to frame industrial policies deliberately to build clusters. Although there are cases, such as Taiwan, China, in which government technology development and industrial policies successfully launched an innovative cluster, in many other instances success has proven more elusive, as in Daeduck and Tsukuba.[55] Highly trained professionals and skilled workers are a major asset, whether or not their presence leads to the formation of clusters. Moreover, an open urban milieu is vital for creativity, and the circulation of human capital from overseas appears to be critical. An advantage East Asia enjoys over many other developing regions is its large diaspora of skilled workers participating in some of the leading North American clusters where they have acquired intangible capital, contacts, and financial wealth. As in Hsinchu Park, Hong Kong (China), and Singapore, these individuals can form the nuclei for cluster development in East Asia—if the institutional environment is hospitable. Finally, these knowledge workers can also provide another essential element of an innovative cluster: links between proto clusters in East Asia and established clusters in

---

55. Not all promotional policies work. So far, lavish tax incentives associated with the Multimedia Super Corridor outside Kuala Lumpur in Malaysia, with $3.7 billion in investment, have been unable to attract a critical mass of top-notch firms, even though other clusters with fewer incentives, such as Penang, are thriving. Ernst (2002) attributes the failure of the Multimedia Super Corridor to its lack of specialized skills and human resources.

Western OECD countries. As long as technological advances are quite localized and the dissemination of cutting-edge findings requires human transmission, contacts among clusters will accelerate the globalization of knowledge.

CHAPTER 7

REDRAWING THE INTERNATIONAL BOUNDARIES OF THE FIRM IN EAST ASIA: THE EVOLUTION OF INTERNATIONAL PRODUCTION NETWORKS

N etworking is widespread in East Asia, and its importance for innovation, technology transfer, cluster development, circulation of skilled workers, and use of information and communications technology (ICT) is undeniable. This chapter discusses the changes in international production networking that could have a significant influence on the prospects of East Asian firms.

The 1990s saw the wholesale reorganization of commercial activities in leading industries such as automobiles, electronics, and textiles. Outsourcing of production, design, and testing and the relocation of production facilities by Japanese and Western firms to economies with cheaper wages had been under way for many years, but the scale of such efforts in the 1990s was unprecedented.

More open borders, the virtual elimination of distance and communications as binding constraints, and the emergence of both China and countries outside East Asia as centers of production have had profound consequences, both for the location of production activities within firms and for the very boundaries of the firms. The major outcomes have been heightened competition, increased commoditization of manufactured products, the emergence of global contract manufacturers outside of East Asia, and a drift of the regional center of gravity toward China. As a result, East Asian first-tier suppliers such as Acer, LG Electronics, Quanta, and Samsung are under heightened pressure to survive and remain competitive.

The changes in corporate organization have created production networks of firms in East Asia. Such changes have resulted in a surge of trade in parts and components, as intermediate products cross borders many times before being finished and shipped off to purchasers (Hummels, Ishii, and Yi 2001; Ng and Yeats 2001). In the East Asian context, such components constitute at least a fifth of manufacturing exports and are concentrated in four tariff lines: electronic components, office machinery parts, switch gear, and telecommunications equipment parts (Ng and Yeats 2001). Trade in parts and components has typically grown 4–5 percent faster than overall trade in East Asia.

What are the implications of these organizational changes for the growth of firms, innovation, employment, and exports in East Asian economies? Thus far, only a few East Asian firms have managed to use their participation in these networks to graduate from merely supplying parts and components to undertaking significant process innovation or improving existing designs. Second, even fewer firms have become manufacturers of original brands (an outcome that reflects their lack of proximity to demanding purchasers in Japan and the West and the reluctance of existing brand manufacturers to partner with potential rivals when intellectual property rights are uncertain). Third, membership in production networks has not yet led to substantial growth in employment and value added—two metrics that should be part of a broader assessment of these networks' developmental impact. For example, as shown in table 7.1, Malaysian firms rely heavily on imported components, and the local value added is modest (Ernst 2002).

Table 7.1 Actual and Projected Share of Value Added by the Electronics Cluster in Malaysia, Various Years, 1994–2005
(percentage)

Sector	1994	2000[a]	2005[a]
Electrical and electronics cluster	27.6	31.7	33.3
Semiconductors	19.0	21.1	21.6
Consumer electronics	5.2	7.2	8.1
Computers	0.6	0.6	0.6

a. Projected share.

Source: Malaysia, Ministry of International Trade and Industry (1996).

Drawing on the seven-country, cross-industry survey of firms conducted for this study and a review of industry case studies, this chapter traces the evolution of international production networks and compares the performance of East Asian firms that are and are not members of them. It then examines the changes in the automobile and electronics sectors and draws policy implications for East Asia's economies.

INTERNATIONAL PRODUCTION NETWORKS

International production networks, or cross-border production networks, have been defined differently by different authors. Borrus, Ernst, and Haggard (2000, p. 2) use the following definition:

> By a lead firm's "cross-border production network" (CPN) we mean the inter- and intra-firm relationships through which the firm organizes the entire range of its business activities: from research and development, product definition and design, to supply of inputs, manufacturing (or production of a service), distribution, and support services. We thus include the entire network of cross-border relationships between a lead firm and its own affiliates and subsidiaries, but also its subcontractors, suppliers, service providers, or other firms participating in cooperative relationships, such as standard setting or R&D [research and development] analysis.

This definition gives prominence to the lead firms in a network and to the activities other than production (service and innovation) that occur within the network. In addition, it is broad enough to include wholly owned subsidiaries, joint ventures, and arm's-length transactions between firms. That is, membership in a network does not require that the lead firm own a stake in every other member of the network—a factor that differentiates these new networks from the more traditional forms of overseas foreign direct investment (FDI) by Japanese firms (Beechler and Bird 1999).

Other authors, such as Ernst (2001a), use the notion of international production networks to shed light on the changing configuration of production in East Asia. For them, "The concept of an IPN [international production network] is an attempt to capture the spread of broader and more systemic forms of international produc-

tion that cover all stages of the value chain; these may or may not involve equity ownership" (Ernst 2001a, p. 228). This definition, too,
emphasizes that such networks cover more than production-related
activities (all stages of the value chain). By contrast, other commentators focus on international production fragmentation, international
production sharing, distributed manufacturing, and dispersed manufacturing.[1]

Given the importance of clusters and agglomeration economies
(chapter 6), it is noteworthy that only a few analyses have emphasized
the role of agglomerations of firms in the location and formation of
international production networks. One such analysis is the detailed
exposition of McKendrick, Doner, and Haggard (2000, p. 8) on the
hard disk drive industry in East Asia:

> Our analysis emphasizes not only agglomeration at several different in-
> vestment sites, but also the network that links firms operating at those
> sites. In the aggregate, we call this network a regional production system.
> Not only does leveraging multiple locations in an international network
> exploit the comparative advantage of different sets of locational assets, but
> it offers an industry a hedge against exchange rate shocks, labor shortages,
> and other supply disruptions.

"Lead Firms" as Drivers of International Production Networks

A wealth of evidence points to the emergence of new organizational
structures underpinning the value chains of several major manufacturing industries (Sturgeon and Lester 2002). These new structures
can best be understood by looking at several interrelated developments. First, the "deverticalization" of value chains—the erosion of
the vertically integrated firm—has led to the emergence of lead firms
that do little, if any, manufacturing in-house and have rapidly expanding appetites for advanced manufacturing services from external
suppliers. Second, increased use of information and communications
technologies throughout the supply chain has extended and accelerated the deverticalization process. Third, advances in logistics have
made possible the dispersion of manufacturing. Fourth, the rapid expansion, growing financial strength, and increasing competence of

---

1. On international production fragmentation, see Cheng and Kierzkowski (2001); on international production sharing, see Ng and Yeats (2001) and Yeats (1997).

the largest suppliers of core manufacturing services have fueled further outsourcing by the lead firms and more consolidation among the suppliers. Fifth, the greater involvement of suppliers early in the design process has strengthened the competitive position of suppliers that locate their engineering activities in close proximity to those of their customers, thereby contributing to the growth of networked clusters close to end users. Sixth, the requirements of World Trade Organization membership and the strengthening of regional trading blocs in Europe and North America have reduced the long-standing impediments to the migration of high-volume production to low-cost sites in these regions—that is, East Europe and Mexico—and to the largest countries of Asia—that is, China and India (World Bank 2000j). Seventh, growth in demand and changes in the nature of demand in end-user markets—in particular, the demand for rapid response and for build-to-order performance—are reinforcing the trend toward regional organization of production systems (Abernathy and others 1999, 2001).

Deverticalization

The deverticalization of firm structures is partly a response to shorter product life cycles as innovation accelerates, the complexity and high cost of new products, and demanding end-user and capital markets— all of which exert new pressures on the entire range of a firm's activities, from R&D to manufacturing to marketing and sales. In response to these pressures and in order to shift risk, firms in a wide range of sectors and locations have sought to outsource so-called non-core functions. Outsourcing has been especially prominent in fast-moving industries such as electronics and motor vehicles, which have a considerable presence throughout East Asia (Fine 1999; Prahalad and Hamel 1990; Quinn and Hilmer 1994).[2]

---

2. The reasons for deverticalization and increased outsourcing in complex assembly sectors include (a) a more intense focus on design and marketing at lead firms, impelled by the rising cost and technological complexity of product development and greater international competition; (b) rising logistical complexity, product variety, and risk as the number of production locations expands; (c) a desire to streamline the manufacturing process and lower in-process inventory in keeping with the tenets of "lean" production (Womack, Jones, and Roos 1990); (d) a drive by lead firms to reduce costs and financial exposure by paying for parts and final products only after they are received from suppliers; and (e) rising competence in supplier firms.

Lead firms have concentrated on the areas and functions they believe to be essential to creating and maintaining their competitiveness (especially in product innovation, marketing, and other activities related to brand development) and have increasingly come to rely on specialized suppliers to provide non-core functions. Firms that develop, market, and sell cars, clothing, and electronic hardware have turned to contractors for production and, increasingly, post–architectural design services.

In principle, by developing production networks, lead firms can revamp their organizations so as to maintain a substantial market presence without the fixed costs and risk of building and supporting a vertically integrated corporate structure. Among their advantages, these production networks are more adaptable to change than are integrated firms,[3] they encourage innovations in business models, and they provide better economic performance in highly competitive or volatile markets (Cooke and Morgan 1993; Powell 1990), especially when falling trade barriers have intensified competitive pressures.[4]

Information Technology

The increasing use of advanced information and communications technologies, many of them Internet based, has made it easier to integrate dispersed value chains both geographically and organizationally. Firms carrying out functions at different points along a value chain

---

3. Another argument often made for the better economic performance of production networks is greater innovativeness. Interpersonal experience garnered through long-term relationships renders information more reliable, resulting in a more innovative environment than that within the modern corporation, which can suppress innovation due to empire building and "information impactedness" (Powell 1990).

4. Falling trade impediments—and international market integration—have other, more subtle, effects on the vertical structure of firms that emphasize the role of transaction costs. When suppliers produce specialized inputs, they can be "held up" by buyers who may try to renegotiate the terms of their contract after the inputs have been produced (Williamson 1971, 1989). Such ex post renegotiation is more likely to occur when the seller cannot find other potential buyers for its product. To cover the losses associated with lower payments on some of their sales, this hold-up problem causes suppliers of inputs to raise prices, which in turn creates an incentive for the buyers to integrate vertically. Falling impediments to international commerce reduce this incentive to integrate vertically by increasing the number of potential overseas buyers for an input, diminishing the severity of the hold-up problem. McLaren (2000) develops these arguments at length, building on Ronald Coase's famous insights about transaction costs and the theory of the firm.

are increasingly able to exchange data, so as to achieve a high degree of conformity with specifications and a tight coordination of productive activities. In the past, achieving such conformity and coordination required firms to locate the relevant functions within their own vertically integrated organization or within tightly controlled networks of subordinate suppliers.

ICT has caused significant changes in the management of supply chains and in the design of products and components. In the management of supply chains, the specific ICT applications include enterprise resource planning systems, business-to-business e-commerce marketplaces, and electronic data interchange. In the design of products and components, the Internet and new digital tools include easier inter-firm and international collaboration among designers, electronic design automation, computer-aided engineering, and computer-aided design. When combined with computer-aided manufacturing systems embedded in numerically controlled and robotic production equipment, these allow firms to give complex product specifications to outside suppliers. Together, these methodologies allow the creation of fully integrated computer-integrated manufacturing procedures that track product quality and inventory and shorten design and production cycles.

Logistics

Advances in the speed of moving goods and major reductions in the costs of doing so have contributed significantly to making deverticalization a reality. Networked systems depend crucially on efficient logistics that enable an optimal degree of specialization, outsourcing, and seamless integration of production. This is because networking involves a major increase in the transport of components, and thin profit margins necessitate small inventories, just-in-time delivery, and flexible schedules.

In East Asia both the volume and the value of airfreight have been growing more than 10 percent a year for the past six years (Carruthers and Bajpai 2002). Airfreight now accounts for 30 percent of East Asia's trade by value. Airfreight forwarding and logistics in Hong Kong (China), Japan, the Republic of Korea, and Singapore compare favorably with those in Europe and the United States. Smaller and newer airports in the region are continuing to offer improved servic-es. At the same time, the capacity of fleet container ships on East Asian routes increased at an average rate of more than 20 percent a year during the 1990s, while competition between shipping lines drove down shipping costs. The trend is toward multimodal trans-port systems packaged with simplified trade documentation and clearances valid across modes. Already a reality in Europe and the United States, these are emerging in the most trade-open countries in East Asia, where third-party logistics (in which manufacturers out-source logistics to specialized service providers) are becoming well established. Countries, like China, that are lagging behind at the mo-ment are headed in the same direction (Shaw and Wang 2002).

Global Contractors

The emergence of global suppliers is enabling lead firms to lessen their dependence on foreign direct investment—which entails setting up wholly owned or joint venture production facilities on foreign soil—and to rely more on the international network of facilities pro-vided by global suppliers. By using this network, lead firms gain the ability to change the location of their suppliers on an ongoing basis without tying up a lot of their own capital. The advantage applies, moreover, whether the lead firms are pursuing low-cost production strategies or manufacture-where-you-sell strategies—both of which are becoming more important with the continuing integration of China into the world trading system. The global contract suppliers, for their part, spread the risks of their investments by cultivating a large and diverse set of purchasers.

These new structures of production are raising the threshold of performance for supplier firms in several areas, including design and engineering, sourcing, the effective use of ICT, and the ability to op-erate in and coordinate among multiple locations, all of which re-quire the building of innovation capability. In the case of supplier firms in East Asia, these requirements amount to the following.

Design and Engineering. Lead firms in the advanced economies are asking their suppliers to take on more responsibility for the design and engineering of products and parts. Suppliers are increasingly being chosen and brought into the development process before products are fully designed. This enables the lead firm to enhance the scope for innovation, diversify the risks, and reduce the costs of development. When suppliers develop prototypes, they typically improve their ability to design products for manufacture and to implement subsequent orders requiring engineering changes. Redesigning products for different markets is also easier and quicker if the suppliers are actively involved from the outset.

All of this requires suppliers to hire more technically qualified personnel and to develop innovation capability, which in turn places a premium on higher-quality education in science and mathematics at secondary schools and on scientific training at universities, the subject of chapter 5.

One of the keys to involving suppliers in the early stages of development is the promise of future business. Lead firms organizing the production of specific product models and generic product platforms increasingly source their inputs from a small number of suppliers or even a single supplier. It is becoming rare for a new supplier to be brought on board after volume production has begun. In industries such as motor vehicles, where models remain in production for two to five years, suppliers win and lose business in large blocks and for long periods. The lead firms try to reduce the market power of suppliers in various ways, for example, by using different suppliers for different models, which prevents the supplier from acquiring economies of scope. Nevertheless, a supplier for a successful model can gain a great deal of leverage.

Information and Communications Technology. Information and communications technologies enable lead firms to ask much more of their established suppliers in the areas of rapid response, design collaboration, lower costs, and close monitoring.[5]

It is not unusual for lead firms to put great pressure on their suppliers to adopt the latest ICT to improve quality, to facilitate the

---

5. Another important feature of recent advances in ICT is the increasing use of synchronous interaction. Previously, integration of ICT resulted in expanded use of e-mail and database sharing. However, with the increase in bandwidth, synchronous interaction, such as real-time data exchange, is now possible (Ernst 2002).

tracking of in-process inventory, and to streamline their order and re-order processes. New ICT systems are expensive and often must be adapted to the specific requirements of the firms that use them. Furthermore, the successful adoption of ICT requires competent vendors and specialized personnel to build and operate the new systems. User firms often must adapt their organizational routines to accommodate the new systems. What is more, the ICT systems of suppliers typically have short life cycles and must be upgraded continually to remain compatible with the systems of their clients. Staying on this treadmill of ongoing capital spending, learning, and organizational change is possible only at considerable effort, expense, and expertise in ICT.

Leading Asian manufacturers and suppliers such as Taiwan Semiconductor and Li and Fung are among the world's most sophisticated users of ICT. These and similar firms have adopted the latest information technologies and, more generally, have successfully improved their design, engineering, and capacity to source components and equipment in line with customer expectations.

By contrast, many smaller firms, especially from the less developed economies of the region, are struggling to keep up, as seen in table 7.2, which reports the very low rates of Internet use by manufacturers in China and the four Association of South East Asian Nations (ASEAN) economies of Indonesia, Malaysia, the Philippines, and Thailand (known as ASEAN-4). Furthermore, smaller companies in China that use the Internet benefit much less in terms of competitive advantage than do larger firms (Riquelme 2002).

Table 7.2 Internet Use by ASEAN-4 and Chinese Manufacturing Firms

Purpose	ASEAN-4		China	
	Number	Percent	Number	Percent
Communication with clients via Internet	101	24	997	6
Communication with suppliers via Internet	102	15	994	5
Percentage of orders via Internet or e-mail				
1999	83	10	945	2
2000	83	14	951	4
2005 (projected)	83	23	956	6

Source: Survey of firms in China and several other East Asian nations conducted by the World Bank during the spring of 2001.

Global Reach of Operations. As lead firms outsource more of the manufacturing, sourcing, and logistics functions that they previously carried out in-house, they increasingly prefer to deal with suppliers with an international reach, for several reasons. First, in many cases the lead firms are marketing their products globally and need support in each market location. Second, they often seek to economize on development costs by creating global platforms that share and reuse many common parts, modules, and subsystems (a phenomenon described later in discussing the auto parts sector). By partnering with a small number of suppliers, or even with a single supplier, they can exploit these economies of scope more fully and avoid the cost of requalifying new suppliers for each new market. Third, cost pressures require purchasing organizations to scan the world for low-cost, high-quality parts, and, to the degree that suppliers are taking on these responsibilities, they too must have global sourcing capabilities. Fourth, the preference for key suppliers to take on a more active role early in the development process requires that they be able to locate at least some of their own design activities in close proximity to those of their purchasers. Some lead firms have given their key suppliers an ultimatum: provide support on a global basis or lose the business entirely.[6]

Providing this kind of support involves coordinating the flow of components, subassemblies, and products across production networks that often span several countries or even continents. Most of the suppliers that have met this challenge have come from Europe, Japan, and the United States—countries where the lead firms locate the bulk of their design activities, where there is a deep pool of management talent with long experience in international operations, and where capital can be easily raised to finance global expansion.

The pressure to expand among contractors has been met partly by internal growth but even more so by aggressive mergers and acquisitions. Acquisitions of competitors in similar lines of business have yielded sudden jumps in geographic coverage. Acquisitions of firms

---

6. According to a manager at a global automotive supplier, "The industry began to change 5–10 years ago. Today it is a requirement to serve platforms—it is part of the bid. If a supplier doesn't have a global strategy, it can't bid. New projects are no longer seen as an opportunity to expand globally—instead, a supplier must have a global base in place to even make a bid. This forces suppliers to have a global supply system in place" (Sturgeon and Lester 2002, p. 17).

with upstream or downstream capabilities have broadened the range of products and services on offer. (Many acquisitions have served both purposes simultaneously.) And acquisitions of customers' facilities have also helped suppliers expand their geographic and functional scope.[7]

For established East Asian manufacturing firms, global reach may be the most challenging of all the demands created by the evolution of international production networks. Very few firms have extended their operations outside East Asia. Few have tried to build an international position through mergers and acquisitions. Indeed, many are still controlled by their founders or the founders' family members, and many lack the managerial expertise needed to operate successfully outside Asia.

The Changing Nature of Demand in Industrial Economies

To see how the specifics of demand are affecting East Asian firms, consider the textile and apparel industry. Until recently—and to a significant degree even today—the demand in American, European, and Japanese markets differed significantly from one another. American buyers looked for local firms able to produce long runs of a product and to sustain consistent quality at relatively low costs. The American buyers arrived with designs in hand and were prepared to instruct the local supplier in exactly how they wanted the goods produced. They usually brought their own samples, patterns, accessories, and virtually all that was needed to start production. In contrast, European buyers looked for firms capable of producing a greater diversity of products in a given season, with smaller batches, and so were willing to pay relatively higher prices. The Europeans expected local firms to have in-house design and sample-making capabilities, which they would use to translate and adapt the designs sent over from Eu-

---

7. For example, Sanmina, an electronics contract manufacturer based in San Jose, California, acquired Nortel's Wireless Electro-mechanical Subsystem Assembly in August 1999. This deal included inventory, production equipment, and 230 employees in manufacturing facilities in Calgary, Canada, and Chateaudun, France, as well as a small engineering design group located in Guyancourt, France. Both the Calgary and Chateaudun facilities were located adjacent to Nortel's wireless system design houses, allowing the production facilities, now owned by Sanmina, to bring new products quickly into production. Sanmina's newly acquired locations in Canada and France can support not only Nortel but also other customers.

rope. Japanese buyers required levels of quality in finishing that exceeded even the European levels; they also required suppliers to go through rather long probationary periods. In practice, very few firms were able to meet all of these requirements, and firms tended to supply just one of these markets.

Today these markets are undergoing major changes. The Harvard Center for Textile and Apparel Research recently examined the revolution in retailing taking place in the United States (Abernathy and others 1999). The U.S. retail sector is becoming more concentrated, and the "lean retailing" practices of the largest retailers have dramatically reduced in-store inventories, avoiding costly end-of-season markdowns for unsold goods. In practice, many retailers now commonly reorder on a weekly cycle based on actual sales by style, color, and size. Weekly sales are examined on Sunday evenings, orders are placed to manufacturers, and goods are delivered to stores ready to display the following Thursday. The consequences for apparel suppliers are far-reaching. As Abernathy and others (1999, p. 84) explain, suppliers must now "label, track, and respond to product orders in real time on the basis of style, color, fabric, and size; exchange (send and receive) information concerning the current status of a retailer's products on an electronic basis; provide goods to a retailer's distribution center that can be efficiently moved to stores—that is, containers with bar codes concerning contents; shipment of products ready for display in retail stores."

For the Asian firms that produce for these behemoth U.S. retailers, the demands for more rapid delivery, lower prices, a larger assortment of products, and better quality have become more difficult to meet, and these producers are having to compete more and more with apparel firms located closer to the United States, notably in the Caribbean and in Mexico. While the productivity and quality of these firms may not match those of Asian companies, their proximity to the U.S. market—and their virtually duty-free status within the Caribbean Basin Initiative or the North American Free Trade Agreement—have made them genuine rivals in some types of clothing (Abernathy and others 1999, p. 236).

To maintain their competitiveness, several Asian textile and apparel firms have established plants in the Dominican Republic, Haiti, Jamaica, Mexico, Nicaragua, and elsewhere in Central America. But in doing so they are facing new difficulties associated with operating in an unfamiliar environment, and some have discovered that the kinds of organization that worked well in Asia are not as effective elsewhere. For example, when visiting researchers observed that the Mexican plants of one Taiwanese apparel firm were half empty, the managers explained that they had counted on being able to draw workers from all over Mexico, just as their plants in China draw workers from many distant provinces. But they found it hard to attract suitable workers willing to leave their family, work outside their home area, and live in a dormitory. As a consequence, this Taiwanese firm faced a serious labor shortage, especially after the Mexican government turned down its request for authorization to bring in Chinese workers (Sturgeon and Lester 2002).

Although the markets of Japan and the West remain crucial for the Asian textile and apparel sector, producing for regional markets is gaining in importance, and a key issue is how well the structure of Asian producers is adapted to these new outlets.[8] Again, the missing capabilities—whether design, fabric production, or retailing and merchandising experience—need to be acquired, and firms begin the process of acquiring them with highly variable initial endowments.

Japanese Supply Chains in East Asia

The supply chains of Japanese firms have taken several distinct, sometimes overlapping, forms. FDI by Japanese firms has influenced the development of industry throughout East Asia for decades. Flows of investment, technology, and training resources from Japan to other East Asian countries have been substantial, and today Japanese firms are sourcing throughout the region on a large scale, although frequently through their own subsidiaries and keiretsu-related firms in which they retain equity stakes. Some firms have developed supply links through acquisition, and some have done so through joint ventures or the licensing of process technologies for the manufacture of inputs and components that have become highly standardized and increasingly unprofitable for Japanese producers. In this manner,

---

8. In 1999, for example, almost two-thirds of Indonesia's exports were destined for Asian markets (Bouillot and Michelon 2001, p. 24).

Japanese firms have pursued the well-known flying geese strategy described in chapter 1.

The technical progress induced by the Japanese model of flying geese has been widely documented for developing countries (see, for example, Encarnation 1999). Amsden (1989) refers to an "apprenticeship," in which other East Asian economies acquire foreign technology through licensing and technical assistance programs, differentiating this from "imitation," which is the copying of foreign technology through tactics such as reverse engineering, a common method in the Asian newly industrializing countries.[9]

However, upgrading via the flying geese model may not eliminate the technological lag. Since the technology thus transferred is invariably one or more generations behind the leading edge, countries that have relied on this strategy remain in low-profit and highly volatile sectors such as low-cost personal computers, computer monitors, scanners, power suppliers, batteries, keyboards, memory, and mass market apparel and footwear products. More profitable product segments where innovation tends to be rapid, such as high-end computers and servers, communications equipment, software, microprocessors, and high fashion apparel and footwear continue to be supplied primarily by American, European, and Japanese firms working closely with advanced end users, which remain concentrated in the industrial economies.

Japanese investments in East Asia accelerated after 1985, and some production platforms were upgraded and expanded to serve export markets in the West.[10] However, the tendency of Japanese firms to

---

9. Amsden (1989, p. 110) argues that the acquisition of advanced production equipment has been a major avenue for industrial upgrading in East Asia. Productivity increases are realized through imports of foreign technology embedded in advanced production equipment. Competitiveness on world markets is enhanced by operating advanced production equipment at scale economies sufficient to minimize unit costs and by learning to use it more efficiently than foreign rivals. As long as the profits from increased output are invested in new equipment that embodies the newest technology, growth can be maintained. Increased output results in greater scale economies and expands the opportunities for learning-by-doing, improving efficiency, increasing wages, and driving growth in the domestic market. Although the state can do a lot to initiate this process, effective application of new technology depends on what happens on the shop floor, which, according to Amsden, helps to explain the importance of managers over entrepreneurs in countries like Korea, which have pursued this manufacturing-led approach to industrial upgrading.

10. Japanese export platforms in Southeast Asia were not as extensive as they might have been, because Japanese firms simultaneously made very large investments within or adjacent to Western markets (Abo 1994; Curry and Kenney 1999).

rely on their own subsidiaries and on Japanese suppliers has limited the opportunities for local firms to upgrade their competencies.[11] To the extent that Japanese firms developed links with local firms, these were usually in smaller and medium-size markets. For example, in Malaysia, the Philippines, and Vietnam, local firms were used as final assemblers and retailers that would work under license, source all components from Japanese firms, and absorb the risk of distributing and selling finished products. In a few cases where the network relationships were of long standing and the local supplier's capabilities were good enough, the local firm was tapped to serve the export market. But such firms were rarely part of the core of the production network and were particularly vulnerable to changes in the lead firm's strategy.

In the future, the prospects for upgrading through links with Japanese lead firms seem more remote than they were in the past. The protracted economic downturn in Japan—combined with the recent downturn in other East Asian economies in 2000–01, the elimination of tariff barriers for finished products in the region, and the saturation of markets for some products in smaller East Asian countries—may cause Japanese firms to centralize production in fewer locations in order to eliminate excess capacity and exploit economies of scale and the advantages of geographically close networking. In many cases, this could mean focusing on production in China at the expense of other East Asian locations, a tendency that became more apparent during 2001–02.

Production Networks as a Means of Upgrading

The literature on supplier-oriented industrialization is somewhat diffuse and eclectic, partly because it tends to emphasize the details of international production networks in specific industries or the efforts of individual firms from a particular home society (see Borrus, Ernst,

---

11. Some analysts have contrasted the closed Japanese production networks in Asia with the relatively open networks led by North American—and to a lesser extent European—firms, which, they argue, have created more opportunities for East Asian firms to upgrade their capabilities (Borrus, Ernst, and Haggard 2000). On the captive, hierarchical character of Japanese-led production networks, see Aoki (1987), Dore (1986), Gilson and Roe (1993), Sako (1989), Sayer (1986), Schonberger (1982), Sturgeon (1999), and Womack, Jones, and Roos (1990).

and Haggard 2000; Dedrick and Kraemer 1998; Dolan and Humphrey 2000; Encarnation 1999; Gereffi 1994, 1999; Kaplinsky 2000; Shimokawa 1999; Tachiki 1999). Although these authors do not focus explicitly on economic development, they often argue that international production networks have contributed much to development in East Asia and elsewhere. In particular, the economies of Hong Kong (China), Singapore, and Taiwan (China), as well as China and some of the ASEAN countries, are said to have upgraded substantially by participating directly in the value chains led by firms from industrial economies.

In supplier-oriented industrialization, domestic suppliers have the opportunity to upgrade their capabilities either by serving the needs of the local affiliates of multinational firms or by supplying lead firms in industrial countries from a distance. In both cases, local firms can often build up research and design competencies of their own. These competencies not only provide new sources of revenue but also eventually enable the firms to develop their own lines of branded products and perhaps even to compete directly with lead firms in the industrial economies.

The upgrading can proceed in stepwise fashion, beginning with the supply of parts and components manufactured to specifications provided by foreign buyers—the so-called original equipment manufacturing (OEM) relationship—followed by the addition of post–conceptual design services to the manufacturing function—known as original design manufacturing (ODM). Once design competencies are well established, the supplier can begin to conceptualize, innovate, develop, and manufacture finished products, first for sale under the brand label of its customers and later marketed under its own brand name. At that point, a local firm can begin to shed the role of supplier and enter what is sometimes referred to as original brand manufacturing (OBM).

For our purposes, it is useful to assess the potential of this upgrading process.[12] Some East Asian firms have begun to make the transition from manufacturing original equipment to producing their own

---

12. For in-depth investigation of the role of the global supply chain in industrial upgrading in Malaysia, see Ernst (2002).

branded items. But the example of Uraco, a Singaporean electronics firm, suggests that the process of upgrading is difficult in practice.

The Case of Uraco. Uraco was founded in 1981 by two Singaporean engineers who had been laid off from the Singaporean subsidiary of the German electronics firm Rollei (Sturgeon and Lester 2002). Observing that the local tool and die industry in Singapore was underdeveloped—as most foreign firms tended to bring their own tooling with them—the two set up some machine tools on a chicken farm owned by the parents of one of the partners. From their experiences at Rollei, the two engineers knew that advanced lathes for precision metal cutting spin very fast but can be stopped quickly to make rapid changes. They retrofitted the inexpensive lathes they had purchased with motorcycle brakes to achieve the same effect. Their new company generated $700,000 in revenues during its first year of operation, mostly by supplying precision metal parts to American producers of disk drives, which were investing heavily in manufacturing in Malaysia and Singapore at the time.

As Uraco grew, it began supplying a wider range of products to the disk drive industry, including precision metal stampings and assembled circuit boards. Most of the company's business was with Seagate, the leading American manufacturer of disk drives, but the company also exported parts to the Philippine operations of Hitachi, Japan's biggest disk drive manufacturer. In 1987 the company, adversely affected by the volatile disk drive and personal computer markets, began the first of many efforts to diversify its base of customers by entering into the distribution of electronics components, eventually winning distributorships from Harris Semiconductor, Motorola, and Siemens. This opportunity arose in Malaysia and Singapore and stemmed from the lack of an adequate conduit to connect local chip assembly operations with the growing subassembly and product-level manufacturing that foreign firms were doing in the region. By 1996 Uraco's revenues had grown to more than $53 million, and the company was operating three factories in Singapore and another five factories in Johor and Selangor, Malaysia. Its main lines of business were the distribution of components, the manufacturing of precision metal parts and simple electronics components such as crystals, connectors, and circuit board assembly, and the provision of warehouse consulting services.

In the mid-1990s the company began to use its experience with electronics components, contract manufacturing, and warehouse management to manufacture and sell products of its own design, including connectors, crystals, automated warehouse vehicles, electronic ballasts for fluorescent lamps, light bulbs, and telecommunications products. Ultimately, these attempts to design and manufacture its own products were not very successful, and Uraco was in deep trouble in 1999 with all-time record losses. It reemerged as Beyonics Technology in 2000 and hired a chief executive officer who had spent 18 years with Flextronics. Half-yearly results released in February 2002 show that Beyonics Technology is profitable again as a specialized electronics contract manufacturer ("Beyonics' New Dream" 2002).

Common Difficulties with Upgrading. Especially for suppliers whose operations are tightly coupled with those of customers in industrial economies, one price of entry into international production networks has been heightened exposure to the risk of abrupt changes in customers' strategies. For example, when Compaq adopted a new strategy of marketing a complete desktop personal computer system for less than $1,000 in 1997, many small manufacturers in Taiwan, China, were forced to close, and those that remained survived only by rapidly shifting production to China.

Developing their own in-house research and design capabilities can give suppliers some protection against uncertainties in the business environment, enabling them to respond more quickly to shifts in demand (and also to capture more of the final price of the product). In fact, some East Asian firms that have assembled the necessary technical and managerial expertise have graduated from OEM to ODM status.

The transition from ODM to brand-name production has been more difficult, however. Certainly there are success stories among Asian brand-name producers. Firms like Fang Brothers and VTech in Hong Kong, China, and Acer and Quanta in Taiwan, China, have developed brands (for example, of laptop computers) for Western markets as well as for markets in Asia.[13] The OBM model has been attractive throughout the region, especially in Taiwan, China, where Acer—until recently one of the leading firms in the Taiwanese computer industry—seems to have made the transition successfully (Dedrick and Kraemer 1998).[14]

But the reality is that numerous firms have retreated from a brand-name strategy back to an ODM or an OEM focus, and for many firms the attempt to upgrade from OEM to ODM and finally to OBM has stalled at the ODM phase (Sturgeon and Lester 2002).[15] Several reasons account for this. First, for ODM manufacturers, the import, sales, marketing, and distribution functions associated with brand-name products are entirely new and costly, especially when penetrating the markets of industrial economies (Sturgeon and Lester 2002). Second, lead firms from the West continue to enjoy substantial design and marketing advantages resulting from their proximity to demanding customers in their home markets. Third, Asian brand-name manufacturers who have retained OEM and ODM production lines have had difficulty reassuring their current or potential clients that their proprietary and competitive position will not be compromised, and these manufacturers have sometimes lost their status as preferred suppliers as a result.[16]

Today the OEM-ODM strategy, important as it has been for industrial upgrading in the region, must itself meet new challenges. Indeed, for the East Asian economies generally, one of the biggest challenges may be the emergence of a new class of highly sophisticated

---

13. Variants of these brands are also sold by Dell and Gateway.

14. The head of a Hong Kong, China, firm that produces both brand-name goods and OEM products for clients observes, "With a label, you take on a series of challenges. It's a baby to continuously enhance. If you work only OEM, if you work only for others, you're taking commands from them. You're on the hand-me-down side. You're not in the decisionmaking seat" (S. Berger and Lester 1997, p. 39).

15. Even Acer struggled and ultimately failed to establish a significant presence in the U.S. market.

16. Acer's chairman Stan Shih acknowledged the problems that its own-brand operations had created for its contract manufacturing business: "In many cases we were in the final list, but...when they made a decision, they picked our competitors in Taiwan [China]" ("Acer Plots Path" 2001). Like other companies that have struggled with the OBM strategy, Acer now appears to be refocusing on its OEM and ODM businesses; it is dividing into an own-brand business and a business that does contract design and manufacturing (see "Reinventing Acer" 2001).

suppliers, mostly U.S. based, that are capable of supporting the manufacturing needs of U.S. and European lead firms around the world. Later in this chapter we describe how East Asian firms are facing this challenge in the electronics and automobile sectors.

Impact of International Production Networks on Development

Most explanations for the spread of international production networks focus on the benefits to the lead firms that organize them (Borrus, Ernst, and Haggard 2000). For example, Hanson and Feenstra (2001) find that Hong Kong, China, firms earned considerable premiums from organizing production networks throughout China and Northeast Asia. The canonical example of a firm that has successfully organized production networks over a wide range of activities is Li and Fung, which had 48 offices in 32 economies in 2000. Li and Fung organizes the production of 6,000 suppliers to meet the demand of 600 customers worldwide (Yusuf and Evenett 2002).

However, the suppliers to lead firms also gain from membership in production networks (Moran 2001; UNCTAD 2001b). Their gains accrue from technology transfer within the network, access to specialized technical and marketing expertise, and the impetus that demanding purchasers provide to enhance productivity and bolster innovation (Porter 2000). For example, Blalock and Gertler (2002) find that Indonesian firms supplying sectors with a large share of foreign ownership saw their total factor productivity rise nearly 10 percent; they attribute the rise to technology transfer within (vertically organized) supply chains.[17]

In assessing the impact of production networks on development for public policy purposes, it is important to distinguish between horizontal spillovers and the effects of FDI within the supply chain. If the effects of FDI are entirely internalized by firms within a supply chain, then—on these grounds—no rationale exists for government promotion of this type of FDI. (Neither is there a case for impeding

---

17. However, their findings could also result from the frequent demands of foreign buyers for price reductions and quality improvements and the continuous pressure to improve performance. These are desirable outcomes, but they are not necessarily associated with technology transfer or with higher profits for the local firms.

such investment; an open FDI regime is still the preferred option.) By contrast, horizontal spillovers can provide a case for government promotion of networks.

Research on the performance of firms in East Asia and elsewhere provides decidedly mixed evidence on the presence of such spillovers.[18] Yet a substantial and growing literature, discussed in chapters 4 and 6, points to the strength of such spillovers in urban clusters and other agglomerations. To the extent that membership in production networks generates horizontal spillovers in urban areas, a case exists for encouraging their spread.

A critical determinant of the developmental impact of international production networks is their durability. Trade reforms are unlikely to be reversed, and technological change will continue to lower transport and communications costs. Even so, production networks might not remain a prominent feature of the Asian-Pacific commercial landscape, because their profitability—and that of any given supplier within a network—also depends on several other factors.

First, the fate of networks is very much tied up with fluctuations in the exchange rate of the leading currencies. Sharp movements in the exchange rate can swamp any of the domestic cost advantages of a given production location.[19] In the 1980s the movement offshore of Japanese industrial electronics firms was precipitated by the surge in the yen after the Plaza Accord (chapter 1). Ernst (2001b) argues that the yen exchange rate played an important role in shaping Japanese electronics networks through the 1990s as well.[20] The susceptibility of production networks to movements in the exchange rate is worth bearing in mind if devaluation of the yen becomes a central component of government policy to revive the Japanese economy.

---

18. For evidence that casts doubt on the importance of horizontal spillovers, see Aitken and Harrison (1999), Blalock and Gertler (2002), and Haddad and Harrison (1993).

19. Governments in the region have placed a premium on maintaining a stable exchange rate. This concern with intraregional exchange rate stability should not be confused with the effects on production networks of fluctuations in the U.S. dollar and Japanese yen.

20. According to Ernst (2001b, p. 93), "Accelerating yen appreciation (from around 240 to the U.S. dollar in 1985 to below 80 in 1995) and the burst of the bubble economy forced firms to cut costs at every stage of the value chain. As a result, Japanese affiliates in East Asia paid steeply rising prices for components and production equipment imported from Japan, wiping out any advantages from lower labor costs. Localization of component sourcing in Asia thus became a necessary prerequisite for sustaining international market share."

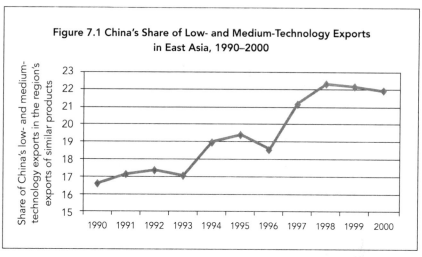

Figure 7.1 China's Share of Low- and Medium-Technology Exports in East Asia, 1990–2000

Source: World Bank, Statistical Information Management and Analysis database.

Another factor determining the profitability and hence the distribution of international production networks within the region is the continued integration of China into the world trading system. The migration of apparel production from Hong Kong, China, and Taiwan, China, and of electronics components production from Japan and Southeast Asia to China has demonstrated the powerful influence that labor costs can have in certain labor-intensive stages of production. These shifts of production into China are partly responsible for China's growing share in the production of low- and medium-tech products exported by countries in East Asia (see chapter 1). By 2000 China's share was about 22 percent, having risen 5 percent during the 1990s (figure 7.1).[21]

In some sectors, increased FDI inflows into China have undoubtedly come at the expense of Southeast Asia. Indeed, Ernst (2002) documents the migration of several leading electronics companies from Penang, Malaysia, to China (table 7.3).[22] Nevertheless, overall total

21. However, interpreting these shifts requires some perspective, not least because the growing share reported in figure 7.1 came about because China's trade in low- and medium-tech goods quadrupled in real terms throughout the 1990s, while this trade flow "only" tripled for the other developing economies in East Asia (Yusuf and Evenett 2002).

22. Malaysia also faces competition from other lower-cost centers of production, including India, the Philippines, and Thailand. This is in addition to competition occurring at the higher end of the electronics parts industry from Korea, Singapore, and Taiwan, China (Ernst 2002).

Table 7.3 Relocation of Leading Electronics Companies from Malaysia to China

Year	Company (product)	Remarks
1998	Read-Rite (hard disk drives)	Penang facility closed and relocated to Thailand and the Philippines (job loss: 4,000)
2000	Seagate (hard disk drives)	Shareholder-driven downsizing; facility closed in Ipoh (job loss: 2,000)
2001	Seagate (hard disk drives)	One plant closed in Prai (job loss: 4,000)
2001 (April)	Motorola	10 percent of its 4,000 employees laid off in its plant in Sungei Way, Selangor (job loss: 400)
2001	Intel	Worldwide work force reduced 5 percent (expected job loss in Malaysia: 500); massive expansion in China
2001	AMD	Job loss in Penang plant: 1,300 (52 percent of worldwide job cuts); massive expansion in China
2001	Dell	Desktop production relocated for Japan market from Penang to Xiamen, China
		Xiamen made the exclusive supply base for Dell's complete product line with the exception of desktops; Penang remains the hub for the rest of Asia-Pacific (main reason: limited flight connections between Malaysia and Japan)
2001	Lucent	Regional technology center closed in Malaysia (job loss: 150)
		Work force cut 50 percent at manufacturing plant

Source: Ernst (2002).

annual flows of FDI to Southeast Asia remained between $15 billion and $20 billion during 1995 to 2000, but FDI to China continued increasing during 2001–02.[23]

Nor are all stages of production likely to move to China. Supply chain managers are reluctant to source all of their inputs from any one nation, preferring instead to diversify the risks of exchange rate instability or supply disruptions across economies. Moreover, rapid growth in wages is beginning to erode some of the cost advantages of locating in the Chinese coastal regions. This emphasizes the point

---

23. On the face of it, there appears—from national statistics of inward FDI—to have been a shift in the regional distribution of FDI toward Northeast Asia in the late 1990s. However, for the most part, this reflects the liberalization of Japan's and Korea's FDI regimes (Yusuf and Evenett 2002). Furthermore, the statistics on inward FDI to China are undoubtedly exaggerated because of the circular movement of funds from mainland China through financial intermediaries in Hong Kong, China, and back into the mainland.

that the long-term commercial viability of these regions will increasingly depend on logistical and communications infrastructure and on the depth of their pool of skilled labor.

SURVEY-BASED EVIDENCE ON THE IMPACT OF PRODUCTION NETWORKS IN EAST ASIA

We now consider two additional pieces of evidence: survey data on high-performing East Asian firms in seven East Asian countries[24] and qualitative evidence from two major sectors where such networks exist: automobile parts and electronics equipment and components.

Based on the survey findings, table 7.4 indicates the prevalence of internationally networked firms in East Asia. Just under a quarter of the firms surveyed in East Asia excluding China (henceforth "non-Chinese firms") are networked, with 10 percent selling both parts and final goods to foreign buyers. The comparable numbers for firms in China (henceforth "Chinese firms") are considerably lower, with 15 percent being networked and 5 percent selling both parts and final goods to foreign buyers, perhaps reflecting China's relatively recent and ongoing integration into the world trading system. The sectoral breakdown of network membership is shown in table 7.5, as is the number of networked firms that do not have significant foreign ownership. Clear differences can be seen between the two samples. In the apparel and leather goods and vehicles sectors, non-Chinese producers are much more likely to be networked than are their Chinese

---

24. The survey of firms undertaken especially for this study examined 1,500 Chinese firms in five cities and also polled 326 firms in six other East Asian economies (Indonesia, Korea, Malaysia, the Philippines, Singapore, and Thailand). Although the questionnaires were very similar for both samples, the data were collected by different entities, a factor that could, in principle, account for any differences between the samples reported here. For survey purposes, a firm was classified as a member of an international production network if its general manager reported that since January 1999, it had (1) used parts specifically supplied by a foreign firm and (2) produced parts for a foreign firm *or* produced final goods to the specifications of a foreign firm. The definition does capture a member of an international production network that received parts from another member of the network, processed or assembled them, and exported them to another network member. The definition does not capture firms that only supplied parts to a network and, therefore, did not import components from abroad. This results in an undercount of the number of networked firms. In contrast, the definition does capture firms that had short-term relationships with both overseas suppliers and purchasers, resulting in an overcount of the number of networked firms.

Table 7.4 Prevalence of Networking among Firms in East Asia

Indicator	Chinese firms	Non-Chinese firms[a]
Number of firms in survey	1,500	326
Number of internationally networked firms	219	76
Percentage of internationally networked firms that		
Import parts and produce parts or final goods for foreign buyers	100.0	100.0
Import parts and produce final goods for foreign buyers	71.2	72.5
Import parts and produce parts for foreign buyers	61.6	72.5
Import parts and produce parts and final goods for foreign buyers	32.2	43.3
Number of firms not internationally networked	1,281	250

a. Firms in Indonesia, Republic of Korea, Malaysia, the Philippines, Singapore, and Thailand.
Source: Survey of firms in China and several other East Asian nations conducted by the World Bank during the spring of 2001.

counterparts. Moreover, among networked firms in the apparel and leather products, consumer products, and vehicle sectors, non-Chinese firms are much less likely than Chinese firms to have significant foreign ownership (10 percent or more).

Overall, however, two-thirds of the firms in both samples have received foreign investments, such that they are more than 10 percent owned by entities abroad. This raises the question of just how much these networked firms depart from the traditional practices of cross-holding and subsidiary ownership in Japanese and U.S. multinationals, respectively.

The networked firms in our samples do conform to some of the important characteristics of international production networks identified in the literature. As figure 7.2 shows, networked firms rely much more on air and ocean shipping for the delivery of their supplies than do non-networked firms. The networked non-Chinese firms obtain less than half of their supplies (measured by value) using surface transport, highlighting the extent of their international links and, possibly, their proximity to international transport connections.[25] Furthermore, networked firms tend to employ specialized lo-

---

25. Dell's decision to relocate its desktop facilities for the Japanese market from Penang to Xiamen, China, was partly based on the limited number of flights between Malaysia and Japan.

Table 7.5 Prevalence of Foreign Ownership among Networked Firms in East Asia, by Sector

| | Chinese firms | | | | | Non-Chinese firms[a] | | | | |
| | Networked firms in the sector | | Networked firms with less than 10 percent foreign ownership | | | Networked firms in the sector | | Networked firms with less than 10 percent foreign ownership | | |
Sector	Number	Percent	Number	Percent		Number	Percent	Number	Percent	
Apparel and leather goods	30	13.5	17	7.7		25	41.7	12	20.0	
Consumer products	27	16.4	13	7.9		3	23.1	2	15.4	
Electronic components	63	31.0	29	14.3		17	39.5	6	14.0	
Electronic equipment	61	31.8	29	15.1		16	48.5	5	15.2	
Vehicle and vehicle parts	38	17.6	12	5.6		15	65.2	3	13.0	
Total	219	21.9	100	10.0		76	44.2	28	16.3	

a. Firms in Indonesia, Republic of Korea, Malaysia, the Philippines, Singapore, and Thailand.

Source: Survey of firms in China and several other East Asian nations conducted by the World Bank during the spring of 2001.

gistics firms to deliver their products in a timely fashion (figure 7.3). This is especially true of networked firms that supply both parts and final goods to foreign firms according to their specifications. These firms may have greater ties to overseas production networks than do firms that produce just parts or final goods for foreign firms. Such firms employ firms that specialize in logistics 85 percent of the time, well over 10 percent more than do non-networked firms.

Finally, networked firms appear to be attracted to the benefits of industrial parks, which typically include better communications infrastructure, less red tape, and, often, duty-free imports (figure 7.4). Among networked firms, non-Chinese firms are overwhelmingly located in industrial parks, compared with a smaller percentage of Chinese firms. Thus forgoing the benefits of such parks does not appear to impose a critical constraint on the participation of Chinese firms in international production networks.

Another way to look at the relation between international production networks and development is to examine performance. As ex-

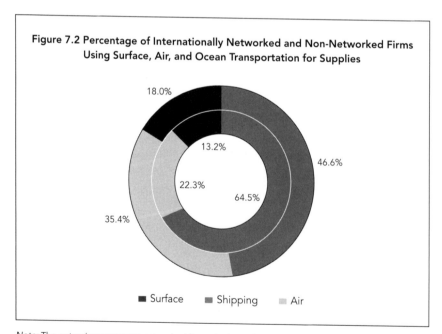

Figure 7.2 Percentage of Internationally Networked and Non-Networked Firms Using Surface, Air, and Ocean Transportation for Supplies

18.0%
13.2%
46.6%
22.3%
64.5%
35.4%

■ Surface   ■ Shipping   ■ Air

Note: The outer ring represents networked firms; the inner ring represents non-networked firms.
Source: Survey of firms in China and several other East Asian nations conducted by the World Bank during the spring of 2001.

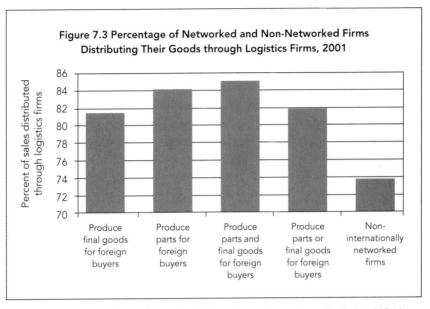

Source: Survey of firms in China and several other East Asian nations conducted by the World Bank during the spring of 2001.

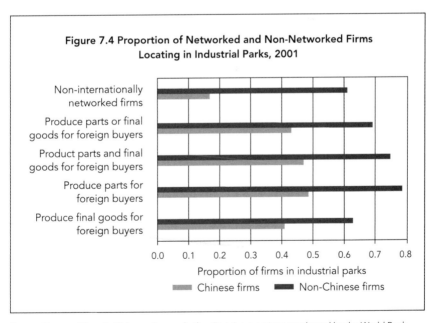

Source: Survey of firms in China and several other East Asian nations conducted by the World Bank during the spring of 2001.

pected, networked firms had a higher median share of sales from exports in 2000 and faster real growth in exports during 1998–2000 (table 7.6). Only in one sector—electronics components in the non-Chinese sample—does the median export growth of non-networked firms exceed that of networked firms. Overall, the findings in table 7.6 are consistent with the view that networked firms are export dynamos.

However, the growth of exports does not seem to have translated into sizable growth of employment (table 7.7). In China both networked and non-networked firms saw little employment growth in 1998–2000. In the other countries in East Asia, although the rate of employment growth was higher in networked firms in apparel and leather goods, consumer products, and electronics equipment, in two sectors—electronics components and vehicles and vehicle parts—the growth rate of employment was higher in non-networked firms.

Likewise, the picture is mixed when one considers growth of value added during 1998–2000 (table 7.7). Even though most sectors saw

Table 7.6 Export Performance of Networked and Non-Networked Firms in East Asia, 2000 (percent)

Sector	Chinese firms		Non-Chinese firms[a]	
	Networked	Non-networked	Networked	Non-networked
Median share of exports, 2000				
Apparel and leather goods	0.911	0.827	0.808	0.700
Consumer products	0.784	0.071	0.500	0.365
Electronic components	0.637	0.750	1.000	0.400
Electronic equipment	0.565	0.084	0.469	0.301
Vehicles and vehicle parts	0.095	0.096	0.769	0.224
Median percentage increase in real exports, 1998–2000				
Apparel and leather goods	21.5	13.8	4.1	4.3
Consumer products	52.2	−14.2	92.5	64.2
Electronic components	53.8	25.4	20.7	65.5
Electronic equipment	97.1	62.5	30.4	18.9
Vehicles and vehicle parts	77.8	56.9	29.1	22.5

a. Firms in Indonesia, Republic of Korea, Malaysia, the Philippines, Singapore, and Thailand.

Source: Survey of firms in China and several other East Asian nations conducted by the World Bank during the spring of 2001.

Table 7.7 Growth of Employment and Value Added of Networked and
Non-Networked Firms in East Asia, 1998–2000

Indicator and sector	Chinese firms		Non-Chinese firms[a]	
	Networked	Non-networked	Networked	Non-networked
Median percentage increase in employment, 1998–2000				
Apparel and leather goods	0.0	5.6	6.2	1.7
Consumer products	0.1	0.0	87.5	11.1
Electronic components	4.7	0.0	18.8	18.9
Electronic equipment	0.6	0.0	23.2	9.4
Vehicle and vehicle parts	1.7	–3.7	5.3	13.1
Median percentage increase in real value added, 1998–2000				
Apparel and leather goods	12.7	–0.7	15.2	1.8
Consumer products	26.2	–18.1	100.0	22.7
Electronic components	34.7	29.3	–2.2	51.1
Electronic equipment	4.3	12.1	6.1	16.8
Vehicle and vehicle parts	24.1	–3.1	33.9	11.7

a. Firms in Indonesia, Republic of Korea, Malaysia, the Philippines, Singapore, and Thailand.
Source: Survey of firms in China and several other East Asian nations conducted by the World Bank during the spring of 2001.

value added grow faster in networked firms, the largest sectors (electronics components and equipment) saw non-networked firms generate more growth of value added during 1998–2000. This unexpected finding, in one of East Asia's most dynamic sectors, may reflect the constant demand of overseas purchasers for lower prices from East Asian suppliers, reducing the extent to which any productivity improvements translate into additional value added.

Networked firms tend to be much more innovative than other firms. Comparing the last two columns of table 7.8 reveals that, in both samples, the percentage of networked firms reporting a given type of innovation after January 1998 is often double that of non-networked firms. It may be that more innovative firms were chosen to become members of international production networks (because they had demonstrated the capacity to break new ground and accommodate change), but the evidence on the sources of firms' innovation in tables 7.8 and 7.9 shows that networking augments their propensity to innovate by drawing on overseas expertise. The evidence is most striking for Chinese firms (table 7.10). Networked firms are much

Table 7.8 Types of Innovation of Networked and Non-Networked Firms in East Asia
(percentage of firms reporting a given type of innovation)

| Survey and type of innovation | Import parts and produce final goods for foreign buyers | Networked firms | | | Non-networked firms |
		Import parts and produce parts for foreign buyers	Import parts and produce parts and final goods for foreign buyers	Import parts and produce parts or final goods for foreign buyers	
Chinese firms					
Introduce new product	64.1	74.6	78.9	65.8	30.4
Enter new business line	35.9	41.0	47.9	35.2	18.0
Introduce process improvement	53.2	59.0	62.0	53.9	25.3
Introduce new managerial technique	66.7	76.1	78.9	68.5	44.0
Introduce new quality controls	72.4	79.1	80.3	74.0	40.3
Non-Chinese firms[a]					
Introduce new product	29.1	33.3	33.3	30.3	10.4
Enter new business line	9.1	18.5	15.2	13.2	4.8
Introduce process improvement	36.4	38.9	36.4	38.2	14.8
Introduce new managerial technique	32.7	29.6	27.3	32.9	6.4
Introduce new quality controls	34.5	25.9	27.3	34.2	12.4

a. Firms in Indonesia, Republic of Korea, Malaysia, the Philippines, Singapore, and Thailand.

Source: Survey of firms in China and several other East Asian nations conducted by the World Bank during the spring of 2001.

Table 7.9 Form of Innovation of Networked and Non-Networked Non-Chinese Firms[a]
(percentage of firms in the non-Chinese sample that used the given form of innovation when introducing a new product or process improvement)

Form of innovation	Product improvement		Process improvement	
	Networked firms	Non-networked firms	Networked firms	Non-networked firms
Developed or adapted in-house	48.7	57.5	60.0	68.0
Transferred from another company in the same corporate group	15.4	15.0	15.0	10.0
Developed in cooperation with a supplier	23.1	35.0	25.0	28.0
Developed in cooperation with direct competitors	2.6	7.5	2.5	0.0
Developed in cooperation with client firms	38.5	25.0	35.0	24.0
Purchased new machines or technology to improve the plant's performance in the national market	25.6	47.5	35.0	40.0
Purchased new machines or technology to improve the plant's performance in the international market	25.6	22.5	35.0	22.0
Introduced its own version of a product already supplied (by another firm) on the national market	15.4	27.5	10.0	20.0
Introduced its own version of a product already supplied (by another firm) on the international market	28.2	7.5	12.5	8.0
Licensed a technology or process from a foreign firm	10.3	12.5	12.5	10.0
Implemented an idea after hiring key personnel	15.4	17.5	17.5	18.0
Implemented an idea from a business or industry association	5.1	15.0	15.0	10.0
Implemented an idea after attending a conference or seminar	10.3	7.5	22.5	6.0
Implemented an idea from a published article	12.8	15.0	10.0	10.0
Implemented an idea after undertaking a study tour	5.1	10.0	7.5	10.0
Implemented an idea recommended by consultants	10.3	17.5	20.0	14.0
Implemented an idea from a university or public institution	7.7	10.0	5.0	8.0
Number of firms in the survey	39	40	40	50

a. Firms in Indonesia, Republic of Korea, Malaysia, the Philippines, Singapore, and Thailand.

Source: Survey of firms in China and several other East Asian nations conducted by the World Bank during the spring of 2001.

Table 7.10 Form of Innovation of Networked and Non-Networked Chinese Firms
(percent of firms in the Chinese sample that used the given form of innovation when introducing a new product or process improvement)

Form of innovation	Product improvement		Process improvement	
	Networked firms	Non-networked firms	Networked firms	Non-networked firms
Developed or adapted in-house	69.6	69.2	60.7	57.8
Transferred from another company in the same corporate group	23.2	14.0	23.8	10.2
Developed in cooperation with a supplier	20.2	18.8	14.3	12.8
Developed in cooperation with direct competitors	3.0	3.5	1.8	2.4
Developed in cooperation with client firms	29.8	25.3	27.4	16.4
Purchased new machines or technology to improve the plant's performance in the national market	53.0	40.4	51.8	36.5
Purchased new machines or technology to improve the plant's performance in the international market	42.3	17.3	41.1	15.5
Introduced its own version of a product already supplied (by another firm) on the national market	15.5	17.5	11.3	11.7
Introduced its own version of a product already supplied (by another firm) on the international market	25.6	14.2	20.8	9.1
Licensed a technology or process from a foreign firm	36.3	12.8	35.7	10.4
Implemented an idea after hiring key personnel	16.7	18.6	15.5	15.0
Implemented an idea from a business or industry association	5.4	3.6	4.2	3.8
Implemented an idea after attending a conference or seminar	8.9	9.0	7.7	7.3
Implemented an idea from a published article	7.7	9.3	8.3	7.7
Implemented an idea after undertaking a study tour	32.1	30.6	32.7	27.9
Implemented an idea recommended by consultants	14.3	10.7	14.3	10.8
Implemented an idea from a university or public institution	14.3	13.1	13.7	11.1
Number of firms in the survey	168	549	168	548

Source: Survey of firms in China and several other East Asian nations conducted by the World Bank during the spring of 2001.

more likely to transfer best practices from other members of a business group, to develop process improvements with client firms (including foreign firms), to purchase new machinery to enhance domestic and international competitiveness, and to transfer technology from foreign firms. Even so, the most common source of innovation for all firms is in-house adaptation or development—suggesting that membership in an international production network augments rather than supplants the existing elements of firms' innovation strategies.

On the assumption that this survey evidence is representative of more dynamic firms within East Asia, the findings here provide a somewhat cautionary view of the developmental impact of international production networks. To be sure, networked firms tend to generate more export growth and innovations. However, these beneficial outcomes do not appear to translate into broad-based increases in direct employment growth. Furthermore, in the sector where such networks are said to be most prevalent—electronics—the growth of value added appears to be slower than in non-networked firms.[26]

Altogether, these findings temper the view that East Asian competitiveness and economic performance will derive a significant and wide-ranging boost from the spread of international production networks.

ELECTRONICS: THE RISE OF
GLOBAL CONTRACT MANUFACTURERS

The global electronics industry throughout the 1990s experienced rapid growth of revenue, consolidation of lead firms, and geographic expansion.

During the 1990s, established North American electronics firms in the computer and networking sectors, such as Apple Computer, Hewlett-Packard, IBM, Lucent, Maxtor, Nortel, and 3Com, moved rapidly to outsource their circuit board and product-level assembly, most notably by selling off many of their domestic and offshore production facilities to the five largest contract manufacturers. At the same time, many newer North American electronics companies, such

---

26. Similar results are found in Malaysia (Ernst 2002).

as Cisco Systems, EMC, JDS Uniphase, Juniper Networks, Network Appliance, Sun Microsystems, and Sycamore Networks, outsourced most of their production from the outset, and their rapid growth during the late 1990s fueled the expansion of the largest manufacturers.

By the late 1990s, major European suppliers of communications infrastructure such as Alcatel, Ericsson, and Nokia had turned to outsourcing.[27] Japanese firms followed. In December 2000 NEC announced that it was selling its cell phone production facilities in England and Mexico to Solectron, while keeping facilities in China and Japan ("NEC to Sell" 2000). In October 2000 Sony announced that it was selling two underused Asian facilities to Solectron—one in Miyagi, Japan, and a second in Kaohsiung, Taiwan, China. In 2002 NEC signed a $2.5 billion agreement with Celestica, and Casio entered into a $1.5 billion arrangement with Flextronics ("Flextronics Signs Up" 2002).

Most of the growth in electronics contract manufacturing has taken place in the very top tier of firms. The five leading electronics contract manufacturers had captured 38 percent of the market by 1999, and their share is expected to reach 65 percent in 2003 (Electronic Trend Publications 2000). All five are based in North America.[28] Using revenue estimates for 2003, table 7.11 reports that these firms collectively have grown at an average annual rate of 33 percent a year since 1995.[29]

The rapid expansion of these contract manufacturers, fueled by the acquisition of customer facilities and competitors as well as by organic expansion of existing and newly established facilities, was aided by

---

27. In 1997 Ericsson made a decisive series of moves, first by outsourcing production to Flextronics, SCI, and Solectron and then by selling its principal domestic production facilities in Karlskorna, Sweden, to Flextronics and a plant in Brazil to Solectron ("Ericsson Telecom Signs Agreement" 1997). Solectron established a local presence in Sweden as well but shifted the bulk of Ericsson's circuit board assembly to its existing network of plants in France, Germany, and Scotland ("Ericsson, CEMs Sign Deals" 1997). In 2000 Ericsson shifted the remainder of its cell phone production to these American contract manufacturers and sold its U.S. production facilities to SCI ("Ericsson Shifts Phone Production" 2000). In 2001 SCI was acquired by Sanmina.

28. Solectron is based in Milpitas, California; Flextronics International is incorporated in Singapore but is managed from its San Jose, California, headquarters; Sanmina/SCI is based in San Jose; Celestica is based in Toronto, Canada; and Jabil Circuit is based in St. Petersburg, Florida.

29. The contract manufacturing market experienced its first-ever decline in 2001, as the electronics sector suffered a global recession. After another slight decline in 2002, the market is expected to resume its growth in 2003 (Electronic Trend Publications 2002).

Table 7.11 Revenue Growth at the Top Five Electronics Contract Manufacturers, 1995 and 2003
(estimates, millions of U.S. dollars)

Company	1995 revenue	Analyst revenue outlook for 2003	Compound annual growth rate (percent)
Solectron	1,679	12,900	34
Flextronics	389	14,100	67
Sanmina/SCI	3,514	9,900	16
Celestica	600[a]	8,000	45
Jabil	686	4,600	31
Total	6,868	49,500	33

a. All Celestica revenues in 1995 were from IBM.
Source: Company annual and quarterly reports.

Table 7.12 Revenue from Acquisitions at the Top Five Electronics Contract Manufacturers, 2002
(estimates, millions of U.S. dollars)

Company	Annual revenue from acquisitions	Analyst revenue outlook for 2002	Percent of revenue from acquisitions
Solectron	8,850	16,470	54
Flextronics	9,500	13,160	72
Sanmina/SCI	13,575	12,140	112
Celestica	5,975	11,250	53
Jabil	625	4,870	13
Total	38,525	57,891	67

Source: Company annual and quarterly reports.

the U.S. stock market boom in the late 1990s, which concentrated 90 percent of market capitalization in the five largest firms. More than two-thirds of the revenues projected for 2002 were expected to come from acquisitions (table 7.12).

Each of the largest electronics contract manufacturers has a global network of plants that includes low-product-mix, high-volume production sites mostly in Asia, East Europe, and Mexico; high-product-mix, medium-to-high-volume production sites in Canada, the United States, and Western Europe; engineering-heavy "new product introduction" centers, often located near an important customer's design activities; and facilities that perform final assembly and product configuration to order or provide after-sales repair service, often located near major transport hubs, such as Amsterdam and Memphis, Tennessee.

All the contract manufacturers have large-scale investments in high-volume production in East Asia, especially in Southeast Asia and China.

The largest electronics contract manufacturer, Solectron, is a case in point. Solectron was concentrated in a single campus in Silicon Valley until 1991, when its key customers, including Hewlett-Packard, IBM, and Sun Microsystems, began to demand global support for their manufacturing and process engineering activities. Within 10 years, Solectron had expanded to nearly 50 facilities worldwide, including nine facilities in East Asia (table 7.13, pages 310–11).[30]

In other instances, North American contract manufacturers expanded in East Asia by acquiring established regional firms.[31] In the future, they are likely to compete directly with, and may already be constraining the growth of, the largest indigenous electronics producers in East Asia.

Estimates by Technology Forecasters, IDC, and Prudential Financial suggest that the five leading manufacturers had captured roughly 13 percent of the global market for circuit board and product-level electronics manufacturing in 2000. A recent Bear Stearns survey of brand-name electronics firms concludes that the rate and size of outsourcing agreements will continue to increase; 85 percent of the firms interviewed were planning further increases in production outsourcing. On average, the branded firms hoped to increase outsourcing to 73 percent of their total production needs, and 40 percent hoped ultimately to outsource 90–100 percent of their final product manufacturing. Based on these projections, the chief executive officers of Celestica and Flextronics expect their annual revenues to approach the $100 billion range in the next 5–10 years, suggesting considerable medium-term growth in this industry despite the global downturn of 2000–02 (Sturgeon and Lester 2002).[32]

---

30. Today this network consists of global and regional headquarters, both high- and low-mix manufacturing facilities, materials purchasing and management centers, new product introduction centers, after-sales repair service centers for products manufactured by Solectron and others, and technology centers to develop advanced process and component packaging technologies.

31. For example, Solectron acquired NatSteel Electronics (Singapore) and Ocean Electronics (Hong Kong, China) in the late 1990s (Ernst 2002).

32. Misgivings have been expressed about the efficacy of outsourcing following the supply chain problems that resulted from the sudden downturn in the electronics industry. But the verdict, after much hand wringing, is that "outsourcing is here to stay" (Lakenan, Boyd, and Frey 2001, p. 65).

Comparison of East Asian Suppliers with North American Contract Manufacturers

How well are East Asia's major electronics suppliers competing with the emerging global suppliers based in the West? How are they responding to the shifts just described? A detailed comparison of two sets of firms is instructive (Sturgeon and Lee 2001). The first set consists of the five largest Taiwanese ODM producers of personal computer–related hardware. Based in the Taipei-Hsinchu corridor, these firms have grown rapidly, bolstered in part by the dense supply base for components that has grown up alongside them. More recently, these firms have moved production of the most price-sensitive products, particularly desktop computers, to China. However, they undertake the design and preproduction stages within their cluster in Taiwan, China. The second set of firms consists of the five largest North American electronics contract manufacturers.

The comparison is particularly interesting because the five Taiwanese ODMs have been among the most successful vehicles of supplier-oriented upgrading in East Asia, while the North American contract manufacturers represent the most clear-cut and striking global suppliers.

The performance of the Taiwanese ODMs and the North American contract manufacturers can be compared along three dimensions: scope of the value chain, scope of products or customers, and geographic scope. The two groups show significant differences in all three dimensions (figure 7.5, page 312).

The Taiwanese ODMs supply a wider range of value chain activities than do the North American contract manufacturers, especially in the area of post–architectural design and development. These Taiwanese firms have become world leaders in bringing personal computer products to market quickly. This is despite the fact that some of their customers, including companies such as Hewlett-Packard, Dell, and Gateway, have retained marketing, product strategy, and much conceptual design; and also despite the fact that ongoing innovation by component producers, such as Intel and Microsoft, dictates most of the standard architectures to which post–architectural design must adhere.

Table 7.13 Solectron's Global Locations and Functions, 2001

Region	Headquarters	Manufacturing facilities	Materials purchasing and management centers	New product introduction centers	Service centers	Technology centers
Americas						
Milpitas, Calif., United States	X	X	X	X	X	
Fremont, Calif., United States		X	X	X		
Austin, Texas, United States		X	X	X		X
Charlotte, N.C., United States		X	X	X		X
Columbia, S.C., United States		X	X	X		
San Jose, Calif., United States		X	X	X		
Atlanta, Ga., United States		X	X	X	X	
Westborough, Mass., United States		X	X	X		
Suwanee, Ga., United States		X	X	X	X	X
Fremont, Calif., United States		X	X			
Everett, Wash., United States		X	X			
Raleigh, N.C., United States		X		X		
Aguadilla, Puerto Rico, United States		X				
Aguada, Puerto Rico, United States		X				
Los Angeles, Calif., United States					X	
Austin, Texas, United States					X	
Memphis, Tenn., United States					X	
Louisville, Ken., United States					X	
San Jose, Calif., United States					X	X
Vaughn, Canada					X	
Calgary, Canada		X				
Guadalajara, Mexico		X	X			
Monterrey, Mexico		X	X	X		
São José dos Campos, Brazil		X	X	X	X	

Location	1	2	3	4	5	6
Hortolândia, Brazil		X			X	
Europe and Middle East						
Reading, United Kingdom	X					X
Bordeaux, France		X	X	X		
Herrenberg, Germany		X	X	X		
Munich, Germany		X	X	X		
Östersund, Sweden		X	X	X		X
Istanbul, Turkey		X	X			X
Dublin, Ireland		X	X		X	
Carrickfergus, Northern Ireland		X	X			
Dunfermline, Scotland		X	X			
East Kilbride, Scotland		X	X			
Timisoara, Romania		X	X			
Asia						
Taipei, Taiwan, China	X	X				
Singapore		X	X	X		
Johor, Malaysia		X	X	X		
Penang, Malaysia		X	X	X		
Suzhou, China		X	X			X
Penang, Malaysia		X	X			
Wangaratta, Australia			X			
Singapore		X				
Liverpool, Australia				X		
Bangalore, India		X				
Tokyo, Japan	X					X
Kanagawa, Japan		X	X	X	X	X

Note: This network consists of global and regional headquarters; both high- and low-mix manufacturing facilities; materials purchasing and management centers; new product introduction centers; after-sales repair service centers for products manufactured by Solectron and others; and technology centers to develop advanced process and component packaging technologies.

Source: Sturgeon and Lester (2002).

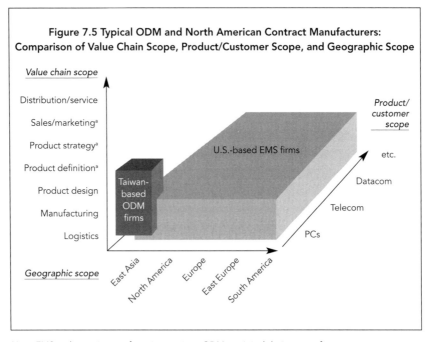

Figure 7.5 Typical ODM and North American Contract Manufacturers: Comparison of Value Chain Scope, Product/Customer Scope, and Geographic Scope

Note: EMS = electronic manufacturing services; ODM = original design manufacturer.

a. Key lead firm functions.

Source: Sturgeon and Lester (2002).

In contrast, the North American contract manufacturers concentrate on the base manufacturing processes that are common to most electronics parts or subsystems, particularly circuit board and product-level assembly. They have been much slower to develop design services, although they are making serious efforts to upgrade them.

The differences in scope of the value chain are related to differences in the scope of products. North American contract manufacturers are able to use the same production processes across a wide range of products, including computers, communications equipment, consumer electronics, electronic instruments, industrial electronics, medical electronics, and electronics for military and aerospace applications. Taiwanese ODMs have thus far concentrated on products where they have built up design capabilities—in categories related to personal computers.

The Taiwanese ODMs and North American contract manufacturers also differ in the geographic scale and scope of their production facilities. Because of their rapid overseas expansion, the largest North American contract manufacturers have many more manufacturing facilities than do Taiwanese ODMs. As they have set up global operations, they have acquired important competencies in logistics and management of the supply chain. The Taiwanese ODMs have virtually all their manufacturing sites in Taiwan, China, and China.

Performancewise, in 1993–99 the total revenues of the top five Taiwanese ODMs increased 36 percent annually, from $1.7 billion to $10.3 billion. During the same period, the comparable revenues of the top five North American contract manufacturers increased 48 percent annually, from $3.3 billion to $33 billion (figure 7.6).

The difference is probably due in part to differences in the range of customers and the scope of products. Thus the focus of the Taiwanese ODMs on a single electronics subsector—personal computers—may have kept their growth below that of the North American contract manufacturers, which were able to expand across a wide spectrum, especially into the burgeoning fields of data communication and medical electronics. Another possible cause of the difference

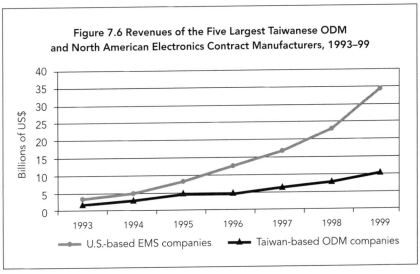

Figure 7.6 Revenues of the Five Largest Taiwanese ODM and North American Electronics Contract Manufacturers, 1993–99

Note: The five largest North American contract manufacturers are Solectron, Sanmina/SCI, Celestica, Flextronics, and Jabil. The five largest Taiwanese ODMs are Acer, Quanta, HonHai, FIC, and Mitac.
Source: Company annual reports.

is the scope of their value chains. Some Taiwanese ODMs have attempted to use their expertise in product design to develop and sell products under their own brand name, but lead firms have been wary of granting them too much business. In at least one case, lead firms reportedly chose to work with North American contract manufacturers, which they perceived to pose a smaller threat because they did far less design work (Sturgeon and Lester 2002).

Lessons for Policymakers

Policymakers can draw lessons from this industry's experience. As well as fostering cluster-bred research and design capabilities (essential for reaching ODM and eventually OBM status), electronics companies may want to extend their global reach and compete directly with contract manufacturers. Policymakers might help them to accomplish this in various ways. First, if the attainment of economies of scale and scope is critical to the competitiveness of electronics firms, policymakers can make market-based mergers and acquisitions easier. National firms are more likely to obtain the financing they need to expand if they conform to the highest possible standards of corporate governance (chapter 2). Because adopting higher standards of corporate governance is costly for any one firm—but beneficial to all if everyone complies—state action can help to overcome this collective action problem. Second, policymakers can promote regional or international agreements that facilitate FDI and protect the rights of investors. Third, policymakers can implement a regime of intellectual property rights that provides swift and effective redress against firms that infringe on their agreements with other firms (chapter 4).

AUTOMOBILE PARTS PRODUCERS IN EAST ASIA

Several parallels exist between the circumstances facing East Asian suppliers of electronics components and the suppliers of automobile components. Auto parts producers around the world are competing to become one of the small number of first-tier suppliers to the dwindling number of car manufacturers. The demands on suppliers—in particular, so-called first-tier suppliers—are increasing and include heavy investments in design capabilities and ICT. In addition, a premium is being placed on global reach (especially the location of R&D facilities with those of lead firms) and on economies of scale.

Auto parts producers in Southeast Asia, in particular, face additional challenges as they confront the prospect of ASEAN-led trade liberalization and the intense competition and shakeout that this will induce. They will have little choice but to embrace such reform, because without it, national markets will remain too small to allow local firms to become global players.

Demand Conditions in East Asia

The market for new cars in Japan, the United States, and Western Europe has been relatively flat for the last decade, with average demand growing at less than 1 percent a year. East Asian countries, excluding Japan, have become the major source of significant future growth; automotive sales in East Asia (excluding Japan) are projected to rise from 9 percent of the world's market to a significantly higher level. The market in Asia has grown more than 45 percent in the last three years ("Back in Gear" 2002). Almost 70 percent of anticipated growth in light-vehicle output between 1999 and 2006 will come from outside North America and Western Europe (PriceWaterhouseCoopers 2000b).

Even within the rapidly growing markets of the developing world, the growth of East Asia's market stands out. Demand for automobiles was growing at about 15 percent yearly before 1997 and is beginning to recover from the crisis. The Asia-Pacific region (excluding Australia and Japan) is projected to account for some 45 percent of incremental global industry volume from 1998 to 2006 and will remain a major market for the future growth of vehicle manufacturers and suppliers (Doner, Noble, and Ravenhill 2002). The largest markets—China and the Republic of Korea—are predicted to double in size in the next decade and, in combination, to reach the size of the Japanese market (table 7.14). Although the volume of markets in the ASEAN countries is smaller, their annual growth rates are expected to be impressive, at 10–20 percent compared to 4–8 percent in China, Korea, or Taiwan (China).

Notwithstanding the growth, the region's markets are fragmented. China has more than 120 vehicle assemblers, most of them producing fewer than 15,000 units per year (Veloso 2000). In ASEAN protective measures favoring assembly over parts manufacture have resulted in a

Table 7.14 Current and Prospective Vehicle Sales for Asian Countries, 1999–2010

Economy	1999	2005	2010
Japan	5,861	6,816	7,000
Korea, Rep. of	1,275	1,948	2,650
China	1,925	3,238	4,673
Thailand	218	687	1,253
Taiwan, China	423	560	638
Malaysia	289	504	747
Indonesia	94	439	696
Philippines	74	244	533
India	830	1,432	2,209
Pakistan	67	99	114
Others	102	148	186
Total	11,158	16,115	20,699

Source: Doner, Noble, and Ravenhill (2002).

proliferation of assembly plants, most of which produce less than 10,000 vehicles a year—well under the 200,000 units thought necessary for efficient scale economies in a single plant (Abrenica 2000; Legewie 2000). Relatively high economies of scale are achieved only in Korea, which historically has limited the number of assemblers; in Thailand, where tax policies have promoted a large market for one-ton pickups; and in Malaysia, where heavy protection has allowed Proton to reach 200,000 units per year. The region also has excess capacity; capacity utilization rates are running between 65 and 75 percent in the region.

Heavy protection adds to the intraregional fragmentation of markets (table 7.15), contrasting starkly with East Asia's open trade regime in electronics. All the East Asian countries except Japan and Korea have significant trade deficits in the production of parts, reflecting the deleterious impact of protection on the international competitiveness of their auto industries.

Current liberalization efforts include the ASEAN Industrial Cooperation Program, launched in 1996, and the ASEAN free trade area, scheduled to cut automotive tariffs to 0–5 percent by 2002 (Malaysia is exempted until 2005).[33] Although many auto manufacturers sup-

---

33. Such efforts are far from new. The desire of auto manufacturers to increase scale economies in their ASEAN operations is reflected in two decades of industrial integration and trade liberalization. These include the government-led ASEAN Industrial Complementation Scheme

Table 7.15 Automotive Tariffs and Nontariff Barriers in Select Economies, 1998

Economy	Average applied tariff rates		Share of imports subject to nontariff barriers	
	Parts	Vehicles	Parts	Vehicles
Indonesia	21.8	86.4	0.0	70.2
Malaysia	16.3	53.1	9.4	81.5
Philippines	11.5	23.3	2.5	40.6
Thailand	42.7	43.3	2.4	44.7
ASEAN average	26.6	47.2	2.8	64.7
Argentina	19.9	29.2	50.0	100.0
Brazil	20.5	47.6	12.7	100.0
Chile	11.0	11.0	0.0	22.8
Uruguay	15.9	20.0	8.0	96.9
Paraguay	9.6	20.0	0.2	0.0
Mercosur average	19.4	32.1	26.2	80.5
Taiwan, China	16.4	30.2	0.7	0.2
Mexico	13.0	14.6	0.0	0.0

Source: Abrenica (2000), based on data from the United Nations Conference on Trade and Development.

port these efforts, the lead firms have shown some differences in strategy. U.S. firms tend to place more emphasis on the success of the ASEAN free trade area, whereas the Japanese firms, especially Honda and Toyota, seem content to operate within the confines of the ASEAN Industrial Cooperation Program, whose projects they dominate (Yap 2001).[34] This reflects the fact that Japanese firms, with their long involvement and relatively strong network of plants and suppliers in the region, had already initiated a division of labor among the four ASEAN countries before the influx of Western firms (table 7.16; see Doner, Noble, and Ravenhill 2002). These arrangements, which develop a country-specific concentration of production across firms (for example, transmissions in the Philippines, engines in Indonesia

(1981) and the company-led Brand-to-Brand Complementation Program in the late 1980s, neither of which succeeded in promoting any significant regional division of labor. The ASEAN Industrial Complementation Scheme had limited impact, covering less than 1 percent of total intra-ASEAN trade. The Brand-to-Brand Complementation Program, while covering more projects, was not accompanied by any significant growth in intra-ASEAN trade. Its progress was hindered further when assemblers scaled back their investments after the 1997 crisis (Legewie 2000).

34. Together, Japanese assemblers (43) and components firms (15) accounted for roughly 60 of the 72 applications approved under the ASEAN Industrial Cooperation Program, as of March 2001.

Table 7.16 Production and Trade of Automobile Parts by Japanese Manufacturers in ASEAN-4 Countries

Economy	Toyota	Mitsubishi	Honda	Nissan	Denso
Thailand	Diesel engines, stamping parts	Casting parts, suspensions	Stamping parts	Engine parts, stamping parts	Starters, alternators
Malaysia	Steering gear, suspensions	Steering gear, stamping parts	Plastic products, suspensions	Steering gear, stamping parts	Air con relay, flasher
Indonesia	Gas engines, cylinder blocks	Engine parts	Cylinder heads, cylinder blocks	Gas engines	Compressors, spark plugs
Philippines	Transmissions, transmission parts	Transmissions	Casting parts	Transmissions, stamping parts	Instrument clusters

Source: Legewie (2000), based on company data.

and Thailand, and steering gear in Malaysia), tend to be bilateral or trilateral and therefore fit into the more limited scope of the ASEAN Industrial Cooperation Program. In fact, one observer argues that such initiatives would have occurred even without any formal regional agreements (Legewie 2000).

Evolving Strategies of Lead Firms: Consolidation and Platform Deproliferation

Certain strategies have become common throughout the industry. First, automobile manufacturers are consolidating. They are merging and developing strategic alliances to enhance their access to volume-generating markets and to expand the set of skills, add competencies, and become more innovative. PriceWaterhouseCoopers anticipates that in the next decade only six assemblers will account for some 80 percent of total vehicle output.[35] Second, auto manufacturers are expanding their global reach. Whereas automakers tended to dominate their home regions through the 1980s, in the 1990s they made significant investments throughout the world, especially in emerging markets, where competition among OEMs is intensifying (Veloso 2000; see also Fine, LaFrance, and Hillebrand 1996).

To meet the needs of these diverse markets while cutting costs, automakers are searching for economies of scale in design and manufacturing by standardizing and reducing the number of automotive "platforms." The goal of this "platform deproliferation" is to increase the range of end products across a smaller number of basic designs and interchangeable modules (PriceWaterhouseCoopers 2000a). This allows firms to contain the growing costs of R&D, design, and other tasks, even as they develop products with sufficient differentiation to meet the fragmented and shifting preferences of consumers.

Modularity and Its Implications for Suppliers

Automakers are performing far fewer functions within their assembly facilities than they did in the past. Assembly workers now bolt to-

---

35. As of 2000, 190 firms were engaged in light-vehicle assembly, of which a much smaller number have global significance. Of the top 20 assemblers operating in 1965, 14 have been taken over or merged. As of 1995, 11 of the top 20 manufacturers have given up some measure of ownership or managerial control (PriceWaterhouseCoopers 2000a).

gether a greater number of large subassemblies of individual components, known as modules, which suppliers have preassembled off-site. Integrated feeder lines, which build up subassemblies such as seats, cockpits, and climate control systems within vehicle assembly facilities, have all but disappeared. Modules now arrive fully assembled on the loading dock of the final assembly plant, ready to be attached to vehicles as they move down the line. This means more production workers in supplier plants and fewer in final assembly plants.

As automakers do less assembly, suppliers do more. For example, they deliver vehicle doors with the glass, fabric, interior panels, handles, and mirrors preassembled or dashboards complete with polymers, wood, displays, lights, and switches. By one estimate, 75 percent of a vehicle's value is contained in only 15 modules (Sturgeon and Lester 2002). If the trend toward modules continues, suppliers will provide automakers with groups of related modules, in so-called module systems. For example, a module composed of seats, interior trim, headliner, dashboard, and cockpit could be supplied as a complete interior system. Figure 7.7 provides a graphic representation of the trend from discrete parts to modules to systems.[36]

The drive toward modularity is associated with consolidation, as first-tier suppliers buy second-tier suppliers to gain the broader range of capabilities they need to supply modules and systems. This is possible because modularity creates natural break points in the value chain, making the integration of suppliers more feasible. However, modularity can also be pursued largely as an in-house strategy, as at Volkswagen, where internal subsidiaries have moved beyond the manufacture of parts to the assembly of modules and systems that are delivered to streamlined assembly plants.

The adoption of modular assembly also encourages the location of assembly plants with supplying plants, because larger modules are

---

36. Some modules encompass contiguous subassemblies, while others do not. For example, seats and heating, ventilation, and air conditioning units encompass physically contiguous subassemblies, while electric or occupant safety features can include a variety of physically discrete components that work together to make up a functional system. Contiguous subassemblies provide the key benefit of assemblyline simplification, while noncontiguous systems do not. Sourcing noncontiguous modules from a single supplier provides an opportunity for automakers to pass the responsibility for system integration and product warranty to suppliers. Industry nomenclature remains to be standardized; some automakers refer to contiguous subassemblies as "modules" and to functionally related noncontiguous parts as "systems."

more difficult and expensive to ship over long distances and are more likely to need just-in-time delivery according to the sequence of cars moving down the assembly line. This trend, in turn, could provide an additional impetus for regional systems of production.

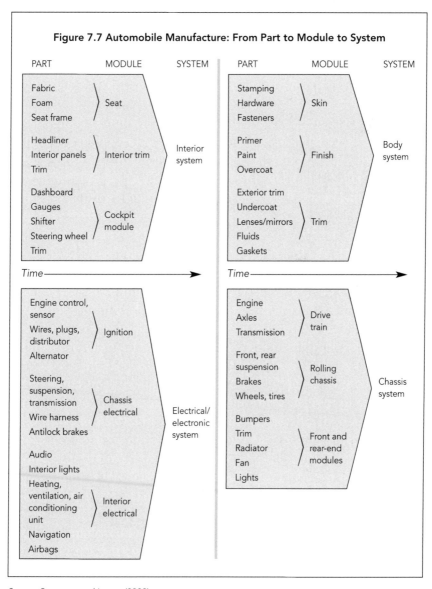

Figure 7.7 Automobile Manufacture: From Part to Module to System

Source: Sturgeon and Lester (2002).

For parts manufacturers in East Asia, the trend toward consolidation, modular production, and platform deproliferation will continue to have important consequences. As assemblers attempt to capture more of the downstream value chain (between themselves and final customers), they compel auto parts suppliers to play a greater role in design and manufacture. As we have seen, suppliers are now expected to meet functional objectives defined by assemblers, to produce or assemble complete modules rather than individual components, and to involve assemblers in the specification of quality systems and production (Humphrey 1998). Given the high transaction costs of outsourcing, assemblers have moved away from arm's-length relations with a large number of suppliers toward closer involvement with a smaller, more select group. To be sure, there is some variation among assemblers on this issue, with Ford cutting its base of suppliers more aggressively than most. But, in general, the consolidation of suppliers is proceeding in parallel with the consolidation of assemblers. This, in turn, implies the emergence of only a small number of independent first-tier suppliers.[37]

Future Prospects for East Asia's Auto Parts Producers

It seems unlikely that many Southeast Asian firms will become first-tier suppliers of auto parts. Not only are they unable to achieve significant economies of scale in regional markets, but the absence of domestic consolidation reduces the production runs for home markets and limits their R&D capacity. This reinforces the case for market-based corporate restructuring, because any impediment to the exit of unviable domestic firms effectively taxes the competitiveness of their viable counterparts.

The auto parts industry has little to gain from the attachment to national champions, as few firms in Southeast Asia can reach the necessary economies of scale within national markets. Worse, such attachments could impede a regional trade reform that might offer the

---

37. In some systems, such as brakes and seats, the global industry is dominated by three or four global producers. Doner, Noble, and Ravenhill (2002), citing PriceWaterhouseCoopers, indicates that the 1,500 first-tier suppliers in 1998 will whittle down to about 150 large system integrators and 450 direct suppliers who will compete largely on price.

prospect of a market large enough to allow such economies. Undoubtedly, ASEAN-led trade reform will create some rationalization, but the leading buyers of parts will almost certainly continue to source a large proportion of inputs locally, to avoid exchange rate risks (Takayasu and Mori 2002).

Another factor to consider is that, to date, many Southeast Asian auto parts companies have barely reached the ODM stage. In their detailed study of Thailand's auto parts industry—the largest in Southeast Asia—Takayasu and Mori (2002) report that Japanese car companies essentially retained control of the production development stage (and thus did not transfer technologies to local Thai firms). To become competitive in a world moving toward first- and second-tier suppliers, local Thai firms will have to achieve international standards of quality, price, and delivery; acquire engineering capabilities that enable them to participate in production planning; plan on supplying markets beyond Thailand so as to reap economies of scale; and employ ITC-based network systems compatible with those of their clients.[38]

Public policy has a role to play here. Governments can augment the supply of engineering talent through education and immigration policies. Further, they can ensure that the nation's ICT infrastructure can support the transmission of the substantial amounts of data that are a necessary component of joint production planning.

The challenges facing Chinese and Korean auto parts producers are less severe. Unlike their Southeast Asian competitors, both China and Korea have sizable domestic markets, which, in principle, could allow them to reap economies of scale. The size of their home markets will continue to attract foreign investors, some of which are likely to seek partners with local firms. Perhaps another advantage enjoyed by Korean parts producers is that some of their principal customers—Korean automobile assemblers—have in the past taken significant steps toward attaining global reach, and this may provide a springboard for the future expansion of Korean parts producers abroad.

---

38. This stage includes the conception of new products, product planning, product engineering (including the creation of prototypes), and responsibility for researching the engineering changes necessary to meet local specifications and production.

OPENNESS AND COMPETITIVENESS

Through their effect on intraregional trade and investment flows, international production networks have been a significant force for integrating national markets in East Asia. These networks have created many opportunities for East Asian firms, some of which have done exceptionally well as a result of their partnerships with firms headquartered in industrial economies.

Previously, these networks were seen primarily as a means for accessing foreign technology and bolstering a nation's base of innovative firms. Opening the economy and attracting FDI were important to generating export growth and improving the quality of that export base through global partnerships.

Today, the emergence of global contract manufacturers from outside East Asia is forcing the consolidation of competing first-tier suppliers and making it imperative for suppliers to acquire a global reach. Whether individual East Asian firms want to pursue this path remains essentially their own decision. But governments, for their part, can help supplier firms to become more globally competitive by (1) making market-based mergers and acquisitions easier; (2) providing the ICT infrastructure needed by first-tier networked suppliers; (3) introducing and enforcing the standards of corporate governance that are required by globally linked firms; and (4) implementing regimes of intellectual property rights to provide credible redress against firms infringing on collaborative agreements with other firms.

CHAPTER 8

INFORMATION AND COMMUNICATIONS TECHNOLOGY IN EAST ASIA'S FUTURE GROWTH

This chapter reviews the role that information and communications technology (ICT) has played in the region's growth and weighs the policy options for stimulating both the production of ICT and its use in the future. It argues that the region's future is linked inextricably with its ability to ensure that ICT is mastered by and readily accessible to the broad mass of the population.

The production and use of ICT have begun to transform patterns of investment and employment in the United States and other globally linked economies. In East Asia the production of ICT is already a major source of export earnings, and some ICT applications are improving productivity.[1] And even though the early predictions of a rapid global economic transformation may be overblown, ICT has begun to yield vitally important economic and social benefits.

For East Asian firms in the highly competitive export industries that supply the bulk of the region's income, profits are frequently a function of membership in international networks that depend on ICT-based products and use ICT to coordinate production, expedite delivery, and embark on collaborative design and research. Firms, regions, and economies that lag in their adoption of ICT will certainly find their competitive position eroded and may even be shut off from

---

1. Singapore, for example, estimates that the introduction of ICT into government services has generated $2.70 for each dollar of expenditure (UNESCAP 1999).

new commercial opportunities. And evidence is accumulating from East Asia, India, the United States, and elsewhere that ICT investments disproportionately strengthen those regions, clusters, companies, and individuals that had greater capacities (measured by skills and manufacturing base) prior to making the investments (Autor, Katz, and Kreuger 1998; Lal 1996).

The innovation that is crucial to the future well-being of the region is unthinkable without ICT. Information and communications technology is at the core of the innovation system in two respects. First, it spans a significant proportion of the innovation occurring worldwide—with product innovation being unusually rapid in the computer industry, for example—and is almost a necessary focus for research and development (R&D) in countries that see innovation as a means to growth.[2] Second, it opens the door to the global storehouse of information and makes it possible to share knowledge in real time over great distances.

Beyond the imperatives of innovation, in time ICT will become a dominant factor in the acquisition of skills and perhaps, through distance education, in the transfer of skills; computer literacy, while no panacea, is becoming essential for individuals and companies seeking to remain competitive in the marketplace. Last but not least, ICT has the potential to realize some long-sought ideals of governance with respect to information sharing, transparency, and accountability.

ELECTRONICS PRODUCTION AND USE IN EAST ASIA

East Asia is in a better position than any other developing region to capture the benefits of advances in ICT. The story of the East Asian miracle starting in the 1980s and continuing through the 1990s was increasingly a story about electronics. In 1985 East Asia other than Japan supplied about 6 percent of world electronics production. By 1998 it was supplying more than 20 percent. By 1998 all economies in the region except Hong Kong, China, had greater shares in world electronics production than they did in world trade (Wong 2001).

---

2. For example, almost a third of productivity growth in the United States can be traced to the computer industry from the early to the late 1990s, and much of this arose from technical progress in the industry (Chun and Nadiri 2002).

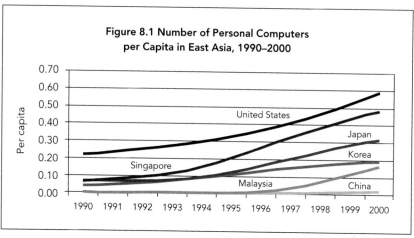

Figure 8.1 Number of Personal Computers per Capita in East Asia, 1990–2000

Source: ITU (2000).

This experience provides the base for a transition to higher-value-added ICT production. Although East Asia has a comparatively small role in the global market for software and applications, it manufactures much of the hardware. For example, although American-owned companies dominate the subsectors responsible for computers and many of their key components, these items are produced mainly in East Asia.[3] In other ICT subsectors, locally owned Asian companies have gained a global foothold.[4]

East Asia's own use of information and communications technology also expanded rapidly in the 1980s and 1990s. Between 1993 and 1998, China Telecom was adding about 14 million new subscribers each year. Ownership of personal computers rose (figure 8.1), and computer use and general computer literacy spread quite rapidly, as the cost of equipment declined and technological refinements, in-

---

3. In 1995 vendors with Asian headquarters accounted for less than 25 percent of world computer sales, compared to 65 percent for North America. Conversely, more than 45 percent of world hardware production was based in East Asia, compared to around 25 percent for North America (Dedrick and Kraemer 1998).

4. Within a decade of launching its first memory chip, Korea's Samsung had become the world leader in flash and memory chip production. This company and LG Electronics have capitalized on their lead in digital technology to become forces in the markets for flat-panel displays and digital mobile telephones. The Chinese company Huawei is becoming a force to be reckoned with in telecommunications switches and other gear.

cluding the availability of programs, keyboards, and printer software adapted for East Asian languages (for example, Haansoft had captured 60 percent of the Korean word-processing market by 2000, pushing Microsoft to second place), made computers and smart mobile phones easier to use. By late 2002 the fixed-line providers—China Netcom and China Telecom—had a customer base of 189 million, while mobile service providers—China Mobile and China Unicom—had 161 million subscribers ("China Telecom IPO" 2002).

East Asia has begun to embrace the technology of the Internet, with e-commerce and e-government applications spreading fast. The number of Internet hosts per capita ranges from less than 1 per 10,000 people in China and Vietnam to more than 1 per 100 in Japan and the Republic of Korea. Public use of the Internet is already ubiquitous in many countries in the region, with 57 million users in China alone by late 2002, the largest in Asia ("China Internet Penetration" 2002), and 26 million daily users in Korea ("South Korea: Broadband" 2003). Ipsos-Reid's survey of Internet use in 30 countries (asking the question "Have you used the Internet in the past 30 days?") finds usage rates in Korea and Singapore of 45 and 46 percent of the population, respectively (although a number of countries have seen usage rates settling at lower levels; Japan at 33 percent, for example).[5] Internet access is on the rise through a variety of locations, such as public libraries and Internet cafes (table 8.1).[6] Government promotion of high-speed broadband access helped to raise the number of broadband subscribers in Korea to 10 million by the end of 2002 ("South Korea: Broadband" 2003).

As East Asian companies have gained experience and are finding it essential to use the Internet for their international transactions, rates

---

5. See cyberatlas.internet.com (May 21, 2001). In some subsectors of ICT, East Asia has the highest levels of use in the world. Japan leads the world in mobile Internet using the i-Mode Internet service provided by NTT DoCoMo. In the first year, 5 million subscribers were attracted to the service, and by April 2000 more than 350 companies were providing mobile online services in the country (Dedrick and Kraemer 2000). By early 2002 the service had 31 million subscribers, or more than a quarter of the Japanese population (see also Yusuf and Evenett 2002).

6. Especially in the poorer countries of the region, Internet use does not necessarily connote household Internet subscription. In many countries, users frequently access the Internet through public facilities, or cybercafes. In China, for example, 11 percent of users access the Internet from cybercafes, as do 43 percent of users in Korea (ITU 2000). In late 2002 China began placing some restrictions on cybercafes and on a range of websites ("Access Denied" 2002; "Beijing Approves New Measures" 2002).

Table 8.1 Locations for Internet Access in East Asia

Location	Leading-edge economies[a]	Advancing economies[b]
Own home	50	37
Someone else's home	46	23
Library, post office, other government building	47	13
Work	38	24
School	15	9
Internet cafe or bar	12	7
Computer or electronics shop	15	8
Other fixed location	11	4
No Internet access	14	30
Never heard of the Internet	4	11

Note: Data are based on 18,713 interviews in 30 countries, in response to the question "Regardless of whether or not you use the Internet, do you currently have access to the Internet from. . . ? "

a. Australia, Canada, Finland, Germany, Netherlands, Republic of Korea, Singapore, Sweden, Switzerland, United Kingdom, and United States. The East Asian countries included are Korea and Singapore.

b. Belgium, France, Hong Kong (China), Italy, Japan, Malaysia, Mexico, and Taiwan (China). The East Asian economies included are Hong Kong (China), Japan, Malaysia, and Taiwan (China).

Source: Ipsos-Reid, "The Face of the Web II: 2000–01: Module 8."

of adoption have started to rise. By April 2000 about half the suppliers in Taiwan, China, had access to the Internet, and 24 percent of manufacturing firms in Indonesia, Malaysia, the Philippines, and Thailand were using the Internet to communicate with their clients (Dedrick and Kraemer 2000; Sturgeon and Lester 2002).

Regional use of the Internet for e-commerce is also rising, but more slowly: 14 percent of Chinese Internet users buy or sell goods on-line, compared to 36 percent of American users (Harwit and Clark 2001).[7] The value of business-to-business Internet commerce in Asia reached about $100 billion in 2000, according to the Gartner Group, which estimates that this is one-fourth of the world total.[8] A number of re-

---

7. However, buying and selling stocks on-line is far more common in China than in the United States, and the Chinese search for jobs on-line to the same extent as do Americans. The inefficient payment system is often cited as the major barrier to engaging in business-to-consumer e-commerce. Some companies have begun to use debit cards as the method of payment, but this practice is restricted to persons living in a specific city (but see "China Internet Penetration" 2002 on the "golden card" system). Since business-to-business transactions rely more on the company's line of credit, lack of an on-line payment system would have little effect on business-to-business compared to business-to-consumer e-commerce (Asia Information Associates 2000, p. 83).

8. See cyberatlas.internet.com.

gional business-to-business e-commerce hubs have already sprung up to serve this market.[9] Other uses of the Internet such as the provision of on-line games and auction services are becoming popular and generating profits in the Republic of Korea, where Internet-based shopping is also on the rise ("Internet Pays" 2002).

Adoption rates and policies governing the ICT sector vary widely within the region (table 8.2). In relation to per capita income, Korea has the highest provision of ICT, while Indonesia and Thailand have relatively low levels of provision. As to the legislative and regulatory infrastructure required to exploit e-commerce, as well as the broader environment for ICT-based business opportunities, table 8.3 shows significant variations in the level of competition, public sector ownership, and regulatory structures in the region.

THE ROLE OF ICT IN PRODUCTIVITY AND COMPETITIVENESS

What is the the potential contribution of ICT to the region's future economic growth, and what are the implications for individual firms?

ICT, Economic Growth, and Productivity

Evidence linking advances in information and communications technology with improved economic performance is widespread. Even skeptics admit that ICT investment has raised the productivity of labor throughout the Organisation for Economic Co-operation and Development (OECD); in the United States, ICT in manufacturing has yielded dramatic gains in total factor productivity. The evidence for ICT-induced gains in total factor productivity in other sectors of the U.S. economy or in other countries of the world is less solid, and it may be too soon to judge the global economic impact of the Inter-

---

9. Advanced Manufacturing On-line, a Singapore-based company, operates an Internet exchange in which companies such as Matsushita, Motorola, and Taiwan Semiconductor are linked with 600 regional small and medium enterprises through a system that allows firms to place orders, share delivery forecasts, and solicit quotes ("Asia's Biz-to-Biz E-Boom" 1999).

Table 8.2 Indicators of ICT Access, Policy, and Capacity

Indicator	China	Hong Kong, China	Indonesia	Japan	Korea, Rep. of	Malaysia	Philippines	Singapore	Thailand	United States	Vietnam
Host density	1		1	269	101	28	2	386	9	2,419	0
Absolute ICT provision	97	8	116	19	21	58	105	13	90	10	122
Relative ICT provision	55	30	94	66	21	43	86	58	95	75	31
Cost/quality	51	25	—	30	8	38	76	14	46	—	—
Competition	40	—	47	1	1	1	1	40	47	—	56
E-leadership	2	—	1	—	2	3	1	—	2	—	1
Human capital	1	—	1	—	2	2	1	—	1	—	1
Information security	2	—	1	—	3	2	2	—	1	—	1
E-business climate	2	—	1	—	3	2	1	—	1	—	1
E-business readiness	4.4	8.3	5.6	7.7	7.2	6.0	4.9	8.3	6.1	8.8	4.2

— Not available.

Note: Host density measures the number of computers with Internet provider addresses attached to the Internet per 10,000 people. "Absolute ICT provision" measures ICT service rollout. It is a rank score out of 149 countries of an index constructed of Internet users per capita, telephones per capita, and mobile telephones per capita. "Relative ICT provision" measures how far behind or ahead a country is in providing ICT services from the level that would be expected at its stage of development. It is a rank score out of 130 countries of the "absolute ICT provision" index compared to the absolute provision index score that would be expected given country income. "Cost/quality" measures the cost and quality of telephony services. It is a rank score out of 111 countries of an index constructed out of the cost of local calls expressed as a percentage of the global average, the cost of international calls expressed as a percentage of the global average, and waiting time for telephone service as a percentage of the global average. "Competition" measures competition in provision of telephony services. It is a rank score based on the presence of duopoly or competition in local, long-distance, and international fixed telephony, mobile analog, and digital services. "E-leadership" measures the government priority given to e-readiness, including factors such as efforts to automate government processes and promote citizen access programs. "Human capital" measures education relevant to e-business, including factors such as quality of and participation in basic education and skills and efficiency of work force. "Information security" measures the strength of the legal underpinnings for e-commerce, including factors such as intellectual property rights, digital signature laws, public key, and computer crimes legislation. "E-business climate" measures the ease of doing e-business, including sector competition, transparency, predictability, and the openness of government and development of the financial sector. "E-business readiness" is a broad-based measure of the attractiveness of doing business in a country, combined with measures of infrastructure availability.

Sources: Economist Intelligence Unit (2000); Kenny (2001b); Kenny (2001a); McConnell International (2000); World Bank (2001a).

Table 8.3 Structure of the Telecommunications Sector in Select East Asian Countries

| Economy | Competition | | | | | | Privatization, incumbent provider | Regulatory institution |
	International	Long distance	Local	Digital cellular	Leased lines	Internet service providers		
Cambodia	D	M	P	C	M	M	SOE	MPT
China	C	C	P	P	C	C	SOE	MPT
Indonesia	P	M	M	C	P	C	P	MPT
Korea, Rep. of	C	C	P	C	C	C	P	IR
Lao PDR	M	M	M	M	P		P	MPT
Malaysia	P	P	P	P	P	P	P	IR
Myanmar	M	M	M	M	M	M	SOE	MPT
Papua New Guinea	M	M	M	M	M	P	SOE	IR
Philippines	C	C	C	C	C	C	SOE	IR
Singapore	C	C	C	C	C	C	P	IR
Thailand	M	M	P	C	P	C	SOE	IR
Vietnam	M	M	P	M	M	P	SOE	MPT

Note: M = monopoly; D = duopoly; C = competition; P = partial competition; SOE = state-owned enterprise; P = private stake; MPT = ministry; IR = independent regulator.

Source: ITU (2001a), updated from World Bank information.

net.[10] Nonetheless, ICT clearly has a growing part to play in promoting economic performance worldwide.[11]

The ratio of price to performance of ICT goods has improved rapidly over the past 20 years, and because of this there has been a significant substitution of ICT capital for other types of capital and labor inputs. During the 1990s business investment in ICT amounted to $2.4 trillion, and between 1999 and the end of the decade the investment in computers accounted for 60 percent of nominal investment in the United States, deepening the U.S. capital stock and expanding output (R. J. Gordon 2002; Temple 2002). The role of ICT in capital stock is increasing throughout the OECD countries: the share of ICT in nominal productive capital stock rose from 2.4 to 3.2 percent in France and from 3.6 to 5.2 percent in the United Kingdom over the 1990s, for example (van Ark 2002). As a result of ICT capital deepening, labor productivity has risen (table 8.4). In the United States, for example, labor productivity has grown 0.85 percent faster since 1995 than in the previous two decades; capital deepening as a result of investment in ICT accounts for perhaps half this growth. The United States has also benefited from increases in total factor (not just labor) productivity due to ICT-related manufacturing.[12]

In general, however, the economywide consequences of ICT investment for total factor productivity, as opposed to labor productivity, remain contentious. Some empirical work at the micro level in the United States finds excess returns to investments in computers across a range of industries (Lehr and Lichtenberg 1999). This finding disappears when other factors such as company reorganization are taken into account (P. A. David 2000). In OECD countries more broadly, although ICT investment has been a source of capital deepening and higher labor productivity in some sectors, there is less evidence vali-

---

10. However, analysis of the experience of 42 U.S. industries during 1985–2000 suggests that the spillover gains from information technology might be more pronounced in service activities (Mun and Nadiri 2002).

11. Some signs of the continuing push exerted by ICT on U.S. productivity during 2001–02 were apparent from the data on non-farm productivity from the third quarter of 2001 to the third quarter of 2002, when productivity rose 5.3 percent ("Productivity in the U.S." 2002).

12. R. J. Gordon (2002), a noted skeptic on the contribution of ICT to economic growth, accepts that the durables manufacturing sector accounted for an increase of 0.89 percent in U.S. total factor productivity growth in the second half of the 1990s, for example.

Table 8.4 Links of ICT Investment and Production to Growth of Gross Domestic Product and Productivity

Sample group	ICT capital contribution				ICT production	
	Ratio to GDP group	As a percentage of total GDP growth	Ratio to labor productivity growth	As a percentage of total labor productivity growth	Total factor productivity contribution to labor productivity growth	Total factor productivity as a percentage of total labor productivity growth
United States	0.95	27	0.66	33	0.50	25
Early 1990s	0.65	23	0.43	29	0.33	23
Late 1990s	1.41	31	0.88	36	0.67	27
Other	0.39	17	0.48	22	0.57	27
Early 1990s	0.25	17	0.36	14	0.43	17
Late 1990s	0.47	15	0.60	33	0.71	40
Total	0.45	19	0.53	25	0.55	26

Note: This table synthesizes data presented in tables 1 and 2 of van Ark (2002), which draw on a number of recent growth-accounting studies. The table uses simple averages of the statistics reported in the two tables for individual countries and the Euroland group of countries, divided into U.S. and non-U.S. studies as well as early (predominantly the first half of the 1990s) and late (predominantly the second half of the 1990s) studies. Given such a simple technique and a small sample of studies, the figures clearly should be used with caution.

dating the growth of total factor productivity.[13] For example, Oulton (2002, p. 371) shows that ICT was responsible for one-half of capital deepening since 1979 in the United Kingdom and accounted for 90 percent of the productivity growth during 1994–98 (a finding broadly supported by Spencer [2000] for 1986–2000); however, Oulton's research does not show that the overall productivity growth rate was any higher, in spite of the spending on ICT.

A wider industrial-country sample at the macro level shows a significant correlation between ICT investment and economic growth (Dewan and Kraemer 1998, 2000), but this is subject to the usual concerns over causality (R. King and Levine 1994). Although a long tradition links stocks of telecommunications capital with subsequent growth,[14] a number of econometric studies challenge the link between the rollout of telecommunications and growth (see, for example, Garcia-Mila and McGuire 1992). Overall, the OECD picture indicates that ICT investment increases labor productivity, but not at an abnormally high rate.

It may be too early to detect the influence of the Internet in recent productivity figures, even for the United States.[15] Statistics thus far show that e-commerce has played only a very small role in productivity growth. The U.S. productivity upturn after 1995 coincided with the launch of e-commerce (Nezu 2000), but even by 1998 e-commerce transactions were equivalent only to 0.5 percent of U.S. gross domestic product (GDP).[16] Generously assuming that the productivity impact of these transactions was as much as 10 percent of their value, e-commerce might have added 0.05 percent to GDP that year. The cumulative faster-than-trend productivity growth from 1995 to 1998 was only about 4.7 percent.

---

13. See also Yusuf and Evenett (2002) for an overview of recent developments in this sector.

14. Canning and Fay (1993), Easterly and Levine (1997), and Hardy (1980) are but three examples from a broader literature; see Forestier, Grace, and Kenny (2001) for a review. Access to telecommunications and "advanced infrastructure" has also been linked to flows of foreign direct investment (Reynolds, Kenny, and Qiang 2001).

15. Some of the effects of the Internet, while benefiting consumers, may never be reflected in productivity statistics or other macroeconomic indicators, yet nonetheless provide significant consumer surplus. Examples include on-line banking, on-line chat rooms, and a range of sites for special interests.

16. Calculated from World Bank (2001a).

The impact of the Internet—and particularly e-commerce—is likely to continue to grow (see "How e-Biz Rose" 2002), and it is apparent in the imports of services by the United States, which are rising 1.7 percent for each 10 percent increase in Internet use (Freund and Weinhold 2002). The benefits of many general-purpose technologies such as the Internet are felt only over a very long time (P. David 2000). Two uses of the Internet might take time to filter through to productivity: its use for strengthening communities of practice and research networks and its use for reshaping firms and production processes through decentralized communication. With e-commerce, if the technology follows the boom-bust-boom pattern of the railway, the car, and the personal computer, an immediate downturn will be followed by rationalization and new growth—evidenced by continued strength in business-to-business sales and new profits in previously loss-making e-businesses such as Amazon.com ("How E-Biz Rose" 2002).

To sum up, ICT investment is widely thought to be impinging strongly on growth, largely through gains in labor productivity. Yet widespread evidence of gains in total factor productivity is only now beginning to accumulate, especially outside the United States. Nonetheless, there is clearly potential for ICT in general and the Internet in particular to play an increasing role in economic growth.

Firms also need to be aware not only of the possible benefits to productivity but also of the threats to their competitiveness if they are unable to keep up with advances in ICT. On-line commerce may be reinforcing the trend toward a reduction in the number of company suppliers, creating losers as well as winners, as discussed in chapter 7.[17] The losing firms are likely to be those that were already behind and slow to adopt technological innovations.[18] For example, among firms that introduced Internet-based management of the supply chain, those that were previously more efficient appear to have gained more than their previously inefficient competitors (World

17. Companies such as Dell and General Electric, which have moved their supply chain management on-line, now have fewer suppliers as a result (Heeks and Kenny 2001).

18. Many foreign firms selling e-commerce solutions to Chinese firms find that, in fact, state-owned enterprises are slow to adopt e-commerce and even resist its adoption in general (Asia Information Associates 2000, p. 98).

Bank 2000d).[19] Advanced regions in Europe seem to have benefited more from the rollout of communications infrastructure than have backward regions, and the production of high-value-added "knowledge goods" has remained concentrated in wealthier regions of the United Kingdom (Cornford 2001).

Implications for East Asia

The effects of ICT production and use on overall productivity growth may be initially more muted in East Asia than in the OECD. On the production side, the 1990s showed no strong relationship between the share of high-tech products in manufacturing exports and productivity growth in the region, suggesting that investment in ICT production did not raise productivity as much in Asia as it did in the United States (APEC 2001; Wong 2001).[20] In addition, ICT production is not correlated with ICT use in the region.[21] And even studies that discern an association between ICT investment and growth in the industrial world tend not to find that link in developing countries (Dewan and Kraemer 2000; Mayer 2000; Pohjola 2001).

A potential reason for the apparent lower return to ICT investment in developing countries is that scale effects are at work—for example, telecommunications and economic growth are related, but only above a threshold level of telephone use (Röller and Waverman 2001). Global surveys of e-commerce also suggest slower rates of penetration in the developing world.[22] And although ICT-enabled

---

19. The complexities of successfully introducing new technologies are well illustrated by a recent Forrester research report: only 40 percent of companies that adopted on-line purchasing systems along with change management programs to help implement the new system actually managed to save money from the new technology. And of companies that introduced new systems without a change management program, only 3 percent managed to save any money ("How E-Biz Rose" 2002).

20. This finding might reflect the poor measurement of productivity increases in the ICT-producing sector in East Asia.

21. The results echo the finding in Colecchia and Schreyer (2001) for 10 OECD countries that there is no apparent link between increases in labor productivity from ICT use and the size of the ICT-producing sector.

22. For example, the effect on Asia as a whole is estimated to be equal to about 1 percent of GDP—one-third of the projected impact in industrial economies—because of barriers to effective exploitation of the technology (UNCTAD 2000). More optimistic commentators suggest that, if these barriers can be overcome, the impact of the Internet in developing countries might be as large as it is in the industrial world (Mann, Eckert, and Knight 2000). In industrial countries,

services will create opportunities for the region, the scale of such opportunities should not be overrated.[23]

Public policymakers in East Asia should not conclude from this that the ICT sector has a low priority. Regardless of the sector's potential contribution to productivity and growth, firms have no option but to keep up with the progress and spread of ICT if they are to remain competitive. What, then, should governments do to support them?

GOVERNMENT SUPPORT IN DEVELOPING ICT PRODUCTION AND USE

Success in the "knowledge-based economy" calls for a healthy business environment, a strong innovation system, a well-balanced intellectual property rights regime, and pervasive human resource development (APEC 2001). Among the factors that determine the level of provision of ICT in a country, by far the most significant is income, with the environment for private investment coming second. The openness of the sector is the third most important factor (Kenny 2001b). The most significant determinants of use are technological barriers, beyond access to the Internet. This is clear from the fact that throughout the developing world only a fairly small percentage of people with access to the Internet use it for e-commerce, with most of these concentrated in the United States and the five largest Western European economies (Kenny 2001c).[24]

Current thinking in East Asia favors significant policy involvement by the state to bolster both the provision and the use of ICT. This

business-to-business commerce is expected to have a long-term impact of about 5 percent of GDP (UNCTAD 2001a).

23. The total global market for ICT-enabled services was only $10 billion in 1998 (World Bank 2001f). India is probably the most successful developing country in attracting ICT-enabled services. According to the International Labor Organization (2001), India's software industry employed 180,000 people in 1998, an impressive performance while still a modest share of the Indian economy (if spillover and "role model" effects are significant, these small numbers could still have large consequences). And major companies such as Infosys, Tata Consultancy, and WIPRO continued growing strongly through 2002, with total sales of $2.5 billion ("Indian IT" 2002).

24. The United States had 105 million users of the Internet in 2002, and the five European economies had 60 million, but membership was rising steeply in Europe ("E-commerce Starts" 2002).

conviction is based partly on a long history of intervention in the sector. In the 1980s, for example, Korea, Singapore, and Taiwan (China) all enacted national strategies to promote the personal computer and electronics industries with support for human capital development, R&D, technology transfer, and industry promotion (Dedrick and Kraemer 1998). Investments in "strategic" industries were supported across the region by state-owned development banks, public sector R&D institutes, industrial parks such as Jurong in Singapore, economic development agencies, tax incentives, technical training, standard-setting for ICT use in government agencies, and export promotion (Mathews and Cho 2000; see also chapter 4).

Perhaps the most important point regarding success in ICT production, whether hardware or software, is that a country's macroeconomic and policy climate must be broadly favorable if marginal interventions in favor of particular industries are to have a useful impact. The record of intervention in the ICT sector reinforces the position taken in chapter 4: the strength of the overall innovation system, rather than interventions targeted at a specific sector or subsector, is what matters (Mathews and Cho 2000). Short-term government policies covering taxation and subsidies are only a small part of the picture that companies look at when choosing to invest in a new ICT venture. A host of factors outside immediate state control—the country's pool of skills and of English speakers, the quality and cost of living, the presence or absence of other companies in the same area—all might stymie a government's efforts to promote a particular sector. And beyond the ICT sector itself, investment, fiscal, and monetary policy and education together play perhaps the predominant role in determining how investors view the attractiveness of a country's policy environment.

Hardware Production

Government intervention to support ICT production is justified on several grounds. High-technology production is based on R&D that has the character of a public good. Production requires a highly skilled work force. Further, ICT production appears to involve cluster effects—hence the emergence of areas such as Bangalore in India and Silicon Valley as centers of ICT innovation.

In a sector as diverse as this, strategies for success have varied, and a single set of rules for policymaking is unlikely to apply. The conditions that underlie the success of German firms in applications related to enterprise software, of Swedish firms in the field of wireless Internet technology, or, more recently, of Korean firms in digital communication technology are associated with technology, company strategies, institutions, and public policy regimes that differ widely from the Silicon Valley model (Casper and Glimstedt 2001). As Dedrick and Kraemer (1998) note in their study of the East Asian computer manufacturing industry,

> Much of the East Asian success has been the result of companies acting in a highly competitive environment with limited government intervention. By contrast, governments outside the region, such as Brazil and India, that tried to develop their own computer industries in isolation from global competition have failed.... The East Asian countries have employed aggressive industrial policies to develop their own computer industries ... investments in human resources, technology development, and infrastructure, as well as strong incentives for investment (foreign and domestic) in computer production.

Nonetheless, some broad lessons can be drawn from experience.

Integration with Global Networks. First, in a field of such rapid technological change, firms need to be fully integrated with global investment, technology, and production networks, as emphasized throughout this study. For this they need a supportive policy environment. The relative success of Singapore, Taiwan (China), and now China over Japan and Korea in computer manufacturing is based on policies that support integration into the global production system, rather than domestic production and export promotion.[25]

Government Support. Successful integration into global networks has involved a significant element of public intervention. In Taiwan, China, public sector laboratories such as the Industrial Technology Research Institute played an important role in obtaining semiconductor technology transfer agreements with source firms in the United States and in disseminating technology to the private sector—to the

---

25. The successful models differed, with Taiwan, China, creating many strong local companies and Singapore attracting U.S. firms.

extent of creating companies where required.[26] Even critics of the role of government intervention in ICT production in the region credit the Industrial Technology Research Institute with helping to overcome capital and scale barriers in an economy made up of small firms with limited R&D capacity (Hobday 2001).[27]

Market Signals. In countries where ICT production has expanded rapidly, there has sometimes been a role for government-backed venture capital funds. Singapore, for example, has a $1 billion fund for "technopreneurs." Such funds have a mixed record in the region, however, as noted in chapter 4. Even Hong Kong's $100 million venture capital fund for ICT ran into difficulties. Although the fund was to be managed by private companies, those selected (perhaps by necessity) were large banks, which failed to find attractive investments (100 of the U.S. companies that launched venture capital funds in the late 1990s had closed them by 2002, and a further 100 were seeking to do so, a clear indication of the riskiness of such activity ["Corporate Venture Investors" 2002]). HSBC's private equity fund, chosen to manage part of the proceeds, gave most of its shares back after making only one investment in the course of a year ("Tiger and the Tech" 2000). It seems that government-backed venture capital funds can operate successfully only in an environment that already favors high-risk, relatively small-scale investments in entrepreneurial operations—an environment that appears to be absent in Hong Kong, China. This suggests that government intervention succeeds where market conditions are already favorable enough for a relatively small intervention to foster results. It is difficult to identify the subsectors that meet these conditions. Singapore's approach in supporting the hard disk drive industry—following market signals to the extent possible, while recognizing the need for some government interven-

---

26. The Legend Computer Group was spawned by China's Institute of Computing Technology and could draw significantly from the pool of talent there. But much of the company's success can be attributed to substantial managerial autonomy, which enabled it to introduce the institute's new discoveries to the marketplace (Lu 2000).

27. Government involvement in R&D is similar in Taiwan, China, to that in a number of other economies successful in ICT production. Finland's National Technology Agency, Tekes, provides funding for R&D and promotes national and international networking. Tekes supports high-risk commercializable R&D efforts by both companies and institutes in particular "strategic areas" (World Bank 2001e).

tion—is likely to be the type of hybrid policy with the greatest chance of creating viable innovative clusters (Hobday 2001).

Focus of Support. In the ICT sector, as with clusters in general, policy intervention should start with a broad focus wherever possible and only narrow down the focus after some degree of comparative advantage has been revealed—a point discussed in chapter 6. The opposite approach of "picking winners" regarding particular technologies has a mixed record in the region (Yusuf 2001).[28] Picking winners is made far harder by the speed of technological change in ICT. Today, for example, wireless fidelity allows mobile access to broadband Internet service, while new technologies allow a fivefold increase in the speed at which data are transmitted over twisted copper wires, offering to enormously increase wireless voice and data transmission over the Internet (see, for instance, "Wireless Act" 2002). These technologies are much cheaper than hardwiring new broadband transmission lines into buildings, as was mandated by Korea's universal broadband access program, for example ("All Net, All the Time" 2002).

Software and Applications

A homegrown software industry often requires generations of product development before programs become profitable; it also requires close interaction with sophisticated end users. To build a software industry and promote ICT applications, countries use two main models.

The first involves attracting major international players to establish regional offices and production facilities. Ireland reaped considerable economic benefits from following this model and now produces 40

---

28. Even an apparent success such as Korea's early adoption of Code Division Multiple Access mobile phone technology is less clearly a success story of government intervention on deeper examination. Korean government agencies and firms committed to this new and untried technology in 1993, while it was still being developed. The technology was licensed from the U.S. inventor firm Qualcomm and developed by two Korean firms; the local market was used as a test bed. By the end of 1996, Korea had the world's largest Code Division Multiple Access network. Nonetheless, some recent observers argue that even this intervention was unnecessary, heavy-handed, and ineffective, in addition to entailing the payment of very high royalties to Qualcomm ("All Net, All the Time" 2002; Hobday 2001). However, this may have paved the way for Korea's development and use of Code Division Multiple Access 2000, which has considerable promise for mobile systems.

percent of all software packaged with personal computers sold in Europe. Ireland's success has been built on significant investments from predominantly U.S. market leaders, including Microsoft and Oracle; the Irish government supported training and adoption of e-commerce by small and medium enterprises (World Bank 2001e). Singapore, an exception for the region, followed this model and built a fairly well-developed base of software manufacturing as a result, drawing on technical and English language skills. In 1995 software production was worth 0.84 percent of GDP in Singapore compared to 0.86, 0.15, and 0.13 in the United States, Japan, and Korea, respectively.

The second model, followed in India, involves having low-cost, high-quality engineers to attract outsourcing work from global players in the industry, competing in the labor-intensive, cost-sensitive areas of coding, testing, web services, and technical support. This model is becoming increasingly difficult to follow as more countries and regions attempt to compete, including Eastern Europe, Russia, and South Africa (World Bank 2001e). Nonetheless, East Asian countries with a strong base of human capital and low wages, such as China, may choose to emulate it ("Building Software" 2002).

To foster East Asia's software industry, public support for domestic use and training and improvements in the regulatory and policy environment for venture capital markets and intellectual property rights are likely to have more impact than traditional means of promoting industry. Countries also need to achieve greater parity in the development of human capital between electronics engineers and computer scientists (Dedrick and Kraemer 1998). Here again, government expenditure and training for ICT professionals should take its cue from market signals and emphasize the quality of general education.

E-Commerce

As ICT suppliers and customers worldwide move to exploit the opportunities generated by e-commerce, East Asia will need more competitive communications, combined with an environment conducive to exploiting ICT. Most companies in the region do not have access to the financial infrastructure needed to trade on-line or have the services of the physical delivery infrastructure to make direct business-to-consumer transactions feasible. While 84 percent of Chinese companies with a computer use e-mail, only 0.1 percent of Chinese enterprises have a website (UNCTAD 2001a). Even in Korea, while 85 percent of small and medium enterprises have Internet access, few engage in e-commerce. The same is true in Hong Kong, China, where the percentage of companies with a web page supporting on-line transactions increased from 3.7 percent in September 1999 to just 3.8 percent in May 2001 (APEC 2001).

Most immediately, e-commerce requires the skills to operate sites and the financial mechanisms for payment.

Skills Development. Basic requirements to exploit the Internet are the skills needed to use and create e-mail applications and websites. Basic skills development is already a priority for many countries across the region—for example, Korea has an ambitious program of subsidized and free Internet training courses and has undertaken to teach more than 11 million students, civil servants, and military personnel how to use computers (World Bank 2000f). Singapore is also active in this respect. There might also be a role for vocational training of ICT professionals, although here the case for intervention is much weaker than it is in general education. English language skills also will remain important for exploiting international e-commerce opportunities, as they are for attracting foreign direct investment and supporting technology spillovers.[29]

Financial Sector Reform. Financial sector reform is perhaps one of the highest priorities for the successful exploitation of e-commerce. In China, for example, the lack of a fully integrated banking network makes it impossible to process transactions across different regions and between different banks. Customers of China Merchants Bank

---

29. It is widely projected that China will have more Internet users than any other country by the end of the decade, which will make Chinese the dominant language on the Internet (Crandall and Litan 2002). Even if the rather optimistic numbers on the Chinese user base come true, this is unlikely. China already has more literate people than any other country, and yet there is no sense that China dominates the world publishing market (although with approximately 100,000 titles and 6 million copies published in 1994, according to UNESCO, it certainly has a significant role). Further, English is far more dominant worldwide among likely users of the Internet (wealthy and well educated) than is Chinese. A sign of the likely continued dominance of English is that about 50 percent of Chinese websites support English, as compared to about 20 percent of U.S. sites that support any language apart from English (Gantz 2001).

can access the bank's websites in 10 cities, for example, but they can buy on-line only from merchants that also bank with China Merchants Bank. Some domestic Chinese sites (such as www.bookmall. com) offer secure electronic transactions, but only to holders of foreign currency credit cards or clients of just five banks. Only 13 percent of on-line transactions are completed with on-line payment in China, compared to 42 percent with cash on delivery and 24 percent with remittances via post offices (UNCTAD 2001a). Regulatory moves in the financial sector that encourage interconnection are likely to be vital in expanding on-line commerce in the country (Kenny 2000b). China's "golden card" program to set up a credit card verification scheme and an interbank, interregion clearing system by 2003 is an important step in this direction (UNCTAD 2001a).

The penetration of credit cards remains very low across East Asia with the exception of Korea (where 40 percent of consumer transactions were with credit cards in 2002), for reasons of low financial sector development, lack of trust, problems with quickly and cheaply verifying consumer creditworthiness, and the preference of consumers for cash payments to avoid taxes. Nonetheless, differences in credit card protection can also be a significant deterrent to card ownership and on-line purchasing. In Taiwan, China, for example, the cardholder is liable for the full amount of any fraudulent transaction and must go to court to obtain redress (Mann, Eckert, and Knight 2000). Compounding the problems with payment is the inadequacy of fulfillment services in China, where a sizable fraction of goods ordered are not delivered and post-sales service is deficient ("E-woes, E-gads" 2002).

THE UNDERPINNINGS OF INFORMATION INFRASTRUCTURE

The cost, quality, and extent of Internet access vary with the cost, quality, and extent of telephone access. Economies with well-regulated, competitive private provision of information infrastructure see lower costs, better service, and wider provision of both telecommunications and Internet services (Forestier, Grace, and Kenny 2001; Kenny 2000a, 2001a; Kubota 2000; Reynolds, Kenny, and Qiang 2001; Wallsten 1999; Wheeler 2000).

To provide inexpensive, high-quality telecommunications and Internet services, the first step for most countries in the region is to complete telecommunications reform. Several examples from within the region show the power of reform to extend access. When Korea removed the government-imposed compulsory two-year subscription period for mobile telephones in April 1999, the number of subscribers in the country expanded by 3 million people within a month (World Bank 2000f). Even in China's far from perfect regulatory and investment environment, limited competition between largely government-controlled operators caused an explosive growth in access to backbone bandwidth.[30]

Regulatory Regimes for ICT in East Asia

For many countries, telecommunications reform entails a significant policy agenda. Malaysia is in some ways a model for regulatory reform, with a Communications and Multimedia Act that visualizes the convergence of information and communications technologies, declares itself pro-competition and technology-neutral, and aims to achieve universal service (ITU 2002b). But Malaysia retains a number of laws and regulations, including limits on foreign ownership, that hinder sector development.

Japan and Korea, which in practice have two of the most liberal and well-regulated markets in the region, are the only two countries in the OECD without an independent regulatory structure. For other countries, including China, Indonesia, Singapore, Thailand, and Vietnam, the issue is one of opening the sector to (international) private competition under the oversight of a regulator with autonomy, significant expertise, and access to resources.

Telecommunications Regulation in China. China, for example, has a unique environment for information infrastructure: a somewhat competitive system among state enterprises (the four major fixed-line carriers—China Mobile, China Netcom, China Telecom, and China

---

30. Between June 1998 and December 2000, the number of operators for leased international bandwidth rose from four to nine, and the share of bandwidth controlled by the largest operator (ChinaNet) fell from 92 to 70 percent; the availability of international bandwidth in China increased from a total of 85 to 2,800 megabits per second (Harwit and Clark 2001).

Unicom—are all owned by various state organs). Not surprising under the circumstances, China's regulatory system lacks transparency and is based on fragmented administrative decrees. The Ministry of Information Industry regulates the sector and controls both China Telecom and China Unicom. Thus far, it has not used this position to ensure that the regulatory system promotes new competition. New telecom regulation put into force in September 2000 should improve the situation somewhat (Qiang 2001).

As a result, despite impressive growth in some areas, costs and access remain far worse than they might be under a reformed market structure. In 1999 leased telephone lines from China Telecom took up 80 percent of the costs of Internet service providers (ISPs), compared to about 6 percent in the United States (Harwit and Clark 2001). Prices have since fallen, but the regulated prices for Internet access, combined with discriminatory tactics against ISPs building their own networks, have left 90 percent of ISPs simply reselling the services of regionally branded ChinaNet Internet connections (Harwit and Clark 2001). This removes other avenues to Internet service competition. For example, even though cable penetration is high in China, regulation prohibits cable operators from offering Internet services, effectively closing down a promising avenue for providing broadband access.[31]

China's accession to the World Trade Organization (WTO) should speed the development of more liberal market structures (as well as allow the phased introduction of minority foreign ownership in information infrastructure), but the WTO Basic Telecommunications Agreement is fairly vague, allowing significant room for interpretation (Qiang 2001). China's government will need to undertake fur-

---

31. By mid-1999 an estimated 80 million Chinese households subscribed to cable television services (Asia Information Associates 2000, p. 28). The prohibition on cable Internet services is largely due to the competition over jurisdiction in China. Internet access and e-commerce typically fall under the jurisdiction of the Ministry of Information Industry and the Ministry of Foreign Trade and Economic Cooperation. Cable television is promoted through the State Administration of Radio, Film, and Television (SARFT). Since it is not in the interest of the Ministry of Information Industry for SARFT to venture into the Internet, it issued regulations in November 1999 prohibiting cable television networks from connecting to the telecom network (Asia Information Associates 2000, p. 15). This is reflected in the survey conducted by China Internet Network Information Center in January 2000, which reveals that 53 percent of Internet users are dissatisfied with their slow connections (Asia Information Associates 2000, p. 29).

ther reform if access to and use of ICT services are to continue growing rapidly.

Telecommunications Regulation in Other Countries. A number of other countries in the region have an even less competitive environment than China.[32] For example, of the East Asian countries listed in table 8.3, only four have open competition in the provision of international gateway services. In Thailand, although reform is ongoing, the two main state-owned operators legally own the entire telecommunications infrastructure, with revenue-sharing agreements binding concession holders (ITU 2002a).

Going beyond competition in the provision of physical infrastructure and allowing new competitive carriers to lease "unbundled network elements"—principally copper-wire access lines—from incumbents and even to share these lines with the incumbents, are particularly important when it comes to extending broadband access. In Japan NTT is now required to provide competitors with access to its subscriber lines, or "local loops." Korea has pushed for the rapid rollout of high-speed lines, and competitors have access to these lines through the telephone network, owned by Korea Telecom, and through cable networks.

Implicit public policies toward vertical integration by telecommunications carriers make a significant difference to competition among Internet service providers. For example, Japan's NTT is forbidden to provide Internet access to its telephone subscribers; as a result, Japan has more than 4,000 ISPs. In contrast, Singapore has only three ISPs, and in Malaysia, Telekom Malaysia controls 69 percent of the ISP market, with the remainder split among only six other operators (ITU 2000, p. 38). The Philippines places no market restrictions on ISPs but does not allow them to build their own infrastructure, so that independent operators are little more than resellers, facing unfair competition from ISPs that are linked to telecommunications operators (ITU 2002c; Yusuf and Evenett 2002).

Environment for Foreign Investment. Several countries in the region, including China, Korea, and Thailand, also lag in providing an attractive environment for foreign investment. In China the decision

---

32. See Noll (2000) for an international overview of telecommunications regulation.

to terminate China-China-foreign (CCF) investments, which had been the major source of funding for China Unicom, muddied the investment climate in 2000.[33] Foreign joint ventures with China Unicom and investments in Internet services have generally not been profitable, yielding an average return on equity of just 3 percent (Qiang 2001). China has thus far relied on the scale of its market to attract foreign investors even under these difficult circumstances. But without greater clarity and investor protection in the sector, future foreign investment could be at risk.

Korea, which met its WTO commitments on foreign ownership in the ICT sector 18 months early, still places some limitations on the foreign ownership of incumbent providers (World Bank 2000f). In the Philippines the constitution limits foreign ownership in utilities to 40 percent (ITU 2002c). In Thailand the government has recently passed a telecommunications law that, while privatizing the two government-owned operators, also tightens the restriction on foreign holdings in local telephone companies from 49 to 25 percent. This threshold is exceeded by three of the top four private operators, however, and the new law is being reconsidered ("Thailand: Telecoms Reforms" 2001). In Malaysia the share of foreign investment after five years of operation is limited to 49 percent (ITU 2002b).

Countries that have allowed foreign investment in ICT have attracted it readily, with resulting improvements in access to quality services. Their experience suggests that limits on foreign ownership should be removed throughout the region.

Universal Service and Cross-Subsidies

Related to reform of the telecommunications sector is the issue of universal service and universal access policies, both for basic telephony and for more advanced services including the Internet. Access to networked services, especially the Internet, remains skewed toward wealthy urban residents across the region (as it does throughout the world).[34]

---

33. CCF allowed foreign companies to take part indirectly in revenue sharing by assisting with the financing and construction of China Unicom's networks.

34. For example, Beijing, with 1 percent of the country's population, had 12 percent of its Internet users in 2000, whereas Tibet, with 0.2 percent of the population, had only 0.03 percent of the country's users (Harwit and Clark 2001).

Policymakers across the region have called for much broader access to telephony and the Internet, especially in rural areas,[35] and a number of countries have instituted ambitious universal service targets. Korea has gone so far as to put in place a program for all homes to have access to high-speed connections of 2 megabits per second (World Bank 2000f).

Appropriate universal access targets are to be lauded. Evidence shows that if network access and use are concentrated among a wealthy minority, this creates a strong force for increasing inequality within countries (Forestier, Grace, and Kenny 2001). Ubiquity of access is especially important where a country plans to offer an increasing number of government-to-citizen services over networks, because the government has to ensure that the persons who most need government services are not excluded from them.

Design of Universal Service Policies. Access policies should be implemented only after basic reform is complete. They should be technology-neutral and appropriate to a country's level of development and to the needs of citizens. They also should be designed to support the delivery of services by the market. Experience offers several lessons.

First, unless the environment for telecommunications is well regulated and competitive, a universal access program is likely to be very costly and to provide significant rents to telecommunications operators. Chile's experience with what may be the model program for reform and access indicates the results that can be achieved if universal access programs are preceded by competition. In 1988 fewer than 20 percent of Chile's households had telephones. With the introduction of private competition and the advance of technology, by 2000 about 75 percent had telephones, and all but 1 percent of the remaining households were served by a public telephone. A government-financed scheme, which used a competitive reverse-auction subsidy to encourage private providers to install public phones in unserved areas, gave 10 percent of households access to a public phone. Under the subsidy scheme, 2.2 million people gained access to telephony at

---

35. For example, Malaysian Prime Minister Datuk Seri Dr. Mahathir Mohamad spoke at length about the need for universal access at the G-15 Summit in Jakarta in May 2001 (see www. sibexlink.com.my/g15/news/31052001.htm).

the cost of $22 million in public funds, which attracted an additional $139 million in private investment (calculated from information in Wellenius 2001). If universal access goals had been imposed or achieved before the introduction of competitive private provision, the costs of that access to the economy (and to the government in particular) would have been much greater.

Second is the need for technology neutrality. Rather than selecting the technology that will deliver universal access to services, regulators should select the services that they believe should be universally accessible and let the market, not the government, choose the most efficient technologies for delivering them. For example, with today's technologies, expanding access to telephony is likely to be far easier using wireless rather than fixed solutions. Yet government rollout obligations have frequently specified expansion targets for fixed networks. As a result, and at great cost, fixed networks have been expanded into areas more efficiently served by mobile systems. These same areas are now served by mobile service providers who can offer cheaper access. This has left some countries with very low capacity utilization of the fixed network. In Thailand, for example, had the government focused on increasing access to telephony rather than on extending the coverage of fixed telephone lines, a good deal of wasted investment in fixed lines might have been avoided. Only 69 percent of the fixed lines in the country are now used.[36] The percentage of households with a telephone doubled between 1996 and 2000, but almost entirely as the result of expanded mobile access. Thailand's largest mobile operator planned to have 91 percent mobile coverage by the end of 2001—in other words, 9 out of 10 people will live in areas served by mobile telephones (ITU 2002a).[37]

Third is the need to assess demand and costs realistically. Near-universal telephone access might be a realistic and valuable goal for

---

36. Two franchises were obligated to install 4.1 million fixed telephone lines between 1993 and 1997. Much of this capacity remains unused because fixed services are more costly and less convenient than the mobile services that now cover the same base of potential subscribers (ITU 2001b).

37. A similar story can be told in the Philippines, where nine mobile and international operators were ordered to install 4 million fixed telephone lines in the period 1993–98. This target was met, but of those 4 million installed lines, only 29 percent were being used in December 2000 (ITU 2002c).

even the poorest countries in the region, but providing Internet access on a nationwide basis is more difficult and expensive than providing telephony—it requires electricity, a computer, a modem, and access to skilled technical support for users.[38]

Universal service (or even access) provisions for the Internet might well provide an unwanted tool to most of the region's citizens—or at least might give priority to the wrong expenditures. In middle-income East Asian countries, people who are not connected to the Internet say that the main reason for their lack of interest is not cost (mentioned by only 7 percent of respondents) but lack of need (mentioned by 41 percent; R. Rose 2002). In Hong Kong (China), Korea, and Singapore, as many as 92 percent of the population know where they can access the Internet if they choose to. Yet, in Korea, less than one-third of the population actually uses the Internet—and in Hong Kong, China, and Singapore the figure is less than half. In Taiwan, China, about 60 percent of the population knows where to access the Internet, yet only 29 percent do so (calculated from R. Rose 2002).

Illiteracy remains an issue in many of the poorer countries in the region, as do technical skills in virtually every country. The language barrier remains significant as well; a recent study conducted in Bangkok, Beijing, Jakarta, Seoul, Singapore, and Tokyo suggests that English speakers are two to four times more likely than others to use the Internet (Kenny 2001a).[39]

Universal access to broadband connectivity might become more important in the future as more sophisticated forms of e-commerce and always-on applications evolve. The importance of broadband to the home is not yet clear from an economic standpoint. By 2001 Korea had 6 million broadband subscribers. Clearly, this service involved costs (including an estimated $1.5 billion for upgrading existing buildings), and the benefits of such access are yet to be conclusively demonstrated.[40]

---

38. In rural Costa Rica, for example, LINCOS's off-grid, solar-powered telecenters providing Internet access have a set-up cost of about $20,000 per computer for a six-computer center. Ongoing costs excluding manpower are about $5,000 per computer per year. How sustainable such costs would be, even given a generous public subsidy, is an open question (Shakeel and others 2001).

39. In 2000 only 11 percent of Internet users in a 30-country sample spoke no English (R. Rose 2002).

40. Pyramid Research (2001) suggests that a main reason for high broadband uptake in Korea is that teenagers and young professionals are using the service in order to support on-line gaming.

Cross-Subsidies. The argument that private access to telephony or the Internet should be cross-subsidized through below-cost rental or free local telephone calls remains largely untested, even in the wealthier countries of the region. Using the revenues from long-distance and international traffic to cross-subsidize the costs of local calls, residential connections, and rental fees does increase home access and use of telephone services, if carried out by a reasonably efficient operator.

However, from a public policy perspective, cross-subsidies raise a number of issues. First, they undermine competitive market structures and greatly increase the burden placed on regulators. Second, they significantly reduce the use of the network (indeed, the demand for *calling* is far more price sensitive than is the demand for *accessing* the network, even in developing countries).[41] Third, the advantage of universal service over (more sustainable) universal public access programs, especially in the poorer countries of the region, is questionable.

In the wealthier countries of East Asia, support for home access to telephony should be transparent and based on general government revenues rather than on hidden cross-subsidies within the dominant carrier. For the poorer countries, a universal access program, modeled on the Chilean competitive reverse-auction scheme, is likely to be more sustainable.

Regarding free local calls, an econometric analysis carried out for this study (Crandall and Litan 2002), based on data for 17 developing countries, suggests that high marginal pricing for Internet access (per minute ISP and telephone charges) bears some relationship to lower usage per month, but the estimated price elasticity of demand is only –0.17. Further, compared to the fixed costs, the marginal cost of Internet access is low. The cost of local calls worldwide, estimated from the International Telecommunications Union, averages about $1.55 per hour (table 8.5). If the marginal value of Internet use is near to $1.55 per hour, so that the marginal cost of access is a significant deterrent, this suggests a great deal about the potential of the Internet as an economically transformative technology.

Singapore's broadband network, which involved a government investment of $300 million, saw a sluggish initial uptake by subscribers because consumers did not consider the significantly higher cost of access worthwhile (Mann, Eckert, and Knight 2000).

41. See Crandall and Waverman (2000) for estimates of the cost of universal service policies. See also Garbacz and Thompson (1997) and Kaserman, Mayo, and Flynn (1990).

Table 8.5 Price of a Three-Minute Local Call, 1990 and 1999
(U.S. dollars)

Country	1990	1999
European Union		
France	0.13	0.11
Germany	0.14	0.11
Portugal	0.05	0.09
Spain	0.04	0.09
United Kingdom	0.26[a]	0.19
North America		
United States[b]	0	0
Canada	0	0
Asia and Oceania		
Australia	0.18[c]	0.16
New Zealand	0[c]	0
China	—	0.01
Hong Kong, China	—	0
Japan	0.06	0.08
Korea, Rep. of	0.03	0.03
Malaysia	0.04	0.02
Philippines	0	0
Singapore	0	0.02
Thailand	0.11	0.07

— Not available.

a. 1992.

b. In a few jurisdictions, such as Chicago, there is a charge per call, but most have flat-rate local residential service.

c. 1991.

Source: ITU (2000).

Free local calling, if targeted at Internet users, is a regressive regulatory measure designed to support the wealthy home computer user at the cost of those with no access to the Internet. Furthermore, industrial countries (like the United States) with free local calling have been unable to sustain the provision of free Internet service. In the United Kingdom, by contrast, the revenue from local calls exceeds the marginal cost by a margin sufficient to sustain ISPs such as Freeserve, which is the largest in the country and, as its name suggests, is free of charge (Graham 2001).

Even if expanding Internet use is seen as a goal worthy of distorting market forces, the presence of such tradeoffs indicates that the policy conclusion in favor of free local calls is hardly self-evident. This is especially true because poor users are more likely to be deterred from having an Internet account by up-front ISP fees than by per minute usage charges.[42]

Regulation of E-Commerce

Moving beyond basic reform of the telecommunications sector and policies for access, the Internet raises a number of policy issues that require responses, in areas including e-commerce law, taxation, privacy, and security. East Asian countries have moved some way toward addressing these concerns, but further work and international agreements are needed.

Laws that grant digital signatures—assents by the parties on-line that are authenticated in a well-recognized manner—the same legal status as handwritten signatures are clearly a prerequisite for e-commerce.[43] Some form of digital signature legislation has been enacted in Hong Kong (China), Korea, Malaysia, Singapore, and Thailand (Crandall and Litan 2002). Digital signature laws were pending in late 2001 in Japan, the Philippines, and Thailand. It is not clear, however, whether the current or proposed laws need supplementation to encourage more e-commerce. Recent initiatives in Mexico, for example, point to the advantages of an approach that also addresses electronic authentication and certification issues. All three of these Asian countries might want to revisit their laws in this light (Mann, Eckert, and Knight 2000).

A particular concern is the security of on-line transactions. Asian consumers reportedly are especially dubious about the security of credit card transactions on-line (Mann, Eckert, and Knight 2000; "Shoppers Lost in Cyberspace" 2001). A recent survey of Malaysian businesses that use e-commerce finds security to be the greatest barrier to expanding e-commerce operations—a concern that is validat-

---

42. Although low-cost local calls may not greatly increase the economic effects of the Internet, high-cost local calls suggest a cross-subsidy from call costs to fixed-line provision. Cross-subsidy from local calls to fixed-line provision is economically inefficient and, especially in the region's less developed countries, unlikely to benefit the poor. But it is a relatively small problem in East Asia.

43. The U.S. Electronic Signatures in Global and National Commerce Act became effective on October 1, 2000. Among other things, the law contains rules and procedures that clarify the legal status of electronic signatures, requiring that the relevant contract be in an electronic form capable of being retained and accurately reproduced. The law does not apply to certain documents governed by state law, notably wills or contracts relating to divorce. Numerous states in the United States, however, have their own versions of a digital signature law.

ed by the extent of credit card fraud on-line in the United States.[44] At least one survey also reports that concern about security is the most frequently cited reason for the relatively low rate of on-line banking among moderate to high-income Asian consumers. Singapore has led the way in passing cyber crime laws to address such concerns, involving some of the severest penalties in the world (Claessens, Klingebiel, and Laeven 2001). Other East Asian governments might follow suit.

A number of other e-finance regulation issues remain to be tackled in the region. As of mid-2001, for example, Korea lacked disclosure requirements for portals, regulation of stored value cards, and separate authorization requirements for virtual electronic finance providers (Claessens, Klingebiel, and Laeven 2001).

Privacy, unlike security, does not yet appear to be a major concern among East Asian Internet users, despite the fact that in some countries (for example, China) governments play an active role in tracking Internet use (Crandall and Litan 2002). In Europe and the United States widespread concern over the confidentiality of on-line activities has resulted in a series of laws and regulations covering (among others) banking, health, and retail sites, of which the European Union (EU) Privacy Directive of 1995 is perhaps the best known. Korea has taken steps in this area, passing legislation that prohibits the transfer of personal data without consent and ordering 500 firms to revise their privacy policies or face fines for violations. The borderless nature of the Internet makes privacy an international issue. Even if local consumers are not deterred by a lack of privacy legislation and protection, the international community might force protection onto the agenda.

China has an especially long way to go regarding Internet legislation. E-commerce in the country remains limited, amounting to less than $100 million in 2000. Only 0.8 percent of the 10 million enterprises in China had a website for e-commerce in 1999 (Qiang 2001). One reason is that e-commerce has been restricted to goods on electronic "marketplaces" maintained by the Ministry of Foreign Trade and Economic Cooperation.[45] Few companies advertising their prod-

---

44. Concern about security is followed by concerns about contractual and financial issues, hackers' intervention, lack of skilled personnel, and privacy (Mukti 2000).

45. Such as www.chinamarket.com.

ucts on the Internet are equipped to accept on-line orders, let alone offer on-line payment facilities, because full regulations on privacy, consumer rights, and recognition of digital signatures have yet to be written.

International Issues

Growing cross-border e-commerce transactions will eventually require the coordination of global laws covering all areas of consumer law and taxation. Different standards regarding a range of products and services (children's toys, pills) will need to be harmonized as global e-commerce expands. If countries decide that local laws apply to Internet transactions, Internet merchants will need to adapt their offerings to 190 different jurisdictions or limit their sales to only a few countries (Crandall and Litan 2002).[46]

Issues of Internet security and privacy might create a barrier to East Asia's integration into global networks of electronic commerce. More than 80 percent of U.S. companies indicate that security is the leading barrier to expanding electronic commerce with their customers and partners (Mann, Eckert, and Knight 2000). However, the concern of businesses with security runs counter to the concern of governments with the ability to monitor transactions for legal and national security reasons, a concern that sharpened further during 2001–02. For example, in Malaysia and Singapore, users must disclose their encryption keys to government agencies or face criminal penalties. China has announced laws requiring foreign firms to register their software with the government (Mann, Eckert, and Knight 2000). Thus concerns regarding national security might place significant burdens on the region's companies in their on-line dealings with overseas clients.

International concerns may create a need to enforce privacy standards. The EU Privacy Directive, for example, threatens the equivalent of a "data embargo" on the export of personal information about

---

46. Another area of cross-border complexity created by the Internet is that of offensive, dangerous, or culturally unacceptable material. In 2001 a French court ordered U.S.-based Yahoo to use geocoding technology (allowing Yahoo to identify the country of approximately 70 percent of its visitors) to prevent French Internet users from gaining access to auctions of Nazi memorabilia and literature.

EU citizens to countries that do not provide adequate privacy protection. If the EU views are to be taken into account, East Asian governments will need to join the international efforts to reconcile various privacy provisions regarding the Internet as well as those bodies that are examining the regulation and taxation of international on-line commercial transactions.

Another question for policymakers worldwide is whether and how on-line commerce should be taxed. At the WTO ministerial meeting in Geneva in 1998, members agreed to a temporary moratorium on imposing customs duties on electronic commerce and products delivered electronically (Mann, Eckert, and Knight 2000). More recently, the EU has begun setting tougher tax rules. All electronic transmissions of "soft goods," including downloaded software and digitized books, for example, are considered services that should be taxed at the appropriate value added tax rate. In contrast to the United States, which does not tax on-line commerce, the European Union has proposed that businesses both within and outside the EU apply, collect, and remit taxes from "soft goods" downloaded by EU entities without an EU value added tax registration (Mann, Eckert, and Knight 2000).

It may be some time before the disparities created by the differences in national tax treatment of e-commerce become a significant practical concern for East Asian nations. At present, trade in digitizable products amounts to less than 1 percent of world trade, less than 1 percent of tariff revenue, and perhaps 0.03 percent of total fiscal revenue. In East Asia, only for Korea and Thailand do tariffs on digitizable products amount to more than 0.15 percent of total government revenue (Mattoo and Schuknecht 2000).[47] In the future, if Asian countries follow the U.S. rather than the European Union model, a significant part of commerce might move on-line to avoid taxes in countries such as Indonesia, whose top rate of value added tax is as

---

47. The electronic delivery of services is probably a more significant issue, accounting for up to 6 percent of world trade and affecting, in particular, China, Korea, and Singapore among developing countries, but few data are available here. Perhaps most important are the principles at stake in the management of world trade via electronic delivery. Preferential treatment of electronic delivery challenges the principle of technological neutrality, which prohibits distinctions between products solely on the basis of means of delivery. This suggests the need for strengthening the General Agreement on Trade in Services in this area (Mattoo and Schuknecht 2000) and for undertaking international reform.

high as 35 percent. And as e-commerce grows, existing tax regimes based on the value added tax and concepts such as permanent establishment are likely to become increasingly difficult to administer effectively and fairly (Mann, Eckert, and Knight 2000). Even if the public-good argument for especially favorable tax treatment of e-commerce is weak—and it will become increasingly distortionary as e-commerce grows—practical considerations might eventually force a change in policy.

USE OF ICT TO IMPROVE GOVERNANCE

The spread of ICT throughout East Asia provides an avenue for governments to strengthen economic rights and accountability, to reduce the transaction costs for businesses, and to enhance the competitiveness of democratic politics.[48] Many East Asian countries have made only a start in this area, although a few have been much quicker off the mark, glimpsing the opportunities. Most countries will find it advantageous to embrace e-governance more fully as computer literacy spreads, societies become extensively wired, Internet access grows, and people come to appreciate the enormous gains it offers in access and convenience.

If ICT can change the government's central nervous system and the nature of its interactions with the public, there is enormous scope for making "government smarter, cheaper, and more effective" (Kettl

---

48. Thus far, however, research in the United States suggests that the Internet is an important means of gathering information but not for conducting political debate, influencing politicians (D. C. King 2002), or raising significant amounts of campaign funds, although these are early days. In fact, the election of Roh Moo Hyun as the president of Korea owed much to the support provided by the younger segment of the population mobilized to vote via the Internet ("Roh's Poll" 2002). Noting that the Internet permits like-minded individuals to seek each other out, one commentator observes, "The rise of homogeneous communities tends not only to decrease interest-group community and increase political fragmentation, but also exacerbates the difficulty of reconciling diverse interests and worldviews . . . the Internet's probable effect will be the intensification of group-centered politics" (Galston 2002, p. 55). Another commentator, writing on the subject of a virtual democracy, notes that even if "e-citizens become more politically engaged and informed, the activity may be confined to a minority. . . . Only a few of the members of the on-line community [in the United States] proved to be engaged in any form of political activity that can claim to be distinctively new. . . . There are persuasive grounds for skepticism, however, toward the more sweeping claims about the power of technology to change democracy as we know it" (Norris 2002, pp. 76–77).

2000, p. 15). Use of the Internet for e-governance can help to strengthen institutions that contribute to the quality of the market environment. It can reduce transaction costs for individuals and businesses, for example, the costs of registering businesses and renewing permits or licenses (Mechling 2002); improve the flow of and access to information from public agencies on a 24-hour basis; strengthen coordination within and among agencies; and reduce paperwork, all of which can make transactions more accurate (Fountain 2002). By encouraging openness and adherence to impersonal rules, the Internet provides a robust mechanism for assuring accountability and, if properly used, for improving the customer service provided by regulatory and monitoring agencies. E-governance can (1) give private entities greater voice and enlarge their range of choices; (2) diminish the power of special interests by reducing the cost of gathering information about policies (Kettl 2000); (3) make government not just more accountable but also more competitive by facilitating the outsourcing of services and increasing the transparency of public sector tendering and contracting arrangements (UNCTAD 2001a); and (4) facilitate decentralization by placing "information and computing power at the operational levels of the hierarchy while making results rapidly transparent at upper levels, [thereby] devolving decisionmaking to operational personnel" (Fountain 2002, p. 121).

However, there are several long steps to realizing the economic and political benefits of e-governance. Much depends on a country's starting point and, especially, its readiness to embark on a number of interlaced reforms, small and large. The Internet and governance cannot be fused without significant advances in computerization, telecommunications development, Internet access, user skills, and organizational changes to embed e-governance within the public sector.

Introducing E-Governance in East Asia

The number of government agencies posting information about their activities on the Internet continues to grow, but the disparities are wide, ranging from two sites in Vietnam to 136 and 169 sites, respectively, in Thailand and Taiwan, China. As expected, governments differ in their capacity to adopt Internet technology. In the relatively advanced economies, including Hong Kong (China), Japan, Korea,

Singapore, and Taiwan (China), the issues are comparable to those in advanced Western countries. In other developing states, such as China, Indonesia, the Philippines, Thailand, and Vietnam, a complementary modernization of government—and provision of Internet access to the general public—must precede an attempt to make full use of the Internet for e-governance.

E-Governance in Singapore. In East Asia, Singapore has taken the lead in using the Internet to organize public services in ways that are clear, accessible, and comprehensive.[49] Its Citizen Service Portal offers citizens electronic assistance in registering births and education as well as retiring from the work force. Altogether, the Singapore government site offers on-line access to officials dealing with more than 100 public programs.

However, the circumstances of the Singapore government are not typical of the region. Singapore has created a relatively efficient modern bureaucracy that delivers a wide range of services to citizens and regulates many activities; it is a city-state that does not face the problems of coordinating a bewildering range of federal systems with those serving geographically dispersed state populations;[50] its GDP per capita is similar or equal to that of France and Germany, greater than that of Canada or the United Kingdom, and much higher than the average for East Asia, indicating not only the level of computer literacy but also the technological awareness of its population.

Government Effectiveness and Quality of Regulation. The pace of ICT adoption and the option of using the Internet are closely correlated with estimates of government effectiveness and quality of regulation. In the ratings of Kaufman, Kraay, and Zoido-Lobatón (2002), Hong Kong (China), Japan, Singapore, and Taiwan (China) are the four leaders and compare favorably with the Western economies. After them come Korea, Malaysia, and Thailand; Indonesia and Vietnam are near the bottom of the list.

---

49. See www.ecitizen.gov.sg.

50. In China, for example, where subnational governments often resist central government edicts and seek to avoid central monitoring and control, the Internet could become a means of bringing all parts of the government system into step by improving information on, for instance, tax collection, imports, credit availability, and production (Asia Information Associates 2000).

Tasks in Computerizing Government Activities. In theory a modern bureaucracy can readily increase its processing efficiency by shifting information from standard paper forms to hard disk. It can further increase efficiency by permitting on-line financial transactions and the use of digital signatures. A prerequisite for computerization is to have well-structured information flows. Standardized forms must already be in widespread use, classifying information according to fixed rules so that it can be readily received, filed, and disseminated. Without a classification system, which does not itself require a computer, information is very difficult to retrieve. The greater the degree of prior standardization, the less effort is required to input routine records into an Internet-based system.[51] Before considering how to computerize the flow of forms required to meet the needs of a given regulation, it is useful to ask: What are the compliance costs of the regulation itself? How much government regulation is necessary and desirable, and thus expedited through Internet clearances, and how much is better repealed rather than transferred to the Internet?

The technology for e-governance can be assimilated quite easily through training courses and through customized software, but the human aspect is much more complex. Changing the mind-set and work habits of entrenched organizations is a slow process and requires the support of people at senior levels. Most civil servants were recruited before the Internet became operational, and their skills and training were established long ago. They will need incentives to increase their use of the instruments available for e-governance. Older civil servants may need training in keyboard skills before they can use e-mail—and if they regard this as inferior work, suitable only for secretaries, their motivation will be low. Newer recruits to the civil service may be computer literate, but, in institutions where seniority counts, they may lack authority. Uncertain support by senior officials

---

51. For example, where a ministry has organizational charts, mission statements, e-mail and telephone directories, and a repertoire of forms, much information will already be in machine-readable form and easily transferred to the World Wide Web. Because public administration is a continuing activity dependent on consistency with what has gone before, records created before a service goes on the Internet will need to be accessed to deal with ICT-based queries, and allowance must be made for transition from old to new retrieval systems. If transactions with citizens and organizations are routinely entered on computers, then databases can incorporate records from past years with minimal effort. If they are not, the transition may be managed more easily by referencing paper and electronic records in tandem.

may act as a brake on Internet use by the public sector, and newer re-cruits with ICT skills may become frustrated and leave for the private sector. Job classification schemes may segregate ICT personnel into separate agencies, making them "outsiders" in the bureaus of govern-ment where their skills must be applied.

As for choosing technology, the senior staff who set the criteria for their agencies' ICT providers must understand what is needed and be able to brief potential suppliers. Experience with installing and up-grading ICT systems shows a high risk that government agencies will choose suppliers whose low price reflects a misunderstanding of what needs to be done.

Introduction of e-governance involves changing some of the tradi-tional ground rules of interaction between the state and the public as well as between agencies within government. A diverse range of stakeholders must be induced to cooperate. Technological advances that lead to more user-friendly software and enhance broadband ac-cess will certainly help, as will the cumulative effects of small, suc-cessfully implemented projects (UNCTAD 2001a). For government-to-government use of the Internet, a precondition is open communication within and between government agencies.

East Asia starts down the road to improving governance with a higher order of skills and infrastructure than most developing regions. Nevertheless, as the industrial countries have discovered, it is difficult to reinvent government even in modern, affluent, democratic states with a participative citizenry. To realize the potential of e-governance to achieve stability and growth will require a major, visible commit-ment from leadership at the uppermost levels of government through to middle management.

CONCLUSION

The opportunities presented by ICT are substantial, but they should not be oversold. The effect of ICT will depend on a country's policy environment and on its efforts to develop an innovation system.

For East Asia, improving the mastery of ICT and providing broad-er access to services are matters of necessity, not choice. For firms de-fending their share of the market, the logic of competition and participation in global production networks makes it essential to keep up with advances in these technologies. Governments, for their part, need to provide policies and services that make this possible.

The most significant determinant of ICT production, access, and use is the state of other sectors and of the macro economy as a whole. Unless these sustain a favorable environment, sector-specific interventions in support of ICT production and use will likely carry high costs for a limited benefit. Experience suggests that government should encourage the production of ICT by providing support for R&D, training, and perhaps some venture capital. But more important is support for expanded access, at least to the basic tools of communication, by reforming the telecommunications sector and universal access programs. Also significant are national and international efforts to regulate and tax e-commerce in a manner that supports the use of technology on a level playing field. There is little justification for devising more active programs of "picking winners" or for offering significant subsidies.

CHAPTER 9

NEXT STEPS FOR EAST ASIA

The next decade is likely to be decisive for East Asia, with the region sustaining and augmenting its past economic successes only if individual countries pursue policies that provide the macroeconomic stability and the institutional foundations needed for growth led by innovation. Without such policies, slower growth closer to the global mean is the likely outcome.[1]

Open economies, especially the smaller ones, will remain vulnerable to external shocks even with rapid growth. But since the 1997–98 crisis the mechanisms for bolstering stability are better understood. They combine exchange rate policy, good management of debt and reserves, and regulation of the banking system to minimize vulnerability. Regional policy cooperation has an important potential role to play in minimizing the risks of crises, providing resources and guidance to countries in difficulty, and reducing the likelihood of contagion.

The potential for stability and growth depends on a country's institutional capacity as well as macroeconomic policies. Most East Asian economies have institutional weaknesses that need to be addressed, in particular weak financial systems, corporate governance practices that put minority shareholders at a disadvantage, laws that favor debtors over creditors, dysfunctional legal systems, ineffectual or ill-defined competition policies, and inadequate rules for protecting contracts and property rights. Strong market institutions reinforce the stabiliz-

---

1. Easterly and others (1993) show that, except in six East Asian countries, there was no correlation between growth rates from one decade to the next, with the overwhelming majority of countries regressing toward a global mean.

ing role of macroeconomic policies and prepare the ground for rapid growth.

Increasingly, growth in the middle- and higher-income countries will depend on fostering innovation capability and providing the means to commercialize innovations readily. Japan's experience and, more recently, that of the Republic of Korea and Taiwan, China, have shown that steady incremental innovation in manufacturing that helps to reduce costs and raise quality, product innovation that enhances market share and increases rents, and, in Japan's case, the occasional "disruptive innovation" can give a country a competitive edge, especially in fast-growing markets with short product cycles.[2] In the future, innovation—particularly product innovation—is likely to become even more central to economic performance in these economies as well as in others such as Malaysia, Singapore, and Thailand.

Innovation in manufacturing will need to be supported by innovation in a wide range of services. At present, service industries in East Asia are less productive and less competitive than those in the United States and Western Europe, and with the share of services in gross domestic product and trade rising steadily worldwide (currently only 12 percent of services produced are traded versus 50 percent of manufactured goods), a productivity gap could soon put a brake on growth. Although information and communications technology (ICT), financial, engineering, consulting, and other producer services are likely to lead the way, East Asia is also ready for a revolution in retailing, wholesaling, and logistics, to name just a few of the traditional service activities that employ large numbers of people.

An open innovation system is emerging as the axis for a dynamic and rapidly growing economy. Innovation capability has many mutually reinforcing parts, and to build it requires policymaking and institution-building efforts across a broad front, plus in certain instances, heavy investment in research and production facilities to keep abreast of rapid developments and accumulate tacit knowledge. Perhaps the most significant recent development is the international and frequently collaborative nature of research taking place at the frontiers of major disciplines (Murtha, Lenway, and Hart 2001). A country's

---

2. On the significance of disruptive technology, see Christensen (1997).

own domestic technical skills, infrastructure, and research and development (R&D) spending remain essential foundations for an innovation system, but international interactions are becoming an increasingly vital complement. Productive research, the pressure to commercialize new findings, and the successful launch of new products or services are demanding a high degree of interaction with researchers, producers, and buyers in leading industrial countries.

CROSS-REGIONAL EXPERIENCE

The experience of Japan and other Northeast Asian countries clearly demonstrates the complementarities between innovation capability, macro policies, and the state of institutions that affect the market. In Japan, although some manufacturing subsectors remained competitive, the rest of the economy stagnated through the 1990s. Total factor productivity grew 2.4 percent a year during 1983–91, but only 0.2 percent a year in 1991–2000, largely because productivity stagnated in the nonmanufacturing parts of the economy.[3] Japan has a highly research-intensive economy—mainly in industry rather than services (Sato 2002)—but the capacity to innovate is not being translated into growth, largely because government policies and corporate actions are only slowly reversing the institutional weaknesses exerting a drag on growth. Japan easily has the potential to realize its modest target of at least 2 percent growth a year (Sato 2002). But this target will remain elusive without a three-pronged policy effort to stimulate domestic demand, reform key institutions, and create a competitive environment that invigorates the service sector.

In contrast to Japan, Korea has brought order to its financial and governance institutions, pursued broadly sound macro policies, and maintained the competitiveness of transport industries while stimulating innovation in electronics and ICT. The ICT sector accounted for 13 percent of gross domestic product and one-fourth of exports in 2001 and is growing rapidly, thanks to the successful adoption of Code Division Multiple Access wireless technology ("Quantum

---

3. The reduction of the workweek since the late 1980s has also contributed to the slowing of growth (Hayashi and Prescott 2002).

Leap" 2002). In general, Korea's innovation system is still narrowly based on the efforts of a few large companies, weakly integrated and relatively closed (Chung 2001). It is too early to say whether Korea's ongoing institutional reforms have succeeded or whether its innovation systems can set the pace for future growth. But the evidence of recovery through 2002 suggests that an approach embracing stabilization policy, institutional reform, and innovation in key sectors will be more potent than a sequential or piecemeal approach.

China's economic performance underscores the effectiveness of interweaving the three major strands of policy. While China's economy has grown faster, on average, than the other leading East Asian economies over the past four years, the limited progress with institutional reforms in finance,[4] corporate governance, and law means that substantial resources are still diverted to activities yielding low returns and raises questions about the future of macroeconomic stability. China has not yet made a suitably wide-ranging effort to craft an adequately funded, open innovation system. Its growth is being led mainly by commoditized manufactured products where the rents are low, and export competitiveness still relies on low costs of labor, land, and other resources. By recognizing the need for policies addressing stability, institutional reform, and the innovation system and tackling these issues together, China could achieve lasting, high growth based on improved productivity and export competitiveness and, at the same time, minimize the risks of domestic crises and problems stemming from external shocks.

A host of scattered developments argues for redoubling the efforts to achieve stability, institutional strength, and innovation capability in Southeast Asia. For example, Singapore and Taiwan, China, are quickly realizing that production of electronic commodities such as personal computers, hard disk drives, and flat-panel displays will not sustain growth. Both are now seeking to move upstream, via design and research, into new areas such as biotechnology and into higher value-adding services. Singapore, for example, has announced a National Biomedical Science Strategy that will lead to an investment of $2 billion in research and teaching infrastructure and attract leading researchers from all over the world to Singapore and expand the work

---

4. The weakness of the financial system is a persistent source of worry ("Finger in the Dyke" 2001; "On the Road" 2002).

force for the biotechnology sector ("Asia's Biotech Tiger" 2002; "Can Money Turn Singapore into a Biotech Juggernaut?" 2002).[5] Side by side, Singapore is selectively deregulating the service sector so that industrial change is firmly backed by the availability of financial and other services.

Malaysia's wage and resource costs are lower than those in Singapore, but Malaysia too is finding that heavy dependence on the manufacture of electronic products is a source of vulnerability and is attempting to spur incremental innovation, create high-tech industrial clusters, and diversify its exports.

Singapore and Taiwan, China, have, for many years, relied on inflows of foreign direct investment and knowledge workers to boost high-tech industry. As they seek to raise the tenor of technological activities, they are working to attract more such resources from overseas. Malaysia, long aware of the advantages stemming from foreign direct investment,[6] also recognizes the need to tap the global pool of technical skills to augment its homegrown innovation capacity. In each case, success will depend on macroeconomic stability, on the credibility of the market, and on legal and other institutions.

Lower-income countries such as Indonesia are confronting the slow decline of footwear and garment industries as foreign producers (such as Nike and Reebok) shift their factories to places where both the costs of production and transactions and the risks of domestic turbulence are lower. As producers move, so do buyers. Indonesia's exports of footwear fell from $2.2 billion in 1996 to $1.5 billion in 2001 ("Just Quit It" 2002). What began as a slowdown in foreign investment inflows, following the 1997–98 crisis, threatens to become far more serious, with longer-run consequences for Indonesia's production, employment, and exports. Without a strong and well-articulated commitment by the authorities to restore stability and remedy the country's glaring institutional weaknesses, Indonesia's manufacturing base runs the very real risk of expanding only slowly, adding to the difficulties of any attempts to create innovation capability.

Thailand's situation is less serious than that of Indonesia, but here, too, the slow pace of institutional reform and an acute shortage of high-level skills are discouraging investments in light consumer in-

---

5. A billion is 1,000 million.

6. Foreign direct investment financed a tenth of Malaysian investment during 1990–95.

dustries and limiting the scope for diversification into more promising high-tech areas. Thailand's few outstanding examples of export success, such as the machinery producer Aapico High-Tech, underscore the key role played by innovation ("Fast Lane to Success" 2002). Thailand also faces uncertainty from a future shakeout of the auto industry, which has a major presence in the country and is encountering global as well as regional excess capacity, the prospect of declining trade barriers, and the incentives that are drawing leading producers to locate in China.

LOOKING FORWARD: 10 POLICY MESSAGES

Each country must pursue a different mix of policies appropriate to its income level, institutional development, recent history, and capacity to frame, finance, and implement policies. Thus Japan's menu of policy choices is very different from Vietnam's. Here we offer 10 policy messages that all the East Asian economies can subscribe to, albeit to varying degrees.

Prudent debt management. The crisis of 1997–98 taught East Asia and the world that a large volume of overall public and private debt is a source of vulnerability, especially when it includes a substantial share of short-term external debt not offset by exchange reserves. Prudent debt management, domestic and foreign, also needs to encompass a government's contingent liabilities, many of which are not transparent but can be highly destabilizing.

Flexible exchange rate management. The vulnerability associated with large debts can be heightened by a fixed exchange rate, and especially an exchange rate regime with a soft peg.[7] Exchange rates should be managed so as to maintain a margin of flexibility (possibly with reference to a basket of currencies) appropriate for the size, openness, and trading relationships of the country.

Regional coordination. With respect to macroeconomic, exchange rate, and reserve policies, the crisis also highlighted the potential benefits from East Asian regional coordination and from swap arrangements that could harness some fraction of the region's vast

---

7. See Goldstein (2002). Corden (2002) also discusses the problems with fixed but adjustable exchange rate regimes in a speculative environment.

foreign exchange reserves (more than $700 billion). The diversity of the region would make a union difficult to achieve in the medium run, but countries can derive sizable gains by focusing their attention on areas—such as trade and financial regulation—where mutual interests are strong enough to overcome the barriers to coordination and harmonization.[8]

Financial reform. Not just the Asian crisis but crises elsewhere have hammered home the costs of weak, underdeveloped, and unregulated financial systems. These are detrimental to growth and to stability. Countries can no longer afford to neglect the restructuring or recapitalizing of banks and the building of market and regulatory institutions. Reform of the financial system will entail relinquishing attempts by government or by business groups to direct the flow of resources from banks. It will run into political opposition, but the potential costs of procrastination are huge. All East Asian countries need to bring their financial reforms to a successful close as soon as possible.

Deregulation and incentives for innovation in services. In many services there is a large and costly productivity and technology gap between East Asian and leading Western countries. Much of the gap derives from East Asia's multitude of regulations and low level of competition in service markets. Although the short-term adjustment could be painful, over the longer run the gains in growth and employment will more than offset any initial dislocations.

Legal reforms to support the market economy. Both financial reform and broader institutional strengthening will be crucially aided by measures that make the legal system an effective instrument for protecting rights and enforcing rules. The time has arrived to put legal reform at the center of the drive to transform the financial sector and corporate governance and to deregulate parts of the economy while stiffening market discipline. Many observers doubt that legal systems can be turned around quickly, and the costs of assigning and enforcing rights are not trivial.[9] But making the legal system a full partner of the market economy is essential.

---

8. The arrangement between China and the Association of South East Asian Nations is a case in point. See also Chirathivat (2002) for an analysis of the gains from this arrangement.

9. Holmes and Sunstein (1999) show that giving legal rights entails costs.

We have emphasized throughout this study that the future performance of the region will hinge on the innovation system—an open innovation system that fully harnesses the potential of ICT. From this follow four further messages.

Resources for innovation. We cannot overemphasize the role of education and research infrastructure in determining the supply of innovation. Human and capital resources will be crucial, as will be mutually fruitful links between centers of research and the business community.

Networks and clusters. For innovative East Asian firms, cooperation, networking, competition, and incentives are no less important. The cost and complexity of advanced research increasingly demand cooperation among players who each bring their own particular knowledge and capabilities to the venture. Commercially successful innovation requires small contributions by many partners and suppliers —even for relatively minor items such as eyeglass frames and toys. Networked producers with access to many services are much better placed to sustain the momentum of innovation. Thus high-tech urban clusters of producers with both a local and a global orientation, hooked into the international channels through which ideas circulate, are intrinsic to the technology landscape.

Competition policies. The forces of demand must complement supply: firms must innovate if they are to survive, grow, and make larger profits. Without the press of competition, the urge to innovate is almost certain to languish. Vigilant domestic, regional, and global trade and competition policies are necessary to keep the system in high gear.

Proactive public policies for innovation. Innovators require incentives, such as tax concessions, assurance of intellectual property rights, stock option schemes for new start-ups, seed money from government, and many others. A robust market system can provide some of the incentives, but government must at times be proactive in order to raise and sustain the pace of innovation.

These are the principal policy messages for East Asian countries as they chart their courses into the twenty-first century.

REFERENCES

The word "processed" describes informally produced works that may not be commonly available through libraries.

Abe, Shigeyuki, and Chung H. Lee. 2001. "China and Japan." In Magnus Blomström, Byron Gangnes, and Summer La Croix, eds., *Japan's New Economy*. New York: Oxford University Press.

Abernathy, Frederick H., John T. Dunlop, Janice H. Hammond, and David Weil. 1999. *A Stitch in Time: Lean Retailing and the Transformation of Manufacturing— Lessons from the Apparel and Textile Industries*. New York: Oxford University Press.

———. 2001. "Globalization in the Apparel and Textile Industries: What Is New and What Is Not?" Background paper for the East Asia Project. World Bank, Washington, D.C. Processed.

Abo, Tetsuo. 1994. *Hybrid Factory: The Japanese Production System in the United States*. New York: Oxford University Press.

Abrams, Richard K., and Michael W. Taylor. 2000. "Issues in the Unification of Financial Sector Supervision." IMF Working Paper 00/213. International Monetary Fund, Washington, D.C. Processed.

Abrenica, Joy V. 2000. "Liberalizing the ASEAN Automotive Market: Impact Assessment." Pacific Economic Cooperation Council project on the ASEAN auto industry.

"Access Denied." 2002. *Far Eastern Economic Review*, September 26.

"Accounting Standards Collaboration." 2002. *Oxford Analytica*, September 26.

"Acer Plots Path to Unbeatable Service." 2001. *Financial Times*, March 30.

Adams, James D. 1990. "Fundamental Stocks of Knowledge and Productivity Growth." *Journal of Political Economy* 98(4):673–702.

Adolf, Huala. 2000. "Trade-Related Aspects of Intellectual Property Rights and Developing Countries." *Developing Economies* 39(1):49–84.

Agarwal, Pradeep, Subir V. Gokarn, Veena Mishra, Kirit S. Parikh, and Kunal Sen. 2000. *Policy Regime and Industrial Competitiveness*. Singapore: Institute of Southeast Asian Studies.

Agarwal, Rajshree, and Michael Gort. 2001. "First-Mover Advantage and the Speed of Competitive Entry, 1887–1986." *Journal of Law and Economics* 44(1):161–77.

Agrawal, Anup, and Jeffrey Jaffe. 2000. *The Post-Merger Performance Puzzle in Advance in Mergers and Acquisitions*. Amsterdam: Elsevier Science.

Ahmad, Ehtisham. 2001. "Governance and Public Expenditure Management Systems—An East Asian Perspective." Paper presented at the East Asia's Future Economy Workshop, Bangkok, Thailand, June 10. Processed.

Aitken, Brian, and Ann Harrison. 1999. "Do Domestic Firms Benefit from Direct Foreign Investment? Evidence from Venezuela." *American Economic Review* 89(3):605–18.

Akaba, Yuji, Florian Budde, and Jungkiu Choi. 1998. "Restructuring South Korea's Chaebol." *McKinsey Quarterly* 4:68–79.

Alesina, Alberto, Ignazio Angeloni, and Federico Etro. 2001. "The Political Economy of International Unions." NBER Working Paper 8645. National Bureau of Economic Research, Cambridge, Mass. Processed.

Alesina, Alberto, and Romain Wacziarg. 1997. "Openness, Country Size, and the Government." NBER Working Paper 6024. National Bureau of Economic Research, Cambridge, Mass. Processed.

"All Net, All the Time." 2002. *Business Week*, April 29.

Allen, Franklin. 2001. "Presidential Address: Do Financial Institutions Matter?" *Journal of Finance* 56(4):1165–75.

"Ally of the People." 2002. *Far Eastern Economic Review*, May 9.

Amsden, Alice H. 1989. *Asia's Next Giant: South Korea and Late Industrialization.* New York: Oxford University Press.

Anderson, Kym. 1995. "Lobbying Incentives and the Pattern of Protection in Rich and Poor Countries." *Economic Development and Cultural Change* 43(2):401–23.

Angrist, Joshua, and Victor Lavy. 2001. "Does Teacher Training Affect Pupil Learning? Evidence from Matched Comparisons in Jerusalem Public Schools." *Journal of Labor Economics* 19(2):343–69.

———. 2002. "New Evidence on Classroom Computers and Pupil Learning." *Economic Journal* 12(October):735–65.

Aoki, M. 1987. "The Japanese Firm in Transition." In K. Yamamura and Y. Yasuba, eds., *The Political Economy of Japan.* Palo Alto, Calif.: Stanford University Press.

Aoki, Reiko, and Yossi Spiegel. 2001. "Pre-Grant Patent Publication, R&D, and Welfare." Working Paper. Tel Aviv University, May. Processed.

APEC (Asia-Pacific Economic Cooperation). 2001. *The New Economy and APEC.* Singapore.

"APEC in Shanghai." 2001. *Financial Times*, October 16.

Arestis, Philip, and Murray Glickman. 2002. "Financial Crisis in Southeast Asia: Dispelling Illusion the Minskyan Way." *Cambridge Journal of Economics* 26(2): 237–60.

ASEAN (Association of South East Asian Nations). 1999–2000. *ASEAN Annual Report.* Jakarta: ASEAN Secretariat.

"ASEAN and China Sign Deal for Free Trade Area." 2002. *Financial Times*, November 5.

ASEAN+3 Ministers. 2000. "Joint Statement of the ASEAN+3 Finance Ministers' Meeting." Chiang Mai, Thailand, May 6. Processed.

Asia Information Associates. 2000. *E-Commerce in China.*

"Asia Learns Size Really Matters." 2001. *Far Eastern Economic Review,* June 7.

"Asia Pacific: Bond Market (A)." 2001. *Oxford Analytica,* November 23.

Asian Development Bank. 2001. *Asian Development Outlook 2001.*

"Asia's Best Companies 2002." 2002. *Financial Asia,* April.

"Asia's Biotech Tiger." 2002. *New Scientist,* September 14.

"Asia's Biz-to-Biz E-Boom." 1999. *Business Week,* October 25.

Atkinson, Anthony B. 1999. *The Economic Consequences of Rolling Back the Welfare State.* Cambridge, Mass.: MIT Press.

Au, Chun-Chung, and Vernon Henderson. 2002. "How Migration Restrictions Limit Agglomeration and Productivity in China." NBER Working Paper 8707. National Bureau of Economic Research, Cambridge, Mass. Processed.

Audretsch, David B., and Maryann P. Feldman. 1994. "Knowledge Spillovers and the Geography of Innovation and Production." CEPR Working Paper 953. Centre for Economic Policy Research, London. Processed.

Auerbach, Alan J., and Daniel Feenberg. 2000. "The Significance of Federal Tax as Automatic Stabilizer." *Journal of Economic Perspectives* 14(3):37–56.

AUTM (Association of University Technology Managers). 1997. *Licensing Survey, FY 1996.* Norwalk, Conn.

———. 2001. *Licensing Survey, FY 2000.* Norwalk, Conn.

Autor, David, Lawrence F. Katz, and Alan B. Krueger. 1998. "Computing Inequality: Have Computers Changed the Labor Market?" *Quarterly Journal of Economics* 113(4):1169–213.

"Back in Gear." 2002. *Business Asia,* September 23.

Backman, Michael. 1999. *Asian Eclipse: Exposing the Dark Side of Business in Asia.* Singapore: John Wiley and Sons (Asia).

Ballou, Dale. 2001. "Pay for Performance in Public and Private Schools." *Economics of Education Review* 20(1):51–61.

Ballou, Dale, and Michael Podgursky. 1998. "Teacher Recruitment and Retention in Public and Private Schools." *Journal of Policy Analysis and Management* 17(3): 393–417.

Bank of England. 1999. *Inflation Report (Summer).* London.

"Banks Put Themselves at Risk in Basle." 2002. *Financial Times,* October 17.

Barro, Robert J. 1991. "Economic Growth in a Cross Section of Countries." *Quarterly Journal of Economics* 106(2):407–43.

———. 1999. "Human Capital and Growth in Cross-Country Regressions." *Swedish Economic Policy Review* 6(2):237–77.

———. 2000. "Democracy and the Rule of Law." In Bruce Bueno de Mesquita and Hilton L. Root, eds., *Governing for Prosperity.* New Haven, Conn.: Yale University Press.

———. 2001. "Economic Growth in East Asia before and after the Financial Crisis." NBER Working Paper 8330. National Bureau of Economic Research, Cambridge, Mass. Processed.

Batten, David F. 1995. "Network Cities: Creative Urban Agglomerations for the 21st Century." *Urban Studies* 32(2):313–27.

Baumol, William J. 2002. *The Free-Market Innovation Machine: Analyzing the Growth Miracle of Capitalism.* Princeton, N.J.: Princeton University Press.

Bayoumi, Tamim, Barry Eichengreen, and Paolo Mauro. 2000. "On a Regional Monetary Arrangement for ASEAN." *Journal of the Japanese and International Economies* 14(2):121–48.

Beardsell, Mark, and Vernon J. Henderson. 1999. "Spatial Evolution of the Computer Industry in the U.S." *European Economic Review* 43(2):431–56.

Beaudry, Catherine, and Peter Swann. 2001. *Growth in Industrial Clusters: A Bird's Eye View of the United Kingdom.* SIEPR Policy Paper 00-38. Palo Alto, Calif.: Stanford Institute for Economic Policy Research.

Beck, Thorsten, Asli Demirgüç-Kunt, Ross Levine, and Vojisl Maksimovic. 2001. "Financial Structure and Economic Development: Firm, Industry, and Country Evidence." In Asli Demirgüç-Kunt and Ross Levine, eds., *Financial Structure and Economic Growth: A Cross-Country Comparison of Banks, Markets, and Development.* Cambridge, Mass.: MIT Press.

Becker, Charles M., Jeffery G. Williamson, and Edwin S. Mills, eds. 1992. *Indian Urbanization and Economic Growth since 1960.* Baltimore, Md.: Johns Hopkins University Press.

Becker, Gary S., and Casey B. Mulligan. 1998. "Deadweight Costs and the Size of Government." NBER Working Paper 6789. National Bureau of Economic Research, Cambridge, Mass. Processed.

Becker, Rob, and Emmanual Pitsilis. 2000. "A Case for Asian Bond Markets." *McKinsey Quarterly* 4.

Bedi, Arjun S., and Ashish Garg. 2000. "The Effectiveness of Private Versus Public Schools: The Case of Indonesia." *Journal of Development Economics* 61(2):463–94.

Beechler, Shon L., and Allan Bird. 1999. *Japanese Multinationals Abroad: Individual and Organizational Learning.* New York: Oxford University Press.

"Beijing Approves New Measures Recruiting Use of Cybercafes." 2002. *Asian Wall Street Journal,* October 14.

Berger, Laurence W., George R. Nast, and Christian Raubach. 2002. "Fix Asia's Bad-Debt Mess." *McKinsey Quarterly* 4.

Berger, Suzanne, and Richard K. Lester. 1997. *Made by Hong Kong.* Hong Kong: Oxford University Press.

Best, Michael H. 2001. *The New Competitive Advantage: The Renewal of American Industry.* New York: Oxford University Press.

"Beyonics' New Dream." 2002. *Smartinvestor,* April 1.

Bhalla, Surjit. 2002. *Imagine There's No Country: Poverty, Inequality, and Growth in the Era of Globalization.* Washington, D.C.: Institute for International Economics.

"A Big Lift from China." 2002. *Business Week,* October 21.

"Billion Gamble." 2002. *Fortune,* November 11.

Bils, Mark, and Peter Klenow. 2000. "Does Schooling Cause Growth?" *American Economic Review* 90(5):1160–83.

Birley, Sue. 2002. "Universities, Academics, and Spinout Companies." *International Journal of Entrepreneurship Education* (April).

Blalock, Garrick, and Paul Gertler. 2002. "Technology Acquisition in Indonesian Manufacturing: The Effect of Foreign Direct Investment." Working Paper. University of California, Berkeley, Haas School of Business. Processed.

Blank, Rebecca M. 2002. "Can Equity and Efficiency Complement Each Other?" NBER Working Paper 8820. National Bureau of Economic Research, Cambridge, Mass. Processed.

Blyth, Mark. 2002. *Great Transformation: Economic Ideas and Institutional Change in the Twentieth Century.* New York: Cambridge University Press.

Boix, Charles. 2002. "The Public Sector in East Asia." Background paper for the East Asia Project. World Bank, Washington, D.C. Processed.

Bora, Bijit, and Edward Graham. 1997. "Can APEC Deliver on Investment?" In Fred Bergsten, ed., *Whither APEC? The Progress to Date and Plans for the Future.* Washington, D.C.: Institute for International Economics.

Bordo, Michael, Barry Eichengreen, Daniela Klingebiel, and María Soledad Martínez-Peria. 2001. "Is the Crisis Problem Growing More Severe?" *Economic Policy* 16(32):51–82.

Borrus, Michael, Dieter Ernst, and Stephan Haggard, eds. 2000. *International Production Networks in Asia.* London and New York: Routledge.

Botero, Juan Carlos, Rafael La Porta, Florencio Lopez-de-Silanes, Andrei Shleifer, and Alexander Volokh. 2003. "Judicial Reform." *The World Bank Research Observer* 18(1).

Bouillot, Jean-Joseph, and Nicolas Michelon. 2001. *China, Hong Kong, Taiwan.* Paris: Documentation Paris, Française.

Bourchier, David. 1999. "Magic Memos, Collusion, and Judges with Attitude: Notes on the Politics of Law in Contemporary Indonesia." In Kanishka Jayasuriya, ed., *Law, Capitalism, and Power in Asia.* London: Routledge.

Bowles, Paul, and Brian MacLean. 1996. "Regional Trading Blocs: Will East Asia Be Next?" *Cambridge Journal of Economics* 20(4):393–412.

Branstetter, Lee, and Mariko Sakakibara. 2001. "Do Stronger Patents Induce More Innovation? Evidence from the 1988 Japanese Patent Law Reforms." *RAND Journal of Economics* 32(1):77–100.

Bray, Mark. 2002. "The Costs and Financing of Education: Trends and Policy Implications." In Asia Development Bank, *Education in Developing Asia*, Vol. 3. Tokyo.

Bresnahan, Timothy F., Erik Brynjolfsson, and Lorin M. Hitt. 2002. "Information Technology, Workplace Organization, and the Demand for Skilled Labor: Firm-Level Evidence." *Quarterly Journal of Economics* 117(1):339–76.

Bresnahan, Timothy, Alfonso Gambardella, Anna-Lee Saxenian, and Scott Wallsten. 2001. *Old Economy Inputs for New Economy Outcomes: Cluster Formation in the New Silicon Valley.* SIEPR Policy Paper 00-43. Palo Alto, Calif.: Stanford Institute for Economic Policy Research.

Brice, Steve. 2002. "Can Asia Compete with China?" *Standard and Chartered Economic and Market Briefing* 92, December 13.

Brown, Byron W., and Carl E. Liedholm. 2002. "Can Web Courses Replace Classrooms in Principles of Microeconomics?" *American Economic Review* 92(2):444–48.

Brusco, Sebastiano. 1992. "Small Firms and Provision of Real Service." In Frank Pyke and Werner Sengenberger, eds., *Industrial Districts and Local Economic Regeneration.* Geneva: International Institute for Labour Studies.

"Building Scientific Networks for Effective Innovation." 2002. *MIT Sloan Management Review* (Spring).

"Building Software Skills in Asia." 2002. *Far Eastern Economic Review*, October 24.

Burkart, Mike, Fausto Panunzi, and Andrei Shleifer. 2002. "Family Firms." NBER Working Paper 8776. National Bureau of Economic Research, Cambridge, Mass. Processed.

"Burying the Competition." 2002. *Far Eastern Economic Review*, October 17.

Callen, Tim, and Warwick J. McKibbin. 2001. "Policies and Prospects in Japan and the Implications for the Asia-Pacific Region." IMF Working Paper WP/01/131. International Monetary Fund, Washington, D.C. Processed.

Calomiris, Charles W. 2002. "Banking Approaches the Modern Era." *Regulation*, Summer 14–20.

"Can Money Turn Singapore into a Biotech Juggernaut?" 2002. *Science*, August 30.

Canning, David, and M. Fay. 1993. *The Effect of Transportation Networks on Economic Growth.* Discussion Paper Series. New York: Columbia University, Department of Economics.

Cao, Cong, and Richard P. Suttmeier. 2001. "China's New Scientific Elite: Distinguished Young Scientists, the Research Environment, and Hopes for Chinese Science." *China Quarterly* 168:960–84.

Caprio, Gerald, and Patrick Honohan. 2001. *Finance for Development.* Washington, D.C.: World Bank.

Caprio, Gerald, and Daniela Klingebiel. 1997. "Bank Insolvency: Bad Luck, Bad Policy, or Bad Banking?" In World Bank, *Annual World Bank Conference on Development Economics*, pp. 79–104. Washington, D.C.

Card, David, and Alan B. Krueger. 1994. "The Economic Return to School Quality: A Partial Survey." Working Paper 334. Princeton University, Princeton, N.J. Processed.

Cargill, Thomas F., and Elliott Parker. 2001. "Financial Liberation in China: Limitations and Lessons of Japanese Regime." *Journal of the Asia Pacific Economy* 6(1):1–21.

Carmichael, Jeffrey. 2001. "Experiences with Integrated Regulation." *Finance Regulator* 3:57–65.

Carnoy, Martin. 2002. "Is Latin American Education Preparing Its Workforce for 21st Century Economies?" Background paper prepared for David de Ferranti, Guillermo E. Perry, Indermit Gill, J. Luis Guasch, and Norbert Schady, eds., *Closing the Gap in Education and Technology.* World Bank, Washington, D.C. Processed.

Carrington, William J., and Enrica Detragiache. 1998. "How Big Is the Brain Drain?" IMF Working Paper 98/102. International Monetary Fund, Washington, D.C. Processed.

Carruthers, Robin, and Jitendra N. Bajpai. 2002. "Trends in Trade and Logistics: An East Asian Perspective." Working Paper 2. World Bank, Transport Sector Unit, East Asia and Pacific Region, Washington, D.C. Processed.

Casper, Steve, and H. Glimstedt. 2001. "Economic Organization, Innovation Systems, and the Internet." *Oxford Review of Economic Policy* 17(2):265–81.

Castells, Manuel, and Peter Hall. 1994. *Technopoles of the World: The Making of Twenty-First-Century Industrial Complexes.* London: Routledge.

Cave, Peter. 2001. "Educational Reform in Japan in the 1990s: Individuality and Other Uncertainties." *Comparative Education* 37(2):173–91.

Caves, Richard E., and Masu Uekusa. 1976. "Industrial Organization in Japan." In H. Patrick and H. Rosovsky, eds., *Asia's New Giant: How the Japanese Economy Works.* Washington, D.C.: Brookings Institution.

"The CEOs Weigh in." 2002. *Business Week*, March 11.

Cermele, Michele, Maurizio Donato, and Andrea Mignanelli. 2002. "Good Money from Bad Debt." *McKinsey Quarterly* 1.

Cervero, Robert. 2001. "Efficient Urbanization: Economic Performance and the Shape of the Metropolis." *Urban Studies* 38(10):1651–71.

Cetorelli, Nicola. 2001. "Competition among Banks: Good or Bad?" *Federal Reserve Bank of Chicago Economic Perspectives* 25(2):38–48.

"Chaebol Counterattack." 2001. *Oxford Analytica*, June 6.

Chang, Ching-His. 2000. "The Reform of the Business Sector: The Case of Taiwan's Financial System." In Takatoshi Ito and Anne O. Krueger, eds., *Deregulation and Interdependence in the Asia-Pacific Region*, pp. 277–352. Chicago: University of Chicago Press.

Chang, Shirley L. 1992. "Causes of Brain Drain and Solutions: The Taiwan Experience." *Studies in Comparative International Development* 27(1):27–43.

Chapman, David. 2000. "Trends in Educational Administration in Developing Asia." *Educational Administration Quarterly* 36(2):283–308.

———. 2002. *Management and Efficiency in Education: Goals and Strategies.* Manila: Asian Development Bank.

Charnes, Abraham, William Cooper, and Shanling Li. 1989. "Using Data Envelopment Analysis to Evaluate Efficiency in the Economic Performance of Chinese Cities." *Socio-Economic Planning Sciences* 23(6):325–44.

Chen, Albert H. Y. 1999. "Hong Kong's Legal System in Transition, 1997–99." In Gungwu Wang and John Wong, eds., *Hong Kong and China: The Challenge of Transition*, pp. 287–320. Singapore: Times Academic Press.

Chen, Andrew Chun, and Jonathan R. Woetzel. 2002. "Chinese Chips." *McKinsey Quarterly* 2.

Chen, Yongmin. 1996. "Impact of Regional Factors on Productivity in China." *Journal of Regional Science* 36(3):417–36.

Chen, Yongmin, and Thitima Puttitanun. 2002. "Intellectual Property Rights and Innovation in Developing Countries." Paper presented at the World Bank Annual Conference on Development Economics, Washington, D.C., April 29. Processed.

Cheng, Leonard K., and Henryk Kierzkowski, eds. 2001. *Global Production and Trade in East Asia*. Boston: Kluwer Academic Publishers.

Cheong, Inkyo. 2002. "Regionalism and FTAs in East Asia." Paper presented at the 2002 Asian Economic Panel Meeting, Keio University, Tokyo, May 13–15. Processed.

"Chile/South Korea: Trade Treaty." 2002. *Oxford Analytica*, October 31.

"China Banking Debt." 2001. *Oxford Analytica*, October 9.

"China: Corporate Bond Market." 2002. *Oxford Analytica*, August 14.

"China Dream." 2002. *Far Eastern Economic Review*, October 10, p. 51.

"China: Internet Penetration." 2002. *Oxford Analytica*, August 14.

"China: M&A Potential." 2002. *Oxford Analytica*, October 31.

China, National Bureau of Statistics. 2000. *Zhongguo Tongji Nianjian 2000 [China Statistical Yearbook 2000]*. Beijing: China Statistics Press.

———. 2001. *Zhongguo Tongji Nianjian 2001 [China Statistical Yearbook 2001]*. Beijing: China Statistics Press.

"China: Pearl River Delta (A)." 2002. *Oxford Analytica*, September 17.

"China: Tax Troubles (A)." 2001. *Oxford Analytica*, December 17.

"China: Telecom IPO." 2002. *Oxford Analytica*, October 23.

"China's President Will Bequeath a Huge Debt Loan to Successors." 2002. *Wall Street Journal*, November 1.

"Chips on Monster Wafers." 2002. *Business Week*, November 4.

Chirathivat, Suthiphand. 2002. "ASEAN-China Free Trade Area: Background, Implications, and Future Development." *Journal of Asian Economics* 13(2):671–86.

"Chohung Bank Put up for Auction by Seoul." 2002. *Financial Times*, November 5.

Choi, Jeong-Pyo, and Thomas G. Cowing. 1999. "Firm Behavior and Group Affiliation: The Strategic Role of Corporate Grouping for Korean Firms." *Journal of Asian Economics* 10(2):195–200.

Chopra, Ajai, Kenneth Kang, Meral Karasulu, Hong Liang, Henry Ma, and Anthony Richards. 2001. "From Crisis to Recovery in Korea: Strategy, Achievements, and Lessons." IMF Working Paper WP/01/154. International Monetary Fund, Washington, D.C. Processed.

Christensen, Clayton M. 1997. *The Innovator's Dilemma: When New Technologies Cause Great Firms to Fail*. Cambridge, Mass.: Harvard Business School Press.

Chuang, Yih-Chyi. 2000. "Human Capital, Exports, and Economic Growth: A Causality Analysis for Taiwan, 1952–1995." *Review of International Economics* 8(4):712–20.

Chun, Hyunbae, and M. Ishaq Nadiri. 2002. "Decomposing Productivity Growth in the U.S. Computer Industry." NBER Working Paper 9267. National Bureau of Economic Research, Cambridge, Mass. Processed.

Chung, Sung-Chul. 2001. "The Research Development and Innovation System in Korea." In Phillipe Laredo and Phillipe Mustar, eds., *Research and Innovation Policies in the New Global Economy*. Cheltenham, U.K.: Edward Elgar.

Claessens, Stijn, Simeon Djankov, Joseph Fan, and Larry Lang. 1999. "Expropriation of Minority Shareholders in East Asia." Working Paper 2088. World Bank, Washington, D.C. Processed.

Claessens, Stijn, Thomas Glaessner, and Daniela Klingebiel. 2001. *E-Finance in Emerging Markets: Is Leapfrogging Possible?* Financial Sector Discussion Paper 7. Washington, D.C.: World Bank.

Claessens, Stijin, Daniela Klingebiel, and Luc Laeven. 2001. "Financial Restructuring in Banking and Corporate Sector Crisis: What Policies to Pursue?" World Bank, Washington, D.C. Processed.

Clarke, Donald C. 1996. "The Creation of a Legal Structure for Market Institutions in China." In John McMillan and Barry Naughton, eds., *Reforming Asian Socialism: The Growth of Market Institutions.* Ann Arbor: University of Michigan Press.

Clarke, George R. G. 2002. "How the Quality of Institution Affects Technological Deepening in Developing Countries." DRG Working Paper. World Bank, Washington, D.C. Processed.

Clarke, George, Robert Cull, María S. Martínez Peria, and Susana M. Sánchez. 2001. "Foreign Bank Entry: Experience, Implications for Developing Countries, and Agenda for Further Research." Policy Research Working Paper 2698. World Bank, Washington, D.C. Processed.

Cline, William. 2002. "Financial Crisis and Poverty in Emerging Market Economies." Working Paper 8. Center for Global Development, Washington, D.C. Processed.

Coglin, Tim. 2002. "Love of Floating." ING Barings. Processed.

Cohen, Stephen S., and Gary Fields. 1999. "Social Capital and Capital Gains in Silicon Valley." *California Management Review* 41(2):108–30.

Cohen, Wesley M., Richard R. Nelson, and John P. Walsh. 2000. "Protecting Their Intellectual Assets: Appropriability Conditions and Why U.S. Manufacturing Firms Patent (Or Not)." NBER Working Paper 7552. National Bureau of Economic Research, Cambridge, Mass. Processed.

Cole, David Chamberlin, and Betty F. Slade. 1996. *Building a Modern Financial System: The Indonesian Experience.* Cambridge, U.K.: Cambridge University Press.

Colecchia, Alessandra, and Paul Schreyer. 2001. "ICT Investment and Economic Growth in the 1990s: Is the U.S. a Unique Case? A Comparative Study of Nine OECD Countries." *Review of Economic Dynamics* 5(2):408–42.

Conger, Jay A., and Edward E. Lawler. 2001. "Corporate Government from Meek to Mighty: Performing in the Boardroom." *Strategy + Business* 25:92–96.

Cooke, Philip. 2000. "Business Processes in Regional Innovation Systems in the European Union." In Zoltan J. Acs, ed., *Regional Innovation, Knowledge, and Global Change.* London: Pinter.

Cooke, Phillip, and K. Morgan. 1993. "The Network Paradigm: New Departures in Corporate and Regional Development." *Environment and Planning D: Society and Space* 11(5):543–64.

Coombes, Paul, and Mark Waston. 2000. "Three Surveys on Corporate Governance." *McKinsey Quarterly* 4.

Cooney, Sean. 1999. "A Community Changes: Taiwan's Council of Grand Justices and Liberal Democratic Reform." In Kanishka Jayasuriya, ed., *Law, Capitalism, and Power in Asia.* London: Routledge.

Corden, W. Max. 2002. *Too Sensational: On the Choice of Exchange Rate Regimes.* Cambridge, Mass.: MIT Press.

Cornford, J. 2001. "The Evolution of the Information Society and Regional Development in Europe." University of Newcastle. Processed.

"Corporate Governance after Enron." 2002. *Finance Asia* (April):24–26.

"Corporate R&D Set Free." 2002. *Technology Review,* December 2002/January 2003.

"Corporate Venture Investors Are Bailing Out." 2002. *Red Herring,* December.

Cortright, Joseph, and Heike Mayer. 2001. *High-Tech Specialization: A Comparison of High-Technology Centers.* Survey Series. Washington, D.C.: Brookings Institution, January.

Crafts, Nicholas. 2000. "Globalization and Growth in the Twentieth Century." IMF Working Paper 00/44. International Monetary Fund, Washington, D.C. Processed.

Crandall, Robert, and Robert Litan. 2002. "The Internet, Telecommunications, and Economic Growth in Asia." Background paper for the East Asia Project. World Bank, Washington, D.C. Processed.

Crandall, Robert, and Leonard Waverman. 2000. *Who Pays for Universal Service? When Telephone Subsidies Become Transparent.* Washington, D.C.: Brookings Institution Press.

Croce, Enzo, and Mohsin S. Khan. 2000. "Monetary Regimes and Inflation Targeting." *Finance and Development* 37(1):48–51.

Cuban, Larry. 2001. *Oversold and Underused.* Cambridge, Mass.: Harvard University Press.

Curry, James. 2000. "San Diego/Tijuana Manufacturing in the Information Age." Paper prepared for San Diego Dialogue: The Global Engagement of San Diego/Baja California. Processed.

Curry, James, and Martin Kenney. 1999. "E-Commerce: Implications for Firm Strategy and Industry Configuration." *Industry and Innovation* 6(2):131–51.

Dahlman, Carl J., and Jean-Eric Aubert. 2001. *China and the Knowledge Economy: Seizing the 21st Century.* Washington, D.C.: World Bank.

David, Paul A. 1985. "Clio and the Economics of QWERTY." *American Economic Review* 75(2):332–37.

———. 2000. "Digital Technology and the Productivity Paradox: After Ten Years, What Has Been Learned?" Stanford University, Palo Alto, Calif. Processed.

David, Paul A., Bronwyn Hall, and Andrew A. Toole. 2000. "Is Public R&D a Complement or a Substitute for Private R&D? A Review of the Econometric Evidence." *Research Policy* 29(4-5):497–530.

"Day of the Shareholder." 2001. *Far Eastern Economic Review,* September 13.

de Fontenay, Catherine, and Erran Carmel. 2001. *Israel's Silicon Wadi: The Forces behind Cluster Foundation.* SIEPR Policy Paper 00-40. Palo Alto, Calif.: Stanford Institute for Economic Policy Research.

de la Fuente, Angel, and Rafael Domenech. 2000. "Schooling Data, Technological Diffusion, and the Neoclassical Model." *American Economic Review* 91(2):323–27.

de Lucio, Juan J., José A. Herce, and Ana Goicolea. 2002. "The Effects of Externalities on Productivity Growth in Spanish Industry." *Regional Science and Urban Economics* 32(2):241–58.

de Vito, Giovanni Nicola. 1995. *Market Distortions and Competition: The Particular Case of Malaysia*. Discussion Paper 105. United Nations Conference on Trade and Development, October, Geneva.

Dedrick, Jason, and Kenneth Kraemer. 1998. *Asia's Computer Challenge: Threat or Opportunity for the United States and the World?* New York: Oxford University Press.

———. 2000. "Asia E-Commerce Report 2000." University of California, Irvine, Center for Research on Information Technology and Organizations. Processed.

Demirgüç-Kunt, Asli, and Ross Levine. 1999. "Bank-Based and Market-Based Financial Systems: Cross-Country Comparisons." Policy Research Working Paper 2143. World Bank, Washington, D.C. Processed.

Dent, Christopher M. 2001. "The Eurasian Economic Axis: Its Present and Prospective Significance for East Asia." *Journal of Asian Studies* 60:731–59.

Deraniyagala, Sonali, and Ben Fine. 2001. "New Trade Theory Versus Old Trade Policy: A Continuing Enigma." *Cambridge Journal of Economics* 25(6):809–25.

Dessus, Sebastian. 2001. "Human Capital and Growth: The Recovered Role of Educational Systems." Policy Research Working Paper 2632. World Bank, Washington, D.C. Processed.

Dewan, S., and Kenneth Kraemer. 1998. *International Dimensions of the Productivity Paradox*. Communications of the ACM 41. Association for Computing Machinery.

———. 2000. "Information Technology and Productivity: Evidence from Country-Level Data." *Management Science* 46.

Dhanani, Shafiq, and Iyanatul Islam. 2002. "Poverty, Vulnerability, and Social Protection in a Period of Crisis: The Case of Indonesia." *World Development* 30(7): 1211–31.

Dimmock, Clive, and Allan Walker. 1998. "Transforming Hong Kong's Schools: Trends and Emerging Issues." *Journal of Educational Administration* 36(5):476–91.

Ding, Weili, and Steven Lehrer. 2001. "The Optimal Policy to Reward the Value Added by Educators: Theory and Evidence from China." Paper presented at the International Conference on Education Reform in China, Harvard University, Cambridge, Mass. Processed.

Djankov, Simeon, Rafael La Porta, Florencio Lopez-de-Silanes, and Andrei Shleifer. 2000. "The Regulation of Entry." NBER Working Paper 7892. National Bureau of Economic Research, Cambridge, Mass. Processed.

———. 2001. "Legal Structure and Judicial Efficiency: The Lex Mundi Project." World Bank, Washington, D.C., October. Processed.

Dodgson, Mark. 2000. "Premium for Science, Technology, and Innovation in Asian Newly Industrializing Economies." In Linsu Kim and Richard R. Nelson, eds., *Technology, Learning, and Innovation.* Cambridge, U.K.: Cambridge University Press.

Dolan, Catherine, and John Humphrey. 2000. "Governance and Trade in Fresh Vegetables: The Impact of U.K. Supermarkets on African Horticulture Industry." *Journal of Development Studies* 37(2):147–76.

Dollar, David, and Aart Kraay. 2002. "Growth Is Good for the Poor." *Journal of Economic Growth* 7(3):195–225.

Doner, Richard F., Gregory W. Noble, and John Ravenhill. 2002. "Production Networks in East Asia's Automobile Parts Industry." Background paper for the East Asia Study. Washington, D.C., World Bank. Processed.

Dore, Ronald. 1986. *Flexible Rigidities: Industrial Policy and Structural Adjustment in the Japanese Economy, 1970–1980.* Palo Alto, Calif.: Stanford University Press.

———. 2000. *Stock Market Capitalism: Welfare Capitalism—Japan and Germany versus the Anglo-Saxons.* New York: Oxford University Press.

Dornbusch, Rudi. 2001a. "Malaysia: Was It Different?" NBER Working Paper 8325. National Bureau of Economic Research, Cambridge, Mass. Processed.

———. 2001b. "A Primer on Emerging Market Crises." NBER Working Paper 8326. National Bureau of Economic Research, Cambridge, Mass. Processed.

"Doubts Grow over South Korea's Credit Craving." 2002. *Financial Times,* November 20.

"Driving Change." 2002. *Far Eastern Economic Review,* September 26.

Duflo, Esther. 2001. "Schooling and Labor Market Consequences of School Construction in Indonesia: Evidence from an Unusual Policy Experiment." *American Economic Review* 91(4):795–813.

Dumais, Glenn Ellison, and Edward L. Glaeser. 1997. "Geographic Concentration as a Dynamic Process." NBER Working Paper 6270. National Bureau of Economic Research, Cambridge, Mass. Processed.

Dun, H., and C. Cai. 2000. "Network Structure: The Organizational Model of the Socks Industry in Datang." In *Zhejiang Jingji [Zhejiang Economy].*

Dyck, Alexander, and Luigi Zingales. 2002. "The Corporate Governance Role of the Media." NBER Working Paper 9309. National Bureau of Economic Research, Cambridge, Mass. Processed.

"East Asia: ASEAN Plus 3 [A]." 2001. *Oxford Analytica,* November 5.

"East Asia: Free Trade Frustrated." 2001. *Oxford Analytica,* April 5.

"East Asia: Trilateral FTA Proposal." 2002. *Oxford Analytica,* November 13.

Easterly, William. 2001. *The Elusive Quest for Growth: Economists' Adventures and Misadventures in the Tropics.* Cambridge, Mass.: MIT Press.

Easterly, William, Michael Kremer, Lant Pritchett, and Lawrence H. Summers. 1993. "Good Policy or Good Luck? Country Growth Performance and Temporary Shocks." NBER Working Paper 4474. National Bureau of Economic Research, Cambridge, Mass. Processed.

Easterly, William, and Ross Levine. 1997. "Africa's Growth Tragedy: Policies and Ethnic Divisions." *Quarterly Journal of Economics* 112(4):1203–50.

———. 2001. "It's Not Factor Accumulation: Stylized Facts and Growth Models." *The World Bank Economic Review* 15(2):177–219.

Eaton, Jonathan, and Zvi Eckstein. 1997. "Cities and Growth: Theory and Evidence from France and Japan." *Regional Science and Urban Economics* 27(4-5):443-74.

Eaton, Jonathan, and Samuel Kortum. 2000. "Technology, Geography, and Trade." Boston University and National Bureau of Economic Research, Cambridge, Mass. Processed.

"E-Commerce Starts to Click." 2002. *Business Week*, August 26.

Economic Strategy Institute. 2001. "The Auto Industry in the Internet Age" (www.econstrat.org/auto_industry.htm).

Economist Intelligence Unit. 2000. *Business Environment Ranking*, reported on the Ebusiness Forum website (www.ebusinessforum.com).

"The Education Shibboleth." 2002. *Economist*, June 8.

Educational Testing Service. 2001-01. *Test and Score Data Summary, 2000-2001: TOEFL*. Princeton, N.J.

Edwards, Sebastian. 1999. "How Effective Are Capital Controls?" *Journal of Economic Perspectives* 13(4):65-84.

———. 2002. "The Great Exchange Rate Debate after Argentina." NBER Working Paper 9257. National Bureau of Economic Research, Cambridge, Mass. Processed.

Edwards, Sebastian, and Alejandra Cox Edwards. 2002. "Social Security Privatization and Labor Markets: The Case of Chile." *Economic Development and Cultural Change* 50(3):465-88.

Edwards, Sebastian, and E. Levy-Yeyati. 2002. "Flexible Exchange Rates as Shock Absorbers: An Empirical Investigation." Working Paper. University of California, Los Angeles. Processed.

Eichengreen, Barry. 1999. *Toward a New International Financial Architecture: A Practical Post-Asia Agenda*. Washington, D.C.: Institute for International Economics.

———. 2001a. "Hanging Together: On Monetary and Financial Cooperation in Asia." Background paper for the East Asia Project. World Bank, Washington, D.C. Processed.

———. 2001b. "Should Emerging Markets Float? Can They Inflation Target?" University of California, Berkeley. Processed.

Eichengreen, Barry, and Michael Bordo. 2002. "Crises Now and Then: What Lessons from the Last Era of Financial Globalizaton?" NBER Working Paper 716. National Bureau of Economic Research, Cambridge, Mass. Processed.

Eichengreen, Barry, and Andrew K. Rose. 1998. "Staying Afloat When the Wind Shifts: External Factors and Emerging-Market Banking Crisis." NBER Working Paper 6370. National Bureau of Economic Research, Cambridge, Mass. Processed.

Electronic Trend Publications. 2000. "The Worldwide Contract Electronics Manufacturing Services Market, Eighth Edition: A Comprehensive Study on the Trends, Issues, and Leading Companies in the Worldwide Market for Contract Electronics Manufacturing Services." San Jose, Calif. (www.electronictrendpubs.com/cems8bro.pdf).

———. 2002. "The Worldwide Contract Electronics Manufacturing Services Market, Tenth Edition: A Comprehensive Study on the Trends, Issues, and Leading

Companies in the Worldwide Market for Contract Electronics Manufacturing Services." San Jose, Calif.

Emery, Robert F. 2001. *Korean Economic Reform: Before and since the 1997 Crisis.* Burlington, Vt.: Ashgate Publishing.

Encarnation, Dennis J. 1999. "Asia and the Global Operations of Multinational Corporations." In Dennis J. Encarnation, ed., *Japanese Multinationals in Asia: Regional Operations in Comparative Perspective.* Japan Business and Economics Series. Oxford: Oxford University Press.

Engelsberg, Paul. 1995. "Reversing China's Brain Drain: The Study-Abroad Policy, 1978–1993." In John D. Montgomery and Dennis A. Rondinelli, eds., *Great Policies: Strategic Innovations in Asia and the Pacific Basin.* Westport, Conn.: Praeger Press.

Engen, Eric M., and Jonathan Skinner. 1992. "Fiscal Policy and Economic Growth." NBER Working Paper 4223. National Bureau of Economic Research, Cambridge, Mass. Processed.

"Enough for Everyone." 2002. *Far Eastern Economic Review,* June 13, pp. 14–18.

Enright, Michael J., Edith E. Scott, and David Dodwell. 1997. *The Hong Kong Advantage.* New York: Oxford University Press.

"Enter the Foreigners: Are Western MBA Schools a Threat to Asia?" 2000. *Asiaweek* (www.asiaweek.com/asiaweek/features/mba/main3.html).

"Ericsson, CEMs Sign Deals." 1997. *Electronic Business News,* July 14.

"Ericsson Shifts Phone Production to Contractors." 2000. *Electronics Weekly,* October 20.

"Ericsson Telecom Signs Agreement with Solectron." 1997. *Electronic Business News,* March 31.

Ermisch, John, and Marco Francesconi. 2001. "Family Matters: Impacts of Family Background on Educational Attainments." *Economica* 68(270):137–56.

Ernst, Dieter E. 2001a. "Evolutionary Aspects: The Asian Production Networks of Japanese Electronics Firms." In Stephan Haggard, Dieter Ernst, and Michael Borrus, eds., *International Production Networks in Asia: Rivalry or Riches?* London: Routledge.

———. 2001b. "Moving beyond the Commodity Trap? Trade Adjustment and Industrial Upgrading in East Asia's Electronics Industry." In R. S. Newfarmer and C. A. Wood, eds., *East Asia: From Recovery to Sustainable Development.* Washington, D.C.: World Bank.

———. 2002. "The Future of Production Networks in the Electronics Sector." Background paper for the East Asia Project. World Bank, Washington, D.C. Processed.

Eskeland, Gunnar S., and Deon Filmer. 2002. "Autonomy, Participation, and Learning in Argentine Schools: Findings and Their Implications for Decentralization." Policy Research Working Paper 2766. World Bank, Washington, D.C. Processed.

"Europe's Low-Tech Schools Fail to Deliver." 2002. *Financial Times,* March 12.

"Europe's Scant Info-Tech Payoff." 2001. *Business Week,* November 19.

"E-woes, E-gads." 2002. *Business China*, April 15.

"Fast Lane to Success." 2002. *Far Eastern Economic Review*, September 12.

Fatas, Antonio, and Ilian Mihov. 2001. "Government Size and Automatic Stabilizers: International and Intranational Evidence." *Journal of International Economics* 55(1):3–28.

Feenstra, Robert C., Gordon H. Hanson, and Songhua Lin. 2002. "The Value of Information in International Trade: Gains to Outsourcing through Hong Kong." NBER Working Paper 9328. National Bureau of Economic Research, Cambridge, Mass. Processed.

Feldman, Maryann P. 2001. "The Entrepreneurial Event Revisited: Firm Formation in a Regional Context." *Industrial and Corporate Change* 10(4):861–91.

Feldstein, Martin. 1998. "Social Security Pension Reform in China." NBER Working Paper 6794. National Bureau of Economic Research, Cambridge, Mass. Processed.

———. 2002. "Economic and Financial Crises in Emerging Economies: Overview of Prevention and Management." NBER Working Paper 8837. National Bureau of Economic Research, Cambridge, Mass. Processed.

Feldstein, Martin, and Jeffrey Liebman. 2000. "The Distributional Effects of an Investment-Based Social Security System." NBER Working Paper 7492. National Bureau of Economic Research, Cambridge, Mass. Processed.

Feldstein, Martin, and Andrew Samwick. 2001a. "The Future of Social Security Pensions in Europe." NBER Working Paper 8487. National Bureau of Economic Research, Cambridge, Mass. Processed.

———. 2001b. "Potential Paths of Social Security." NBER Working Paper 8592. National Bureau of Economic Research, Cambridge, Mass. Processed.

Felipe, Jesus. 2000. "Convergence, Catch-up, and Growth Sustainability in Asia: Some Pitfalls." *Oxford Development Studies* 28(1):51–69.

Ferguson, Niall. 2001. *The Cash Nexus: Money and Power in the Modern World*. New York: Basic Books.

Figlio, David N., and Maurice E. Lucas. 2000. "Do High Grading Standards Affect Student Performance?" NBER Working Paper 7985. National Bureau of Economic Research, Cambridge, Mass. Processed.

"Financial Times EMBA 2002." 2002. *Financial Times*, October 14.

"Financial Times MBA 2003." 2003. *Financial Times*, January 20.

Findlay, Christopher. 2001. "Old Issues in New Regionalism." Pacific Economic Paper 311. Australia-Japan Research Center.

Fine, Charles H. 1999. *Clockspeed: Winning Industry Control in the Age of Temporary Advantage*. London: Little, Brown.

Fine, Charles H., John C. LaFrance, and Don Hillebrand. 1996. *The U.S. Automobile Manufacturing Industry*. Washington, D.C.: U.S. Department of Commerce, Office of Technology Policy.

"A Finger in the Dyke." 2001. *Far Eastern Economic Review*, December 20.

Finn, Michael G. 1997. *Stay Rates of Foreign Doctorate Recipients from U.S. Universities.* Oak Ridge, Tenn.: Oak Ridge Institute for Science and Education.

Fischer, Stanley. 2001. "Exchange Rate Regimes: Is the Bipolar View Correct?" *Finance and Development* 38(2):18–21.

Fisher, Franklin. 2000. "The IBM and Microsoft Case: What's the Difference?" *American Economic Review* 90(2):180–83.

"The Flat Screen Is the Future." 2002. *Far Eastern Economic Review*, August 22.

"Flextronics Signs up for Deal in Japan." 2002. *Financial Times*, May 15.

Fölster, Stefan, and Magnus Henrekson. 2001. "Growth Effects of Government Expenditure and Taxation in Rich Countries." *European Economic Review* 45(8): 1501–20.

Forestier, Emmanuel, Jeremy Grace, and Charles Kenny. 2001. "Can Information and Telecommunications Technologies Be Pro-Poor?" Paper presented at World Bank Economists' Forum, May 3–4.

Fountain, Jane E. 2002. "Toward a Theory of Federal Bureaucracy for the Twenty-First Century." In Elaine C. Kamarck and Joseph S. Nye, eds., *Governance.com: Democracy in the Information Age.* Washington, D.C.: Brookings Institution Press.

Frankel, Jeffrey. 1997. *Regional Trading Blocs in the World Economic System.* Washington, D.C.: Institute for International Economics.

Fratianni, Michele, and John Pattison. 2000. "An Assessment of the Bank for International Settlements." In International Financial Institution Advisory Commission, *Expert Papers.* Washington, D.C.: U.S. Government Printing Office.

Freund, Caroline, and Diana Weinhold. 2002. "The Internet and International Trade in Services." *American Economic Review* 92(2):236–40.

Fuji Research Institute. 2002. "Kokunai Sangyou no Kudoka wo Do Kangaeru ka [What to Make of the 'Hollowing-Out'?]" Fuji Research Institute, April. Processed.

Fujita, Masahisa, and Jacques-François Thisse. 2002. *Economics of Agglomeration.* New York: Oxford University Press.

Fukase, Emiko, and Will Martin. 2001. *Free Trade Area Membership as a Stepping Stone to Development: The Case of ASEAN.* Discussion Paper 421. Washington, D.C.: World Bank.

Gallini, Nancy, and Suzanne Scotchmer. 2002. "Intellectual Property: When Is It the Best Incentive System?" In Adam Jaffe, Joshua Lerner, and Scott Stern, eds., *Innovation Policy and the Economy*, Vol. 2. Cambridge, Mass.: MIT Press.

Galston, William A. 2002. "The Impact of the Internet on Civic Life: An Early Assessment." In Elaine Ciulla Kamarck and Joseph S. Nye Jr., eds., *Governance.com: Democracy in the Information Age.* Washington, D.C.: Brookings Institution Press.

Gálvez, Antonio, Mercedes Maqueda, Manuel Martínez-Bueno, and Eva Valdivia. 2000. "The Scientific Publication Trends and the Developing World." *American Scientist* 88.

Gambe, Annabelle R. 2000. *Overseas Chinese Entrepreneurship and Capitalist Development in Southeast Asia.* New York: St. Martin's Press.

Gani, Azmat, and Michael D. Clemes. 2002. "Services and Economic Growth in ASEAN Economies." *ASEAN Economic Bulletin* 19(2):155–69.

Gantz, John. 2001. *eWorld Survey: Perception Versus Reality.* Framingham, Mass.: IDC.

Garbacz, Christopher C., and Herbert G. Thompson. 1997. "Assessing the Impact of FCC Lifeline and Link-Up Programs." *Journal of Regulatory Economics* 11(1):67–78.

García-Mila, T., and T. J. McGuire. 1992. "The Contribution of Publicly Provided Inputs to States' Economics." *Regional Science and Urban Economics* 22:229–41.

Gereffi, Gary. 1994. "The Organization of Buyer-Driven Global Commodity Chains: How U.S. Retailers Shape Overseas Production Networks." In Gary Gereffi and M. Korzeniewicz, eds., *Commodity Chains and Global Capitalism.* Westport, Conn.: Praeger.

———. 1999. "International Trade and Industrial Upgrading in the Apparel Commodity Chain." *Journal of International Economics* 48(1):37–70.

Geroski, Paul A., and Hossein Samiei. 1998. "Agglomeration Economies, Technology Spillovers, and Company Productivity Growth." CEPR Working Paper 1867. Centre for Economic Policy Research, London. Processed.

Gibson, William. 2001. "My Own Private Tokyo." *Wired Archive*, September 9.

Gilbert, John, Robert Scollay, and Bijit Bora. 2002. "Assessing the Implications for East Asia of New Regional Trading Development in the Asia-Pacific." Background paper for the East Asia Project. World Bank, Washington, D.C. Processed.

Gill, Indermit S., Fred Fluitman, and Amit Dar, eds. 2000. *Vocational Education and Training Reform: Matching Skills to Markets and Budgets.* New York: Oxford University Press.

Gill, Idermit S., and Cho-Son Ihm. 2000. "Republic of Korea." In Indermit S. Gill, Fred Fluitman, and Amit Dar, eds., *Vocational Education and Training Reform: Matching Skills to Markets and Budgets.* New York: Oxford University Press.

Gilson, Ronald J., and Mark J. Roe. 1993. *Understanding the Japanese Keiretsu: Overlaps between Corporate Governance and Industrial Organization.* Palo Alto, Calif.: Stanford University, Stanford Center for Economic Policy Research.

Ginarte, Juan C., and Walter G. Park. 1997. "Determinants of Patent Rights: A Cross-National Study." *Research Policy* 26(3):283–301.

Glaeser, Edward. 1997. "Learning in Cities." NBER Working Paper 6271. National Bureau of Economic Research, Cambridge, Mass. Processed.

Glaeser, Edward, and Andrei Shleifer. 2001. "The Rise of the Regulatory State." NBER Working Paper 8650. National Bureau of Economic Research, Cambridge, Mass. Processed.

Glaeser, Edward, H. D. Kalla, and Jose A. Scheinkman. 1992. "Growth in Cities." *Journal of Political Economy* 100(6):1126–52.

Glaeser, Edward, Jed Kolko, and Albert Saiz. 2000. "Consumer City." NBER Working Paper 7790. National Bureau of Economic Research, Cambridge, Mass. Processed.

Glenn, H. Patrick. 2000. *Legal Traditions of the World: Sustainable Diversity in Law.* New York: Oxford University Press.

Glennerster, Howard. 2002. "United Kingdom Education, 1997–2001." *Oxford Review of Economic Policy* 18(2):120–36.

Glewwe, Paul. 2002. "Schools and Skills in Developing Countries: Education Policies and Socioeconomic Outcomes." *Journal of Economic Literature* 40(2):436–82.

Glick, Reuven, and Andrew Rose. 1999. "Contagion and Trade: Why Are Currency Crises Regional?" *Journal of International Money and Finance* 18(4):603–17.

Globerman, Steven. 2000. "Trade Liberalisation and the Migration of Skilled Professionals and Managers: The North American Experience." *World Economy* 23(7):901–22.

Godo, Yoshihisa. 2002. "Accumulation of Education in Modern Economic Growth: A Comparative Study among Korea, Japan, and USA." Paper presented at World Bank seminar, May 7. Processed.

Goldman Sachs Global Equity Research. 2002. "Technology, Asia Pacific." July 12.

Goldstein, Morris. 1998. *The Asian Financial Crisis*. Washington, D.C.: Institute for International Economics.

———. 2002. *Managed Floating Plus*. Washington, D.C.: Institute for International Economics.

Gooptu, Sudarshan. 2001. "Public Contingent Liabilities in East Asia: A Source of Fiscal Risks in the New Economy." World Bank, Washington, D.C. Processed.

Gordon, Robert J. 2002. "Technology and Economic Performance in the American Economy." NBER Working Paper 8771. National Bureau of Economic Research, Cambridge, Mass. Processed.

Government of Japan. 2001. "Exchange Rate Regimes for Emerging Market Economies." Discussion paper jointly prepared by French and Japanese staff for the ASEM Finance Ministers' Meeting, Kobe (www.mof.go.jp/english/asem/aseme03i2.htm).

Graham, Edward A. 2001. "The Assessment: Economics of the Internet." *Oxford Review of Economic Policy* 17(2):145–58.

Green, C. C., and Kristin B. Zimmerman. 2002. "Science and Technology Policy in Action: How GM Created a Global Laboratory Network." *Technology in Society* 24(1-2):77–82.

Green, David Jay, and J. Edgardo Campos. 2001. "Fiscal Lessons from the East Asian Financial Crisis." *Journal of Asian Economics* 12(3):309–29.

Greenaway, David, Wyn C. Morgan, and Peter W. Wright. 2002. "Trade Liberalization and Growth in Developing Countries." *Journal of Development Economics* 67(1):229–44.

Griliches, Zvi. 1992. "The Search for R&D Spillovers." *Scandinavian Journal of Economics* 94:29–47.

Grossman, Gene M., and Edwin Lai. 2002. "International Protection of Intellectual Property." NBER Working Paper 8704. National Bureau of Economic Research, Cambridge, Mass. Processed.

Gruber, Jonathan, and David Wise. 2001. "An International Perspective on Policies for an Aging Society." NBER Working Paper 8103. National Bureau of Economic Research, Cambridge, Mass. Processed.

———. 2002. "Social Security Programs and Retirement around the World: Micro Estimation." Massachusetts Institute of Technology, July 27. Processed.

Gruen, D., and J. Simon, eds. 2001. *Future Directions for Monetary Policies in East Asia.* Sydney: Reserve Bank of Australia.

Gupta, P., D. Mishra, and R. Sahay. 2000. "Output Response during Currency Crises." International Monetary Fund, Washington, D.C. Processed.

Haddad, Mona, and Ann Harrison. 1993. "Are There Positive Spillovers from Direct Foreign Investment? Evidence from Panel Data for Morocco." *Journal of Development Economics* 42(1):51–74.

Haggard, Stephan. 2000. *The Political Economy of the Asian Financial Crisis.* Washington, D.C.: Institute for International Economics.

"Haier Reaches Higher." 2002. *Fortune,* September 16, pp. 42–46.

Hall, Bronwyn H., and John van Reene. 1999. "How Effective Are Fiscal Incentives for R&D? A Review of the Evidence." NBER Working Paper 7098. National Bureau of Economic Research, Cambridge, Mass. Processed.

Hall, Peter A., and David Soskice, eds. 2001. *Varieties of Capitalism: The Institutional Foundations of Comparative Advantage.* New York: Oxford University Press.

Hanson, Gordon H., and Robert C. Feenstra. 2001. "Intermediaries in Entrepôt Trade: Hong Kong Re-Exports of Chinese Goods." NBER Working Paper 8088. National Bureau of Economic Research, Cambridge, Mass. Processed.

Hanushek, Eric. 2002a. "The Failure of Input-Based Schooling Policies." NBER Working Paper 9040. National Bureau of Economic Research, Cambridge, Mass. Processed.

———. 2002b. "The Long-Run Importance of School Quality." NBER Working Paper 9071. National Bureau of Economic Research, Cambridge, Mass. Processed.

Hanushek, Eric, John F. Kain, and Steven G. Rivkin. 1999. "Do Higher Salaries Buy Better Teachers?" NBER Working Paper 7082. National Bureau of Economic Research, Cambridge, Mass. Processed.

Hanushek, Eric, and Dennis Kimko. 2000. "Schooling, Labor-Force Quality, and the Growth of Nations." *American Economic Review* 90(5):1184–208.

Hanushek, Eric, and Javier A. Luque. 2002. "Efficiency and Equity in Schools around the World." NBER Working Paper 8949. National Bureau of Economic Research, Cambridge, Mass. Processed.

Hanushek, Eric, and Steven Rivkin. 2001. "Does Public School Competition Affect Teacher Quality?" NBER Working Paper. National Bureau of Economic Research, Cambridge, Mass. Processed.

Hardy, Andrew P. 1980. "The Role of the Telephone in Economic Development." *Telecommunications Policy* 4(4):278–86.

Harris, Stuart. 2000. "Asian Multilateral Institutions and Their Response to the Asian Economic Crisis: The Regional and Global Implications." *Pacific Review* 13:495–516.

Harryson, Sigvald. 2002. "Why Know-Who Trumps Know-How." *Strategy + Business* 27:16–21.

Hart, Stuart L., and Clayton M. Christensen. 2002. "The Great Leap." *MIT Sloan Management Review,* Fall 51–56.

Harwit, Eric. 2002. "High-Technology Incubators: Fuel for China's New Entrepreneurship?" *China Business Review* 29(4):26–29.

Harwit, Eric, and D. Clark. 2001. "Shaping the Internet in China." *Asian Survey* 41:3.

Hashimoto, Takehiko. 1999. "The Hesitant Relationship Reconsidered: University-Industry Cooperation in Postwar Japan." In Lewis M. Branscomb, Fumio Kodama, and Richard Florida, eds., *Industrializing Knowledge: University-Industry Linkage in Japan and the United States*. Cambridge, Mass.: MIT Press.

Hatch, Walter, and Kozo Yamamura. 1996. *Asia in Japan's Embrace: Building a Regional Production Alliance*. Cambridge, U.K.: Cambridge University Press.

Hayashi, Fumio, and Edward C. Prescott. 2002. "The 1990s in Japan: A Lost Decade." Processed.

Head, Keith, and John Reis. 1998. "Immigration and Trade Creation: Econometric Evidence from Canada." *Canadian Journal of Economics* 30(1):47–62.

Heeks, Richard, and Charles Kenny. 2001. "Is the Internet a Technology of Convergence or Divergence?" World Bank, Washington, D.C. Processed.

Heller, Peter S. 1999. "Aging in Asia: Challenges for Fiscal Policy." *Journal of Asian Economics* 10(1):37–63.

Helpman, Elhanan. 1993. "Innovation, Imitation, and Intellectual Property Rights." *Econometrica* 61(6):1247–80.

Hemming, Richard, Selma Mahfouz, and Axel Schimmelpfennig. 2002. "Fiscal Policy and Economic Activity during Recessions in Advanced Economies." IMF Working Paper 02/87. International Monetary Fund, Washington, D.C.

Hemp, Paul. 2001. "Managing for the Next Big Thing: An Interview with EMC's Michael Ruettgers." *Harvard Business Review*. January 1, 2001.

Henderson, John V. 1986. "Efficiency of Resource Usage and City Size." *Journal of Urban Economics* 19(1):47–70.

———. 1988. *Urban Development: Theory, Fact, and Illusion*. Oxford: Oxford University Press.

Henderson, John V., and Aril Juncoro. 1996. "Industrial Centralization in Indonesia." *The World Bank Economic Review* 10(3):513–40.

Henderson, John V., T. Lee, and Y. J. Lee. 2001. "Scale Externalities in Korea." *Journal of Urban Economics* 49(3):479–504.

Henderson, Rebecca, Adam Jaffe, and Manuel Trajtenberg. 1995. "Universities as a Source of Commercial Technology: A Detailed Analysis of University Patenting, 1965–1988." NBER Working Paper 5068. National Bureau of Economic Research, Cambridge, Mass. Processed.

Henning, C. Randall. 2002. "East Asian Financial Cooperation." Institute for International Economics, Washington, D.C. *Policy Analyses in International Economics* 68.

Henry, David, and Joel Lexchin. 2002. "The Pharmaceutical Industry as a Medicines Provider." *Lancet*, November 16, 360:1590–95.

"High Tech in China." 2002. *Business Week*, October 28.

Hill, Hal. 2000a. "Indonesia: The Strange and Sudden Death of a Tiger Economy." *Oxford Development Studies* 28(2):117–39.

———. 2000b. *The Indonesian Economy*. Cambridge, U.K.: Cambridge University Press.

———. 2002. "Technology and Innovation in Developing East Asia: An Interpretive Survey." Background paper for the East Asia Project. World Bank, Washington, D.C. Processed.

———. Forthcoming. "Philippine Industrialization: Trends, Patterns, and Issues."

Hobday, Mike. 2001. "The Electronics Industries of the Asia Pacific: Exploiting International Production Networks for Economic Development." *Asia-Pacific Economic Literature* 15(1):13–29.

Hoffmaister, Alexander W. 2001. "Inflation Targeting in Korea: An Empirical Investigation." *IMF Staff Papers* 48(2):317–43.

Holmes, Stephen, and Cass R. Sunstein. 1999. *The Cost of Rights: Why Liberty Depends on Taxes*. New York: W. W. Norton.

Holsey, Cheryl M., and Thomas E. Borcherding. 1997. "Why Does Government's Share of National Income Grow? An Assessment of Recent Literature on the U.S. Experience." In Dennis C. Mueller, ed., *Perspectives on Public Choice: A Handbook*, pp. 562–89. New York: Cambridge University Press.

Hong Kong, China, Education and Manpower Bureau. 2001. *Quality of Education: Policy Objective and Key Result Areas*.

Hoschka, Tobias. 2001. "Thailand Builds a Bond Market." *McKinsey Quarterly* 4.

"How e-Biz Rose, Fell, and Will Rise Anew." 2002. *Business Week*, May 13.

"How Location Clusters Affect Innovation." 2002. *MIT Sloan Management Review*, Fall.

"How to Fix Corporate Governance." 2002. *Business Week*, May 6.

Hoxby, Caroline. 2000. "Does Competition among Public Schools Benefit Students and Taxpayers?" *American Economic Review* 90(5):1209–38.

Hsiao, F. S. 1982. "Wo-Guo Chanye Jizhonglu Zhi Ceding Yu Fenxin [The Measurement of Industry Concentration in Taiwan]." *Taipei City Bank Monthly* 13(5).

Hsueh, Li-min, Chen-kuo Hsu, and Dwight Perkins. 2001. *Industrialization and the State: The Changing Role of the Taiwan Government in the Economy, 1945–1998*. Cambridge, Mass.: Harvard University Press.

Hu, Albert Guangzhou. 2001. "Ownership, Government R&D, Private R&D, and Productivity in Chinese Industry." *Journal of Comparative Economics* 29:136–57.

Hu, Albert Guangzhou, and Adam B. Jaffe. 2001. "Patent Citation and International Knowledge Flow: The Cases of Korea and Taiwan." NBER Working Paper 8528. National Bureau of Economic Research, Cambridge, Mass. Processed.

Hu, Albert Guangzhou, and Gary H. Jefferson. 2002. "FDI Impact and Spillover: Evidence from China's Electronic and Textile Industries." *World Economy* 25(8):1063–76.

Hughes, James, Michael Moore, and Edward A. Snyder. 2002. "Napsterizing Pharmaceuticals: Access, Innovation, and Consumer Welfare." NBER Working Paper 9267. National Bureau of Economic Research, Cambridge, Mass. Processed.

Hughes-Hallett, Andrew, and Diana Weymark. 2002. "The Cost of Heterogeneity in a Monetary Union." CEPR Working Paper 3223. Centre for Economic Policy Research, London. Processed.

Hui, Kai-Lung, and I. P. L. Pong. 2002. "On the Supply of Creative Work: Evidence from the Movies." *AEA Papers and Proceedings* (May):217–20.

Hummels, David, Jun Ishii, and Kei-Mu Yi. 2001. "The Nature and Growth of Vertical Specialization in World Trade." *Journal of International Economics* 54(1):75–96.

Humphrey, John. 1998. "Assembler-Supplier Relations in the Auto Industry: Globalization and National Development." University of Sussex, Institute of Development Studies, Brighton. Processed.

Hunt, Robert M. 2001. "You Can Patent That? Are Patents on Computer Programs and Business Methods Good for the New Economy?" *Business Review* (Q1):3–15.

"Hynix Tightens Its Belt While Seoul Hopes for the Best." 2001. *Financial Times*, November 24–25.

Ianchovichina, Elena, and Will Martin. 2001. "Trade Liberalization in China's Accession to the World Trade Organization." Policy Working Paper 2623. World Bank, Washington, D.C. Processed.

"IBM on Target with New Chip." 2002. *Financial Times*, December 16.

IMF (International Monetary Fund). 2001. *World Economic Outlook*. Washington, D.C., October.

———. 2002. *World Economic Outlook*. Washington, D.C.

"In India, a Bit of California." 2000. *Far Eastern Economic Review*, November 2.

"India: Patent Potential." 2002. *Oxford Analytica Brief*, July 17.

"Indian IT's New Faces." 2002. *Far Eastern Economic Review*, November 14.

"Indonesia: Poverty Reduction a Post-Suharto Victim." 2002. *Oxford Analytica Brief*, April 10.

"Industry Baffled by Honda's Plans in China." 2002. *New York Times*, July 12.

"Infineon's Head Gloomy on Outlook for D-RAM Sector." 2001. *Financial Times*, November 26.

"Innovation Takes Off If Colleges, Businesses Link." 2002. *Japan Times*, November 14.

Institute of Developing Economies and Korea Institute for International Economic Policy. 2000. *Toward Closer Japan-Korea Economic Relations in the 21st Century*. Tokyo: Institute of Developing Economies.

Institute of International Education. Various years. *Open Doors*. New York.

International Labor Organization. 2001. *World Employment Report 2001: Life at Work in the Information Economy*. Geneva.

International Organization for Migration. 2000. *World Migration Report 2000*. New York: United Nations.

"The Internet Pays Off." 2002. *Far Eastern Economic Review*, October 31.

"Investors Vent Anger at Samsung Plan." 2002. *Financial Times*, February 27.

Ipsos-Reid. 2001. "The Face of the Web II: 2000–01: Module 8."

Iredale, Robyn. 2000. "Migration Policies for the Highly Skilled in the Asia-Pacific Region." *International Migration Review* 34:882–906.

Irwin, Douglas A., and Mark Tervio. 2002. "Does Trade Raise Income? Evidence from the Twentieth Century." *Journal of International Economics* 58(1):1–18.

Ito, Takatoshi. 2001. "Growth, Crisis, and the Future of Economic Recovery in East Asia." In Joseph E. Stiglitz and Shahid Yusuf, eds., *Rethinking the East Asian Miracle*. New York: Oxford University Press.

Ito, Takatoshi, Eiji Ogawa, and Yuri Sasaki. 1998. "How Did the Dollar Peg Fail in Asia?" NBER Working Paper 6729. National Bureau of Economic Research, Cambridge, Mass. Processed.

Itoh, Akihiro. 2002. "Higher Education Reform in Perspective: The Japanese Experience." *Higher Education* 43(1):7–25.

ITU (International Telecommunications Union). 2000. *Telecommunication Indicators*. Geneva.

———. 2001a. *Trends in Telecommunications Reform 2001*. Geneva.

———. 2001b. *World Telecommunications Development Report 2001*. Geneva.

———. 2002a. "Bits and Bahts: Thailand Internet Case Study." Geneva. Processed.

———. 2002b. "Multimedia Malaysia: Internet Case Study." Geneva. Processed.

———. 2002c. "Pinoy Internet: Philippines Case Study." Geneva. Processed.

Iversen, Torben, and David Soskice. 2001. "An Asset Theory of Social Policy Preference." *American Political Science Review* 95(4):875–92.

Izushi, Hiro. 1999. "Can a Development Agency Foster Cooperation among Local Firms? The Case of the Welsh Development Agency's Supplier Association Program." *Regional Studies* 33(8):739–50.

Jacob, Brian A. 2002. "Accountability, Incentives, and Behavior: The Impact of High-Stakes Testing in the Chicago Public Schools." NBER Working Paper 8968. National Bureau of Economic Research, Cambridge, Mass. Processed.

James, Estelle, Elizabeth M. King, and Ace Suryadi. 1996. "Finance, Management, and Costs of Public and Private Schools in Indonesia." *Economics of Education Review* 15(4):387–98.

"Japan Asks Why More Yen Don't Yield More Products." 2002. *Science*, May 17.

"Japan/China Hollowing Out." 2002. *Oxford Analytica*, February 12.

"Japan: Education Reforms (A)." 2002. *Oxford Analytica*, June 6.

"Japan: Growth Calculations." 2002. *Oxford Analytica Brief*, September 10.

Japan, Ministry of Education, Culture, Sports, Science, and Technology. 2000. "Japanese Government Policies in Education, Science, Sports, and Culture."

"Japan: Tackling NPLs." 2002. *Oxford Analytica Brief*, September 16.

"Japan's Bad Banks." 2002. *Financial Times*, January 29.

"Japan's High-Tech Hope." 1999. *Business Week*, May 31.

Jefferson, Gary H., and Zhong Kaifeng. 2002. "R&D and Innovative Capabilities in East Asia." Background paper for the East Asia Project. World Bank, Washington, D.C. Processed.

Jepsen, Christopher, and Steven Rivkin. 2002. "What Is the Tradeoff between Smaller Classes and Teacher Quality?" NBER Working Paper 9205. National Bureau of Economic Research, Cambridge, Mass. Processed.

JETRO (Japan External Trade Organization). 2000. *White Paper on Foreign Direct Investment 2000.*

———. 2001. *White Paper on Foreign Direct Investment 2001.*

———. 2002. *White Paper on Foreign Direct Investment 2002.*

Jiménez, Emmanuel, and Yasuyuki Sawada. 1999. "Do Community-Managed Schools Work? An Evaluation of El Salvador's EDUCO Program." *The World Bank Economic Review* 13(3):415–41.

Jin, Jang C., and Louis Yau. 1999. "Research Productivity of the Economics Profession in East Asia." *Economic Inquiry* 37(4):706–10.

Joh, Sung Wook. 2001. "Korean Economic Crisis and Corporate Governance System." Korean Development Institute. Processed.

Johnson, David R. 2002. "The Effect of Inflation Targeting on the Behavior of Expected Inflation: Evidence from an 11-Country Panel." *Journal of Monetary Economics* 49:1521–38.

Jovanovic, Boyan, and Peter L. Rousseau. 2002. "Moore's Law and Learning-by-Doing." NBER Working Paper 8762. National Bureau of Economic Research, Cambridge, Mass. Processed.

"Just Quit It." 2002. *Far Eastern Economic Review*, September 12.

Kaburagi, Shinji, Shiro Izuishi, Takeshi Toyoda, and Mayumi Suzuki. 2002. "The Outlook for Japanese Foreign Direct Investment." *JBICI (Japan Bank of International Cooperation) Review* 6:1–57.

Kalaitzidakis, Pantelis, Theofanis P. Mamuneas, and Thanasis Stengos. 2001. *Rankings of Academic Journals and Institutions in Economics.* Discussion Paper 2001-10. University of Cyprus, Department of Economics.

Kamarul, Bahrin, and Roman Tomasic. 1999. "The Rule of Law and Corporate Insolvency in Six Asian Legal Systems." In Kanishka Jayasuriya, ed., *Law, Capitalism, and Power in Asia.* London: Routledge.

Kaminsky, Graciela, and Carmen Reinhart. 1999. "The Twin Crises: The Causes of Banking and Balance-of-Payments Problems." *American Economic Review* 89(3):473–500.

Kang, Moo-Sub. 1999. "Opening New Horizons for Lifelong Learning at the Tertiary Level: the Introduction of the Educational Credit Bank System." *Higher Education Management* 11(2):31–41.

Kang, Moon-Soo. 2000. "Financial Deregulation and Competition in Korea." In Takatoshi Ito and Anne O. Krueger, eds., *Deregulation and Interdependence in the Asia-Pacific Region.* University of Chicago Press.

Kaplinsky, Raphael. 2000. "Globalisation and Unequalisation: What Can Be Learned from Value Chain Analysis?" *Journal of Development Studies* 37(2):117–46.

Kapur, Devesh. 2001. "Diasporas and Technology Transfer." Background paper prepared for the *Human Development Report*, United Nations Development Programme, New York. Processed.

Kaserman, David L., J. W. Mayo, and J. E. Flynn. 1990. "Cross Subsidization in Telecommunications: Beyond the Universal Service Fairy Tale." *Journal of Regulatory Economics* 2:231–49.

Kassim, Azizah. 1998. "The Case of a New Receiving Country in the Development World: Malaysia." Paper presented at the Technical Symposium on International Migration and Development, The Hague. Processed.

Kaufman, Robert R., and Alex Segura-Ubriergo. 2001. "Globalization, Domestic Politics, and Social Spending in Latin America: A Time-Series and Cross-Section Analysis, 1973–97." *World Politics* 53:553–87.

Kaufmann, Daniel, Aart Kraay, and Pablo Zoido-Lobatón. 2002. "Governance Matters II: Updated Indicators for 2000/01." World Bank, Washington, D.C. Processed.

Kawaguchi, Akiyoshi, and Denis Lander. 1997. "Internationalization in Practice in Japanese Universities." *Higher Education Policy* 10(2):103–10.

Kawai, Masahiro. 2002a. "Exchange Rate Arrangements in East Asia: Lessons from the 1997–98 Currency Crisis." *Monetary and Economic Studies* (Special edition, December):1–38.

———. 2002b. "Financial System Reconstruction and Reform in Crisis-Affected East Asia." Background paper for the East Asia Project. World Bank, Washington, D.C. Processed.

Kawai, Masahiro, Richard Newfarmer, and Sergio Schmukler. 2001. "Crisis and Contagion in East Asia: Nine Lessons." Working Paper 2610. World Bank, Washington, D.C. Processed.

Keister, Lisa A. 2000. *Chinese Business Groups: The Structure and Impact of Interfirm Relationships during Economic Development.* New York: Oxford University Press.

Keller, Wolfgang. 2002. "Geographic Location of International Technology Diffusion." *American Economic Review* 92(1):120–42.

"Kelly Puts Some Spark into IBM Unit." 2002. *Financial Times,* November 20.

Kenney, Martin, Kyonghee Han, and Shoko Tanaka. 2002. "Venture Capital Industries in East Asia." Background paper for the East Asia Project. World Bank, Washington, D.C. Processed.

Kenny, Charles. 2000a. "Expanding Internet Access to the Rural Poor." *Information Technology for Development* 9:25–31.

———. 2000b. "The Information Economy in China." In *Utilities Development in China.* Washington, D.C.: World Bank.

———. 2001a. "Is the Internet a Useful Tool for Poverty Relief?" World Bank, Washington, D.C. Processed.

———. 2001b. "Prioritizing Countries for Assistance to Overcome the Digital Divide." *Communications and Strategies* 41:17–36.

———. 2001c. "Should We Try to Bridge the Global Digital Divide?" In J. Alleman, ed., *The Digital Divide.* New York: Columbia Institute for Tele-information.

Kettl, Donald F. 2000. *The Global Public Management Revolution: A Report on the Transformation of Governance.* Washington, D.C.: Brookings Institution Press.

Khan, B. Zorina, and Kenneth L. Sokoloff. 2001. "History Lessons: The Early Development of Intellectual Property Institutions in the United States." *Journal of Economic Perspectives* 15(3):233–46.

Kim, Chungsoo. 2001. "Perceptions on Free Trade: The Korean Debate over the Japan-Korea Free Trade Agreement." Center for Northeast Asian Policy Studies. Processed.

Kim, Eun Mee. 1997. *Big Business, Strong State: Collusion and Conflict in South Korean Development, 1960–1990.* New York: State University of New York Press.

Kim, Linsu. 1995. "Absorptive Capacity and Industrial Growth: A Conceptual Framework and Korea's Experience." In Bon-Ho Koo and Dwight H. Perkins, eds., *Social Capability and Long-Term Economic Growth.* New York: St. Martin's Press.

Kim, Sukkoo. 2000. "Urban Development in the United States, 1960–1990." *Southern Economic Journal* 66(4):855–80.

Kim, Yun-Hwan. 2001. "The Asian Crisis, Private Sector Saving, and Policy Implications." *Journal of Asian Economics* 12(3):331–51.

King, David C. 2002. "Catching Waters in the Web." In Elaine Ciulla Kamarck and Joseph S. Nye Jr., eds., *Governance.com: Democracy in the Information Age.* Washington, D.C.: Brookings Institution Press.

King, Elizabeth M., Berk Ozler, and Laura B. Rawlings. 1999. "Nicaragua's School Autonomy Reform: Fact or Fiction?" Working Paper on Impact Evaluation of Education Reforms 19. World Bank, Washington, D.C. Processed.

King, Robert, and Ross Levine. 1994. "Capital Fundamentalism, Economic Development, and Economic Growth." *Carnegie-Rochester Series on Public Policy* 40:259–92.

Kingdon, Geeta, and Francis Teal. 2002. "Does Performance-Related Pay for Teachers Improve Student Performance?" Working Paper. Department of Economics, University of Oxford. Processed.

Kingston, William. 2001. "Innovation Needs Patents Reform." *Research Policy* 30(3): 403–23.

Kirk, Donald. 1999. *Korean Crisis: Unraveling of the Miracle in the IMF Era.* New York: St. Martin's Press.

Kneller, Robert. 1999. "Intellectual Property Rights and University-Industry Technology Transfer in Japan." In Lewis M. Branscomb, Fumio Kodama, and Richard Florida, eds., *Industrializing Knowledge: University-Industry Linkage in Japan and the United States.* Cambridge, Mass.: MIT Press.

Kong, Qingjiang. 2000. "China's WTO Accession: Commitments and Implications." *Journal of International Economics Law* 3(4):655–90.

Kongsamut, Piyabha. 1999. "Philippines: Preparations for Inflation Targeting." IMF Working Paper WP/01/99. International Monetary Fund, Washington, D.C. Processed.

Koo, Chung M. 2002. "Fiscal Sustainability in the Wake of the Economic Crisis in Korea." *Journal of Asian Economics* 13(4):659–69.

"Korea, Japan Likely to Conclude Free Trade Agreement in 2005." 2002. *Korea Herald,* October 14.

Korea, Ministry of Education. 2001. *Education for the Future.* Seoul.

"The Korean Renaissance: Lessons for a Humbled Japan." 2002. *Financial Times,* October 25.

Kose, M. Ayhan, and Kei-Mu Yi. 2001. "International Trade and Business Cycles: Is Vertical Specialization the Missing Link?" *American Economic Review Papers and Proceedings* 91(2):371–75.

Krueger, Alan, and Mikael Lindahl. 1999. "Education for Growth in Sweden and the World." *Swedish Economic Policy Review* 6(2):289–339.

———. 2001. "Education for Growth: Why and for Whom?" *Journal of Economic Literature* 39(4):1101–36.

Krueger, Anne O., and Jungho Yoo. 2001. "Chaebol Capitalism and the Currency-Financial Crisis in Korea." Paper prepared for the Korea Conference, National Bureau of Economic Research, Cambridge, Mass., February 9. Processed.

Krueger, Dirk, and Krishna B. Kumar. 2002. "Skill-Specific Rather Than General Education: A Reason for Slow European Growth?" Working Paper 02-7. University of Southern California, Department of Finance and Business Economics, Los Angeles. Processed.

Krugman, Paul. 1991. *Geography and Trade.* Leuven, Belgium: Leuven University Press.

———. 1998. "What Happened to Asia?" Massachusetts Institute of Technology, Cambridge, Mass. Processed.

Krumm, Kathie L., and Christine P. Wong. 2002. "Analyzing Government Fiscal Risk Exposure in China." In Hana Polackova Brixi and Allen Schick, eds., *Government at Risk.* New York: Oxford University Press.

Kubota, K. 2000. "The Effects of Market Conditions and Policies on Performance in Telecommunications Sector: Some Evidence." World Bank, Washington, D.C. Processed.

Kuroda, Atsuo. 2002. "The Rise of China and the Changing Industrial Map of Asia." *Journal of Japanese Trade and Industry* (September-October):14–18.

Kuroda, Haruhiko, and Masahiro Kawai. 2002. "Strengthening Regional Financial Cooperation in East Asia." Paper presented at the seminar on Regional Economic, Financial, and Monetary Cooperation: The European and Asian Experiences, Frankfurt, April 15–16. Processed.

Kwan, Chi Hung. 2002a. "Overcoming Japan's China Syndrome." *Journal of Japanese Trade and Industry* (September-October):26–29.

———. 2002b. "The Rise of China and Asia's Flying-Geese Pattern of Economic Development: An Empirical Analysis Based on U.S. Import Statistics." Research Institute of Economy, Trade, and Industry. Japan. Processed.

"Kyoto." 2002. *Times Literacy Supplement,* January 4, p. 13.

La Porta, Rafael, Florencio Lopez-de-Silanes, and Andrei Shleifer. 2000. "Government Ownership of Banks." NBER Working Paper 7620. National Bureau of Economic Research, Cambridge, Mass. Processed.

La Porta, Rafael, Florencio Lopez-de-Silanes, Andrei Schleifer, and Robert Vishny. 1998. "Law and Finance." *Journal of Political Economy* 106(6):1133–55.

Ladd, Helen F. 2002. "School Vouchers: A Critical View." *Journal of Economic Perspective* 16(4):3–24.

Lai, Pingyao. 2002. "Recent Trends in Foreign Direct Investment in China." Background paper for the East Asia Project. World Bank, Washington, D.C. Processed.

Lakdawalla, Darius. 2001. "The Declining Quality of Teachers." NBER Working Paper 8263. National Bureau of Economic Research, Cambridge, Mass. Processed.

Lakenan, Bill, Daren Boyd, and Ed Frey. 2001. "Why Cisco Fell: Outsourcing and Its Perils." *Strategy + Business* 24:54–65.

Lal, K. 1996. "Information Technology, International Orientation, and Performance: A Case Study of Electrical and Electronic Goods Manufacturing Firms in India." *Information Economics and Policy* 8(3):269–80.

Lall, Sanjaya. 2000a. "Technological Change and Industrialization in the Asian NIEs." In L. Kim and R. R. Nelson, eds., *Technological Learning and Economic Development: The Experience of the Asian NIEs.* Cambridge, U.K.: Cambridge University Press.

———. 2000b. "The Technological Structure and Performance of Developing Country Manufactured Exports, 1985–98." *Oxford Development Studies* 28(3): 337–69.

Lall, Sanjaya, and Manuel Albaladejo. 2001. "The Competitive Impact of China on Manufactured Exports by Emerging Economies in Asia." United Nations Industrial Development Organization, Geneva. Processed.

Lamfalussy, Alexander. 2000. *Financial Crises in Emerging Markets.* New Haven, Conn.: Yale University Press.

Landes, David. 1999. *The Wealth and Poverty of Nations: Why Some Are So Rich and Some So Poor.* New York: W. W. Norton.

Lardy, Nicolas L. 2002. *Integrating China into the Global Economy.* Washington, D.C.: Brookings Institution Press.

Lau, Ho-Fuk, and Sebastian Green. 2001."The Electronics Industry: Can Manufacture Continue in Hong Kong?" *World Economy* 24(8):1075–90.

Lavy, Victor. 2002. "Evaluation of the Effect of Teachers' Performance Incentives on Pupil Achievement." *Journal of Political Economy* 110(6).

"Law Set to Push Indonesian Debtors over the Edge." 1998. *Financial Times*, August 20.

Lawlor, Andrew, Herman Chein, Jason Conway, and Yanyan Zhang. 2002. "Cluster Development in Beijing and Shanghai." Background paper for the East Asia Project. World Bank, Washington, D.C. Processed.

Lee, Jisoon. 2001. "Education Policy in the Republic of Korea: Building Block or Stumbling Block?" Working Paper 22648. World Bank Institute, Washington, D.C. Processed.

Lee, Jong-Wha. 1998. "Capital Goods Imports and Long-Run Growth." *Journal of Development Economics* 48(1):91–110.

Lee, Jong-Wha, and Robert Barro. 1997. "School Quality in a Cross-Section of Countries." NBER Working Paper 6198. National Bureau of Economic Research, Cambridge, Mass. Processed.

Lee, Kuan Yew. 1998. *The Singapore Story: Memoirs of Lee Kuan Yew.* Singapore: Prentice Hall.

Lee, Yung Joon, and Hyoungsoo Zang. 1998. "Urbanization and Regional Productivity in Korean Manufacturing." *Urban Studies* 35(11):2085–99.

Legewie, Jochen. 2000. "Driving Regional Integration: Japanese Firms and the Development of the ASEAN Automotive Industry." In Verena Blechinger and Jochen Legewie, eds., *Facing Asia: Japan's Role in the Political and Economic Dynamism of Regional Cooperation.* Munich: Iudicium.

Lehr, Bill, and Frank Lichtenberg. 1999. "Information Technology and Its Impact on Productivity." *Canadian Journal of Economics* 32(2):335–62.

Lerner, Josh. 1999. "The Government as Venture Capitalist: The Long-Run Effects of the SBIR Program." *Journal of Business* 72(3):285–318.

———. 2000. "150 Years of Patent Protection." NBER Working Paper 7478. National Bureau of Economic Research, Cambridge, Mass. Processed.

———. 2002. "Patent Protection and Innovation over 150 Years." NBER Working Paper 8977. National Bureau of Economic Research, Cambridge, Mass. Processed.

Lessig, Lawrence. 2001. *The Future of Ideas.* New York: Random House.

"Lessons in Learning." 2002. *Far Eastern Economic Review,* February 28.

Lever-Tracy, Constance, David Ip, and Noel Tracy. 1996. *The Chinese Diaspora and Mainland China: An Emerging Synergy.* London: Macmillan.

Levin, Herry M. 1998. "Education Vouchers: Effectiveness, Choice, and Costs." *Journal of Policy Analysis and Management* 17(3):373–92.

Levine, Ross. 1997. "Financial Development and Economic Growth: Views and Agenda." *Journal of Economic Literature* 35(2):688–726.

Levinson, James. 1996. "Competition Policy and International Trade." In J. N. Bhagwati and R. E. Hudec, eds., *Fair Trade and Harmonization.* Cambridge, Mass.: MIT Press.

Li, Feng, and Jing Li. 1999. *Foreign Investment in China.* London: Macmillan.

Liang, Xiaoyan. 2001. *China: Challenges of Secondary Education.* Secondary Education Series 22856. Washington, D.C.: World Bank.

Lim, Youngil. 1999. *Technology and Productivity: The Korean Way of Learning and Catching Up.* Cambridge, Mass.: MIT Press.

Lin, Chang Li, and Ramkishen S. Rajan. 2000. *Regional Versus Multilateral Solutions to Transboundary Environmental Problems: Insights from the Southeast Asian Haze.* Discussion Paper 41. Centre for International Economic Studies, Adelaide University.

Lincoln, Edward J. 2001. *Arthritic Japan: The Slow Pace of Economic Reform.* Washington, D.C.: Brookings Institution Press.

Lindeman, David C. 1996. "Introduction." In Peter A. Diamond, David C. Lindeman, and Howard Young, eds., *Social Security: What Role for the Future*. Washington, D.C.: National Academy of Social Insurance.

Lindert, Peter H. 1992. "Historical Patterns in Agricultural Policy." In Peter Timmer, ed., *Agriculture and the State*, pp. 23–92. Ithaca: Cornell University Press.

Lindgren, Carl-Johan, J. T. Balino, Charles Enoch, Anne-Marie Gulde, Marc Quintyn, and Leslie Teo. 2000. *Financial Sector Crisis and Restructuring: Lessons from Asia*. IMF Occasional Paper 188. Washington, D.C.: International Monetary Fund.

Linnan, David K. 1999. "Insolvency Reform and the Indonesian Financial Crisis." *Bulletin of Indonesian Economic Studies* 35(2):107–37.

"A Little Sympathy." 2001. *Far Eastern Economic Review*, July 26.

Liu, Jin-Tan, James Hammitt, and Chyongchiou Jeng Lin. 2000. 'Family Background and Returns to Schooling in Taiwan." *Economics of Education Review* 19(1):113–25.

Lloyd, Peter J., and others. 2002. "Harmonizing Competition Policies in the East Asian Region." University of Melbourne. Processed.

Loeb, Susanna, and Marianne Page. 2000. "Examining the Link between Teacher Wages and Student Outcomes: The Importance of Alternative Labor Opportunities and Non-Pecuniary Variations." *Review of Economics and Statistics* 82(3): 393–408.

Loungani, Prakash. 2000. "Comrades or Competitors? Trade Links between China and Other East Asian Economies." *Finance and Development* 37(2):34–36.

Lu, Qiwen. 2000. *China's Leap into the Information Age*. New York: Oxford University Press.

Lubman, Stanley. 1999. *Bird in a Cage: Legal Reform in China after Mao*. Palo Alto, Calif.: Stanford University Press.

Lucas, Robert E. B. 2002. "Diaspora and Development: Highly Skilled Migrants from East Asia." Background paper for the East Asia Project. World Bank, Washington, D.C. Processed.

Lybeck, Johan A. 1988. "Comparing Government Growth Rates: The Non-institutional Versus the Institutional Approach." In Johan A. Lybeck and Magnus Henkerson, eds., *Explaining the Growth of Government*. Amsterdam: North-Holland.

Magretta, Joan, with Nan Stone. 2002. *What Management Is*. New York: Free Press.

Mako, William P. 2001. "Corporate Restructuring Strategies: Recent Lessons." Paper presented at the Asian Regional Seminar on Financial Reform and Stability, Hyderabad, India. March 29. Processed.

Malaysia, Ministry of Education. 2001. *The Malaysian Smart School Blueprint*. Kuala Lumpur.

Malaysia, Ministry of International Trade and Industry. 1996. *Second Industrial Master Plan*. Kuala Lumpur.

Malecki, Edward J. 2000. "Network Models for Technology-Based Growth." In Zoltan J. Acs, ed., *Regional Innovation, Knowledge, and Global Change*. London: Pinter, A Cassell Imprint.

Mann, Catherin, Sue Eckert, and Sarah Knight. 2000. *Global Electronic Commerce.* Washington, D.C.: International Institute for Economics.

Manning, Chris. 2002. "Structural Changes, Economic Crisis, and International Labor Migration in East Asia." *World Economy* 25(3):359–85.

Mansfield, Edwin. 1991. "Academic Research and Industrial Innovation." *Research Policy* 20(1):1–12.

Manzano, George. 2001. "Is There Any Value Added in the ASEAN Surveillance Process?" *ASEAN Economic Bulletin* 18(1):94–102.

Markusen, Ann, Karen Chapple, Greg Schrock, Daisaku Yamamoto, and Pingkang Yu. 2001. "High-Tech and I-Tech: How Metros Rank and Specialize." Hubert H. Humphrey Institute of Public Affairs, University of Minnesota. Processed.

Martin, Michael O., Ina V. S. Mullis, Eugenio J. Gonzalez, Kelvin D. Gregory, Teresa A. Smith, Steven J. Chrostowski, Robert A. Garden, and Kathleen M. O'-Connor. 1999. *TIMSS 1999 International Science Report.* Boston: Boston College, Lynch School of Education, International Study Center.

Martinez, Patricia. 2002. "Malaysia in 2001." *Asian Survey* 42(1):133–40.

Maskus, Keith E. 1998. "The International Regulation of Intellectual Property." *Weltwirtschaftsliches Archiv* 134:186–208.

———. 2000. *Intellectual Property in the Global Economy.* Washington, D.C.: Institute for International Economics.

———. 2001. "Intellectual Property Protection and Capital Markets in the New Economy." Paper presented at the 27th Pacific Trade and Development Conference, Canberra, Australia, August 20–22. Processed.

Maskus, Keith E., and Christine McDaniel. 1999. "Impacts of the Japanese Patent System on Productivity Growth." *Japan and the World Economy* 1(11):557–74.

Maskus, Keith E., and M. Penubarti. 1997. "Patents and International Trade: An Empirical Study." In Keith E. Maskus, P. Hooper, E. E. Leamer, and J. D. Richardson, eds., *The International Economic Legacy of Robert M. Stern.* Ann Arbor: University of Michigan Press.

Mathews, John A. 1999. "A Silicon Island of the East: Creating a Semiconductor Industry in Singapore." *California Management Review* 41(2):55–74.

Mathews, John A., and D. Cho. 2000. *Tiger Technology: The Creation of a Semiconductor Industry in East Asia.* Cambridge, U.K.: Cambridge University Press.

Mattoo, A., and L. Schuknecht. 2000. "Trade Policies for Electronic Commerce." Policy Resarch Working Paper 2380. World Bank, Washington, D.C. Processed.

Mayer, J. 2000. "Globalization, Technology Transfer, and Skill Accumulation in Low-Income Countries." WIDER Working Paper 150. World Institute for Development Economic Research, United Nation University, Helsinki, Finland. Processed.

McBurnie, Grant, and Christopher Ziguras. 2001. "The Regulation of Transnational Higher Education in Southeast Asia: Case Studies of Hong Kong, Malaysia, and Australia." *Higher Education* 42(1):85–105.

McConnell International. 2000. *Risk E-Business: Seizing the Opportunity of Global E-Readiness* (www.mcconnellinternational.com).

McCulloch, Neil, L. Alan Winters, and Xavier Cirera. 2001. *Trade Liberalization and Poverty: A Handbook.* London: Centre for Economic Policy Research.

McKendrick, David G., Richard F. Doner, and Stephen Haggard. 2000. *From Silicon Valley to Singapore: Location and Competitive Advantage in the Hard Disk Drive Industry.* Palo Alto, Calif.: Stanford University Press.

McKibbin, Warwick, and Hong-Giang Le. 2002. "Which Exchange Rate Regime for Asia?" Paper prepared for the conference on Future Financial Arrangements in Asia, AJRC, CCER, Beijing, March 2–25. Processed.

McKinnon, Ronald. 2000. "The East Asian Dollar Standard, Life after Death?" *Economic Notes* 29(1):31–82.

———. 2001. "After the Crisis, the East Asian Dollar Standard Resurrected: An Interpretation of High-Frequency Exchange Rate Pegging." In Joseph E. Stiglitz and Shahid Yusuf, eds., *Rethinking the East Asian Miracle.* New York: Oxford University Press.

McLaren, John. 2000. "Globalization and Vertical Structure." *American Economic Review* 90(5):1239–54.

Mechling, Jerry. 2002. "Information Age Governance: Just the Start of Something Big?" In Elaine Ciulla Kamarck and Joseph S. Nye Jr., eds., *Governance.com: Democracy in the Information Age.* Washington, D.C.: Brookings Institution Press.

Mesa-Lago, Carmelo, and Katharina Muller. 2002. "The Politics of Pension Reform in Latin America." *Journal of Latin American Studies* 34:687–715.

Mezzoleni, Roberto, and Richard R. Nelson. 1998. "The Benefits and Costs of Strong Patent Protection: A Contribution to the Current Debate." *Research Policy* 27(3):273–84.

Mills, E. S., and Charles M. Becker. 1986. *Studies in Indian Urban Development.* New York: Oxford University Press.

Mingat, Alain. 1998. "The Strategy Used by High-Performing Asian Economies in Education: Some Lessons for Developing Countries." *World Development* 26(4): 695–715.

Mishkin, Frederic S. 2000a. "Inflation Targeting in Emerging-Market Countries." *American Economic Review* 90(2):105–09.

———. 2000b. "Prudential Supervision: Why Is It Important and What Are the Issues?" NBER Working Paper 7926. National Bureau of Economic Research, Cambridge, Mass. Processed.

———. 2001. "Financial Policies and the Prevention of Financial Crisis in Emerging Market Countries." NBER Working Paper 8087. National Bureau of Economic Research, Cambridge, Mass. Processed.

"Missing Generation Leaves Hole in Fabric of Research." 2002. *Science,* October 25.

Miwa, Yoshiro, and J. Mark Ramseyer. 2002. "Banks and Economic Growth: Implications from Japanese History." *Journal of Law and Economics* 45(1):127–64.

"The Mod Squad." 2002. *Far Eastern Economic Review,* November 7.

Mody, Ashoka. 2002. "Is FDI Integrating the World Economy?" International Monetary Fund, Washington, D.C. Processed.

Mok, Ida Ah Chee, and Paul Morris. 2001. "The Metamorphosis of the 'Virtuoso': Pedagogic Patterns in Hong Kong Primary Mathematics Classrooms." *Teaching and Teacher Education* 17(4):455–68.

Moran, Theodore H. 2001. *Parental Supervision: The New Paradigm for Foreign Direct Investment and Development.* Washington, D.C.: Institute for International Economics.

———. 2002. "The Relationship between Trade, Foreign Direct Investment, and Development: New Evidence, Strategy, and Tactics under the Doha Development Agenda Negotiations." Prepared for the ADB study Regional Integration and Trade: Emerging Policy Issues for Selected Developing Member Countries. Asian Development Bank, Tokyo. Processed.

Moss, David A. 2002. *When All Else Fails? Government Is the Ultimate Risk Manager.* Cambridge, Mass.: Harvard University Press.

Mowery, David C. 1999. "The Computer Software Industry." In David C. Mowery and Richard R. Nelson, eds., *Sources of Industrial Leadership.* Cambridge, U.K.: Cambridge University Press.

Mowery, David C., Richard R. Nelson, Bhaven N. Sampat, and Arvids A. Ziedonis. 1999. "The Effect of the Bayh-Dole Act on U.S. University Research and Technology Transfer." In Lewis M. Branscomb, Fumio Kodama, and Richard Florida, eds., *Industrializing Knowledge: University-Industry Linkage in Japan and the United States.* Cambridge, Mass.: MIT Press.

Mowery, David C., and Arvids A. Ziedonis. 2002. "Academic Patent Quality and Quantity before and after the Bayh-Dole Act in the United States." *Research Policy* 31(3):399–418.

Mukti, N. A. 2000. "Barriers to Putting Businesses on the Internet in Malaysia." *Electronic Journal of Information Systems in Developing Countries* 2(6):1–6.

Mullis, Ina V., Michael O Martin, Eugenio J. Gonzalez, Kelvin D. Gregory, Robert A. Garden, Kathleen M. O'Connor, Steven J. Chrostowski, and Teresa A. Smith. 1999. *TIMSS 1999 International Mathematics Report.* Boston: Boston College, Lynch School of Education, International Study Center.

Mun, Sung-Bae, and M. Ishaq Nadiri. 2002. "Information Technology Externalities: Empirical Evidence from 42 U.S. Industries." NBER Working Paper 9272. National Bureau of Economic Research, Cambridge, Mass. Processed.

Murtha, Thomas P., Stefanie Ann Lenway, and Jeffery A. Hart. 2001. *Managing New Industry Creation.* Palo Alto, Calif.: Stanford University Press.

Muta, Hiromitsu. 2000. "Deregulation and Decentralization of Education in Japan." *Journal of Education Administration* 38(5):455–67.

Nabeshima, Kaoru. 2002a. "Quality of Secondary Education in East Asia." World Bank, Washington, D.C. Processed.

———. 2002b. "Technology Transfer in East Asia." World Bank, Washington, D.C. Processed.

Nam, Il Chong, and Soogeun Oh. 2001. "Asian Insolvency Regimes from a Comparative Perspective: Problems and Issues for Reform." In OECD, *Insolvency Systems in Asia: An Efficiency Perspective.* Paris.

National Science Foundation. 1997. *1997 SESTAT.* Washington, D.C.: National Science Foundation, Division of Science Resources Studies.

———. 1998. *International Mobility of Scientists and Engineers to the United States—Brain Drain or Brain Circulation?* Issue Brief 98-316. Washington, D.C.

———. 2000. *Science and Engineering Indicators 2000.* Washington, D.C.

———. 2001a. *Human Resource Contributions to U.S. Science and Engineering from China.* Issue Brief. Washington, D.C.: National Science Foundation, Division of Science Resources Studies, Washington, D.C.

———. 2001b. "NSF Division of Science Resource Studies, 1995 Survey of Doctorate Recipients." Special unpublished tabulation prepared by N. Kannankutty, May 1. Processed.

———. 2002. *Science and Engineering Indicators 2002.* Washington, D.C.

Neal, Derek. 2002. "How Vouchers Could Change the Market for Education." *Journal of Economic Perspectives* 16(4):25–44.

"NEC to Sell Cell Phone Plants in Mexico." 2000. *Bloomberg News,* December 12.

Nelson, F. Howard. 1994. "International Comparison of Teacher Salaries and Conditions of Employment." In National Center for Education Statistics, *Developments in School Finance,* pp. 111–27. Washington, D.C.

Nelson, Richard R. 2000. "National Innovation Systems." In Zoltan J. Acs, ed., *Regional Innovation, Knowledge, and Global Change.* London: Pinter, A Cassell Imprint.

Neville, Warwick. 1998. "Restructuring Tertiary Education in Malaysia: The Nature and Implications of Policy Change." *Higher Education Policy* 11(4):257–79.

"The New Frontier." 2001. *Far Eastern Economic Review,* December 6.

"A New Workshop." 2002. *Economist,* October 12.

Nezu, R. 2000. "E-Commerce: A Revolution with Power." Organisation for Economic Co-operation and Development, Paris. Processed.

Ng, Francis, and Alexander Yeats. 2001. "Production Sharing in East Asia: Who Does What for Whom, and Why?" In Leonard K. Cheng and Henryk Kierzkowski, eds., *Global Production and Trade in East Asia.* Boston: Kluwer Academic.

Ng, Yew-Kwang. 2000. *Efficiency and Public Policy with a Case for Higher Public Spending.* New York: Palgrave Macmillan.

Nicolas, Françoise. 2000. "Is There a Case for Single Currency within ASEAN?" *Singapore Economic Review* 44(1):1–25.

Noble, Gregory W., and John Ravenhill, eds. 2000. *The Asian Financial Crisis and the Architecture of Global Finance.* Cambridge, U.K.: Cambridge University Press.

Nolan, Peter. 2001. *China and the Global Economy: National Champions, Industrial Policy, and the Big Business Revolution.* New York: Palgrave.

———. 2002. "China and the Global Business Revolution." *Cambridge Journal of Economics* 26(1):119–37.

Nolan, Peter, and Jin Zhang. 2002. "The Challenge of Globalization for Large Chinese Firms." *World Development* 30(12):2089–107.

Noland, Marcus, and Howard Pack. 2002a. "Industrial Policies and Growth: Lessons from International Experience." Paper presented at the fifth annual conference

Challengers of Economic Growth, Central Bank of Chile, Santiago, November 29–30. Processed.

———. 2002b. *Reconsidering the Washington Consensus: The Lessons from Asian Industrial Policy.* Washington, D.C.: Institute for International Economics.

Noll, Roger G. 2000. "Telecommunications Reform in Developing Countries." In Anne O. Krueger, ed., *Economic Policy Reform: The Second Stage.* Chicago: University of Chicago Press.

Noorbakhsh, Farhad, Alberto Paloni, and Ali Youssef. 2001. "Human Capital and FDI Inflows to Developing Countries: New Empirical Evidence." *World Development* 29(9):1593–610.

Norris, Pippa. 2002. "Revolution, What Revolution? The Internet and U.S. Elections, 1992–2000." In Elaine Ciulla Kamarck and Joseph S. Nye Jr., eds., *Governance.com: Democracy in the Information Age.* Washington, D.C.: Brookings Institution Press.

Norville, Elizabeth. 1998. "The 'Illiberal' Roots of Japanese Financial Regulatory Reform." In Lonny E. Carlile and Mark C. Tilton, eds., *Is Japan Really Changing Its Ways? Regulatory Reform and the Japanese Economy.* Washington, D.C.: Brookings Institution Press.

Odagiri, Hiroyuki. 1999. "University-Industry Collaboration in Japan: Facts and Interpretation." In Lewis M. Branscomb, Fumio Kodama, and Richard Florida, eds., *Industrializing Knowledge: University-Industry Linkage in Japan and the United States.* Cambridge, Mass.: MIT Press.

OECD (Organisation for Economic Co-operation and Development). 1998. "Alternative Approach to Financing Lifelong Learning: Country Report of Korea." Paris. Processed.

———. 2000a. *Learning to Bridge the Digital Divide.* Paris.

———. 2000b. *Trends in International Migration.* Paris: SOPEMI.

———. 2000c. *Where Are the Resources for Lifelong Learning?* Paris.

———. 2001a. *Economics and Finances for Lifelong Learning.* Paris.

———. 2001b. "The Impacts on Innovation and Economic Performance of the International Mobility of Highly Skilled Workers." COM/DSTI/DEELSA. Paris, May.

———. 2001c. *Innovative Clusters: Drivers of National Innovation Systems.* Paris.

———. 2001d. *International Mobility of Highly Skilled Workers: From Statistical Analysis to the Formulation of Policies.* Paris.

———. 2001e. *Knowledge and Skills for Life: First Results from PISA 2000.* Paris.

———. 2001f. *Science, Technology, and Industry Outlook.* Paris.

———. 2002. *Education at a Glance: OECD Indicators 2002.* Paris.

Oh, Deog-Seong. 2002. "Technology-Based Regional Development Policy in Taedok Science Town, Korea: Case Study of Taedok Science Town, Taejon Metropolitan City, Korea." *Habitat International* 26(2):213–28.

Ohmae, Kenichi. 2002. "Profits and Perils in China.Inc." *Strategy + Business* 26:68–79.

Okada, Yosuke, and Shigeru Asaba. 1997. "The Patent System and R&D in Japan." In Akira Goto and Hiroyuki Odagiri, eds., *Innovation in Japan*. New York: Oxford University Press.

Okazaki, Tetsuji. 2001. "The Government-Firm Relationship in Postwar Japan: The Success and Failure of Bureau Pluralism." In Joseph E. Stiglitz and Shahid Yusuf, eds., *Rethinking the East Asian Miracle*. New York: Oxford University Press.

"On the Road to Ruin." 2002. *Far Eastern Economic Review*, November 14.

Oulton, Nichlas. 2002. "ICT and Productivity Growth in the United Kingdom." *Oxford Review of Economic Policy* 18(3):363–79.

Pack, Howard. 2002. "Education for East Asian Growth: Deepening or Widening?" Background paper for the East Asia Project. World Bank, Washington, D.C. Processed.

Pacon, Ana Maria. 1996. "What Will TRIPS Do for Developing Countries?" In Friedrich-Karl Beier and Gerhard Schricker, eds., *From GATT to TRIPS: The Agreement on Trade-Related Aspects of Intellectual Property Rights*. Munich: Max Planck Institute.

Parente, Stephen L., and Edward Prescott. 2000. *Barriers to Riches*. Walras-Pareto Lectures 3. Cambridge, Mass.: MIT Press.

Park, S. O. 1991. "High-Technology Industries in Korea: Spatial Linkages and Policy Implications." *Geoforum* 22:421–31.

Park, Yung Chul, and Jong-Wha Lee. 2001. "Recovery and Sustainability in East Asia." NBER Working Paper 8373. National Bureau of Economic Research, Cambridge, Mass. Processed.

Park, Yung Chul, and Chi-Young Song. 2001. "Institutional Investors, Trade Linkage, Macroeconomic Similarities, and Contagion of the Thai Crisis." *Journal of the Japanese and International Economies* 15(2):199–224.

Parry, Taryn Rounds. 1997. "Achieving Balance in Decentralization: A Case Study of Education Decentralization in Chile." *World Development* 25(2):211–25.

"Pass the Chalk." 2002. *Economist*, October 24.

Penner, Rudolph G., Isabel V. Sawhill, and Timothy Taylor. 2000. *Updating America's Social Contract: Economic Growth and Opportunity in the New Century*. New York: Columbia University, American Assembly.

"People's Republic of Capital." 2002. *Red Herring*, November.

Perkins, Dwight. 2002. "Industrial Policy Versus the Rule of Law in East and Southeast Asia." Background paper for the East Asia Study. World Bank, Washington, D.C. Processed.

"Philippines: Slowing Economy." 2002. *Oxford Analytica*, August 27.

"Pinch of Piracy Wakes China upon Copyright Issue." 2002. *New York Times*, November 1.

Pinto-Duchinsky, Michael. 2002. "Financing Politics: A Global View." *Journal of Democracy* 13(4):69–86.

Pistor, Katharina, and Phillip A. Wellons. 1998. *The Role of Law and Legal Institutions in Asian Economic Development, 1960–1995*. Hong Kong: Oxford University Press.

Pitsilis, Emmanuel, David A. von Emloh, and Yi Wang. 2002. "Filling China's Pension Gap." *McKinsey Quarterly* 2.

Pohjola, Matti. 2001. "Introduction." In Matti Pohjola, ed., *Information Technology, Productivity, and Economic Growth*. Oxford: Oxford University Press.

Porter, Michael E. 1998a. "The Adam Smith Address: Location, Clusters, and the New Microeconomics of Competition." *Business Economics* 133(1):7–14.

———. 1998b. "Clusters and the New Economics of Competition." *Harvard Business Review* 76(6):77.

———. 2000. "Location, Competition, and Economic Development: Local Cluster in a Global Economy." *Economic Development Quarterly* 14(1):15–34.

Porter, Michael E., and Scott Stern. 2001. "Innovation: Location Matters." *MIT Sloan Management Review* 42(4):28–36.

Powell, W. 1990. "Neither Market Nor Hierarchy: Network Forms of Organization." *Research in Organizational Behavior* 12:295–336.

Prahalad, C., and G. Hamel. 1990. "The Core Competence of the Corporation." *Harvard Business Review* 3:79–91.

PriceWaterhouseCoopers. 2000a. *The Second Automotive Century: Executive Summary*.

———. 2000b. "Value Realisation in a Consolidating Global Automotive Sector."

Pritchett, Lant. 2001. "Where Has All the Education Gone?" *The World Bank Economic Review* 15(3):367–91.

"Productivity in U.S. Jumps 4 Percent." 2002. *Asian Wall Street Journal*, November 8.

Prudhomme, Remy, and Chang-Woon Lee. 1999. "Size, Sprawl, Speed, and the Efficiency of Cities." *Urban Studies* 36(11):1849–58.

Pyramid Research. 2001. "Broadband: Leaps in Asia." *Pyramid Research Perspective*.

Qiang, C. 2001. "Building the Information Infrastructure." In Carl Jo Dahlman and Jean-Eric Aubert, eds., *China and the Knowledge Economy: Seizing the 21st Century*. Washington, D.C.: World Bank.

"Quantum Leap." 2002. *Far Eastern Economic Review*, July 18.

"Quarterly Chronicle and Documentation: Economic Affairs." 2002. *China Quarterly* 171(September):793.

Quibria, M. G. 1999. "Challenges to Human Resource Development in Asia." *Journal of Asian Economics* 10(3):431–44.

———. 2002. *Growth and Poverty: Lessons from the East Asian Miracle Revisited*. ADB Institute Research Paper 33. Tokyo: Asian Development Bank.

Quigley, John M. 1998. "Urban Diversity and Economic Growth." *Journal of Economic Perspectives* 12(2):127–38.

Quinn, James Brian, and Frederick G. Hilmer. 1994. "Strategic Outsourcing." *MIT Sloan Management Review* 35(4):43–56.

Quintyn, Marc, and Michael W. Taylor. 2002. "Regulatory and Supervisory Independence and Financial Stability." IMF Working Paper 02/46. International Monetary Fund, Washington, D.C. Processed.

Radelet, Steven, and Jeffrey Sachs. 1998a. "The East Asian Financial Crisis: Diagnosis, Remedies, Prospects." *Brookings Papers on Economic Activity* 1:1–74.

————. 1998b. "The Onset of the East Asian Financial Crisis." NBER Working Paper 6680. National Bureau of Economic Research, Cambridge, Mass. Processed.

————. 2000. "What Have We Learned, So Far, from the Asian Financial Crisis?" Background paper for the project on Exchange Rate Crisis in Emerging Market Countries: The Korean Currency Crisis. National Bureau of Economic Research, Cambridge, Mass., February. Processed.

Rajan, Raghuram, and Luigi Zingales. 2001. "The Influence of the Financial Revolution on the Nature of Firms." CEPR Working Paper 2782. Centre for Economic Policy Research, London. Processed.

Ramesh, M., and Ian Holliday. 2001. "The Health Care Miracle in Southeast Asia: Activist State Provision in Post-Colonial Hong Kong, Malaysia, and Singapore." *Journal of Social Policy* 30(4):637–51.

Ramstetter, Eric D. 1998. "Export Propensities and Foreign Ownership Shares in Southeast Asian Manufacturing." In F. Gerard Adams and Shinichi Ichimura, eds., *East Asian Development: Will the East Asian Growth Miracle Survive?* Westport, Conn.: Praeger.

Ratliff, John M. 2002. "NTT DoCoMo and Its i-mode Success: Origins and Implications." *California Management Review* 44(3):55–71.

Rauch, James E., and Vitor Trindade. 2002. "Ethnic Chinese Networks in International Trade." *Review of Economics and Statistics* 84(1):116–30.

Rauch, James E., and Joel Watson. 2002. "Entrepreneurship in International Trade." NBER Working Paper 8708. National Bureau of Economic Research, Cambridge, Mass. Processed.

Ravallion, Martin. 2002. "Have We Already Met the Millennium Development Goal for Poverty?" World Bank, Washington, D.C. Processed.

Ravenscraft, David J., and F. M. Scherer. 1987. *Mergers, Sell-offs, and Economic Efficiency.* Washington, D.C.: Brookings Institution Press.

Reich, Robert B. 2002. *I'll Be Short: Essential Ideas for Getting America to Work.* Boston: Beacon Press.

"Reinventing Acer." 2001. *Far Eastern Economic Review*, May 24.

"Return of the Behemoths." 2001. *Far Eastern Economic Review*, October 11.

Reynolds, Taylor, Charles Kenny, and Christine Zhen-wei Qiang. 2001. "Telecommunications Infrastructure and Foreign Direct Investment: An Empirical Analysis." World Bank, Washington, D.C. Processed.

Rhee, Yeongseop, and Woosik Moon. 2002. "Asian Monetary Cooperation: Ideas Past and Future." Sookmyung University and Seoul National University. Processed.

Richards, John E. 2001. "Clusters, Competition, and Global Players in ICT Markets: The Case of Scandinavia." SIEPR Policy Paper 00-46. Palo Alto, Calif.: Stanford Institute for Economic Policy Research.

Richardson, H. W. 1993. "Efficiency and Welfare in LDC Mega-Cities." In A. M. Parnell and J. D. Kasarda, eds., *Third World Cities: Problems, Policies, and Prospects.* Newbury Park: Sage Publications.

Rigby, Darrell, and Chris Zook. 2002. "Open-Market Innovation." *Harvard Business Review* (October):80–89.

Riquelme, Hernan. 2002. "Commercial Internet Adoption in China: Comparing the Experience of Small, Medium, and Large Enterprises." *Internet Research* 12(3): 276–86.

Rodríguez, Francisco, and Dani Rodrik. 2000. "Trade Policy and Economic Growth: A Sceptical Guide to the Cross-National Evidence." In *NBER Macroeconomic Annual.* Cambridge, Mass.: MIT Press.

Rodrik, Dani. 1997. *Has Globalization Gone Too Far?* Washington, D.C.: Institute for International Economics.

———. 1999. "The New Global Economy and Developing Countries: Making Openness Work." Policy Essay 24. Washington, D.C.: Overseas Development Council.

"Roh's Poll Win a Generational Earthquake." 2002. *Financial Times,* December 23.

Röller, Lars-Hendrik, and Leonard Waverman. 2001. "Telecommunications Infrastructure on Economic Development: A Simultaneous Approach." *American Economic Review* 91(4):909–23.

Rose, Andrew K. 1998. "Limiting Currency Crises and Contagion: Is There a Case for an Asian Monetary Fund?" University of California, Berkeley. Processed.

Rose, Richard. 2002. "Openness, Impersonal Rules, and Continuing Accountability: The Internet's Prospective Impact on East Asian Governance." Background paper for the East Asia Project. World Bank, Washington, D.C. Processed.

Rouse, Cecilia. 1998. "Private School Vouchers and Student Achievement: An Evaluation of the Milwaukee Parental Choice Program." *Quarterly Journal of Economics* 113(2):554–602.

Rozman, Gilbert. 2002. "Can Confucianism Survive in an Age of Universalism and Globalization?" *Pacific Affairs* 75(1):11–37.

Saggi, Kamal. 2002. "Trade, Foreign Direct Investment, and International Technology Transfer: A Survey." *The World Bank Research Observer* 17(2):191–235.

Sakakibara, Eisuke, and Sharon Yamakawa. 2002. "Regional Integration in East Asia: Challenges and Opportunities." Background paper for the East Asia Project. World Bank, Washington, D.C. Processed.

Sakakibara, Mariko, and Michael E. Porter. 2001. "Competing at Home to Win Abroad: Evidence from Japanese Industry." *Review of Economics and Statistics* 83(2):310–22.

Sako, M. 1989. "Competitive Cooperation: How the Japanese Manage Inter-firm Relations." London School of Economics, Industrial Relations Department. Processed.

Sala-i-Martin, Xavier. 2002. "The World Distribution of Income (Estimate from Individual Country Distributions)." NBER Working Paper 8933. National Bureau of Economic Research, Cambridge, Mass. Processed.

"Samsung Tries to Snatch Sony's Crown." 2002. *Far Eastern Economic Review,* October 10.

Sandee, Henry, Ross Kities Andadari, and Sri Sulandjari. 2000. "Small Firm Development during Good Times and Bad: The Jepara Furniture Industry." In Chris

Manning and Peter van Dierme, eds., *Indonesia in Transition: Social Aspects of Reformasi and Crisis*. Singapore: Institute of Southeast Asian Studies.

Santiago, Paulo. 2001. "Teacher Shortage." *OECD Observer*, March 30.

Sato, Kazuo. 2002. "From Fast to Last: The Japanese Economy in the 1990s." *Journal of Asian Economics* 13(2):213–35.

Sato, Yukio. 2001. "The Structure and Perspective of Science and Technology Policy in Japan." In Phillipe Laredo and Phillipe Mustar, eds., *Research and Innovation Policies in the New Global Economy*. Cheltenham, U.K.: Edward Elgar.

Sauvé, Pierre. 2002. "Collective Action Issues in Investment Rule-Making." Background paper for *Global Economic Prospects 2003: Investment to Unlock Global Opportunities*. World Bank, Washington, D.C. Processed.

Saxenian, Anna-Lee. 1994. *Regional Advantage: Culture and Competition in Silicon Valley and Route 128*. Cambridge, Mass.: Harvard University Press.

———. 1999. *Silicon Valley's New Immigrant Entrepreneurs*. San Francisco: Public Policy Institute of California.

———. 2000. "Taiwan's Hsinchu Region: Imitator and Partner for the Silicon Valley." SIEPR Policy Paper 00-44. Palo Alto, Calif.: Stanford Institute for Economic Policy Research.

Saxenian, Anna-Lee, and Jinh-Yuh Hsu. 2001. "The Silicon Valley–Hsinchu Connection: Technical Communities and Industrial Upgrading." *Industrial and Corporate Change* 10(4):893–920.

Sayer, A. 1986. "New Developments in Manufacturing: The Just-in-Time System." *Capital and Class* 30:43–72.

Schmitz, Hubert. 1997. "Collective Efficiency and Increasing Returns." IDS Working Paper 5. University of Sussex, Institute of Development Studies, Brighton. Processed.

Schmitz, Hubert, and Khalid Nadvi. 1999. "Clustering and Industrialization: Introduction." *World Development* 27(9):1503–14.

Schonberger, Richard. 1982. *Japanese Manufacturing Techniques*. New York: Free Press.

"School Daze in Japan." 2002. *Far Eastern Economic Review*, May 9.

Schopf, James C. 2001. "An Explanation for the End of Political Bank Robbery in the Republic of Korea: The T+T Model." *Asian Survey* 41(5):693–715.

Scollay, Robert, and John Gilbert. 2001. *New Regional Trading Arrangements in the Asia Pacific?* Policy Analyses in International Economics 63. Washington, D.C.: Institute for International Economics, May.

Scott, Alan J. 1988. *Metropolis: From the Division of Labor to Urban Form*. Berkeley: University of California Press.

"Search 500,000 Documents." 2002. *Forbes*, June 24.

Segal, Adam. 2003. *Digital Dragon*. Ithaca, N.Y.: Cornell University Press.

"Seoul, Singapore to Study FTA." 2002. *Asian Wall Street Journal*, November 8.

"Seriously Big Science." 2002. *Far Eastern Economic Review*, November 14.

"Seven Former Imperial Universities Receive High Share." 2002. *Yomiuri Shimbun*, October 3.

Shakeel, H., M. Best, B. Miller, and S. Weber. 2001. "Comparing Urban and Rural Telecenter Cost." *Electronic Journal on Information Systems in Developing Countries* 4(2):1–13.

Shanmugaratnam, Tharman. 2002. "IT in Learning: Preparing for a Different Future." Speech given at ITOPIA, SICEC, Suntec City, Singapore, July 24. Processed.

Shaw, Stephen M., and Feng Wang. 2002. "Moving Goods in China." *McKinsey Quarterly* 2.

Shimokawa, Koichi. 1999. "New Trend for Component Modules in Japan." *Japanese Automotive News*.

Shleifer, Andrei, and Robert W. Vishny. 1997. "A Survey of Corporate Governance." *Journal of Finance* 52(2):737–75.

———. 2001. "Stock Market Driven Acquisitions." NBER Working Paper 8439. National Bureau of Economic Research, Cambridge, Mass. Processed.

"Shoppers Lost in Cyberspace." 2001. *Far Eastern Economic Review*, February 22.

Shukla, V. 1996. *Urbanization and Economic Growth*. Delhi: Oxford University Press.

Sidorenko, Alexandra, and Christopher Findlay. 2001. "The Digital Divide in East Asia." *Asian-Pacific Economic Literature* 15(2):18–30.

"Singapore Banking Mergers." 2001. *Oxford Analytica*, July 4.

"Singapore in Free-Trade Pact with Australia." 2002. *Financial Times*, November 4.

Singapore, Ministry of Education. 2001. *Masterplan for IT in Education*.

Skeldon, Ronald. 1997. *Migration and Development: A Global Perspective*. Harlow: Addison Wesley/Longman.

Skoggard, Ian A. 1996. "The Indigenous Dynamic in Taiwan's Postwar Development: The Religious and Historical Roots of Entrepreneurship." In *Taiwan in the Modern World*. New York: M. E. Sharpe.

Smith, Heather, ed. 2000. *Looking Forward: Korea after the Economic Crisis*. Sydney: Asia Pacific Press.

Song, Jaeyong. 2002. "What Is Behind the Surge in Korean Patenting?" Paper presented at the Asian Development Forum, Seoul, November 4. Processed.

"South Korea: Broadband Boom." 2003. *Oxford Analytica*, January 2.

"South Korea: Burdened Banks." 2001. *Oxford Analytica*, November 13.

"South Korea's Chaebol Counterattack." 2001. *Oxford Analytica*, June 6.

"South Korea/China, Deepening Ties." 2001. *Oxford Analytica*, November 20.

"South Korea: Corporate Governance." 2002. *Oxford Analytica*, January 15.

"South Korea: Curbing Credit." 2002. *Oxford Analytica*, October 28.

"South Korea: Entrepreneurial Fresh Air." 2001. *Economist*, January 13.

"Southeast Asia: Attempts to Invigorate Corporate Bond Markets." 2002. *Oxford Analytica*, October 25.

"Southeast Asia: Bankruptcy Law." 2000. *Oxford Analytica*, August 21.

"Southeast Asia: Bond Issues." 2002. *Oxford Analytica*, October 25.

"Southeast Asia: China Challenge." 2002. *Oxford Analytica*, January 8.

"Southeast Asia: Consolidating Banks." 2002. *Oxford Analytica*, March 1.

"Southeast Asia: Public Pension Plans." 2002. *Oxford Analytica*, July 19.

Spence, A. Michael. 1996. "Science and Technology Investment and Policy in the Global Economy." In Ralph Landau, Timothy Taylor, and Gavin Wright, eds., *The Mosaic of Economic Growth*. Palo Alto, Calif.: Stanford University Press.

Spencer, Peter. 2002. "The Impact of ICT on UK Productive Potential 1986–2000: New Statistical Methods and Tests." *The Manchester School Supplement* 1463–6786:107–26.

"State Intervention." 2002. *Oxford Analytica*, October 25.

Steinfeld, Edward S. 2002. "Chinese Enterprise Development and the Challenge of Global Integration." Background paper for the East Asia Project. World Bank, Washington, D.C. Processed.

Stern, Scott, Michael E. Porter, and Jeffery L. Furman. 2000. "The Determinants of National Innovation Capacity." NBER Working Paper 7876. National Bureau of Economic Research, Cambridge, Mass. Processed.

Stiglitz, Joseph E., and Shahid Yusuf, eds. 2001. *Rethinking the East Asian Miracle*. New York: Oxford University Press.

Stinebrickner, Todd R. 2002. "An Analysis of Occupational Change and Departure from the Labor Force: Evidence of the Reasons That Teachers Leave." *Journal of Human Resources* 37(1):192–216.

Stone, Mark R. 2000. "Large-Scale Post-Crisis Corporate Sector Restructuring." IMF Policy Discussion Paper PDP/00/7. Washington, D.C.: International Monetary Fund.

"Strategic Planning Perspectives." 2002. *Business Asia*, November 4.

Strauss, Robert P., Lori R. Bowes, Mindy S. Marks, and Mark R. Plesko. 2000. "Improving Teacher Preparation and Selection: Lessons from the Pennsylvania Experience." *Economics of Education Review* 19(4):387–415.

Stubbs, Richard. 2002. "ASEAN Plus Three: Emerging East Asian Regionalism?" *Asian Survey* 42(3):440–55.

Sturgeon, Timothy. 1999. "Turnkey Production Networks: Industrial Organization, Economic Development, and the Globalization of the Electronics Manufacturing Supply Base." Ph.D. diss. University of California, Berkeley, Department of Geography.

Sturgeon, Timothy, and Ji-Ren Lee. 2001. "Industry Co-Evolution and the Rise of a Shared Supply-base for Electronics Manufacturing." IPC Working Paper 01-003. Massachusetts Institute of Technology, Cambridge, Mass. Processed.

Sturgeon, Timothy, and Richard Lester. 2002. "Global Value Chains and the Future of East Asian Development." Background paper for the East Asia Project. World Bank, Washington, D.C. Processed.

"Sub-Continental Drift." 2000. *AsiaWeek*, December 15.

Sueyoshi, Toshiyuki. 1992. "Measuring the Industrial Performance of Chinese Cities by Data Envelopment Analysis." *Socio-Economic Planning Sciences* 26(2):75–88.

Tachiki, Dennis S. 1999. "Exploiting Asia to Beat Japan: Production Networks and the Comeback of U.S. Electronics." In Dennis J. Encarnation, ed., *Japanese Multinationals in Asia*. New York: Oxford University Press.

"Taiwan Acts to Slim Down Banking Sector." 2001. *Financial Times*, October 30.

Taiwan, China, Ministry of Education. 1999. *1999 Progress Report*.

Takayasu, Kenichi, and Minako Mori. 2002. "East Asia's Automobile Industries in the Global Strategies of Vehicle Assemblers." Background paper for the East Asia Project. World Bank, Washington, D.C. Processed.

Tanzi, Vito, and L. Schuknecht. 2000. *Review of Public Spending in the 20th Century: A Global Perspective*. New York: Cambridge University Press.

Tavares, Jose, and Romain Wacziarg. 2001. "How Democracy Affects Growth." *European Economic Review* 45(8):1341–78.

Taylor, Peter J., and D. R. F. Walker. 2001. "World Cities: A First Multivariate Analysis of Their Service Complexes." *Urban Studies* 38(1):23–47.

"Technology and You." 2002. *Business Week*, September 9.

"Techtronic Branding Breaks New Ground for Hong Kong." 2001. *Financial Times*, November 26.

Teece, David J. 1986. "Profiting from Technological Innovation: Implications for Integration, Collaboration, Licensing, and Public Policy." *Research Policy* 15(6):285–305.

Temin, Peter. 2002. "Teacher Quality and the Future of America." NBER Working Paper 8898. National Bureau of Economic Research, Cambridge, Mass. Processed.

Temple, Jonathan R. W. 2001. "Generalizations That Aren't? Evidence on Education and Growth." *European Economic Review* 45(4-5):905–18.

———. 2002. "The Assessment: The New Economy." *Oxford Review of Economic Policy* 18(3):241–64.

Tenev, Stoyan, and Chunlin Zhang. 2002. *Corporate Governance and Enterprise Reform in China: Building the Institutions of Modern Markets*. Washington, D.C.: World Bank.

Terada, Takashi. 2001. "Directional Leadership in Institution-Building: Japan's Approaches to ASEAN in the Establishment of PECC and APEC." *Pacific Review* 14:195–220.

"Thailand: Asset Management (A)." 2002. *Oxford Analytica*, October 25.

"Thailand: Deeper in Debt." 2002. *Business Asia*, Janaury 28.

"Thailand: Family Fortunes." 2002. *Oxford Analytica*, August 19.

Thailand, Ministry of Education. 2000. *Assessment on Education for All*.

"Thailand: TAMC Not Enough to Resolve Bad Debt Problem." 2002. *Oxford Analytica*, October 25.

"Thailand: Telecoms Reforms Could Harm Privatization." 2001. *Oxford Analytica*, November 14.

"Tide Turns for Seagate Technology." 2002. *Far Eastern Economic Review*, May 2.

"The Tiger and the Tech." 2000. *Economist*, February 5.

Tilak, Jandhyala B. G. 2001. "Building Human Capital: What Others Can Learn." Working Paper 37166. World Bank Institute, Washington, D.C. Processed.

Timmer, Marcel. 2000. *The Dynamic of Asian Manufacturing: A Comparative Perspective in the Late Twentieth Century*. Cheltenham, U.K.: Edward Elgar.

Trajtenberg, Manuel. 2000. "R&D Policy in Israel: An Overview and Reassessment." NBER Working Paper 7930. National Bureau of Economic Research, Cambridge, Mass. Processed.

"The Tug of War for Asia's Best Brains." 2000. *Far Eastern Economic Review*, November 9.

UNCTAD (United Nations Conference on Trade and Development). 2000. *Building Confidence: Electronic Commerce and Development*. New York.

———. 2001a. *E-Commerce and Development Report 2001*. New York: United Nations.

———. 2001b. *World Investment Report 2001*. Geneva.

———. 2002. *World Investment Report 2002*. Geneva.

UNDP (United Nations Development Programme). 2001. *Human Development Report*. Geneva.

UNESCAP (United Nations Economic and Social Commission for Asia and the Pacific). 1999. *Economic and Social Survey of Asia and the Pacific, 1999*. Development Research and Policy Analysis Division (unescap.org/drpad/pub3/svy5e.htm). Bangkok, Thailand.

UNESCO (United Nations Educational, Scientific, and Cultural Organization). 2001. *World Data on Education*. Geneva.

"Unfinished Recession." 2002. *Economist*, September 28.

United Nations Population Division. 2000a. *Replacement Migration: Is It a Solution to Declining and Aging Population?* New York.

———. 2000b. *World Population Prospects: The 2000 Revision* (esa.un.org/unpp).

———. 2001. *World Urbanization Prospects: The 2001 Revision* (esa.un.org/unpp).

van Ark, Bart. 2002. "Measuring the New Economy: An International Comparative Perspective." *Review of Income and Wealth* 48(1):1–14.

Vegas, Emiliana. 2002."School Choice, Student Performance, and Teacher and School Characteristics: The Chilean Case." Policy Research Working Paper 2833. World Bank, Washington, D.C. Processed.

Veloso, Francisco. 2000. "The Automotive Supply Chain: Global Trends and Asian Perspectives." Background paper for the project on International Competitiveness of Asian Economies: A Cross-Country Study. Massachusetts Institute of Technology, Cambridge, Mass. Processed.

Vettiger, Peter, and Gerd Binnig. 2003. "The Nanodrive Project." *Scientific American*, January, 47–53.

Vietnam, General Statistical Office. 2000. *Statistical Yearbook, 2000*. Hanoi: Statistical Publishing House.

Viren, Malti, and Markku Malkamaki. 2002. "The Nordic Countries." In Benn Steil, David G. Victor, and Richard R. Nelson, eds., *Technological Innovation and Economic Performance*. Princeton, N.J.: Princeton University Press.

Volpin, Paolo. 2002. *Governance with Poor Investor Protection: Evidence from Top Executive Turnover in Italy*. CEPR Discussion Paper 3231. London: Centre for Economic Policy Research.

Wade, Robert. 1990. *Governing the Market: Economic Theory and the Role of Government in East Asian Industrialization.* Princeton, N.J.: Princeton University Press.

Wallsten, Scott J. 1999. "An Empirical Analysis of Competition, Privatization, and Regulation in Africa and Latin America." World Bank, Washington, D.C., May. Processed.

————. 2000. *The Role of Government in Regional Technology Development: The Effects of Public Venture Capital and Science Parks.* SIEPR Policy Paper 00-39. Palo Alto, Calif.: Stanford Institute for Economic Policy Research.

Wang, Jici. 2001. *Innovative Spaces: Enterprise Clusters and Regional Development [in Chinese].* Beijing: Peking University Press.

Wang, Jici, and Xin Tong. Forthcoming. "Industrial Clusters in China: Alternative Pathways towards Global-Local Linkages." Forthcoming in a UNU/TECH book on innovation in China. United Nation University, Helsinki. Processed.

Wang, Jici, Huasheng Zhu, and Xin Tong. 2001. "Industrial Districts in a Transitional Economy: The Case of Datang Sock and Stocking Industry in Zhejiang, China." Paper presented at the residential conference of the IGU Commission on the Organization of Industrial Space, Turin, Italy. Processed.

Wang, Mark Yaolin. 2002. "The Motivations behind China's Government-Initiated Industrial Investment Overseas." *Pacific Affairs* 75(2):187–206.

Wang, Pien, and Pui San Chan. 1995. "Advantages, Disadvantages, Facilitators, and Inhibitors of Computer-Aided Instruction in Singapore's Secondary Schools." *Computers in Education* 25(3):151–62.

Warr, Peter. 2002. "Economic Recovery and Poverty Alleviation in Indonesia." Paper presented at the Young Economists' Seminar, Jakarta, Indonesia, May 29. Processed.

Wei, Shang-Jin. 2000. "Local Corruption and Global Capital Flows." *Brookings Papers on Economic Activity* 2:303–54.

Weidenbaum, Murray, and Samuel Hughes. 1996. *The Bamboo Network: How Expatriate Chinese Entrepreneurs Are Creating a New Economic Superpower in Asia.* New York: Martin Kessler Books.

Wellenius, Bjorn. 2001. "Closing the Gap in Access to Rural Communications: Chile, 1995–2002." Discussion Paper 430. Washington, D.C.: World Bank.

Wenglinsky, Harold. 1998. "Does It Compute? The Relationship between Educational Technology and Student Achievement in Mathematics." ETS Policy Information Report. Educational Testing Service, Princeton, N.J. Processed.

Wesley, Michael. 2001. "APEC's Mid-Life Crisis? The Rise and Fall of Early Voluntary Sectoral Liberalization." *Pacific Affairs* (Summer):185–204.

Westhead, Paul, and Stephen Batstone. 1998. "Independent Technology-Based Firms: The Perceived Benefits of a Science Park Location." *Urban Studies* 35 (12):2197–219.

"What Makes Sally Learn?" 2001. *Business Week*, August 27.

Wheeler, D. 2000. "A Research Contribution to the World Bank's ICT Sector Strategy." World Bank, Washington, D.C. Processed.

"When the Best Brains Go Abroad." 2001. *IEEE Spectrum*, October.

White House, Office of the Press Secretary. 2000. "Information Technology, Research, and Development: Information Technology for the 21st Century." Washington, D.C. Processed.

"Why Korea's Success May Come at a High Price." 2002. *Financial Times*, October 25.

"Why Small Banks Survive." 2001. *Far Eastern Economic Review*, October 18.

"Why Tech's Heavyweights Still Can't Crush the Small Fry." 2002. *Business Week*, November 4.

Williamson, John. 1999. "The Case for a Common Basket Peg for East Asian Currencies." In Stefan Collignon, Jean Pisani-Ferry, and Yung Chul Park, eds., *Exchange Rate Policies in Emerging Asian Countries*. London: Routledge.

Williamson, Oliver E. 1971. "The Vertical Integration of Production: Market Failure Considerations." *American Economic Review* 61(2): 112–23.

———. 1989. "Transactions Costs Economics." In Richard Schmalansee and Robert Willig, eds., *Handbook of Industrial Organization*. New York: North Holland.

"Wired Schools." 2000. *Business Week*, September 25.

"Wired Schools, Wired Nations." 2001. *Economist*, November 8.

"Wireless Act." 2002. *Red Herring*, October.

Wirtz, Jochen. 2000. "Growth of the Service Sector in Asia." *Singapore Management Review* 22(2):37–54.

Wirtz, Jochen, Christopher H. Lovelock, and Abul Kasim Sajjadul Islam. 2002. "Service Economy Asia: Macro Trends and Their Implications." *Nanyang Business Review* 1(2):6–18.

Wise, David A. Forthcoming. "Introduction." In Seiritsu Ogura, Toshiaki Tachibanaki, and David A. Wise, eds., *Labor Markets and Firm Benefit Policies in Japan and the United States*. Chicago: University of Chicago Press.

Witte, Johanna. 2000. "Education in Thailand after the Crisis: A Balancing Act between Globalization and National Self-Contemplation." *International Journal of Educational Development* 20(3):223–45.

Wiwattanakantang, Yupana. 2001. "Controlling Shareholders and Corporate Value: Evidence from Thailand." *Finance Journal* 9(4):323–62.

Woessmann, Ludger. 2000. "Schooling Resources, Educational Institutions, and Student Performance: The International Evidence," Kiel Working Paper 983. Kiel Institute of World Economics, Kiel, Germany. Processed.

———. 2001. "New Evidence on the Missing Resource-Performance Link in Education." Kiel Working Paper 1051. Kiel Institute of World Economics, Kiel, Germany. Processed.

Wolman, Harold, and David Spitzley. 1996. "The Politics of Local Economic Development." *Economic Development Quarterly* 10(2):115–50.

Womack, J., D. Jones, and D. Roos. 1990. *The Machine That Changed the World*. New York: Rawson Associates.

Wong, Poh-Kam. 2001. "ICT Productivity and Diffusion in Asia: Digital Dividends or Digital Divide?" UNU/WIDER Discussion Paper 2001/8. Helsinki, Finland: World Institute for Development Economic Research, United Nations University.

Wonnacott, Ronald. 1996. "Trade and Investment in a Hub-and-Spoke System Versus a Free Trade Area." *World Economy* 19(3):237–52.

Wood, Adrian, and Kersti Berge. 1997. "Exporting Manufactures: Human Resources, Natural Resources, and Trade Policy." *Journal of Development Studies* 34(1):35–39.

World Bank. 1993. *The East Asian Miracle: Economic Growth and Public Policy.* New York: Oxford University Press.

———. 1998a. *East Asia: Road to Recovery.* Washington, D.C.

———. 1998b. "Indonesia Public Expenditure Review." Report 18691-IND. World Bank, Washington, D.C., October 7. Processed.

———. 2000a. "China: Managing Public Expenditures for Better Results." Report 20342-CHA. World Bank, Washington, D.C., April 25. Processed.

———. 2000b. "Corporate Restructuring in ASEAN: Lessons from Indonesia, Malaysia, Philippines, and Thailand." Paper presented at the Surveillance and Financial Cooperation Workshop, ASEAN, Bangkok, Thailand, September 18–19. Processed.

———. 2000c. *East Asia: Recovery and Beyond.* Washington, D.C.

———. 2000d. *Global Economic Prospects 2001.* Washington, D.C.

———. 2000e. "Higher Education in Developing Countries: Peril and Promise." World Bank, Washington, D.C., February. Processed.

———. 2000f. "Korea's Transition to a Knowledge-Based Economy." Report 20346-KO. World Bank, Washington, D.C. June 29. Processed.

———. 2000g. "Philippines: Judicial Reform." Project Concept Document. World Bank, Washington, D.C. Processed.

———. 2000h. "Reforming Public Institutions and Strengthening Governance." World Bank, Washington, D.C., November. Processed.

———. 2000i. *Thailand Secondary Education for Employment.* Vol. 1: *A Policy Note.* Washington, D.C.

———. 2000j. *Trade Blocs.* New York: Oxford University Press.

———. 2000k. *World Development Report 1999/2000.* New York: Oxford University Press.

———. 2001a. "E-Government: A Guide." World Bank, Washington, D.C., March. Processed.

———. 2001b. *Finance for Growth: Policy Choices in a Volatile World.* New York: World Bank and Oxford University Press.

———. 2001c. "Financial and Corporate Restructuring in East Asia: An Update." Paper presented at the eighth meeting of the Manila Framework Group, Beijing, March 28–29. Processed.

———. 2001d. *Global Economic Prospects and the Developing Countries 2002.* Washington, D.C.

———. 2001e. "Republic of Tunisia: Information and Communications Technology Strategy Report." World Bank, Washington, D.C. Processed.

———. 2001f. "Urban Poverty in the East Asia Region: A Preliminary Desk Review with Particular Focus on the Philippines, Indonesia, and Vietnam." World Bank, East Asia Urban Development Unit, Washington, D.C. Processed.

———. 2002a. *Constructing Knowledge Societies: New Challenges for Tertiary Education.* Washington, D.C.

———. 2002b. *Global Economic Prospects and the Developing Countries 2003: Investing to Unlock Global Opportunities.* Washington, D.C.

———. 2002c. *Lifelong Learning in the Global Knowledge Economy.* Washington, D.C.

———. 2002d. "Making Progress in Uncertain Times (Regional Overview)." World Bank, East Asia and Pacific Region, Washington, D.C. Processed.

———. 2002e. "Thailand Country Assistance Strategy." World Bank, Washington, D.C.

World Bank. Various years. *World Development Indicators.* Washington, D.C.

World Bank, East Asia Region. 2001. *East Asia Update (October).* Special Focus: Public Financial Accountability in East Asia and Renewing Trade as an Engine for Growth and Poverty Reduction. Washington, D.C.

———. 2002. *East Asia Update: Regional Overview (November).* Washington, D.C.

World Bank and IMF (International Monetary Fund). 2001. *Government Bond Markets.* Washington, D.C.

World Intellectual Property Organization. 1994. IP/STAT/1994/B. Trademarks and Service Marks. Geneva.

———. 1999. IP/STAT/1999/B. Marks. Geneva.

"World Teacher Crisis Looms, Say Reports." 2002. *South China Morning Post,* October 5.

Wu, Hsiu-Ling, and Chein-Hsun Chen. 2001. "An Assessment of Outward Foreign Direct Investment from China's Transitional Economy." *Europe-Asia Studies* 53(8):1235–54.

Wyplosz, Charles. 1999. "International Financial Instability." In Inge Kaul Isabellenberg and Marc A. Stern, eds., *Global Public Goods.* New York: Oxford University Press.

Xu, Xinpeng, and Ligang Song. 2000. "Export Similarity and the Pattern of East Asian Development." In P. J. Lloyd and Xioguang Zhang, eds., *China in the Global Economy,* pp. 145–64. Northampton, U.K.: Edward Elgar.

Yamawaki, Hideki. 2001. "The Evolution and Structure of Industrial Clusters in Japan." Working Paper 37183. World Bank Institute, Washington, D.C. Processed.

Yap, Chips. 2001. "Will Malaysia Ever Open Up?" *Automotive Resources Asia* (www. auto-resources-asia.com/experts).

Yeats, Alexander. 1997. "Does Mercosur's Trade Performance Raise Concerns about the Effects of Regional Trade Arrangements?" Working Paper 1729. World Bank, Washington, D.C. Processed.

Yeung, Yue-man. 2001. "The Competitiveness of Hong Kong, Shanghai, and Singapore in the Era of Globalization." In *A Tale of Three Cities.* Hong Kong, China: Hong Kong Institute of Asia-Pacific Studies.

Yi, Zeng, and Linda George. 2000. "Extremely Rapid Ageing and the Living Arrangements of Old Persons: The Case of China." United Nations UN/POP/AGE/2000/8. United Nations, New York. Processed.

Yoo, Seong Min, and Sung Soon Lee. 1997. "Evolution of Industrial Organization and Policy Response in Korea, 1945–1995." In Dong-Se Cha, Kwang Suk Kim, and Dwight H. Perkins, eds., *The Korean Economy 1945–1995: Performance and Visions for the Twenty-first Century.* Seoul: Korea Development Institute Press.

Yoon, Bang-Soon L. 1992. "Reverse Brain Drain in South Korea: State-Led Model." *Studies in Comparative International Development* 27(1):4–26.

Yoshihara, Mariko, and Katsuya Tamai. 1999. "Lack of Incentives and Persisting Constraints: Factors Hindering Technology Transfer at Japanese Universities." In Lewis M. Branscomb, Fumio Kodama, and Richard Florida, eds., *Industrializing Knowledge: University-Industry Linkage in Japan and the United States.* Cambridge, Mass.: MIT Press.

Yoshitomi, Masaru, and Sayuri Shirai. 2000. "Technical Background Paper for Policy Recommendations for Preventing Another Capital Account Crisis." Tokyo: Asian Development Bank Institute.

Young, Alwyn. 2000. "The Razor's Edge: Distortions and Incremental Reform in the People's Republic of China." NBER Working Paper 7828. National Bureau of Economic Research, Cambridge, Mass. Processed.

Yu, Tzong-Shian, and Dianqing Xu, eds. 2001. *From Crisis to Recovery: East Asia Rising Again?* Singapore: World Scientific Publishing.

Yusuf, Shahid. 2001. "East Asian Miracle at the Millennium." In Joseph Stiglitz and Shahid Yusuf, eds., *Rethinking the East Asian Miracle.* New York: Oxford University Press.

Yusuf, Shahid, and Simon Evenett. 2002. *Can East Asia Compete? Innovation for Global Markets.* New York: Oxford University Press.

Yusuf, Shahid, Simon Evenett, and Weiping Wu, eds. 2002. *Facets of Globalization: International and Local Dimensions of Development.* Washington, D.C.: World Bank.

Yusuf, Shahid, Ho-Chul Lee, and Akifumi Kuchiki. 2002. "Reviving Japan's Economy: A Suggestion for a Consumer-Oriented Policy." DECRG Working Paper. World Bank, Washington, D.C. Processed.

Yusuf, Shahid, and Weiping Wu. 1997. *The Dynamics of Urban Growth in Three Chinese Cities.* New York: Oxford University Press.

———. 2002. "Pathways to a World City: Shanghai Rising in an Era of Globalization." *Urban Studies* 39(7):1213–40.

Zhao, Yaohui, and Jianguo Xu. 2002. "China's Urban Pension System: Reforms and Problems." *Cato Journal* 21(3):395–414.

Zhou, Y. 1988. "On the Relations between the Industrial Output Level of City and the Scale of City." *Jingji Yanjiu [Economic Research]:* 74–79.

Zook, Matthew A. 1999. "The Web of Production: The Economic Geography of Commercial Internet Content Production in the United States." Processed.

INDEX

Abernathy, F.H., 227n6, 283

Access policies for telecommunications, 350–52

Acer, 290

Adolf, H., 135n65

Advanced Manufacturing On-line, 330n9

AFTA (ASEAN Free Trade Agreement), 95

Aging of the population and lifelong learning, 217

Agrawal, A., 77n57

Agricultural trade: barriers to liberalization, 125; free trade agreements, 130

Aiwa, 20n33

Alesina, A., 12n19

Alford, William, 85n68

AMCs (asset management corporations), 53, 54n25, 55

Amsden, A.H., 285, 285n9

Angeloni, I., 12n19

Angrist, J., 196n17, 200

APEC (Asia Pacific Economic Cooperation), 98; bilateral trade agreements, 96; competition policy initiatives, 138; FDI initiatives, 134; financial cooperation initiatives, 117; foreign direct investment promotion, 134; free trade initiatives, 124; members, 96n4

ASEAN (Association of South East Asian Nations), 12; auto industry (*See* Automobile parts producers); CMI and, 103n18; competition policy initiatives, 138; FDI initia-

tives, 133; financial cooperation initiatives, 117; free trade initiatives, 123–24, 125n51; intellectual property initiatives, 136; Internet use rate, 280; members, 95n2; tariff exclusions, 125–26; two-way trade with China, 99n10

ASEAN+3, 118–19

ASEAN-4, 23n39

ASEAN Free Trade Agreement (AFTA), 95

ASEAN Industrial Complementation Scheme, 316–17n33

ASEAN Industrial Cooperation Program, 316–19

Asian Swap Arrangement, 103n18, 104

Asia Pacific Economic Cooperation. *See* APEC

Asset management corporations (AMCs), 53, 54n25, 55

Association of South East Asian Nations. *See* ASEAN

Astra International, 57n27

Auerbach, A.J., 10n13

AU Optronics, 26n42

Australia, 256, 258t, 259

Automobile parts producers: consolidation and platform deproliferation, 319; future prospects, 322–23; intraregional fragmentation of markets, 315–19; market growth, 315, 316t; modularity and its implications, 319–21; public policy and, 323; summary, 322–23.

Ballou, D., 198n21

Bangladesh, 139

Bank for International Settlements, 115

Banking sector: cause of 1997 crisis, 12; consolidation, 63–65; foreign ownership pros and cons, 14–15; prudential regulation and, 62–63; recapitalization progress, 65–66; regulatory system need, 15; strategies for improvement, 13–14

Bank restructuring: asset management corporations, 53, 55; incentive schemes, 54; in Indonesia, 56–57; in Korea, 54–56; mediation, 54

Bankruptcy legislation: industrial policies and, 73–76; reform need, 70–73

Basle Capital Accord, 113n33, 114, 116n38

Basle Committee, 114, 116

Baumol, W.J., 141, 143

Bayh-Dole Act, 174–75

Bayoumi, T., 11–12n18

Beardsell, M., 228n8

Beck, T., 83n64

Best, M.H., 226

Beyonics Technology, 289

Bhalla, S., 4n3

Bils, M., 144n3, 182n2

Blalock, G., 291

Bogor Declaration, 134

Boix, C., 42n9

Bond markets, 112–13

Bora, B., 120n45, 128, 130n57

Borcherding, T.E., 45n13

Borrus, M., 273

Brand-to-Brand Complementation Program, 316–17n33

Bretton Woods, 98

Brown, B.W., 220

Brusco, S., 253

Callen, T., 21

Cambodia: inflation targeting, 109; tariffs, 127

CAMEL, 13

Canon, 20n33, 158

Cao, C., 204

Capital Accord (Basle), 113n33, 114, 116n38

Capital investment and innovation, 147–48. *See also* Foreign direct investment; Venture capital

Caribbean, 2, 3t

Casio, 306

Celestica, 306

CEPT (Common Effective Preferential Tariff), 125–26

Cermele, M., 70n46

Chapman, D., 192

Chen, Y., 230n11

Chiang Mai Initiative (CMI): goals and considerations for, 104–5; surveillance and conditionality need, 105–6; surveillance process role, 118–19

China: asset management corporations, 53, 54n25; auto industry prospects, 323; banking sector, 12–14, 63–64; bank recapitalization progress, 65–66; bankruptcy system, 72; barriers to effective corporate governance, 68–69; CMI reserves, 104; coauthors of scientific articles, 210; competition policy, 163; competition with other Asian countries, 23–25, 26–27; contingent liabilities, 49–50; cost advantages in manufacturing, 23; current economic status, 368; economic crisis impact, 4; e-governance in, 361n50; exchange rate management, 11; FDI and technology transfer, 152–53; financial sector reform, 344–45; fiscal reforms,

ABOUT THE AUTHORS

Shahid Yusuf is research manager in the Development Economics Research Group at the World Bank.

M. Anjum Altaf is a senior economist in the East Asia Urban Development Sector Unit at the World Bank.

Barry Eichengreen is the George C. Pardee and Helen N. Pardee Professor of Economics and Political Science, University of California, Berkeley.

Sudarshan Gooptu is a senior country economist (China) in the East Asia Poverty Reduction and Economic Management Sector Unit at the World Bank.

Kaoru Nabeshima is an economist in the Development Economics Research Group at the World Bank.

Charles Kenny is an economist in the Global Information and Communications Division at the World Bank.

Dwight H. Perkins is the Harold Hitchings Burbank Professor of Political Economy and director of the Harvard Asia Center at Harvard University.

Marc Shotten is a consultant in the Development Economics Research Group at the World Bank.